PREHISTORIC
LANCASHIRE

PREHISTORIC LANCASHIRE

DAVID BARROWCLOUGH

The
History
Press

For Alan and Gillian Barrowclough

First published 2008

The History Press Ltd
The Mill, Brimscombe Port
Stroud, Gloucestershire, GL5 2QG
www.thehistorypress.co.uk

British Library Cataloguing in Publication Data.
A catalogue record for this book is available from the British Library.

ISBN 978 0 7524 4708 7

Typesetting and origination by The History Press Ltd.
Printed in Great Britain

CONTENTS

There rolls the deep where grew the tree,
Oh, Earth, what changes hast thou seen!
There where the long street roars hath been
The stillness of the central sea.
The hills are shadows and they flow
From form to form and nothing stands;
They melt like mist, the solid lands,
Like clouds, they shape themselves and go.

Tennyson

ACKNOWLEDGEMENTS

This work has only been possible because of the support and assistance that I have received from friends and colleagues in Cambridge and Lancashire too numerous to mention individually. Thanks go to the President and Fellows of Wolfson College, Cambridge and to Marie Louise-Sørensen, Elizabeth DeMarrais, Simon Stoddart, Colin Renfrew and Graeme Barker in the Department of Archaeology at Cambridge University. Special mention should also be made of Richard Bradley, external examiner of my doctoral thesis and to Caroline Malone who introduced me to Tempus (now The History Press). In Lancashire I was made welcome by the many local museums and I am grateful for their patience in allowing time-consuming access to their collections. Particular mention must go to Peter Iles, County Archaeologist for Lancashire, to Ron Cowell at the National Museums and Galleries on Merseyside and Rachel Newman of Oxford Archaeology North, all of whom kindly gave access to their data. In addition there are a number of private individuals who gave freely of their time. Malcolm Bain was particularly helpful on the subject of early mining on the Anglezarke uplands; Ben Edwards on his excavations at Bond's Farm, Pilling; Ann Hallam for discussion of the regional ceramic assemblage; Gordon Roberts for introducing me to the footprints on Formby Beach; and Robert Williams for discussion of his Mesolithic site and providing the cover art. Most of all I would like to thank John and Julie Hallam for their hospitality and intellectual support. John has had a life-long love of Lancashire's prehistory and I am fortunate to have had the benefit of his encyclopedic knowledge. The book has benefited from access to John's unpublished excavations, and has also benefited from the comments of Mary Chester-Kadwell who kindly assisted with the illustrations.

The discussion draws upon the following sources: the Astley Hall Farm urns at Astley Hall; objects from the Furness area at the Barrow Dock Museum; Blackburn Museum; Noon Hill material at Bolton Museum; Whitelow urns at Bury Museum; extensive collection of flints and local finds at Rochdale Museum; White Hall urns at Darwen Library; Fleetwood for Over Wyre finds courtesy of the Fylde Country Life Preservation Society; local Fylde Coast finds at Grundy Museum and Art Gallery, Blackpool; the Highfurlong Elk, Bleasdale urns and timbers, and Preston Dock finds at Harris Museum, Preston; Kate's Pad and Heysham Head material at Lancaster City Museum; the Museum of Lancashire, Preston; metalwork finds and the Alderley Edge shovel at Manchester University Museum; local metalwork finds and Ribchester urns at Ribchester Museum; the Blackheath urns at Todmorden Library; the Burnley Moors finds at Towneley Hall Museum and Art Gallery, and the Winmarleigh Hoard at Warrington Museum. This book also draws upon the Portable Antiquities Scheme data and that of the Historic Environment Record's of Lancashire, Greater Manchester, Merseyside, Cumbria and Cheshire, for which I am grateful.

CHAPTER I

INTRODUCTION

This study attempts to provide a synthesis of the prehistoric archaeology of Lancashire. I, like many before, have been frustrated that there was no up-to-date account of the county's archaeology. This concerned me for several reasons, though mainly because it has meant an over-reliance on such texts that do exist, which, because of their age, lacked discussion of more recent excavations. This has led to the proliferation of misconceptions about the region's archaeology, in particular that it was in some way a 'black hole' in prehistory. This book therefore takes the opportunity to publish, often for the first time, details of excavations that have in some cases only been hinted at in previous works, and in other cases not known of at all. Also fully published for the first time is a suite of Accelerator Mass Spectrometry (AMS) radiocarbon dates for the county's Early Bronze Age burial assemblages, which allows us to better consider the developments that took place throughout the prehistoric period against the backdrop of a regional chronology. Regionality is a theme that has interested me for some time and which I am pleased to say is becoming increasingly important in studies of British prehistory. Building on the work of archaeologists active in the county, and in particular that of Ron Cowell working in West Lancashire and Merseyside, it has been possible to begin to develop a narrative that stands for the past, and that begins to answer the question which first brought me to the study of archaeology: 'What was life like in Lancashire in the past?'

Prehistoric Lancashire spans the period from the end of the last Ice Age to the arrival of the Romans, a span of over 8000 years. For convenience and ease of comparison, the traditional terms for the divisions of the prehistoric period – Mesolithic, Neolithic, Bronze Age and Iron Age – have been adopted with the addition of subdivisions, such as Early Bronze Age, used to further refine the chronology. The discussion is, however, led by the archaeology, rather than terminology, thus the discussion of the so-called 'hillforts' – defended hilltop enclosures – spans the whole of the later prehistoric period from Late Bronze Age to Early Iron Age. It is felt that this retains clarity whilst also addressing the complexity of the archaeological record.

Within these broad period divisions it is possible to further subdivide the periods into numerous phases (Burgess 1979; Burgess 1980; Burgess 1988; Needham 1996; Needham *et al* 1997; Gibson and Kinnes 1997; Garwood 1999). Although there are many different systems of phases that are sometimes contradictory, it is possible to distinguish between those chronologies

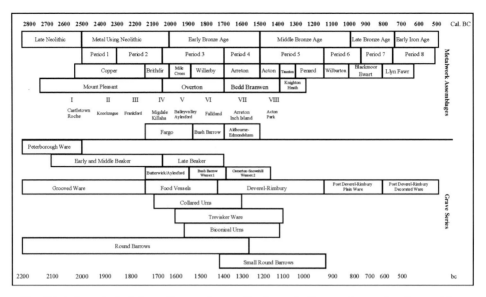

1 Simplified chronological chart of concordances of major periodisations for metalwork assemblages and major burial traditions in England and Wales from the Late Neolithic to Early Bronze Age. *Burgess 1979, 1980, 1988; Needham 1996; Needham et al 1997; Gibson and Kinnes 1997; Garwood 1999*

based on metalwork assemblages and the grave series based on ceramic evidence. In each case several attempts have been made at defining different phases and the results are subject to ongoing debate. For the purposes of the current discussion a concordance has been produced (*1*) which reconciles the different sequences with each other and with a timeline marked in both years cal BC and BC. Throughout the study I refer to radiometrically dated sites and artefacts in years cal BC, applying the latest calibration curve, OxCal v3.8 (Stuiver *et al* 1998; OxCal v3.8, Bronk Ramsey 2001) to both new dates and to existing published dates in order to be consistent.

The layout of what follows is therefore basically chronological, with one exception: before dealing with the prehistory I have devoted a chapter to consideration of the history of archaeological research in Lancashire – Chapter 2. In the absence of a published history I felt it necessary to set what follows in some sort of historic and theoretical framework. Lancashire has a long tradition of local flint collecting and in the nineteenth century was at the forefront of national debates concerning the origins of the Mesolithic. More recently the county's upland bogs and lowland mosses provided the preserved remains that made pioneering palynological studies possible.

Chapter 3 deals with the post-glacial colonisation and Mesolithic exploitation of Lancashire. Evidence for the Late Upper Palaeolithic is scarce in northern Britain as the ice sheets took longer to retreat from there than they did further south. Nonetheless, the north of the county has produced a number of interesting finds, the most impressive of which was the discovery of an elk at Highfurlong near Poulton-Le-Fylde. The find was remarkable because with it were two barbed hunting points, one of which was still embedded in the skeleton of the elk. During the Mesolithic the activities of mobile hunter-gatherer communities can be discerned from the many flints found in the Central Pennines. Most of these finds consist of stray flints, collected rather than excavated from surface scatters. What is needed to develop our understanding of the way these hunters lived their lives can only be provided by the archaeological context. The opportunity is taken here to publish three excavated Mesolithic sites for the first time: Nab End in the Central Pennines, Marles Wood on the Ribble at Ribchester and the lowland site of Mawdesley in West Lancashire (courtesy of John Hallam). These contrasting locations, when considered in the context of research undertaken in the Alt-Ditton valley on Merseyside (Cowell 2000a, 2000b), make it possible to begin to understand the different types of activities undertaken and the extent of mobility among hunter-gatherer-fisher communities.

Turning to the Neolithic, the evidence for occupation in Lancashire still needs to be developed. What are most distinctive about the period in many parts of Britain are the communal burial monuments, few of which are known from the county. Those that we have, such as Pikestones and Calderstones, are unfortunately in a state of ruin. That is not to say that we lack evidence completely, because important palynological studies inform the debate on the introduction, timing and extent of cereal cultivation. I am also able to present new evidence of Neolithic settlement beneath the Late Bronze Age defended settlement at Portfield, only partially published before (courtesy of John Hallam). Furthermore I submit my latest finds and research for a burial monument at Peel, Lytham, first identified by Robert Middleton (Middleton et al 1995, 91–99). Overall, the evidence for the Neolithic has striking similarities with that of the Mesolithic, which suggests that the population remained relatively mobile.

This sense of continuity in the face of technological innovation is a theme I have previously identified (Barrowclough 2007) and it continues into the Early Bronze Age, the subject of Chapter 5. The earthworks and monuments are the most visible testament to the prehistoric occupation of Lancashire and are widely spread across the county. Many so-called barrows were destroyed at the end of the nineteenth century and the early part of the twentieth, and the literature has often bemoaned the lack of scientific excavation. I have therefore taken this chapter as an opportunity to present the details of two more recent excavations – those of Astley Hall Farm and Carrier's Croft, Pendleton (again courtesy of John Hallam). I have also reviewed the older excavations, many of which now have the benefit of modern osteological and radiocarbon analysis (Barrowclough 2007). These data underpin a renewed analysis of the period, which includes consideration of the regional chronology, grave good assemblages and demography in the context of what we know about settlement and domestic activity during this period.

The next chapter progresses to the Middle and Late Bronze Age, and focuses on the deposition of metalwork. The break between Early and Late Bronze Age is one of the more obvious disjunctures in the archaeological record. It is still not at all clear why the longstanding Early Bronze Age burial practices came to an end, although suggestions that it may have something to do with a deteriorating climate are supported by the local environmental evidence. The advent of popular metal detecting combined with more consistent reporting, thanks in part to the Portable Antiquities Scheme, has led to an increase in the number of finds of this period (see below). Using all the available evidence it has been possible to discern a distinct regional flavour to metalwork deposits in Lancashire. Moving beyond simplistic observations about the absence of large hoards, and an almost total absence of certain weapon types, such as swords, it has been possible to identify particular local associations between certain types of metalwork and certain rivers and bogs.

Chapter 7 is concerned with the Late Bronze Age and pre-Roman Iron Age, with a particular focus on the evidence for settlement which builds upon important work undertaken by Ron Cowell in Merseyside in recent years. The so-called hillforts of the Pennines and limestone uplands are the best known evidence for this period and the chapter presents the previously unpublished details from excavations that took place intermittently at Portfield, Whalley, between the 1960s and 1980s (courtesy of John Hallam). Attention is also directed towards previously unpublished observations as to the location of the *Portus Setantiorum*. The location of the port, and thus the tribe itself, has long been contested and what is presented here will no doubt contribute to the debate.

The book concludes with a consideration of what people throughout history have known and felt about Lancashire's past (Chapter 8). Historic documents are often quiet on the subject of the county's former inhabitants, perhaps marking a general attitude of disinterest about the meaning of archaeological remains. Occasionally, events arise which demonstrate that attitudes of fear and disdain were prevalent, and at other times attitudes were of interest or reverence. Interest in the 'past in the past' has been seen as becoming increasingly important elsewhere in Britain, and Lancashire has its part to play in developing this area of research.

Before considering the archaeological evidence for prehistory in Lancashire, I need first say something about the physical environment of the county. To do so is more than to set the scene, as the physical environment shapes and has been shaped by human activity in a complex series of interactions through the millennia. The changing environment is one important connecting thread between the people that inhabit it in different periods. Particularly in non-industrial, non-literate societies, inhabiting a landscape requires an engagement with the properties of that environment and the constraints and opportunities that it presents. Those properties transcend the boundaries of world view, language and culture that may separate the inhabitants of that landscape in one period from those that inhabited it in another. The physical environment is therefore an enduring, but not unchanging, frame of reference and holds considerable promise as a platform of shared understanding across time (Barrowclough 2005, 39–54; 2007).

During the last two decades there has been a growing recognition that the way the landscape has been perceived by past societies may have been highly culture specific. Different ways of thinking about the landscape result in very different ways of organising it physically. This realisation led to a shift away from the generalising models of spatial organisation that had been sought in the 1970s. The new challenge has been how to retrieve these idiosyncratic cognitive elements from the material record. Christopher Tilley, Richard Bradley and Colin Renfrew have all suggested alternative approaches to the problem. I have previously adopted a contextual approach that is multi-scalar and draws upon elements of these different approaches in order to construct an interpretation that, whilst grounded in empirical research, remains flexible enough to account for individual perception (Barrowclough 2007).

Many of the issues and questions that may be raised about life in prehistoric times are, to a large extent, tied to the relationship between the area's prehistoric inhabitants and its environment. A useful place to begin addressing these questions is at a consideration of the key characteristics of the physical environment and the processes that have changed it over time. A sound grasp of these processes is useful for two reasons. First, the physical environment defined the constraints and opportunities which faced its prehistoric inhabitants. An understanding of the processes that altered the environment over time, and the timescales over which they took place, will make it clearer which elements of the environment may have been different from the conditions that may be observed today, and which elements have remained largely unchanged. A second reason is that the dynamics of the physical environment through human as well as natural agencies may also determine which parts of the prehistoric material record are destroyed or preserved, as well as the circumstances in which they are discovered. This may in turn determine when patterns in the known evidence may be representative of the original patterns, and when they may be misleading artefacts of selective preservation or discovery.

Lancashire lies on the west side of Britain in the north-west of England, 290km north-west of London (London to Manchester) and 354km south of Glasgow (Glasgow to Manchester). For the purposes of this study, the focus is on the historic county of Lancashire, which comprised the Hundreds of Lonsdale, Amounderness, Leyland, Blackburn, Salford and Derby. Lonsdale in the north includes the district of Furness in the west and in the east Lancaster, nearly as far south as Pilling. The Hundred of Amounderness, meaning 'Oak Covered Swamp', covers the Fylde Coast and the Over Wyre District, Garstang and the Bleasdale Fells, down to Ashton-on-Ribble near Preston. The Hundred of Leyland lies south of the River Ribble and includes Southport and much of West Lancashire. The Hundred of Blackburn covers East Lancashire to the Yorkshire border and includes Burnley and Pendle. The Hundred of Salford includes Manchester and the whole of south-east Lancashire, whilst the Hundred of Derby takes in the remaining area of south-west Lancashire including Liverpool and much of what is now referred to as Merseyside. This book therefore includes the modern-day county of Lancashire along with Merseyside and Greater Manchester; it also includes the southern part of Cumbria (2). It is, however, sometimes necessary to consider areas beyond these boundaries, as the prehistoric occupants of the region also occupied parts of adjoining counties, in particular Cheshire and West Yorkshire. The surface area of this enlarged region totals 16,647 sq km.

TOPOGRAPHY

The topography of Lancashire is often dramatic, with the Cumbria Fells and Pennine Hills at one extreme and the extensive lowland plains on another (2). Topographically it straddles the divide between the Highland and Lowland Regions of Britain (Fox 1932), enabling a wide diversity of vegetation zones within. The most extensive areas of land are those at elevations below 60m, which account for a quarter of the total surface area. These are the lowland, coastal plains of Lancashire and Cheshire, beyond which the ground rises rapidly in the uplands. The patterns of relief and drainage are closely controlled by geological structure (colour plate 1).

The volcanic uplands of Cumbria are eroded Palaeozoic rock with associated intrusive granites, slates and tuffs (Broadhurst 1985). They are ringed in the south by carboniferous limestone, which accounts for 16 per cent of the total surface area and forms the headlands of Morecambe Bay,

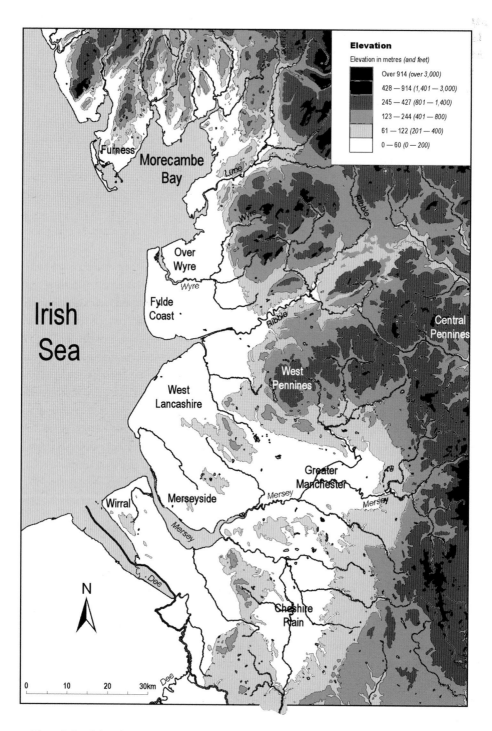

2 The relief and drainage of Lancashire. The Pennine chain runs from north to south and drains to the west over the coastal plain into the Irish Sea

which extend into North Lancashire, where they merge with the Pennines. The Pennines consist of a dissected plateau (*colour plate 2*). The highest points in Lancashire – Leck Fell (627m), Ward's Stone (561m), Pendle Hill (557m), Boulsworth Hill (517m) and Winter Hill (456m) – are also the county's most prominent landscape features. The high plateau, a characteristic 'table top' mesa formation over 428m OD, covers 23 per cent of the region's surface. The rocks are monoclinal, tilted gently towards the east but cut off in the west. Consequently many of the highest points are found along the scarped edges close to the western boundary running the length of the region. They are mainly composed of Millstone Grit, 22 per cent of the total, but also of significance are carboniferous coal measures, 16 per cent of the total.

West of the Pennine uplands lie the Lancashire and Cheshire plains, where the bedrocks are chiefly tertiary red sandstone and marls of the Sherwood Sandstone and Mercia Mudstone Groups (formerly known as Bunter Sandstone and Keuper Marl) (Edwards and Trotter 1954). Unlike the uplands where cover is either completely absent, very thin, or comprised of blanket peat, in the lowlands superficial geology is significant. The dominant cover – 30 per cent – is boulder clay, also known as glacial till (*colour plate 3*) derived from glaciation during the last Ice Age (Hains and Horton 1969; Smith and George 1961; Hall and Folland 1967; Kear 1985; Worsley 1985) and containing flint and chert pebbles, which probably derive from submarine cretaceous rocks. The hummocky surfaces of these quaternary deposits result in poor drainage and the frequent development of meres and basin peat mosses (*c*.6 per cent of the total) which are of archaeological significance because of their potential for good preservation of organic material. For instance at Lindow Moss, near Wilmslow Cheshire, several bog bodies have been discovered (Turner 1986). In coastal areas of West Lancashire superficial deposits of blown sand are frequent (2 per cent), as are those of alluvium (6.45 per cent) which also extend along lower reaches of the major rivers. More significant archaeologically are deposits of glacial sand and gravel, which occur as slightly raised 'islands' of better drained soil within the boulder clay.

DRAINAGE

The region is bisected by the major river systems of the Lune, Wyre, Ribble, Irwell–Mersey and Dee. These erode deep cloughs and valleys in the uplands before meandering to coastal estuaries where they deposit their load. The river systems affect the archaeological record, erosion destroying sites close to the riverbank in upland areas and sedimentation covering sites in the lowlands. For example, along the course of the River Ribble, the archaeological site of Ribchester is being destroyed by erosion, and at Preston Docks alluvial sediments over 10m deep covered the remains of Neolithic and Bronze Age activity.

RECONSTRUCTING ENVIRONMENTAL CHANGE THROUGH THE LATER PREHISTORIC PERIOD

Human activities have played an important role in modifying the landscape of Lancashire. At different times agricultural exploitation, building and quarrying, dredging and land

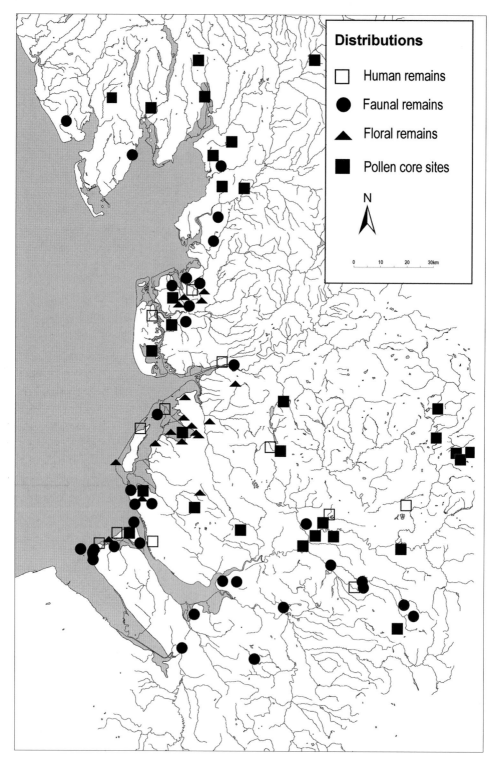

3 Reconstruction of the later prehistoric environment. The prehistoric coastline is shown shaded. The location of pollen sites, fossilised flora and fauna of Late Neolithic and Bronze Age date are also shown

reclamation have all contributed to the human reshaping of the contemporary environment in response to larger-scale climate change. In this section an attempt is made to consider the *longue durée* of environmental change, reconstructing the sequence of change from the last glaciation through to the later prehistoric period. A large body of literature exists cataloguing the palynological sequence of individual sites in both upland bogs and lowland mires and mosses (*3*). Taking this evidence in combination with radiocarbon dates it was possible to reconstruct the sequence of change across the region, in both upland and lowland environments (Barrowclough 2007).

The Late Upper Palaeolithic, *c.*11000 to 8000 BC, is marked by the final retreat of the ice belonging to the Devensian glaciation. As the climate warmed and the ice cap melted, there was a rise in sea level, an increase in rainfall and consequently significant changes in vegetation. The natural woodland vegetation passed through a series of successions as it adapted to climate change. At first on the drier land an open birch, juniper and willow scrub with a rich herbaceous flora developed, but this was ultimately replaced by more open grassland with less stable soil conditions.

Lancashire in the Early Mesolithic, *c.*8000–6500 BC, looked somewhat different to today (*4*). The warming of the climate that had begun in the Late Upper Palaeolithic continued to melt the ice cap, causing sea levels to rise. In *c.*8000 BC the coastline lay *c.*20m below OD (Tooley 1974, 33). This produced a coastline drawn roughly along a line from just west of Anglesey to west of Walney Island in Morecambe Bay, forming a belt of now-submerged land more than 20km wide (Tooley 1985, Fig 6.1). The evidence of this forest can still be seen in West Lancashire, where farmers regularly plough up moss stocks or bog oaks from the fields on the moss lands. The buried forest can also be seen occasionally at Hightown near Formby due to erosion at the mouth of the Alt. In 1636 the Reverend Richard James wrote in his book *Iter Lancastrense*:

> … and in some places, when ye sea doth bate down from ye shore, tis wonder to relate how many thousands of trees now stand black broken from their roots, which once dry land did cover, whence turfs Neptune yields to show he did not always to these borders flow.

By *c.*5200 BC the sea level had risen to 2m below OD, and Britain had become an island (Tooley 1974; 1978; 1985). Palaeoenvironmental evidence reveals that the open grassland of the Late Devensian III, *c.*11000–9500 BC, was succeeded in the Early Mesolithic, firstly by juniper, willow and birch scrub, then by woodland of oak, elm, birch, hazel and lime. In many areas swamp, and subsequently fen, formed behind the present coastal zone and in poorly drained hollows within inland and upland areas.

From *c.*7000–6000 cal BC we see the first possible evidence for human and/or perhaps animal interference with the natural vegetation of the county that continued throughout the Late Mesolithic, *c.*6500–4000 cal BC (Chambers and Elliot 1989). There is evidence that suggests that surface vegetation was being burnt. Discrete bands of charcoal have been found in peat deposits, often dated to the period (see Bain 1991; Middleton *et al* 1995; Hall *et al* 1995; Leah *et al*, 1997; Taylor *et al* 1994). These bands often correlate with brief changes in pollen diagrams, for example at Thwaite House Moss (Middleton *et al*, 1995, 182–190), suggesting

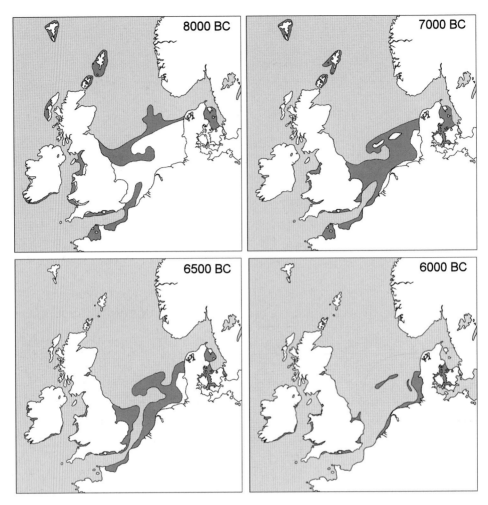

4 Changing sea level following the retreat of the last ice sheets, showing the process of separation of Britain from the continent. *After Bradley 2007, fig. 1.4 based on B; Coles 1998; Shennan and Andrews (eds) 2000*

small clearance events followed by woodland regeneration dominated by alder which spread throughout the county at this time.

During the Neolithic, *c.*4500–2350 cal BC, there was an expanse of dry woodland interspersed with carr wetlands on the lowland, and on the upland edge there was mixed vegetation (*colour plate 4*). This provided a habitat for aurochs, wild boar and deer. The primary forest of *Quercus* sp. (oak), *Alnus* sp. (alder) and *Corylus* sp. (hazel) covered much of the lowland, as well as the Pennines, to *c.*500m (Middleton *et al* 1995; Hall *et al* 1995; Leah *et al* 1997). The Pennines range in height, some hills have tops below 500m and so were forested, others are higher and, in the area above 500m, the cover was made up of hazel and *Betula* sp. (birch) which form a scrub vegetation (Bain 1991).

The primary forest was subject to human activity. This was small-scale *landnam* activity, which consisted of a family or group clearing a small area of forest so that they could grow cereal (Tooley 1978; Bain 1991). This was more at the scale of a garden than a farm. These small clearances were farmed for a few years until the topsoil was depleted of nutrients, at which point the family would then move a few kilometres to another area and clear a new plot. The original clearance would then be left to regenerate. It would regenerate as secondary forest, comprised of alder, birch, oak and hazel, with a more open canopy than the primary cover. By *c*.2850 cal BC almost all the region was covered by secondary forest (Middleton *et al* 1995; Hall *et al* 1995; Leah *et al* 1997).

Remnants of primary forest existed on hillsides and isolated valleys only. Human activity has been identified in occasional clearances used for cereal cultivation, although the more open canopy of the secondary woodland was ideal for animals such as deer which judging by the distribution of flint arrowheads (*colour plate 5*) must have been hunted. Whilst much of the lowland was covered by this deciduous forest, in some places there were natural depressions in the clay which became waterlogged, creating inland wetlands in what is now Manchester (Hall *et al* 1995). The vegetation here would be fen, with alder trees being common in other, wetter, areas, such as by the sides of rivers like the Irwell and on the lower slopes of the uplands.

During this period there was a significant rise in sea level associated with the Lytham VI marine transgression, dated to 4450–3697 cal BC (Tooley 1971; 1978; 1985). During this period the sea level rose by up to 5m. The effect on the very flat coastal plain was dramatic but localised. The Lytham-Skippool valley, on the Fylde Coast, and Martin Mere in West Lancashire were flooded. What are now Blackpool and Southport were separated from the mainland, becoming the two largest of several islands stranded by the rise in sea level (5). Around these flooded islands there would be reed-swamp type vegetation of salt-tolerant plants that are found today around the coast and mudflats (Middleton *et al* 1995).

During the Early Bronze Age, *c*.2350–1400 cal BC, there was a major clearance by the inhabitants of the upland plateaux, by the end of which the forest had largely disappeared (*colour plate 6*). The principle means of clearance was fire, used to create pasture for animals, although there was some small-scale cereal cultivation (Howard-Davis *et al* 1988; Barnes 1982; Bain 1991). On the upland plateaux the thin soils soon started to deplete and the beginning of blanket bog formation, *Ericoid* sp. (heather), can be seen, but this is localised at this stage. Remnant woodland persisted on the sides of the Pennines and in the deeply incised valleys. This woodland was composed of alder, oak, birch and hazel trees. There was also some localised bracken growing on the hillsides, perhaps between the open plateau grasslands and the remnant woodland.

On the lowlands, secondary woodland was cleared to enable small-scale cultivation of cereal (Middleton *et al*, 1995; Hall *et al* 1995; Leah *et al* 1997). In Merseyside the distribution of stone axes suggests that clearance was concentrated around the slopes of the sandstone ridges close to the estuary (see Chapter 5).

On the coast the marine transgression associated with zone 1 had ended and sea levels had begun to fall, up to 5m locally but more usually by only 1–2m. As the sea level fell, extensive creeks, mud flats and salt marsh formed around the coast of West Lancashire, particularly in the Ribble Estuary. These carried *Chenopodiacea* (goosefoot), reeds, bulrushes, freshwater reed swamp and *Gramineae* (grasses), but would have been largely treeless, resembling the Dutch polders of today. They would have afforded seasonal grazing for wild cattle – auroch – whose hoof-prints have been found in preserved sediments on the coast at Formby (Roberts forthcoming and pers.

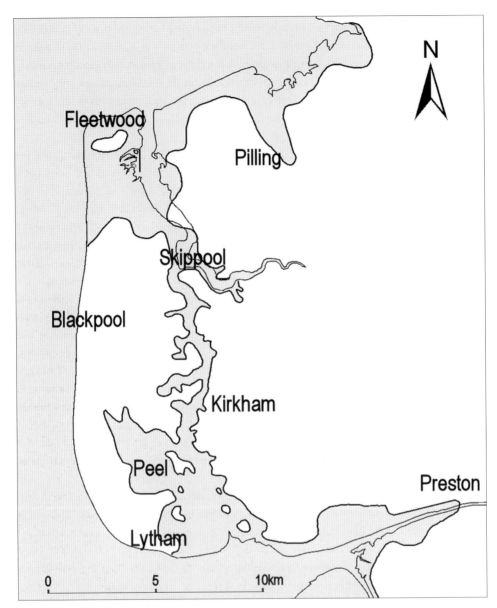

5 The Fylde coast. During the Neolithic the sea level was *c*.5m higher than present levels, flooding much low-lying ground especially in the Lytham-Skippool valley and creating a number of small islands

comm.). On the interior facing sides of the now-dry islands of the Lytham-Skippool valley and Southport, peat-forming communities colonised the still-wet channels that had once separated the areas of what are now Blackpool and Southport from the mainland. Here carr woodland of willow and alder grew, and humans prevented the re-growth of larger trees by regularly burning the cover. There may have been some small-scale cereal cultivation but largely it was kept under control to maintain grazing for animals. On the former islands themselves there would have been thick tree cover dominated by oak (Tooley 1971; 1978; 1985).

In the Over Wyre coastal area carr woodland was inundated by freshwater flooding. This was a one-off episode but it left the long-lasting effect of a waterlogged landscape (Middleton *et al* 1995). Here reeds, cotton grass and rannoch rush started to grow. The human response to this was to construct a wooden trackway – Kate's Pad – several kilometres long, so as to permit continued access to the area. This was made of oak cut with metal axes. In the interior of the coastal plain there was little change from the Neolithic period. Forest, largely secondary, remained dense and damp, oak dominated. There were small infrequent woodland disturbances of quite low intensity signalling human slash-and-burn clearances, creating forest glades for cereal. Some areas of the lowlands may have become heath, with heather and birch more common at the margins of the wetlands (Hall *et al* 1995; Leah *et al* 1997).

The period of *c.*1400–600 cal BC, the Middle and Late Bronze Age, is dominated by a change in climate, becoming wetter and cooler. Climatic deterioration meant that bogs expanded and became more prevalent in the lowland valleys and inland mires as well as on the upland plateaux (*colour plate 7*). This led to a reduction in the agricultural productivity of the land. The human response was to retreat from the wetter upland and the wetter coastal areas to a core area in the middle and upper reaches of the rivers. For the first time we see clearance around some of the central (inland) mossland (wetland) areas, which were used for mixed agriculture. In the uplands, remnant woodland that had covered the hill and valley sides in the Early Bronze Age may have regenerated and extended its cover in the absence of humans. Woodland was never able to recolonise the plateau tops because large areas of peat bog bordered by heathland now dominated these (Tallis and McGuire 1972; Bain 1991). The plateaux may still have been suitable for summer grazing, following the model of alpine transhumance grazing, with cattle/sheep being wintered in the foothills and taken to the higher ground in the summer. The upland wet heath species were *Ericoid* sp. (heather), *Cyperaceae* sp. (sedges) and *Sphagnum* sp. (sphagnum moss). The trees on the flanks were alder, oak and birch. In the surrounding foothills there may also have been flourishing communities of alder, oak, birch and possibly hazel woodland.

In the lowlands the bogs that had started to form in the Early Bronze Age grew and were dominated by wet heath type plants – *Polytrichum, Sphagnum* (moss), *Aubconnium* and *Hylocomium* (Middleton *et al* 1995). Within the bog, areas of slightly higher and therefore drier ground created islands on which birch dominated. Beyond the edge of the bogs there was still secondary forest dominated by oak. There is evidence that near the edge of the bogs some of the woodland was cleared to create open grassland, perhaps an anthropogenic response, replacing the grassland grazing that had been lost to bog. This was maintained by deliberate burning. The bog itself was no longer suitable for humans and people avoided this soggy difficult terrain. It is in this period that metalwork deposition peaked in these wetlands (see Chapter 6). The processes at work in the Late Bronze Age continued into the Iron Age, *c.*600 cal BC to cal AD 43 (*colour plate 8*). Woodland cover was significantly reduced to create extensive areas of pasture for grazing animals, particularly cattle.

LANDSCAPE CHANGE AND SITE PRESERVATION

The processes that have just been considered have to a large extent determined which parts of the prehistoric material record were preserved and then discovered. In order to assess whether the known sample of sites may be considered as representative of the original population, it is useful to consider it against the background of the dynamics of the landscape.

Our present knowledge of the material record of the later prehistoric period of the region is rather uneven, both in terms of chronological distribution and in terms of classes of data. Many burial monuments dating to the Early Bronze Age have survived, only compromised in part by the efforts of early antiquarians. Domestic contexts for the same period, on the other hand, have proved elusive, primarily because domestic huts were built using much lighter methods of construction than those employed in funerary structures. In contrast, for the Late Bronze Age and Early Iron Age our knowledge of funerary practices is scant, perhaps as a consequence of shifting funerary practices in this period, whilst we have increasing evidence for settlement in both defended hilltop enclosures and open farmsteads due to their more durable construction. More significantly for the later period is the wealth of metalwork found either singly or in hoards, often interpreted as the product of ritual deposition.

The effect of these shifts in cultural practices in the later prehistoric period has resulted in a heavily biased repertoire of evidence, making direct comparison between one class of data across the whole period extremely difficult, with the possible exception of copper-alloy metalwork. This problem should not be allowed to obscure the fact that the remarkable survival of a considerable number of prehistoric artefacts, monuments and sites of different classes is also one of the greatest strengths of the evidence, which may present valuable opportunities for the researcher. The changing interrelationship between different classes of data remains our best evidence for gaining insights into the changing socio-spatial organisation of the prehistoric period, and is the subject of the following chapters.

Before pursuing this line of investigation, it is useful to try to establish whether the known sample of archaeological data is representative of the overall picture and to what extent it may have been distorted by selective destruction and discovery. Clarke's fundamental categories of pre-depositional, depositional, post-depositional and retrieval processes (Clarke 1973) provide useful pegs for a discussion of the known sample. Some of the characteristics and processes that may have influenced the deposition, preservation and retrieval of the archaeological record will be considered in turn.

DEPOSITION

Monumental earthworks are by their very nature durable structures. The choice of raw material, location and size ensured their presence in the landscape was permanent. Cultural biographies of these monuments reveal that they were often multi-phased, with re-use in the early medieval period not uncommon. For example, the site of an Early Bronze Age barrow at Southworth Hall Farm, Cheshire was re-used as an inhumation cemetery in the first millennium AD (Freke and Holgate 1988; Freke and Thacker 1988). The effect of such re-use is that throughout the period of their use, they tended to grow in extent and mass and consequently became more conspicuous. Domestic sites, with the exception of Late Bronze Age defended enclosures – 'hillforts' – present a sharp contrast. The limited evidence that excavation has revealed suggests ephemeral structures of light timber construction which leave little impact on the landscape, for example two roundhouses excavated at Oversley Farm, Wilmslow (Thompson 1999). Both stone and copper-alloy tools are durable and both have been preserved in large numbers, in part because of their intentional deposition which ensured they were protected for posterity.

PRESERVATION AND DESTRUCTION

A variety of different processes, both natural and anthropogenic, have the potential to destroy or hide sites and monuments (see Kristiansen 1985). Natural processes actively at work in the region include sedimentation and to a lesser extent erosion. Anthropogenic causes that have had a significant impact are urbanisation and mechanised agriculture. These will be considered in turn.

Sedimentation

As we have already seen, the region is bisected by a number of powerful river systems originating in the Pennine uplands. The erosive strength of these rivers is evidenced by the deeply cut valleys in their upper reaches, for example Lunesdale, Wyresdale and Ribblesdale. Consequently they are responsible for the deposition of thick sediments in their lower reaches which mask the archaeological record. For example, during construction of Preston Docks, archaeological remains of human crania, along with red deer bones, radiocarbon dated to the Neolithic and Early Bronze Age, were found at depths of more than 10m below river sediments. In the same river, copper-alloy weapons of Middle Bronze Age date have been recovered when dredging the river channel. While sedimentation has the potential to preserve archaeological material, it also makes recovery by standard excavation techniques impossible.

The formation of peat mosses similarly preserves copper-alloy metalwork and also some organic remains, but again identification of remains is difficult. Peat is also strongly acidic and as a consequence, whilst wooden artefacts and human skin preserve well, human bone does not. This has resulted in the preservation of a number of 'bog bodies', most famously in recent years that from Lindow Moss, but also the destruction of bone in inhumed burials on acidic moorland soils. Cremated bone is not destroyed to the same extent. The burial record is therefore biased toward cremations rather than inhumations.

Erosion

Complementary to processes of sedimentation is that of erosion. In the upper reaches of the major river systems, river channels are constantly being re-cut and deepened. Potentially this could destroy much archaeology. However, in practice this does not seem to have been a great problem. The situation along the coastline is much more serious. The first map of the Fylde, which is Saxon for 'field', was published about the year 1500. It shows that the coastline at Fleetwood extended about a mile further out into Morecambe Bay than it does now and two miles further out into the Irish Sea at Rossall Point. From Bispham, south to the mouth of the Ribble at Lytham, the coast was one mile further out than today. At that time the area was worked by the inhabitants of the villages of Waddam Thorp, which lay a mile out from the present Squires Gate, and Singleton Thorpe, which was located at Singleton Skeer, a bank of shingle off Cleveleys. There was also Ross Hall, which lay off the present coast beyond the present Rossall College. In 1532 there was a large inundation by the sea which swept inland for two miles, covering all the land from about the present Bloomfield Road, Blackpool, right down to the Ribble Estuary, and inland to near Hawes Side Lane, Blackpool. Waddam Thorp was washed away and there is no record of any of the residents surviving. This land was covered by the sea for many years, eventually receding to form the present coastline, adding a strip of land about one mile wide to the coast which was useless for years because of the salt residue.

In the mid 1550s there was another inundation by the sea further north in which Singleton Thorp was destroyed, this time many of the inhabitants seemed to have escaped, settling at what is now Singleton village. In Thornber's *Historical Account of Blackpool* (1837) he quotes the sixteenth-century antiquarian Roger Dodsworth as saying

> In the reign of Mary, 1554, a sudden eruption of the sea took place at Rossall Grange. A whole village called Singleton Thorpe was swept away by its fury. The inhabitants were obliged to flee from the ancient spot and erected their tents at a place called Singleton to this day.

It is said that all that remained visible of their former village was

> … a huge stone which is said to have stood near the inn … tradition says that the stone formed, at one time, the centre of a Druidical circle … said to have stood near the inn and to which travellers were in the habit of tying their horses whenever they visited the hostelry … there is also a belief that the iron ring in the stone to which the horses were tied has actually been seen. The stone itself is still called Penny Stone, the belief being, that their horses being tethered, the travellers would call for and drink their penny pints of beer, for which the inn was famous.
>
> Langley Roberts 1931; 49

By 1610 the shape of the coast had changed considerably as shown in John Speed's map of Lancashire (*colour plate 9*). In 1877 C.E. de Rance recorded finding horse troughs and shippons (or cow sheds) full of sea water in the sand. In September 1893 Alfred Halstead described in his booklet *Singleton Thorpe: A buried village on the Blackpool Coast* his recent expedition which had revealed the remains of a cobbled building, its roof and a wooden lintel, approximately four miles north of Uncle Tom's Cabin and half a mile south of Rossall. Three years later Halstead continued the search, this time with Mr Pearson, Ben Bowman of *The Blackpool Times* and J. Whiteside. The four men took carts, equipment and labourers with them and, during low tide, conducted excavations roughly three-quarters of a mile west of the cliffs at Bispham. Tree tops were uncovered stretching to about half a mile north of Cleveleys, parts of which were taken home for souvenirs, along with doorposts and what appeared to be the previously mentioned lintel.

Similarly, south of the River Ribble at Formby Point the coastline has undergone change. There was extensive coastal erosion during the eighteenth century up to about 1830. There was an inundation in December 1720 flooding over 267ha of land and demolishing or damaging 150 houses at North Meols, and in 1739 a sandstorm buried the village of Ravenmeols. This trend reversed dramatically in the mid nineteenth century, when

Formby Point moved out, accreting about 300m around its whole arc, only for erosion to begin again from the late 1880s. It is now thought that the current phase of erosion at Formby was initiated by a significant increase in the frequency of storm-force westerly winds and wave energy in the late nineteenth century. Successive cycles of erosion and accretion seem to have been the norm since the last Ice Age along the coast, which makes life difficult for the archaeologist attempting to map the prehistoric landscape. What it is safe to say is that the fixed coastline as we know it is a product of modern sea defences and bears little resemblance to the fluid coastline that was the experience of previous generations of its inhabitants.

Urbanisation

During the nineteenth century, the north-west of England experienced a sustained period of urbanisation with the development of the metropolitan centres of Liverpool, Manchester, Bolton, Preston and Blackburn. The rapid building boom took place outside contemporary planning regulation and no provision was made for the protection of archaeological sites. Records of barrow disturbance and total destruction are numerous, revealing both an interest in, and recognition of, these ancient remains whilst acknowledging the need to destroy them in the name of progress, a desire which sits uneasily with modern attitudes. Fortunately the industrialisation of the region was accompanied by a plethora of literary and scientific societies who saw it as their duty to record the destruction of these monuments. Although the monuments are long lost, records, and in many cases artefacts, survive. Research of these archives, along with those of local newspapers and museum archives, form the basis of the database of artefacts and sites used in the discussion which follows.

Agriculture

Along with the growth of the urban centres went a growth in population which led to increased agricultural activity in Lancashire. Much of the region, as we have seen, is given over to grassland, ideal for dairying. The heavy clay soils are poorly drained making cereal yields low. The effect of this is two-fold: first, archaeological remains are preserved under grassland where otherwise they may be destroyed by plough action, but on the other hand, because the land is not being ploughed, stray finds, which often lead to the discovery of sites, are few and far between. Where arable agriculture is practiced, notably on the Fylde Coast, Over Wyre, West Lancashire and in parts of Cheshire, stone and metal objects have been regularly found. The bias is further compounded by modern metal-detecting practices, which favour ploughed soil over pasture, reinforcing the biased pre-existing distributions.

Retrieval

Retrieval is the third important filter between past activity and the known material record (Renfrew 1979, 152; Fraser 1983, 235–261). If the recognition of metal artefacts, stone artefacts and settlement over time is plotted as a graph, the importance of the amateur archaeologist and lay public become readily apparent (6). The recognition of ancient objects and places when plotted produces a curve, which follows the three-stage model proposed by Fraser (1983, 240–246). During the first phase, from 1750 to 1850, the number of sites and artefacts recorded increases only slowly. During the second phase the number of recorded sites

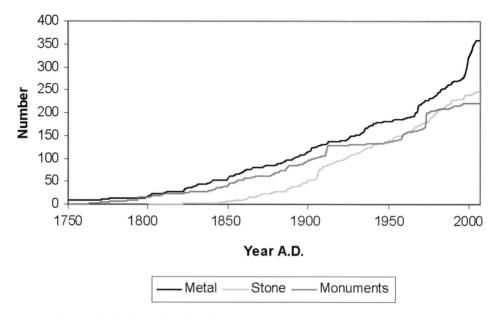

6 Cumulative totals for the number of artefacts/sites recorded since 1750 in Lancashire.
Metal = 358 Stone = 245 Monuments = 221 N = 824

increases rapidly, from 1850 until 1970. The leap in recognition is a consequence of a number of factors. These include the industrialisation of urban centres and the associated works of construction, which disturbed archaeological material, and also an increased awareness of the antiquity of society and an associated interest in archaeological sites and artefacts, evidenced by the formation of local archaeological societies, but not confined to them. Thirdly, the formation of a network of local museums, and later, legal protection for archaeological sites, encouraged the identification, recording, and preservation of sites and artefacts.

The third stage, from the 1970s onwards, is characterised by a sharp levelling off in the number of newly recognised sites. In Fraser's model, it is suggested that this stage is reached when the number of recognised sites is nearing the limit of potentially recognisable sites (Fraser 1983, 243). The tendency towards levelling off occurred first for monuments, beginning in the 1920s. There was a step increase in the late 1960s (the result of field survey producing a large number of new sites in southern Cumbria) but since then the trend has been level. This suggests that the sample of monuments closely reflects the total number of potentially recognisable monuments. Stone implements also show a tendency towards levelling off with the number of new finds slowing down in the last 10–15 years. One of the stated premises of the model is that fieldwork techniques remain unchanged. In the case of metalwork, a significant change has taken place with the advent of metal detecting. This change is clearly visible in the plot. The number of new finds had been slowing in line with Fraser's model. Yet since the 1990s there has been a rapid rise in the number of new finds. This reflects both the popularity of metal detecting as a hobby and also the steps taken to ensure that such finds are recorded, particularly the activity of the Portable Antiquities Scheme.

ASSESSING THE SAMPLE

The archaeological record for Lancashire and the surrounding area consists of 347 stone tools, 230 monuments (earthworks) and 46 settlement sites (Barrowclough 2007). The artefacts, sites and monuments known at present are the ones that have filtered through the processes of deposition, preservation and retrieval that have been considered above. These considerations are useful to help create a better informed judgement of the extent to which the known sample may be considered representative of the original population. The number of known artefacts and monuments was large enough to permit statistical analysis of their distributions (Barrowclough 2007).

PRIMARY FIND CONTEXT

The samples of known funerary monuments, and of stone and metal tools and weapons, are most promising as representative samples of human activity that went on across the region during the prehistoric period. Analysis of the primary find context of funerary monuments revealed that antiquarian/amateur activity and field survey were most important in discovering monuments; surface finds, ploughing and gardening were the most common way to find stone tools; and metal detecting, construction, farming and quarrying were the main source of metal finds (Barrowclough 2007, Figs 4.14, 4.15, 4.16).

A practical way to assess whether the sample was representative is to consider collection strategies adopted in historical periods that may have introduced bias into the record. In order to do this the distribution of all known finds was plotted against modern land-use (*colour plate 10*). In each case fewer artefacts and monuments were found on grassland and moorland than would have been expected from a random distribution and many more were found in urban, arable and woodland contexts (Barrowclough 2007). This suggests that finds are associated with human activity of one sort or another, for example ploughing, coppicing and settlement. Object discovery is therefore biased toward populous locations and those types of agricultural activity that involve disturbance of the soil.

SITE DESTRUCTION AND PRESERVATION: CONCLUSIONS

It is certain that some monuments and artefacts have been destroyed and lost, but the total sample size is sufficiently large to enable one to use it to make some sort of interpretation of past human activity. It is clear that there exists a bias in the primary find context of the archaeological record. Certain locations, arable land and urban areas, are over-represented whilst pasture and moorland tend to be under-represented. This bias will have to be taken into account when interpreting the analysis in the following chapters.

CHAPTER 2

THE FIRST ARCHAEOLOGISTS
IN LANCASHIRE

A SHORT HISTORY OF PREHISTORY IN LANCASHIRE

Antiquarian interest

From the eighteenth century onwards, antiquarian research was a valued pursuit for gentlemen with the required time and income to cultivate and indulge their passion for antiquities. That passion was a reflection of taste and an instrument of competition amongst both aristocrats and gentry. It mattered to be able to converse about the contents of a cabinet of curiosities. To be knowledgeable on such matters bestowed a certain standing within polite society. The earliest archaeological records are the product of antiquarian interest in the county. In his *Itinerary* (Hearne 1710) Leland records travelling through Lancashire in the sixteenth century as part of his national tour, recording as he went points of geographical, historical and antiquarian interest. Subsequently, others, for example William Camden (1971 [1586]) found an interest in the prehistory of the region. The former's notes are relatively few and the publications of both were concerned more with Roman than with prehistoric archaeology. This interest in the Roman period rather than prehistory reflects general antiquarian attitudes in the county (Harrison 1910).

Perhaps Lancashire's most famous eighteenth-century connoisseur and collector was Charles Towneley (1737–1805) of Towneley Hall, Burnley (Coltman 2006). Johann Zoffany, who had previously executed *The Tribuna of the Uffizi*, was commissioned by Towneley (*colour plate 11*) to depict him with highlights of his collection brought together in his London home in Park Street (now Queen Anne's Gate). Most of his collection was purchased in Italy, often from excavations around Rome. The excavation sites attracted the well-heeled British travellers on the Grand Tour, and soon a fever for collecting developed that dominated elegant taste throughout Europe. This domination of 'high culture' by classical interests was at the expense of interest in the prehistory of Lancashire. The journeys made by Leland and Camden are best viewed as precursors to the larger European Grand Tours made by Towneley and did little to advance interest in the region's prehistoric archaeology.

The earliest records of local finds of Bronze Age date are those dealt with by middle- rather than upper-class collectors. In his work *The Natural History of Lancashire, Cheshire and the Peak in Derbyshire* (1700), Dr Charles Leigh, a practising physician from Manchester, refers, amongst

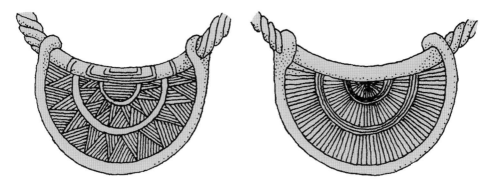

7 Gold pendant found in the River Irwell, Manchester. Interpreted as depicting the rays of the sun on the face (left) and those of the moon on the reverse (right). The object was in the possession of Sir Ashton Lever, but since the dispersal of his collection it has been lost. *Source: Phelps 1915, 192*

other things, to the discovery of eight dugout canoes at Martin Mere, Lancashire, and of a whetstone and metal axe found at Sawick (Salwick) Moss. The Rev. John Whitaker recorded the first perforated stone axe found in Lancashire. In his *History of Manchester* (1771, pl. 16 fig. 3) he describes, with illustration, a 'stone-formed head of a British battle-axe' in his possession and later deposited in the private museum of Sir Ashton Lever at Alkrington, and a bronze palstave known as the 'Mancunian Celt', which had been found in a bog outside the city.

Sir Ashton Lever (1729–1788) was an avid collector of all sorts of things. An article in the *Gentleman's Magazine* of May 1773 records a visit to his museum, which comprised 'upwards of one thousand three hundred glass cases containing curious objects placed in three rooms, besides four sides of rooms shelved from top to bottom with glass doors before them'. His interests and tastes were wide ranging, and the magazine notes that 'There are a great number of antique dresses and parts of dresses of our own and other nations – near two hundred spears and warlike instruments, ancient and modern'. In addition 'He collected all kinds of natural objects' including birds and birds eggs (Hird 1912, 205). Lever was a magnet for those who had stumbled across archaeological artefacts in the county and as a consequence his museum soon became the largest collection of prehistoric objects from Lancashire, including, for example, a gold pendant of probable Early Bronze Age date, found in the Irwell (7; Barrowclough 2007, 51 fig. 5.5). His museum was 'one of the sights of Lancashire' (Hird 1912, 205). In 1774 the museum moved to London where it was named 'The Holophusicon'. It was located in Leicester House in Leicester Square, the mansion of the Sidneys, Earls of Leicester, and it was said that 'sixteen rooms and various passages and staircases were filled with Sir Ashton's curiosities' (Hird 1912, 206).

The museum operated successfully for 11 years during which Sir William Hamilton (husband of Nelson's mistress) said that in different journeys to and from Naples, where he was ambassador, he had seen every public and private museum in Holland, France, Germany, Italy and Sicily, and he thought Sir Ashton Lever's collection was in every respect the finest (Hird 1912, 206). Unfortunately, Lever spent so much money on the museum that he was eventually forced to sell it in order to make ends meet. The collection was considered to be of such national importance that a campaign was begun to save it for the nation. A parliamentary committee was even established with the remit of investigating ways of keeping it, which valued the collection at £53,000. In 1783 Ashton offered it to the British Museum for much less but the trustees declined to buy it (Hird 1912, 207–8). There then followed protracted negotiations with a view to finding a way to keep the museum collection together. Finally, in 1785, the House of Commons passed a special Act of Parliament to enable Lever to sell the collection by lottery with a total of 36,000 tickets, each selling for a guinea. Unfortunately only 8000 tickets were sold and Lever was forced to sell a collection valued at £53,000 for only £8,000. The winner was a Mr Parkinson who rehoused the museum in the Rotunda located near to Blackfriars Bridge on the south side of the Thames. Over time it fell into neglect and in 1806 the entire collection was put up for public auction with 7879 lots being sold between 5 May and 18 July. In the process a collection of national importance was dispersed. As far as Lancashire is concerned, the sale scattered what would otherwise have been a major resource for archaeologists. Through time many objects have found their way back to the county, being bought by museums and private collectors based in Lancashire, but many have been lost forever, including the Irwell gold pendant.

In the Fylde area, William Thornber (1837) records the destruction of several earthworks on the Fylde along with numerous stray finds of metalwork. Thornber was born in Poulton-Le-Fylde in 1803, attending first Baines' Free School, then Giggleswick Grammar School, and finally Trinity College, Oxford; he was ordained and became curate incumbent at St John's, Blackpool. He was said to be of athletic build, 6ft tall and full of energy. His interests in archaeology and history were stimulated by his travels in the Giggleswick and Craven areas as a young man. He wrote the *History of Blackpool and its Neighbourhood* (1837) and also contributed articles to the *Transaction of the Historical Society of Lancashire and Cheshire* on the early history of Lancashire. His records are invaluable for their information on the destruction of several Early Bronze Age barrows on the Fylde as well as for his description of prehistoric trackways across Pilling Moss in the Over Wyre district. Local collectors could afford neither the Grand Tour nor to collect classical antiquities, yet they still had aspirations to enter the realm of the connoisseur. They therefore made what they could of the local finds; it is these collections that form the backbone of the contemporary collections of the nineteenth-century municipal museums.

The late nineteenth and early twentieth centuries

Toward the end of the nineteenth century, approaches to Lancastrian prehistory underwent a fundamental transformation. This transformation is inseparable from the political and economic changes of the period. The rapid industrialisation of Lancashire had led to an influx of people from the countryside into the city conurbations, which developed around the Lancashire coalfields. This drastic upheaval of longstanding ways of life had been observed at first hand in Preston by Charles Dickens whose experiences there form the basis of *Hard Times* (1995 [1854]), and then in Manchester by Friedrich Engels whose ideas (Engels 1986 [1884]) had influenced the writing of Karl Marx. He proposed that society had evolved through stages, taking his cue from the evolutionary principle outlined by Charles Darwin. A key figure in the nineteenth-century evolutionary debate was the comparative anatomist Sir Richard Owen (1804–1892). Most famous for coining the term 'Dinosauria' in

1842, Owen, a native of Lancaster who went on to found the Natural History Museum in London, was a passionate opponent of Darwin (White 2002). Although he ultimately found himself on the losing side of the evolutionary debate, his contribution to evolutionary anatomy and the study of differences between humans and apes was fundamental to the archaeological enquiry into the origins of human beings (Rupke 1994). In particular, the idea of deep time before the biblical flood, of stratigraphic dating and of typology and classification is central to archaeological science today. These political and scientific ideas had repercussions for the subsequent development of archaeology both nationally and in the region.

A near contemporary figure was Anatole von Hugel (1854–1928). Being a Roman Catholic, he was excluded from the ancient universities but was able to study at Stonyhurst College, Lancashire, a Jesuit foundation, between 1871 and 1873. He was advised to undertake a long sea voyage for his health, and decided to visit the Pacific, making an ethnographic study of Fiji (Haddon and Maudslay 1928). On his return to England he soon made contacts in Cambridge and in 1884 he was appointed first curator of what was then called the Museum of General and Local Archaeology, a post he held for 38 years. He acquired a 'considerable and comprehensive knowledge of British stone and bronze implements, and was greatly interested in Saxon pottery and personal ornament' (Haddon and Maudslay 1928, 169). His collection of archaeological artefacts is largely held in the Museum of Archaeology and Anthropology, Cambridge, however the Museum and Library at Stonyhurst College also includes a number of prehistoric artefacts donated by him, including a small number from Lancashire.

Interest in the prehistoric archaeology of Lancashire continued to be largely the preserve of local men, often but not exclusively drawn from the middle classes. North of the Sands in Furness, Harper Gaythorpe (1850–1909), an engraver and illuminator, is noteworthy for his promotion of archaeology in Furness through his publications, for example *Prehistoric Implements in Furness*, *Notes on the Bronze Celts from Urswick and Bronze Spearhead from Piel Castle* and *Prehistoric Implements in Furness*. In this period interests began to coalesce around common principles, and questions and work became more focused. Law and Horsfall discovered flints on their local moors and recognised that they were prehistoric tools, associating them with the Neolithic, as the term 'Mesolithic' had not yet come into use. They sent specimens to John Evans who supported them in their theory that the flints were the work of prehistoric people. He drew their attention to the fact that the very small and delicately chipped flints, many of which had been found on March Hill, were, as far as he knew, the smallest implements that had ever been found in this country. This prompted them to begin a series of investigations 'to ascertain the distribution and mode of occurrence of these Neolithic flints'. Their conclusions were published in a brief account, which has become a classic (Law and Horsfall 1882). They list 34 sites on the Pennine moors and ridges in both Lancashire and West Yorkshire, around Todmorden, Halifax and Huddersfield where they found flint and worked chert. They made a number of important observations which still hold true today: that flints are found in the sandy subsoil beneath the peat; on some moors the flints are widespread and are found wherever there are erosion patches; and in most places the vast majority of the flints are found on the southern aspect of the moors and ridges – an observation often repeated by future writers.

This process was aided by the formation of local and regional archaeological societies, some with their own journals, which provided an outlet for publication of their studies, for example the Lancashire and Cheshire Antiquarian Society founded in 1883. Prehistoric archaeology featured prominently at the first annual meeting held on 4 January 1884 when Prof. Dawkins gave, as his presidential address, 'Lancashire and Cheshire in Prehistoric Time'. Dawkins, who was appointed curator of Manchester Museum in 1869 and professor of geology at Owens College (now Manchester University) in 1874, did much to stimulate interest in archaeology in Lancashire. In the same year Dr H. Colley March's reading of his influential paper *The Flint Implements of the Pennines in East Lancashire* also acted to stimulate greater activity on the part of the society's members in looking into the evidence of early humans in the region. Colley March was a medical practitioner in Rochdale and an outstanding local archaeologist. His was a more anthropological approach: having read all the important books on the subject of 'early man' he was aware of recent ideas on human origins and threaded his way with remarkable insight among the cultural and chronological controversies of the day. In his paper he gives a general survey of the various periods of prehistory and relates the flint finds of the Pennines to the Mesolithic period. He, too, had explored the moors and had made some interesting finds, but although he was a careful worker, as his well-labelled flint collection (Rochdale Museum) indicates, he did not record details in the manner of Law and Horsfall. His address to the Lancashire and Cheshire Antiquarian Society puts forward an interesting discussion on the comparison of flint finds from the moors of East Lancashire with similar finds from Brittany.

Other collectors working quietly in the Pennines included W.H. Sutcliffe, who reported his finds from around Rochdale (Sutcliffe 1897) including a small hoard of graphite. James Binns, a quarryman from Halifax, was a knowledgeable prehistorian. Ling R. Roth relates:

> When the celebrated Berlin botanist, Count von Solmes Laubach, visited Halifax he was much struck with Binns knowledge and ability and on his departure gave Mr William Cash the sum of Three Pounds for him with the words: "We should not in Germany let a man like that remain a quarryman, James Binns was only one more example of the neglect with which scientific men are treated in England."
>
> Roth 1906

During this early period it had become well known to the interested public that the remains of prehistoric or 'Neolithic' people were to be found on the Pennine moors. The newly formed Lancashire and Cheshire Antiquarian Society and Rochdale Literary and Scientific Society, and to a lesser extent the Yorkshire Archaeological Society, published papers, held discussions and organised visits to these moorland sites. Outside these societies we catch glimpses of other collectors and investigators, such as James Binns, George Marsden, Ammon Wrigley, Emmott and several other working men who loved roaming the moors in search of flints. Whilst the geological position of these flints had been established, typological distinctions and wider geographical associations were to be the concern of the years that followed.

It is obvious from the papers read at the meeting of the Lancashire and Cheshire Antiquarian Society and the exhibits put on show in the Gallery of the Whitworth Institute, in January 1903, that interest in local flint remains was widespread among its members. Although the flint implements were still regarded as Neolithic, it was soon

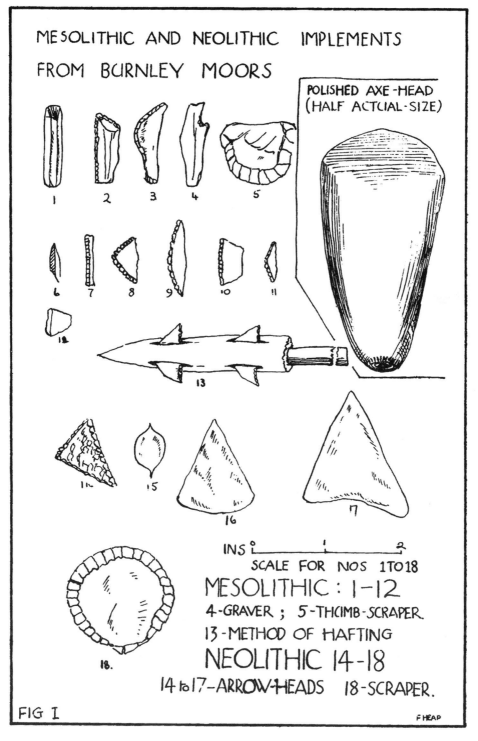

MESOLITHIC AND NEOLITHIC IMPLEMENTS FROM BURNLEY MOORS

POLISHED AXE-HEAD (HALF ACTUAL-SIZE)

INS
SCALE FOR NOS 1 TO 18

MESOLITHIC : 1-12
4-GRAVER ; 5-THUMB-SCRAPER
13-METHOD OF HAFTING

NEOLITHIC 14-18
14 to 17-ARROW-HEADS   18-SCRAPER.

FIG I   F HEAD

8 Examples of the different types of flint implements found on the Pennine moors, Burnley.
Walter Bennett 1946, 12

recognised that they had a different morphology to other implements and belonged to an early phase of the period (8). A conference was devoted to the subject in 1903 at which the Rev. R.A. Gatty stated: 'The first idea which these implements suggested was that they were the work of a small race, pygmies in fact, and he had given them the name of pygmy flints for that reason'. Even though he skates over the implications of this connection between race and tool size, and goes so far as to make it sound unlikely, the name stuck and has persisted in some quarters ever since. Gatty was quite convinced that these pygmy flint implements belonged to the Neolithic because he was finding them in the Scunthorpe area on blown sands, three metres above the peat in which well-defined Neolithic remains had been found.

On the other hand, Colley March was finding them sometimes three metres below the surface of the peat on the Lancashire moors. He accounted for this disparity by pointing out that peat deposits were not altogether trustworthy for dating, a fact that was to be proved in later years. His main emphasis was on the typological homogenity of these 'pygmy' implements, no matter what their stratification. He sums it up by saying, 'Their characteristics are as distinct as the arrowheads and scrapers of Neolithic times'. He had collected pygmies, in the 1870s, from the fields of Bradfield but no one would accept them as flint implements until Carlyle, of the Archaeological Survey of India, brought back the same type of pygmies from the Vindhya Hills in central India. Gatty found them identical with his, except that the Indian ones were made of chalcedony and not flint. He then found that similar types had been discovered on the Pennines near Rochdale in Lancashire, and on the blown sands around Scunthorpe in Lincolnshire. He had also found them in Lakenheath, Cambridgeshire, on sites similar to those at Scunthorpe. At Lakenheath, however, there was a more varied collection of flints of all periods and the pygmies were mixed with the flints of later periods.

Gatty makes the general observation, from the various sites he knew and had visited, that the makers of the pygmy flints preferred a barren, sandy common to more fertile places. He draws attention to a paper by Pierpont in which it was stated that in some places pygmy flints had been found with no other flints near them and were never found associated with polished tools. Gatty paralleled this with some of his finds from Scunthorpe and Carlyle's from India. He could not suggest what these pygmies were used for, found as they were over such a wide area, but agreed, incorrectly, with Canon Greenwell that there was a connecting link between the Indian and the West European pygmies. They erroneously believed that they could not possibly have developed independently, because the assemblages included at least four distinct types, common to both areas.

Colley March, now retired to Dorset, sent a paper (March 1905) and specimens to the meeting. He had nothing more to say about the Rochdale area but linked the finds there with some he had found on the island of Capri: broken pygmies and tiny cores of obsidian, and others from Port St Mary, Isle of Man. Of the latter place he says,

> … he found, a foot [30cm] beneath the surface soil a compact layer of rubble about 3 inches [c.7.5cm] thick in which were fixed by calcareous cement a number of implements, flakes and cores of flint.

Several pygmies of delicate working were amongst them. W.H. Sutcliffe (1905) put forward a system of classification of local implements and drew special attention to the pygmies. He supported an observation in Colley March's paper concerning two pygmies found in Staffordshire barrows by the late Mr Batsman by adding that one had been found by him in Hades Hill Barrow (Sutcliffe 1899), associated with partially cremated bones. The pygmy itself was unburnt.

Nine years later, in 1912, a further special meeting on pygmy flints was held, this time at the Manchester Museum, together with an exhibition of pygmy flints, collected from all over the world. This was a further development of the interest raised in 1903 and some new ideas were forthcoming. Sutcliffe and Parker (1912) put forward a theory for the use of pygmy flints, maintaining they were implements used in the making of clothes from skins. They suggested that flaying knives, scrapers and piercers, were obvious implements for such a purpose, and that the pen knife pygmies, with their hafts, shoulders and points, were very reminiscent of carding teeth used in the cotton industry. The pygmies, therefore, were part of a composite implement for breaking down fibres and softening animal skins. Their users inserted a number of these penknife pygmies in a block of wood and produced it along with a skin for demonstration. The crescentic microliths they declared to be fish throttles, and, in support of this theory, pointed out that the number of reservoirs and streams of the present time was indicative of a good water catchment area which in prehistoric times would have provided good fishing.

It was Colley March who suggested that the 'midget' makers (he objected to the term 'pygmy' because of its unproven racial associations) preceded the Neolithic and suggested they should be called 'Mesolithic' (March 1912). He put this idea forward on the grounds of the Egyptian, Indian, Mediterranean and European connections, and pointed to the fact that they are invariably found in earlier levels than Neolithic. Colley March, judging the more successful flint work, believed Mesolithic people to have been 'artistic'; in this he saw a further link with the hunting communities of the Upper Palaeolithic who were renowned for their artistic achievements. Here was, in his opinion, another reason why they should be considered separate from the Neolithic. In contrast to Colley March, Gatty (1912) stood by his term 'pygmy', and found 'a pleasing fascination in imagining such little implements to have been the work of a mythical race of small men'. He had shown his flints to the authorities at the museum in Brussels whose collection contained pygmy implements identical to his own but found on Palaeolithic sites in France and Belgium. A later exchange of views with Dr Sturge, and an examination of his large collection, seemed to confirm their Palaeolithic connection. Gatty drew attention to the smallness of these pygmy implements (some triangular forms from Scunthorpe were only 5mm long) and also to the great numbers of them both at Scunthorpe and Lakenheath. He stated that Mr Carlyle described finding several thousand of them in the cave earths of the Vindya Hills; but he is no nearer to defining their purpose.

Professor Boyd Dawkins agreed with Sutcliffe and Parker on the use of the penknife pygmy flints. As to their date, he would have nothing to do with Colley March's 'Mesolithic', but firmly declared that they were Neolithic, associated with neoliths (scrapers, knives, arrowheads etc.) in miniature. He pointed out, quoting Dechelette, that in some parts of France pygmy flints were found with polished stone axes, and in Italy, Spain and Belgium with Neolithic implements. He does say, however, that '... very likely they were used in various stages of civilization and that they were not limited to one period'.

A few months later in 1912, a loan exhibition of Local Flint Implements was displayed in the Bankfield Museum, Halifax. In an accompanying booklet only the barbed-and-tanged and leaf-shaped arrowheads and associated forms were described in detail, stating merely that pygmy flints were found in considerable numbers on the moors (Kendal and Roth 1912).

With this exhibition we come to the end of the first 40 years of flint collecting in the Pennines. In the last nine years of this period microliths or 'pygmy' flints had been recognised, many suggestions had been made as to their possible use, and something of their wide geographical distribution recognised, but we had no more detailed descriptions of finds in the manner of Law and Horsfall. This is a pity because from the list of exhibitors at these two exhibitions alone it is obvious that much collecting was taking place. It is also a pity that we do not hear more of Charles Roeder's finds from Kersal Moor and the other slight eminences in and around Manchester (Roeder 1907). He describes them as Neolithic and his mention of small cores suggests they may be similar to the Pennine and Scunthorpe finds. If so, these sites would have been very important from the point of view of Mesolithic distribution. Unfortunately, the finds, once in Salford Museum, have disappeared and the sites, which are situated in heavily populated areas, can no longer be examined. In these nine years there was plenty of interest and ideas but not sufficient archaeological facts to support them. There is a limit to what can be learnt from surface flint collecting. Excavation was needed.

The First World War acted as a major disjuncture in archaeology, as in many other aspects of British life. After the war nothing more was heard of the personalities and interests described above and the role of the Lancashire and Cheshire Antiquarian Society as a centre for Mesolithic interests ended. Future work was undertaken by individuals, independently publishing their discoveries and observations in whatever journal or proceedings they considered most appropriate. At the same time enthusiastic flint collectors were still (and still are) at work amassing material, most of which has never been properly studied or published and is now lost to archaeology. At Rishworth three generations of the Darby family, who worked to maintain the reservoirs on the moors above Marsden, created the Darby flint collection between 1930 and 1997. Their work on the moors gave then an unrivalled knowledge of many of the classic Mesolithic sites. The collection was studied and published by a number of researchers from the 1930s onwards, including an undergraduate from the University of Nottingham, Paul M. Rawson, who numbered and documented the collection. In the same area the eponymously named G. Marsden was one of the small band of working men who roamed the moors in search of flints and other prehistoric remains, often in the early morning before they begun their work. He discovered the Bronze Age cist and urns on Pule Hill, Marsden.

Francis Buckley, a local solicitor and JP, began collecting flints in France during the 1914–18 war, but his period of greatest activity was in the Pennines from 1918 until about 1924. He often worked alone, and with no more equipment than he could carry with him on the bus. His most important excavation was at Warcock Hill, where he was assisted by Woodhead and

Erdtman, a pioneer of palynology. Pollen analysis was undertaken on the site, the first time that an attempt had been made to date flints other than by typology. His views of the Pennine Mesolithic became mainstream when included in the British Museum's *Stone Age Guide* (Smith 1926, 91ff) and Grahame Clark's *The Mesolithic Age in Britain* (1932). Clark writes:

> … many collectors have worked over the [Pennine] sites, but little or no advance in knowledge was achieved until … Francis Buckley of Greenfield began to devote himself assiduously to their study … the writer wishes to acknowledge the wealth and accuracy of the information (Buckley) placed at his disposal.
>
> Clark 1932, 21

J.G. Clark's book represents the first time that an attempt had been made to bring together the wide variety of Mesolithic finds from this country and subject them to careful study. In dealing with the Pennines Clark concentrates almost entirely upon what he called the Huddersfield region and the work of Francis Buckley. He put forward an interesting account of the basic differences between Buckley's 'broad' and 'narrow' blade industries, along with his observations on the subject of patination. Although not agreeing with all of Buckley's ideas he did, however, emphasise the similarity between the 'broad' blade assemblies and the early Tardenoisian as represented by the lower levels at Zonhoven, Belgium, which in turn have analogies with finds from lower levels at Remouchamps, which immediately succeeds the Magdalenian period. On these grounds Clark asserts that these broad blade industries are very early. He regards the narrow blade industries as a more local, British, development, and accounts for the mixture of the two, which Buckley found on the same site at Lominot 4, by postulating either spontaneous evolution or the influence of geometry upon earlier non-geometric forms. In addition to the published Lancastrian finds, flints have been found by collectors on the Bolton and Bury Moors, the Bowland Fells, Pendle Hill, and on the moors around Colne and Burnley. Some of these finds are preserved in the local museums.

Many of the collectors who jealously guarded their flints did so because, in their eyes, they belonged to the liberty of the free open moorlands, which to them was almost sacred ground. Profane strangers and their interests were, consequently, not always welcome. Amman Wrigley, flint collector, local historian and poet from Rochdale, expressed his very strong feelings for the moors in his poem on a barbed-and-tanged arrowhead found on Pule Hill, written in his native Saddleworth dialect (Wrigley 1911). For the medics, lawyers, and local men who joined the newly formed societies and contributed to early journals, what had formerly been curios now became categories of object and classes of site (for example, Harrison 1892). Scientific description and classification was the order of the day and during much of the nineteenth and twentieth centuries, questions of culture sequence and chronology attracted considerable attention and often drove research agendas. Those agendas were varied. The details of local history, how the past was written on familiar ground, were paramount for some. A number of studies of the archaeology of local areas were produced. In 1933, Dr A. Raistrick published an article in the Yorkshire Archaeological Journal giving a useful summary of previous work done in the Pennines and also distribution maps recording new sites as well as those previously published (Raistrick 1933). He describes some of the new sites in the text and furnishes the first detailed survey of Mesolithic distribution in the north of England, although the main emphasis is upon sites in the Yorkshire Dales and north-eastern England.

G.B. Leach published a collection of flint implements from the erosion patches on the Worsthorne Moors, near Burnley, Lancashire (Leach 1951). Here, Mesolithic and Bronze Age flints were found under similar conditions, and pollen analysis of the overlying peats showed little significant difference. As all these remains were picked up from erosion patches there is no knowing whether the Bronze Age finds were embedded in the peat and had weathered out, or whether they were contained in the podsol layer beneath. Further, it is questionable whether Leach is justified in describing the finds from his Site 3 as Bronze Age, as there is nothing distinctively Bronze Age about them. Nevertheless, the fact remains that on these moors he found an impressive mixture of material from different periods even though at present their relationship is not very clear. This is obviously an area where future investigation might be profitable. Apart from the flints the only find of possible Mesolithic connection was half of a macehead with hour-glass perforation similar to stone found at Wakefield. Other examples were Fishwick's (1889) and later Richmond's (1926) studies of Rochdale, and Sobee's of Pilling and the Over Wyre district (1953).

For others, it was not so much the local connection but how that evidence added fuel to the fire of broader debates about evolution and history that was of interest (for example, March 1887). For yet others, and even now, antiquities were simply valued because, like books, they 'furnish a room'. It is to this time that we can point for the beginnings of the divergence between popular understanding of the past and scientific knowledge about it. During the course of the twentieth century the frame of reference for archaeology shifted at the level of academic discourse, away from regional studies and local histories, in favour of national narratives, developed increasingly in European context. The archaeology of Lancashire was subsumed into wider narratives, where it was included, if at all, as part of wider surveys of British prehistory which often took the form of catalogues of object types (for example Clarke 1970; Longworth 1984; Roe 1966).

Cooperation, which had existed between archaeologists and an interested public, broke down during this period, particularly in the post-war years. The Lancashire and Cheshire Antiquarian Society, as one measure of the bridge between public and profession, had begun with close ties to archaeologists. The Society had encouraged and assisted excavation and fieldwork with the aim of establishing a Museum of Local Archaeology and History. Field survey had been undertaken by members of the Society, for example at the stone circles on Extwistle and Worsthorne Moors (Anon 1893). It had funded the excavations of Wilfred Jackson, who was based at Manchester Museum, at Dog Holes Cave, Warton Crag over three years (Jackson 1909; 1910; 1912); it made a further grant to him for excavation of a timber circle at Bleasdale, near Garstang (Dawkins 1900, 114–124) and then in 1933 for preservation work at the site. In the austerity of the post-war era these relationships broke down and then, as the agenda of academic archaeologists shifted away from local and regional studies, the need for the relationship was no longer there.

The later twentieth century

Dislocation between professional archaeologists and the public entered a new phase in the last quarter of the twentieth century with the emergence of professional archaeological units. The origins of the region's units were in the university archaeology departments of Manchester, Liverpool and Lancaster. At Liverpool, Professor Terrence Powell undertook excavations at Broadbank, Burnley; Skelmore Heads, Ulverston and Storrs Moss in North Lancashire. Also out of Liverpool came Ann Hallam's study of the region's prehistoric pottery (1990) and Peter Davey and Eric Forster's study of Bronze Age metalwork (1975). Increased professionalism first marginalised, and then almost brought to an end, the long-standing tradition of amateur society-led excavations, one of the last ones being Whinstanley's Bolton Archaeological Society excavation of Noon Hill (Rosser 1958).

Walter Bennett (1889–1983) was History Master at Burnley Grammar School and a prolific writer of local histories. Not only did he write a comprehensive four-volume *History of Burnley* (1946), which became the standard history of the town, he also wrote histories of Burnley Grammar School, Marsden and Nelson, a book on the Lancashire Witches and an edition of the Churchwardens' Accounts of St Peter's Church. The first volume of his *History* contained descriptions of the local archaeology focusing on the earthworks and finds from the moors in the vicinity of Burnley (*9*). This was followed in 1951 by his own excavation of an Early Bronze Age funerary monument at Mosley Heights (*10*; Bennett 1951).

Those amateurs with an interest in field archaeology found an outlet in the metal-detecting clubs that formed during the late 1970s. This further served to distance public from professional archaeologists. The latter were mistrustful of a technique which they often believed to be no more than treasure hunting; the former felt increasingly closed off from news of archaeological discoveries, accounts of which were increasingly limited to 'grey' literature. I believe that too often communication has been reduced to the level of public lectures delivered by professional archaeologists to community groups, rather than genuine conversation.

The most prolific archaeologist in Lancashire in the latter half of the twentieth century was John Hallam (*11*). Born near Accrington he took his first degree in Ancient History and Philosophy at the University of Manchester before his love of the Pennines, and particularly of the Mesolithic flints, led him to the University of Liverpool. His thesis *The Mesolithic of the Central Pennines* (1960) was followed by a Leverhulme Research Fellowship, also at Liverpool, and continued research into the prehistory of Lancashire. He lectured in archaeology at both Manchester and Liverpool Universities' Extra Mural departments and also directed numerous excavations within the county, including the important Mesolithics site at Marles Wood, Ribchester; Mawdesley, West Lancashire; West Nab, West Yorkshire; the Early Bronze Age sites at Astley Hall Farm, Chorley and Carriers Croft Pendleton; and the later prehistoric 'hillfort' of Portfield, Whalley. Most notable was the discovery of a Late Glacial elk along with barbed points at Highfurlong, Poulton-Le-Fylde (Hallam *et al* 1973). The elk had been hunted, but not killed, as evidenced by the injuries left on the skeleton by the hunting party's arrows. During the 1970s Hallam was consultant archaeologist to the Central Lancashire New Town and subsequently ran the Central Lancashire Archaeological Research Unit working throughout the county. The chapters which follow are greatly enhanced by the data derived from those excavations, much of which is published here for the first time. In addition to the

9 Illustration of funerary urns found on the moors around Burnley. *Bennett 1946, 18*

10 Excavations at Mosley Heights in 1950, directed by Walter Bennett (extreme right). *Photograph: Towneley Hall Museum and Gallery*

11 John Hallam during excavations of a prehistoric cairn on Anglezarke, Lancashire. *Photograph: J. Hallam*

publication of individual sites he published *The Surviving Past* (1988) describing the excavations and artefacts unearthed during the construction of the New Town and 'The Prehistory of Lancashire' an overview of the county's prehistory in the *Archaeological Journal* (1970).

The decline in amateur archaeological societies at the end of the twentieth century was paralleled in a similar decline in the number of prehistoric sites that were excavated. Commercial archaeological units, dependant upon developer-funded rescue work, only rarely had an opportunity to excavate Early Bronze Age burials, but where they did, for example at Borwick (Olivier 1987) and Allithwaite (Wild 2003), the standard of excavation was much higher than previously. Developer-funded work was also responsible for new insights into settlement patterns with important new sites found ahead of the construction of Manchester Airport's second runway (Garner 2001) and the A5300 road development on Merseyside (Cowell 2000a). Most research took the form of archaeological survey, first in the uplands of Anglezarke (Howard-Davis 1996) and then in a series of surveys of the region's wetlands (Hall *et al* 1995; Middleton *et al* 1995; Leah *et al* 1997). These provided much detailed work on pollen cores. Lancashire has often found itself at the forefront of environmental archaeology because of the wealth of its wetland resource, both upland and lowland. Significant contributions have been made by Malcolm Bain on the Anglezarke uplands, John Tallis, Verona Conway, Harry Godwin, Winifred Pennington, Frank Oldfield, Michael Tooley on changing sea levels around the Lancashire coast, Peter Cundhill in south-west Lancashire, Brian Barnes in his study of the Central Pennines and of the elk from Highfurlong, Alan Hibbert at Red Moss, Judith Turner in North Lancashire, G.W. Dimbleby, J.G. Evans in his work with land snails, Donald Walker in his study of the wooden trackway 'Kate's Pad', and Dr Woodhead.

The amateur still has a role to play. Metal detecting has given rise to a huge increase in the amount of Bronze Age material, discussed further in Chapter Six. The Mellor Archaeological Trust has led a renewed interest in community archaeology with its excavations of the largely Iron Age settlement at Mellor, an example of how professional and academic archaeologists can work successfully with the local community as equal partners.

INTERPRETATIONS

A number of accounts have attempted to formulate an interpretation for the post-glacial settlement of the region. An equally prevalent concern throughout the first half of the twentieth century was the cultural and racial origin of the region's prehistoric inhabitants. European prehistory during this period was dominated by culture-historical models, which often sought racial explanations for differences in material culture. The models invoked to explain the Lancastrian evidence were no exception.

The driving force behind the review of funerary urn types undertaken by Colley March (1887) was to understand human descent. His ideas were clearly conceived within the ideas of racial origin prevalent at the time. He divided the urns into three groups on typological grounds, which he associated with Celts, Teutons and Romans, 'all descendents of one Aryan family' (1887, 272). The Second World War brought about a sharp reaction against this line of investigation, which disappeared from the research agendas of the region. March's study was one of a number of accounts that attempted to explain the changes that we see in the archaeological record of Lancashire in terms of the invasion and migration of people. External influence from the continent was the mechanism suggested by Dawkins (1876, 1–7) to explain changes in technology. Jackson (1935) drew on Fox's notion of the Highland Zone to explain changes in material culture – 'the Beaker folk, invaders from the Rhinelands … brought with them a characteristic type of pottery' (1935, 76) – and to identify trade links – 'the discovery of three flat bronze axes near Whalley is taken as evidence of a trade route linking Ireland – the El Dorado of the west in the Bronze Age' – with Yorkshire, via the Ribble and Aire Gap, and ultimately with Denmark and north Germany (Jackson 1935, 82). Likewise in his study of the prehistory of Burnley, Walter Bennett (1946) inferred the movement of people – 'invaders from the Continent [who] introduced a knowledge of how to make bronze' – from material culture types to explain change. Lancashire north of the Sands was dealt with separately by R.G. Collingwood (1933) as part of the archaeology of Cumberland and Westmorland, but along with the theories of the time his interpretation invoked settlement of the region from outside. He envisioned the arrival by sea of 'Neolithic' people on the west coast, whilst 'Beaker folk' migrated from the north-east of England travelling up the Eden valley (1933, 191). The Iron Age was similarly interpreted in terms of 'Celtic invasions', from the Rhine into the Marne Valley and then to eastern England and then Lancashire (Sayce 1956, 3).

The most developed model explaining cultural change in the region was proposed by Bu'Lock (1961). Although he was working within the paradigm of culture-history, which fits uneasily with contemporary approaches, he was the first to recognise that Lancashire's archaeological record has to be explained in the context of the region, and that models imported from elsewhere in Britain cannot be applied uncritically. His interpretation is worth considering in detail as it identifies some of the main characteristics of the region's archaeological record and offers an interpretation that forms the basis of our current understanding. He argued that the north-west of England was a native enclave with its own distinctive 'North Western' styles of pottery surrounded by areas in which the single-grave Food Vessel tradition was either wholly predominant, as in the Peak District and east of the Pennines, or far more influential in amalgamation, as in North Wales, south-west Scotland and Ireland. This defined 'a geographic integrity sufficient to warrant the designation of a North Western Culture in Early Bronze Age England' (Bu'Lock 1961, 38).

According to his model the Neolithic population of pastoralists and hunters shared a common cultural heritage with their contemporaries around the northern shores of the Irish Sea, an idea that has recently received new currency in discussion of the Irish Sea Province (Fowler and Cummings 2003; see also Raftery 1972). He accounted for this in part by the trading of stone axes from the Cumbrian 'factories', and partly on common antecedents, expressed materially through burial rites and monuments, and the associated ceramics. Whilst 'Beaker folk' colonised adjacent areas of Yorkshire and Derbyshire, establishing distinct cultural communities, the north-west of England retained its native traditions, which give it a distinct character. In the east of England he saw a fusion of immigrant and native elements out of which emerged the 'Food Vessel folk', groups of whom penetrated into the north-west in small numbers, following routes favoured by the trade in Irish bronzes. These immigrants are marked by single-grave burials under round barrows.

By the time that the Wessex Culture had established itself in the south the native tradition in the north-west had reached the stage referred to as the 'Pennine Urn Period', that is the North Western Style of Collared Urns. This period was marked by an expansion of the population of the north-west which, fuelled by its part in the bronze trade, was able to expand eastwards into the 'Food Vessel area' of the Peak District. He saw the 'native tradition' as experiencing a resurgence associated with either the absorption or the displacement of the food-vessel single grave groups.

The timing of his publication was unfortunate, coming just as culture-history interpretations were going out of fashion. In the 1970s and 80s, palaeoenvironmental research and models based on environmental determinism came to the fore (for example Hibbert *et al* 1971; Barnes 1975; Jacobi *et al* 1976; Cundhill 1981). According to them Lancashire was an environmentally marginal environment of lowland wetlands and upland bogs making subsistence difficult. Within the region ground-breaking work was undertaken by Barnes, synthesising archaeology and palaeoenvironmental evidence: 'In uplands like the Central Pennines, marginal areas so far as human occupation is concerned, environmental factors played the dominant role' (Barnes 1982, 13). Typology and chronology were similarly interpreted within a framework of geographical determinism for the Bronze Age of West Yorkshire, which includes parts of the region under investigation, by Manby and Turnbull (1986). These interpretations were strongly influenced by geographical determinism originating in the work of Fox (1932) in his book *The Personality of Britain*. This saw the lowlands of Lancashire and the Cheshire Plain as an intrusion into what was an otherwise highland zone (see Dimbleby 1975). As such it was to be expected that influences were likely to be received from the south-east, and also from areas around the Irish Sea coast. The uplands of the Pennines as part of the highland zone were prone to influences from Yorkshire and Scotland channelled through the upland valleys of, for example, the Ribble and Aire gaps (see for example Jackson 1935, 82).

More recent accounts have moved away from such deterministic interpretations. In a discussion of the later prehistoric archaeology of Merseyside, in the context of recent fieldwork, Ron Cowell (1991b) argues that explanations of the region's data do not fit well with models developed for sites in southern Britain. He identifies the need to devise interpretative models specific to the region. Attempts at this have been made for the Romano-British period. Matthews (2001) explicitly rejects models based on south-eastern England, and questions the core-periphery model that dominated interpretations of the Iron Age since the late 1970s, in his study looking at the consumption of material culture and how it worked to create distinct identities for people in the north-west. Nevell (2003b) offered a contextual study of settlement in the Mersey Basin in the Romano-British period. A similar contextual approach to interpretations of the Late Neolithic, Bronze and Early Iron Age of Lancashire has been suggested by my own work (Barrowclough 2007), and in what follows.

DISCUSSION

The above review has traced some of the encounters with Lancashire's prehistory over the past four centuries. It did not set out to give an exhaustive account, but selected some key contributions that are representative of the history of ideas about Lancashire's prehistoric evidence. Present-day attitudes to Lancashire's prehistory are the result of this stratification of ideas. In this sense, the history of Lancashire's archaeology reflects the history of prehistoric archaeology nationally. One of the reasons that this review is useful is that an understanding of how archaeological knowledge has been constructed allows one to identify the strengths and weaknesses in our interpretations more readily. One of the outstanding concerns that have emerged is a disjuncture between popular and scientific knowledge. Regional and national journals have become increasingly specialised. Aimed at professional archaeologists, they are written in increasingly technical language, and are often inaccessible to the general reader. A second is the dislocation of archaeology from the regional context, seen in national narratives drawing upon evidence from other parts of Britain. This largely replaced understanding of the past based upon a reading of the regional archaeological record. Prehistoric archaeology became an activity for outsiders from which the communities living closest to these remains were often excluded. Another dislocation is the decontextualisation of Lancashire's archaeological record from the surrounding landscape. Beginning with the earliest collectors the emphasis has been on removing artefacts from the landscape and placing them first in private and then in public museum collections. These collections form the basis of the various artefact corpora which group objects according to the categories that archaeologists create – placing, for example, the grouping of urns from different locations together, or separating objects that were found together into different corpora. The tendency to treat different classes of data in isolation from each other and from the landscape is not a trait that is particular to Lancashire; it is a tendency that has characterised approaches to prehistoric archaeology in Europe until fairly recently (Watson 2001, 296).

The series of disjuncture and dislocations outlined above are all interrelated. The creation of archaeological understanding is inseparable from the social context in which it occurs. The practices of archaeological investigation and site management that have been outlined were recognisably modelled on the mainstream paradigms of their period. They often became inseparable from the values that were driving research in the wider context of British archaeology. This array of global and local processes went far to create a sound foundation for the understanding of Lancashire's prehistory. Inevitably, it also had its limitations, some of which have been the focus of the present chapter. Such limitations are, of course, easier to recognise from the vantage point of the present. From our position we are better placed to begin to address some of these gaps in our knowledge.

CHAPTER 3

LIVING OFF THE LAND: THE LATE UPPER PALAEOLITHIC AND MESOLITHIC HUNTER-GATHERER OCCUPATION

INTRODUCTION

The last Ice Age came to an end *c.* 10000 years ago. Tundra landscapes that supported reindeer herds were colonized by birch and soon became thick deciduous woodland with dispersed fauna including red deer, auroch and wild pig. Sea levels rose so that Britain, formerly a peninsula of Europe, had become an island by 8500 years ago. In this rapidly changing environment people continued to live by hunting and gathering for several thousand years until agriculture became established.

Stray finds indicate little other than the presence of Mesolithic people. Scatters of stone tools and the debris from their manufacture are the most abundant features of the record of the Mesolithic. The type artefacts from the period are microliths: small blades usually of flint that have been retouched occur in a range of shapes and sizes. Microliths are often found in their hundreds if not thousands and were probably components of a wide range of tools including hunting equipment. The Early Mesolithic, the period before 8500 years ago, was dominated by 'broad blade assemblages'. These are collections of relatively large microliths either shaped like isosceles triangles or described as 'obliquely blunted points'. Later Mesolithic assemblages, after *c.* 8500 BP, are usually dominated by much smaller microliths in a wider variety of forms which are termed 'narrow blade assemblages' and include needle points and scalene triangles.

LATE GLACIAL

The earliest evidence for human hunter-gatherer occupation of Lancashire dates to the Late Upper Palaeolithic, *c.* 16000–8000 BC. The evidence is sparse as the ice sheet did much to obliterate and cover earlier landscapes and the sites that must have once existed. As a consequence it is impossible to reconstruct any meaningful pattern of occupation. Although limited, the Late Upper Palaeolithic material from Lancashire is the earliest evidence for settlement this far north and as such is of national importance. Elsewhere in northern England it is rare to find artefacts of this period, with only two cave sites in the Yorkshire Pennines providing similarly limited evidence (Cowell 1996, 30). The main sites are found in the southern part of Britain with the exception of an important number of cave sites in Derbyshire (Jacobi 1980).

The evidence for the first, post-glacial occupation of Lancashire comes from sites around the shores of Morecambe Bay. A single flint blade from Badger Hole Cave, Warton, has parallels with lithic material from Kirkhead Cave (Ashmead and Wood 1974; Gale and Hunt 1985, 1990; Salisbury 1986), which has been dated to the Late Devensian zone III, *c.*11000–9500 BC (Young 2002). Radiocarbon dating of elk antlers, considered by Gale and Hunt (1985) to be associated with the artefacts in Kirkhead Cave, produced a date of 11027–10077 cal BC (10650 ±200 BP). To the north-east, at the mouth of the River Kent, three Upper Palaeolithic blades have come from Lindale Low (Salisbury 1988; Hodgkinson *et al* 2000). A further 80 lithic implements of Late Upper Palaeolithic date were excavated from Bart's Shelter, Furness, including a shouldered point (Jacobi in Hodgson and Brennand 2006, 25). The faunal assemblage at Bart's Shelter included reindeer and elk, and it was the excavation of the latter across the bay at High Furlong, Poulton-Le-Fylde near Blackpool, that provided the earliest evidence for human occupation of the county. The skeleton of a male elk, between four and six years old, displaying injuries consistent with hunting activity (*12 & 13*) and associated with two bone points (*14*), was recovered within shallow water deposits (Barnes *et al* 1971; Hallam *et al* 1973; Hallam pers. comm.). The condition of the lesions on the bones suggest that the elk had been attacked by hunters on two separate occasions, the first 14 days

12 Anthony Stuart excavating the elk's metatarsal. *Photograph: John Hallam*

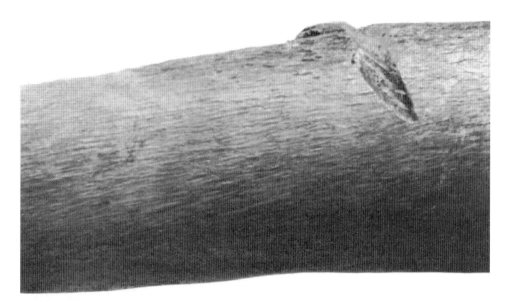

13 Lesion on rib, small cut. *Photograph: John Hallam*

before the second. A barbed point found embedded in the elk's left hind leg (*15*) appeared to
have been shot from a bow. Other injuries penetrating the rib cage were consistent with it
being struck by flint-tipped implements, and those to the left fore foot which severed the
tendons, with it being struck with an axe. Despite the severity of the hunt the elk managed to
escape capture only, perhaps weakened by the attack, to drown in a shallow lake. During the
Late Upper Palaeolithic the vegetation around the Fylde consisted of 'park tundra' composed
of large, open, herbaceous vegetation with scattered copses of shrubs and trees, including
birch, with fen vegetation along the sides of lakes. When examined, the elk was found to be
due to shed its antlers (*16*). As male elk only shed their antlers during the winter we can be
confident that the hunt seems to have taken place at that time, most probably between
December and February. The skeleton was dated to 13500–11500 cal BC (Jacobi *et al* 1986;
Middleton *et al* 1995, 87). Although this date has recently been slightly refined towards the
later end of this spectrum (Jacobi in Hodgson and Brennand 2006, 25) the evidence places it
within the Late Devensian II warm interstadial period.

MESOLITHIC

The potential of Mesolithic evidence from north-west England is amongst the best in the
country because of the combination of upland and lowland sites, both in significantly large
numbers, with detailed pollen studies which provide a range of associated evidence. In North
Lancashire assemblages occur at Bart's Shelter where Early Mesolithic microliths, some
composed of volcanic tuff, were excavated along with a bone or antler point dated to
6210–6190 cal BC (Jacobi in Hodgson and Brennand 2006, 26). North of Lancaster at both

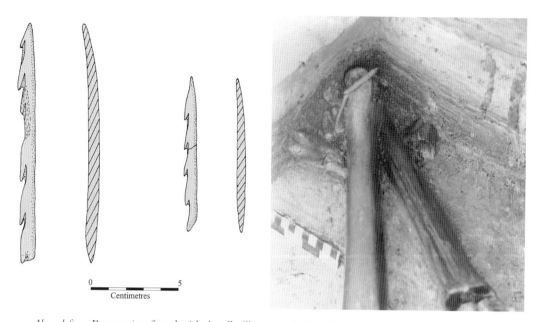

Above left 14 Bone points found with the elk. *Illustration: B.J.N. Edwards*

Above right 15 Metatarsal under excavation with barbed point 2 in situ. *Photograph: John Hallam*

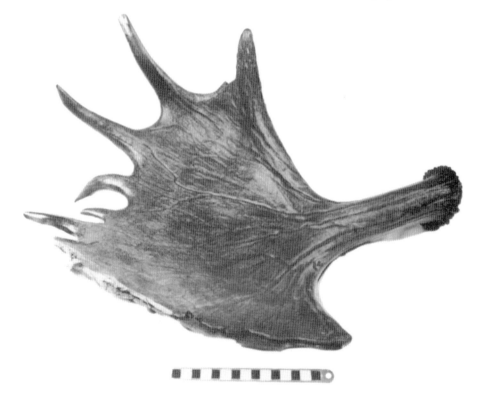

16 Left antler, dorsal view. *Photograph: John Hallam*

17 Eroding Mesolithic site on the River Lune at Halton, North Lancashire. *Photograph: Robert Williams*

Borwick (Olivier 1987) and Levens Park (Cherry and Cherry 2000) assemblages of Late Mesolithic and Early Neolithic date were found sealed beneath burial mounds suggesting repeated use of some locations through the Mesolithic and into the Neolithic (Hodgson and Brennand 2006, 26). The source of the lithics manufactured from volcanic tuff in the north of the region is believed to be glacial drift originating from the central Cumbrian Massif (Bradley and Edmonds 1993).

Surveys along the course of the River Lune have located Mesolithic activity at Halton, the Crook O'Lune (*17*) and at Hornby (Penney 1978; Williams 1998; Oxford Archaeology North 2002a). Over 1400 artefacts (Hodgson and Brennand 2006, 26) have been found in the area. The majority comprise waste material, such as single-platform cores, although tools do occur and these include burins, microliths and crudely made leaf-shaped arrowheads. Chert and flint were present in more or less equal proportions, with some of the most intricate tools being made from chert.

West of Lancaster along the coast at Heysham Head, 1262 largely Late Mesolithic implements, including 23 complete blades, were excavated from an area of 32 square metres. The excavators reported that the lithic assemblage consisted of both complete products and waste flakes, leading them to suggest that this was a permanent settlement rather than a seasonal occupation site (Salisbury and Shepperd 1994). Further south in the Over Wyre district three small possibly Late Mesolithic assemblages are known from Friars' Hill, a sand hill in Stalmine Moss (Middleton *et al* 1995, 54). The hill would have provided dry land within a mosaic of changing environments, making it an ideal base for a hunting and fishing economy. South of Morecambe Bay material of possible Late Mesolithic provenance has been

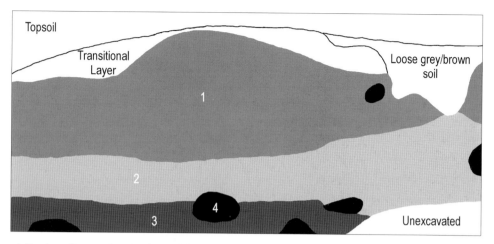

18 Section of excavation, Marles Wood, Ribchester. 1: Yellow-orange compacted loam with occasional charcoal flecks containing the majority of the implements. 2: Yellow/orange loose crumbly soil. 3: Orange/brown sticky clay, very compacted with few artefacts. 4: Very loose orange loam

identified either side of the Ribble Estuary, close to Lytham at Peel, and also at Banks near Southport (Middleton 1990; Cowell 1991a; 1991b; 1992; Cowell and Innes 1994; Middleton *et al* 1995). Further inland along the River Ribble at Marles Wood, Ribchester, a further Late Mesolithic site has been excavated by John Hallam (pers. comm.). This site lies on the south bank of the River Ribble; and like the sites along the Lune, the bank is revealed by erosion of the river, which at present is about 4.5m below the excavation. As this site has not previously been published it justifies further consideration for the light that it can shed on activities at similar sites in both the Ribble and Lune valleys.

A lithic assemblage of 339 implements was excavated containing 27 pieces of chert and 82 of flint, composed of both waste and artefacts. The majority of the pieces came from context II, a yellow-orange compacted loam with occasional charcoal flecks (*18*). The chert was of several varieties: the majority of pieces were of a coarse, brown-speckled, black chert occurring naturally in pebbles from the riverbed. In addition there were 20 examples of a fine black type similar to Derbyshire chert, and a very few pieces of Cheshire rhyolite. The flint ranged in type from a brown translucent form to a grey/white or orange opaque variety. The origin of the flint is questionable: some of the pieces retain cortex, suggestive of pebble flint, but whether this occurred in river debris or had been brought to the site deliberately is unknown.

The cores were all of chert and were heavily worked with long flake/blade scars averaging 25–30mm in length in the majority. Core trimming flakes were well represented showing previous flake removal. Cortex was found on part of two of the flint trimming flakes, which ranged in size from 30–15mm. There were 14 whole blades again of both chert and flint with virtually no evidence of either use or secondary working. Twelve bulbar ends were found, seven of flint, a proportion which may show the preference of flint in the production of implements, assuming bulbar ends are evidence of microlith production. No conventional micro-burins were present in the assemblage but since microliths did occur this may possibly reflect a technique of microlith production not yet recognised, which might have invloved snapping the blade cleanly rather than notching before snapping (Hallam pers comm.). Eight segmented forms (middles of blades) were present as well as six distal ends. It is not possible to determine whether these distal ends were the result of deliberate or accidental snapping since all were very thin and delicate.

The utilised pieces fall into four groups: first, those with cutting or 'knife' edges, shown by worn edges and use scars. These consist of flakes, blades and irregular lumps. One blade had wear scars on one edge and a notch cut in the opposite edge. The second group were those pieces with notches, around which are use scars. The third group, those artefacts with graver facets on a projecting point. These have been made on flakes and fragments and all bear polished facets. The final group were those with borer points of which there were four pieces with sharpened tips and polished facets, two of which appear to have been deliberately worked to a pre-set pattern and may thus qualify as tools. There were also two gravers and ten microliths, seven of flint and three of chert of the speckled brown black type. This is the only group in which flint predominates, suggesting the superior working properties of this material over chert. The high standard of flaking on the microliths contrasts with the lack of other finely made implements, suggesting that the prime aim of the chipping activities was microlith production. Of the 10 microliths, five were rod-shaped and only two were unbroken, both of which bear trimming on both long edges and are of similar length and width: 15–20 x 4mm. The microliths include an obliquely blunted point; a point with a shallow oval notch on the butt, possibly suggestive of hafting; two scalene triangles, one 16 x 5mm and less than 3mm thick which is the most finely worked chert piece on the site; and an ultra-narrow form of a scalene triangle in grey/brown flint with a very sharp point. The latter two can certainly be seen as missile or projectile points.

The microliths of small, geometric type, i.e. scalene triangles and narrow rods, place the site within the Late Mesolithic. The concentration of lithic material within a small area identifies the site as an in situ chipping floor. The presence of microliths and gravers to the exclusion of other tool types such as scrapers, which are well represented on many Mesolithic sites, suggests that only a limited range of activities were taking place at the site. The lithic remains bear witness to a riverbank activity in which equipment was made perhaps for fishing and hunting along the bank. The discovery of further flint and chert pieces along a footpath that follows the river suggests that this stretch of the river, which passes through a narrow gorge, was a customary fishing place.

Since the excavation of Marles Wood a number of other Mesolithic sites have been discovered along the course of the Ribble. Field survey has identified a second site on the north bank of the Ribble, at Talbot's Field, Ribchester. Seventy-five lithic artefacts were found, scattered over a large area measuring 5.5 x 9m, as a result of plough action. Although disturbed and broken it was possible to identify among the assemblage, which consisted of chert with just six flint pieces, two blades and a speckled-brown/black chert core identical to those found at Marles Wood. Mention should also be made of Mesolithic material found on the Ribble at Walton-le-Dale, Preston, below the Roman occupation layers. The material is local pebble, Pendleside chert and white Yorkshire flint, much of which is very similar to the

19 Excavation of Mesolithic flint from the sand quarry at Mawdesley. *Photograph: John Hallam*

type found at Marles Wood. There were a total of 160 pieces with the flint to chert proportion in an approximately 2:1 ratio. Included in the assemblage were 2 cores, 22 blades, 7 knives, 2 scrapers and a scalene point indicative of the later Mesolithic period. The general characteristics of the Mesolithic assemblage suggest a blade, rather than flake industry, whilst the inclusion of larger, broader blades reflects a combination of types of blade industry, possibly of different phases of occupation. There are certainly some affinities with the material from Marles Wood, especially the waste and the microlith types, but the total collection perhaps has its closest parallels with upland sites (e.g. Smithills Moor, Bolton), which also contain this non-homogenous type of assemblage. This may suggest a wider range of activities were taking place at Walton-le-Dale than at the sites further along the river at Ribchester.

A number of lowland sites lie south of the Ribble in West Lancashire and on Merseyside. Small lithic scatters have been found lying on islands of sandy soil at Halsall and Downholland, inland of Formby (Middleton 1997). In the same area excavations on the moss edge at Mawdesley (*19*) (Middleton *et al* 1995, 87; Hallam pers. comm.) have revealed an important habitation site. Originally a slight sandy island standing a few metres above the surrounding countryside, about half a mile east of the River Douglas, the centre of the hillock was excavated commercially for sand extraction.

Lithic material from Mawdesley is comprised of flint and chert (*20*). The flint appears to have been derived from several sources: pebbles from the local drift; grey patinated flint, typical of the Lincolnshire chalk; and fine, clear brown flint, found in parts of North and East Yorkshire. The assemblage included scrapers, gravers, cutting implements, microliths and cores as well as waste.

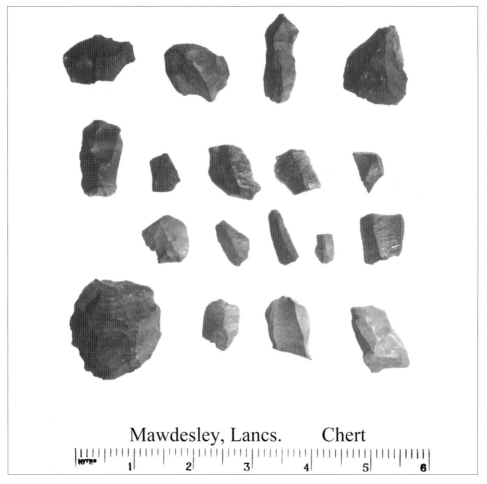

Mawdesley, Lancs.   Chert

20 Examples of chert implements from the Mesolithic site of Mawdesley, Lancashire. *Photograph: John Hallam*

Palaeobotanical investigation of the peat deposits to the north and south of the hillock have shown that a layer of charcoal occurred below the old land surface (Barnes pers. comm.). It is associated with increase in oak pollen at 40 and 35cm, both at the expense of pine and prior to an increase in alder pollen. This occurs at a time when the microliths may have been deposited. The evidence suggests that the Mesolithic inhabitants were using fires to clear woodland, revealing something of the impact that people had upon the landscape.

Further light has been shed on Mesolithic occupation in the lowlands by a series of excavations allied to survey work in southern Lancashire, Merseyside and Cheshire (Cowell and Philpott 2000; Cowell and Innes 1994; Hallam pers. comm.; Middleton 1993; Middleton and Tooley in prep.). The Alt-Ditton valley (*21*), a *c*.25km-long glacial channel, has perhaps the greatest density of Mesolithic sites in lowland Lancashire. The valley provides a worked example of how the population exploited the landscape, which may be used to aid understanding of other lowland sites in the county. Seasonal patterns of wild resource

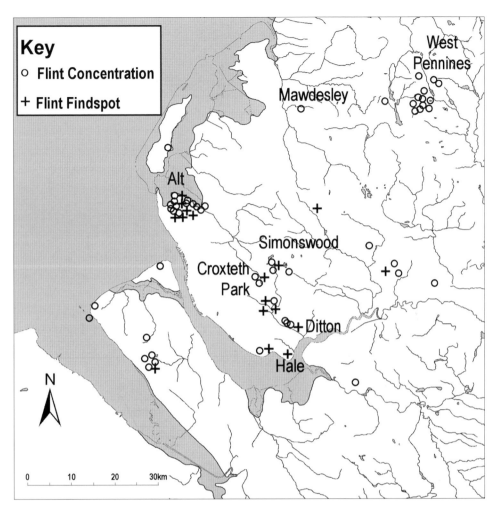

21 Mesolithic sites in the lowlands of West Lancashire and Merseyside. *Distribution after Cowell 2000b*

exploitation in the valley shed light on the degree of mobility, and the nature of differently structured settlements (Cowell 2000b, 165–8).

The area was attractive to hunter-gatherers because of its proximity to the tidal Mersey and the route that the valley created through the wooded landscape from the Mersey into the interior and then to the estuary and coast at Altmouth. The location was ideal for hunting game, drawn to the river for water, and for fishing, with both fresh and saltwater species available around the confluence of the Ditton and Mersey. Around the banks of the rivers were opportunities to gather bird's eggs and wetland plants, and also flint, which occurs in the boulder clay. Wildfowl were probably also available on the sandy reaches of the Mersey at low water.

Sites at Ditton Brook (Site I and the South Site), are small in both size and quantity of lithic material, implying that only a few people occupied them at any given time. They probably represent small camps for mobile hunters and may encompass a variety of special task sites associated with hunting and butchering of wild animals (Cowell 2000b). There is little evidence for the primary reduction of pebble flint nodules at any of the sites investigated in the area. This implies that the bulk of the struck flint on these sites was prepared elsewhere and brought to the site in partially reduced form. This type of site is also represented at several other locations further to the north along the Alt-Ditton channel where the river valley skirts the western side of the central mosslands between Croxteth and Simonswood (Cowell 1991a). To the east the occasional concentration of flintwork exists but the site density and overall distribution of struck lithics in the landscape decreases markedly (Cowell and Innes 1994). Several pollen sites from the western side of the wetlands adjacent to the Alt-Ditton channel show small, short-lived, openings in the woodland cover during the Late Mesolithic, which may be the result of small task groups such as these. At Simonswood Moss such results are associated with a lens of charcoal which indicates that burning of the woodland may have been taking place (Cowell and Innes 1994), as is widely seen in the Pennine uplands (Jacobi et al 1976; Bain 1991).

The density of surface flint sites increases dramatically along the channel to the north, within c.4km of the present mouth of the River Alt and adjacent coastal strip (Cowell and Innes 1994). These sites are represented by flint concentrations around the lower Alt with relatively high proportions of cores and primary reduction material within small assemblages. These coastal sites, along with the site at Banks on the Ribble (Middleton and Tooley in prep.), are probably the best candidates for lowland residential sites, representing larger groups in more extended occupation. They seemed to combine the collection and initial preparation of beach pebbles with more 'domestic' activities. Thus, it is argued that the southern part of Merseyside was mainly supportive of task-based foraging groups from core residential areas to the north and perhaps to the west. The site of Mawdesley (Hallam pers. comm.; Middleton 1993) may be of importance here, as it appears to have the characteristics of some coastal sites but includes many more microliths than is common on sites to the south-west, suggesting that it may have been residential.

The North Wirral has long been known to provide evidence for settlement in the lowlands during the period c.7500–6500 BC (Hume 1863; Roeder 1900; Varley 1964; Cowell 1992). Settlements are represented by the Early Mesolithic sites of Greasby Copse and Thurstaston Dungeon (Cowell 1992), which cover over 200 square metres. A range of flint and chert implements were excavated, the source of the Gronant chert from which they were made lies within the limestone hills on the western side of the Dee estuary. The evidence from these sites suggests that groups living on the Wirral spent part of the year in the uplands of North Wales where they obtained the various cherts from which they made their stone tools. After c.6500 BC this link appears to have been broken and more local flint sources were used. Prior to this, sea levels were lower and the Dee estuary would have been further out towards Anglesey, so that crossing the Dee valley into the uplands would have been a reasonably quick and simple operation. Later, following a rise in sea level and the development of thicker and denser woodland, mobility would have been hindered. Thus flint from the local rivers and the coasts, which from c.5000 BC would have been near to its present location, became the dominant sources of raw material supply.

The Central Pennine uplands of Lancashire and Yorkshire have produced one of the greatest concentrations of Mesolithic sites in the country. More than 540 sites have been recorded above 366m OD (Jacobi *et al* 1976, 308). Most of the upland scatters are dominated by microliths, often forming more than 90 per cent of the assemblage, with the greatest concentration being found in an area of slightly less than 245 square kilometres between Saddleworth and Marsden (*22*; Barnes 1982). This seems to be a genuine reflection of Mesolithic use rather than a bias in collecting (Barnes 1982, 23). The Central Pennines are at their narrowest at this point, the area above 366m OD being little more than half a mile in width on Standedge. Other upland sites have been found to the west on the Rossendale moors (e.g. Garstang 1906, 215; Baldwin 1903), to the north on the moors east of Burnley and north of Calderdale (e.g. Deans 1933; Leach 1951; Watson 1952, 30–5). Other excavations lie near Milnrow at Windy Hill and Piethorn Brook (Poole 1986) and at Rushy Brow, Anglezarke (Howard-Davies 1996) with other excavations just beyond the Lancashire borders in West Yorkshire (Radley and Mellars 1964; Stonehouse 1986).

The sites largely occur where erosion of the post-Mesolithic peat overlying mineral soil has taken place and therefore lack secure stratified context. The majority of the evidence consists of small, usually discrete, scatters of flints over 15–20 square metres. Where excavation has taken place (Barnes 1982; Buckley 1924; Radley and Mellars 1964; Stonehouse 1986; Hallam pers. comm.) upland sites are generally represented by circular arrangements of struck flint over small areas, often with hearths or evidence of burning (Spikins 1995; 1996; 2002; Poole 1986; Howard-Davis 1996). Structural evidence may be represented by small stake-holes or circular arrangements of stone. Although wood and bone must have been used, their relative importance is unknown; as such organic materials would have decayed long ago.

It is noticeable that in the Central Pennines Mesolithic sites tend to occur in groups, sometimes of more than 50 find spots on a single hillside, as in the Dean Clough and White Hill area, or sometimes smaller clusters as at Buckley's Warckock Hill North and Badger Slack sites (Barnes 1982). Elsewhere to the north and south (Davies 1941–3; Radley and Marshall 1963, 95) sites seem to be more widely scattered. Their location is similar to those of the Central Pennine sites, with off-summit hillocks and ridges, and sunny slopes between 350–450m being favoured. These are sheltered localities overlooking spring heads or damp hollows which would be attractive to wild animals. Very occasionally 'caves' or shelters between large boulders on rocky hilltops or edges were utilised. Flint implements were found at 450m OD in a cave among large boulders overlooking the Widdop valley, north of Calderdale (Wilkinson 1911).

On West Nab (*23*) waste flints and blades struck from a single core were found in a sheltered location (Hallam pers. comm.). The site overlooks the Wessenden Head road, some 230m from the summit and facing a north-easterly direction at an elevation of between 450–490m. Its elevated position suggests it was a small 'look out' site, to distinguish it from the larger camp sites where thousands of flints have been found including scrapers, gravers, knives and utilised blades and flakes. Excavation revealed a small chipping floor composed almost entirely of fine, grey, flinty chert. This material represented the remains of the flaking of one nodule. Reject microliths and a worked point were the only tool-types present: there were no scrapers, gravers, knives or utilised pieces.

In the different climatic and vegetational conditions of Mesolithic times the site would have been part of a summit heathland overlooking lower land covered in woodland. The

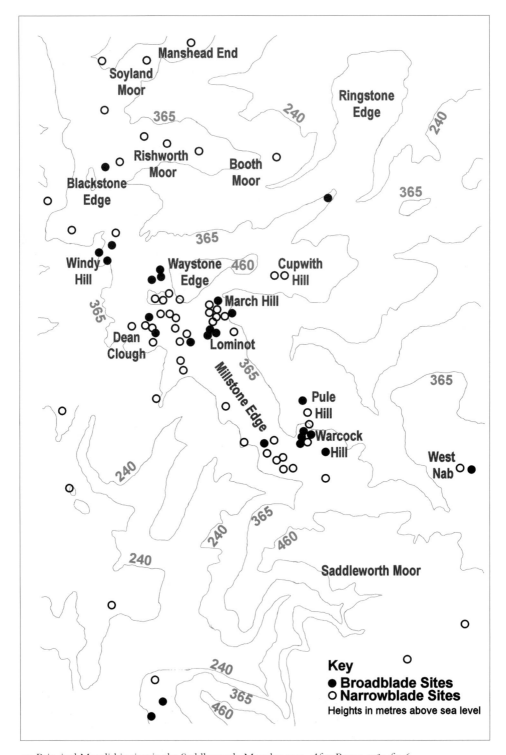

22 Principal Mesolithic sites in the Saddleworth–Marsden area. *After Barnes 1982, fig. 6*

23 West Nab site looking westwards. *Photograph: John Hallam*

24 Refitting of flakes from West Nab Mesolithic site. *Photograph: John Hallam*

flint knapper appears to have squatted with their back to the large rock, the flint chippings falling on the heathland grasses. As they worked they would be facing eastwards looking out over the Meltham valley and Meltham Brook. Immediately below was a pass, which now carries the road from the Isle of Skye to Meltham, but in the Mesolithic may have been a route for migrating deer. A nodule had been systematically worked producing a scatter of flakes, blades and waste. The residual core was found $c.2.5$m from the centre of the chipping floor from where it had presumably been cast away. Some flakes were selected from which blades were struck and from some of these microliths were fashioned. The material may represent the knapping of one person, probably on a single visit, and the clutch of flints in a cavity may signify an intention to return. The flinty-chert, which is most likely from East Yorkshire, varies in shade throughout the nodule along fault or stress lines that would have made it difficult to work. Several pieces could be refitted around residual cores and other fragments (*24*) and showed very clearly the knapper's difficulties with this piece of flint. Flaking platforms were struck wherever it was thought there was a chance of a decent blade, often frustrated by the fault lines running through the nodule. In some cases blades were struck off the prepared nodule, in other cases largish flakes were trimmed down along their dorsal ridges.

A suitable blade was fashioned into an isosceles microlith 15 x 10 x 50mm thick to a point. The embryo microlith was then snapped off from the parent blade. It was the technique of 'snapping off' that had to be done at the right place to obtain the correct length and width that caused the knapper difficulties. The ones that failed are the rejected specimens recovered in the excavation.

The working floors of the upland sites are sharply defined, and there is seldom an indefinite scattering of flint over a wide area (Buckley 1921, 5). This distribution gave rise to the idea of circular emplacements or camping sites, particularly since 'fire pits' and hearths were found on the same spots. On Warcock Hill Buckley found in one place traces of what seemed to him to indicate a group of four shelters, represented by circular clusters of worked flints, each occupying about four square yards, and in another place a single cluster with a shallow fire pit nearby. At the Badger Slack site he found a litter of burnt birch and ling overlying such a cluster of flints, suggesting the remains of an actual shelter (Buckley 1923; Clark and Rankine 1939, 104). Hearths are recorded regularly on almost all workshop sites, together with burnt flints or with flints focused upon them (e.g. Radley and Mellars 1964, 6; Radley 1974, 3–9; Stonehouse 1972, 36; Stonehouse 1976, 15; LAS 1976), possibly suggesting the working of flint with the aid of fire. Buckley found three fire pits in a line on Warcock Hill, each about four inches deep, dug into the shale bedrock and containing charcoal (*25*); another example occurred on March Hill Site 2 (Mss. 1924). Although the nature of the peat cover has led to a dearth of obvious structures associated with the hearths, the slight evidence that has been found does suggest that these sites were the temporary shelters where flints were prepared. The comparative lack of 'domestic tools', in particular scrapers, and also burins, indicates that these were hunting camps rather than true occupation sites where skins might be processed and bone and antler worked. The evidence includes stake holes at Broomhead Moor 5, some with wedging stones and carbonised wood fragments, and at the same site one area had been purposely cleared of stones while another had crude paving, the latter feature

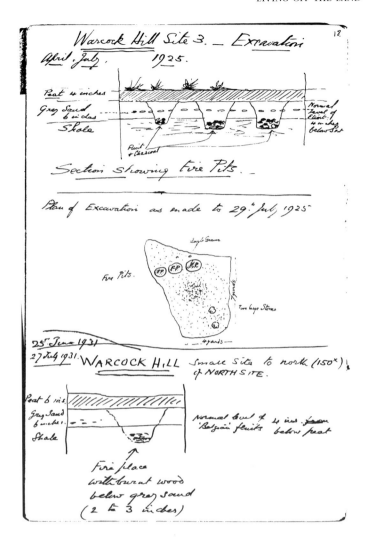

25 Notes on the excavation of Warcock Hill, near Marsden by Francis Buckley. *Source: Drawing Book 9, page 18*

also being found at Dunford Bridge A and Sheldon (Radley 1974, 3; Radley 1968, 29). No postholes were found at Deepcar, though it is possible that posts were wedged among a roughly circular arrangement of stones, which coincided with the maximum flint density (Radley and Mellars 1964, 5–7). These posts might have supported a windbreak. Evidence of similar crude structures is also suggested at Unstone (Courtney 1978). A stone structure forming an arc with flint assemblages within a hearth outside has been excavated at Rishworth Drain 2.

Most sites were small and occupied perhaps only for a single season. An example of this would be the previously unpublished site at Beaver, Wycoller in Lancashire (*26*; Hallam pers. comm.). The assemblage consisted of unpatinated grey-brown-black flint and grey flint with inclusions, consistent with an origin in Yorkshire. Also present was a patinated flint, grey and black chert and a few pieces of burnt flint. Many pieces of flint and chert were calcined, and traces of charcoal were recovered during excavation. Whilst there was no sign of reddening to

26 Excavation of the Mesolithic site at Beaver, Wycoller. In the centre is Julie Hallam. *Photograph: John Hallam*

suggest localised burning, testing showed that some fragments of grey-looking gritstone were found when sectioned to be red inside suggesting that there had been some burning on site (Hallam pers. comm.).

Other sites were larger, possibly having been revisited several times, like the famous sites on March Hill, White Hill, Warcock Hill and other localities on the Saddleworth-Marsden moors. A parallel for this type of site was excavated at Unstone, outside Lancashire in eastern Derbyshire. A multi-phase occupation, separated by short periods of abandonment, each lasting possibly only a few years was discovered (Courtney 1978). This suggested that the Lancashire sites may represent the conflation of a number of 'residential units' (Jacobi 1978, 325).

These upland camps were the site of production of various forms of projectile head. The earlier Mesolithic was characterised by Buckley's 'broad blade' industry (Radley and Mellars 1964, 19ff; Mellars 1973, 15): comparatively large microliths of non-geometric form which belong to the North European 'Maglemosian technocomplex', representing for the most part the tips and barbs of wooden arrows. The later Mesolithic featured the introduction of a greater and more specialised range of smaller geometric microlithic forms of the 'narrow blade' industry, which may represent insets for barbed spearheads of a character similar to those which were manufactured earlier from bone and antler, and which they may have replaced (Mellars 1976b, 396). Francis Buckley's excavation of 'a row of 35 flints in a straight line (like the teeth of a saw) and occurring at intervals of 1½ to 2 inches [3½–5cm]' on the southern slopes of White Hill led to suggestions that they represented the barbs inset into a wooden shaft, the latter having perished in the acidic conditions (Petch 1924, 29; Buckley Mss 1923). A much greater number of narrow blade sites exist, indicating a possible expansion of the population during the Mesolithic or, alternatively, internal displacement from the former coast as sea levels rose (Jacobi 1976).

The broad blade industry, recognised from more than 100 locations in the Central Pennines (Jacobi 1978, 295), was dominated by the manufacture of simple, obliquely blunted points (often retouched on the leading edge) with rarer elongated isosceles triangles and convex-backed blades. Radley and Mellars (1964, 19–20) pointed out the 'Maglemosian affinities' of this group, comparing the content of these upland sites with Deepcar, Thatcham, Colne Valley and Broxbourne. The industry is also comparable with Maglemosian sites in the south-west (Wainwright 1960).

The typological diversity of Buckley's narrow blade industries has been discussed by Radley (Radley 1974, 1). He divided these Later Mesolithic sites into three distinct groups, each distinguished both typologically and by the proportions of the raw materials used (Switsur and Jacobi 1975, 33). The largest group, dominated by small scalene triangles, Switsur and Jacobi's 'March Hill' type, is represented, for example, by Buckley's assemblages from March Hill and Windy Hill Site 5, and by the Dunford Bridge A and Broomhead Moor 5 sites. This group is known from both upland and lowland locations in the Pennines and also the Cleveland Hills and North Lincolnshire, and along the Durham and Cumberland coasts (Switsur and Jacobi 1975, 33). The second group, dominated by straight rod-like microliths, blunted along one or two sides, is known only from high ground in the Pennines and Clevelands. In the Central Pennines it is represented by the assemblages from Buckley's Rocher Moss 1, Dean Clough and Warcock Hill 4 sites, as well as Dunford Bridge B. The third group, with many trapezoids, is known in northern England only from two or three sites, all undated, at Buckley's White Hill North site, and at Red Ratcher (Stonehouse 1976) both in the Central Pennines, and at Beeley Moor in North Derbyshire (Radley 1974, 1).

Of particular interest is the fact that the distinction between broad and narrow blade industries is reflected not only in the typology of the microliths but also in the raw materials used. Broad blade assemblages were manufactured almost entirely from white or grey flint. Examination of Maglemosian sites in the Pennines has demonstrated that most of the cortex remains showed a pebble origin and could, therefore, be from the Yorkshire coast (Radley and Marshall 1963, 401). Jacobi points out that the proportions of this white flint on these Pennine sites (between 80 per cent and 99 per cent) are as high as those on sites adjacent to the flint sources (Jacobi 1978, 304), the implication being that this type of flint was either more highly favoured or more easily acquired by the manufacturers of these broad blade implements. In contrast the narrow blade industries were generally worked in better quality translucent flint (Buckley 1922; Radley and Mellars 1964, 18), usually brown or deep grey in colour. This flint occurs in drift on the Yorkshire coast, and examples with a pebble origin have been found at Dunford Bridge Site A, evidence coming from the milky chalk adhering to some pieces (Radley 1974, 7). There is also much evidence to show that the use of chert increased as time progressed. Radley (1968, 31–3) has examined the use of chert as a raw material on Mesolithic sites in the South Pennines, and discovered that there were at least five varieties of chert available from local Pennine limestones.

The distribution of flint types and of specific microlith shapes strongly suggest that the same population inhabited both the Central Pennines and the Lincolnshire lowlands in the Mesolithic, or that the two groups at least came into contact (Jacobi et al 1976, 310). 'Intermediate' sites occur in the area of the Hatfield Marshes (Radley and Marshall 1963, 92; Buckland and Dolby 1973). The distance in a straight line from the Early Mesolithic site at Sheffield Hill, north of Scunthorpe on Lincoln Edge (May 1976, 33–5), to the Marsden Moors is 90km across what would have been swampy or densely forested tracts in the

27 Location of prehistoric activity on the coast at Formby. (a) *Grus grus* (red deer) track. (b) *Capreolus capreolus* (roe deer) track. (c) Hoof print of *Bos primigenius* (auroch) showing distal sesamoid bone impressions. *Photograph: G. Roberts*

Thorne and Hatfield Marshes, the Trent lowlands and the Coal Measure foothills. The distance from the Yorkshire Wolds, on the other hand, across the Vale of York is 100km and from the coast near Flamborough Head 130km, but an easier routeway, and one much frequented in later prehistoric times, would be provided by the comparatively well-drained end moraines of York and Escrick. Supplies of flint are therefore just as likely to have come from the Wolds of Yorkshire as they are from Lincolnshire.

To the west of the Pennines intermediate, 'foothill', and lowland sites occur on the sands and gravels in the Manchester area (Garstang 1906, 215) and in the Irwell valley at Radcliffe (Spencer 1950–1); outside Lancashire they are found on the sandstone scarp of Alderley Edge (Varley 1932, 51; Varley 1964, 21). Sites within the Pennine foothills occur at Tatton (Higham and Cane 1999), Manchester Airport (Thompson 1998) and Mellor (Redhead and Roberts 2003). A small flint assemblage, including an axe sharpening flake, was excavated at Radcliffe in the Irwell valley. The site at Tatton Park has produced an Early Mesolithic flint scatter associated with a natural hollow (Higham and Cane 1999).

Much of the evidence considered so far is concerned with subsistence practices. This is inevitable given the bias towards lithic assemblages. As a result comparatively little has been said about other aspects of daily life because we simply lack the archaeological evidence. There is one rather dramatic exception to this, which consists of a series of human footprints preserved in compacted silts and muds along the modern coast at Formby Point (Roberts *et al* 1996; *27*). Some of the footprints date to the later Mesolithic and indicate activity in an intertidal environment (Gonzalez *et al* 1997). The prints, which include those of both adults and children, are interspersed with tracks left by roe and red deer, auroch and wading birds. Close study of these prints has the potential to reveal much about human activity during the later Mesolithic.

Using the formula developed by Louise Robbins (1986; 1987) for estimates of height, the mean adult male height was estimated to be 1.66m, and for females 1.45m (Gordon Roberts pers. comm.; Barrowclough 2007, 118). By way of comparison mean male and female heights of later prehistoric populations from Denmark are 1.66m and 1.53m respectively (Waldron 1989). Female stature estimates for Formby are therefore some 80mm less than the North European, Danish, average (and 40mm shorter than the expected universal average). This may be explained by considering the age of the women who left the prints. Abduction of the big toe from the second toe is an indicator of age. In unshod cultures, the degree of hallux abduction can become more pronounced with increasing years. Examination of the female prints for indicators of abduction, and therefore age, reveals that imprints made by fully-grown, adult females are rare. This evidence coincides with gait analyses of female trails, which indicate that it was mainly younger women and older female children that were present on the foreshore (Roberts pers. comm.).

The analysis has only been possible because bare-footed men, women and children have made the prints. One well-defined impression of a healthy foot, a young male *c.*1.33m tall, even appears to show the pointed 'drag' caused by uncut toenails (*28*; Roberts pers. comm.). For the most part prints are those of unshod people, but not all. In some cases there is the suggestion that some form of light footwear was being worn. In these cases instead of the clear imprint made by individual toes the front of the foot has a rounded appearance obscuring

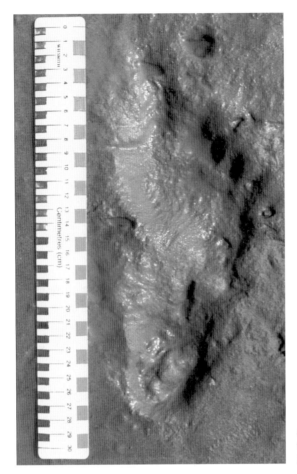

28 An unshod male footprint showing the 'drag' caused by an uncut toenail.
Photograph: G. Roberts

individual toes (Roberts pers. comm.). This is consistent with a form of light moccasin (*29*). It may be that this footwear was worn more often, but that the watery environment of the foreshore led people to remove shoes as a matter of course.

One key advantage that can be gained by studying unshod prints, especially those made on warm summer days during low tide when the fresh prints had chance to harden before being quickly filled in by sand, is that individual anatomical characteristics are revealed. Not only does this aid determination of biological sex and height, it also reveals certain abnormalities. Consideration of these reveals something of prehistoric attitudes toward disease and medical conditions in the living that are otherwise inaccessible to archaeologists.

One young man, *c.*1.55m tall, (*30 & 31*) had deformed feet where either one toe was missing or two toes had fused (Gordon Roberts pers. comm.). A plaster cast taken of the left foot clearly showed that the metatarsals had collapsed and that there had been a compensatory thickening of the *peroneus longus* and the *tibialis posterior* tendons. A similar condition is found in the feet of a young woman, *c.*1.46m tall. Her second and third toes were fused. She also had pronounced abduction of the *hallux* (big toe), which is often associated with walking unshod (Gordon Roberts pers. comm.). The prevalence of genetic abnormalities in the feet of the

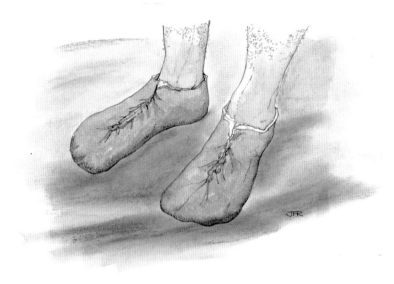

29 Reconstruction of possible moccasin worn by the prehistoric population. *Illustration: Joanna Richards*

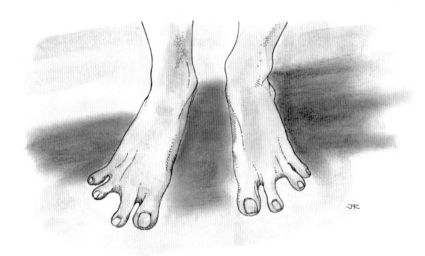

30 Reconstruction of feet with four toes based on footprints from Formby Point. *Illustration: Joanna Richards*

people of Formby may be indicative of a closed population in which inbreeding led to increased genetic abnormalities.

Division of labour appeared to be based on a combination of biological sex (not to be confused with gender, the social construction of sex, Sørensen 1991; 1992) and age. The hunting and management of animals was the domain of adult and adolescent men, whilst the collection of shellfish was that of young women, children and adults, who because of pregnancy or physical disabilities, were excluded from other work. Female prints were generally found aligned north–south, that is parallel to the shore-line. Estimates for the speed at which they

31 Prehistoric footprints, Formby Point.
(a) Footprint of young male, c.1.53m tall,
abduction between the first and second toes.
(b) Left foot of adult female, c.1.67m tall,
displaying indications of ectrodactyly (claw
foot). (c) Right foot of adolescent female,
with congenital bursitis; her gait suggests that
she may have been pregnant.
Photographs: G. Roberts

were travelling were ~3 km hr⁻¹, consistent with walking pace and food-gathering activities, such as collecting shrimps, razor clams and other sea food from the flats, and the collection of bird eggs from among the reed beds bordering the lagoon and creaks. If this is correct it raises the question, where were the more mature adult females? One possibility is that they were engaged in different activities perhaps based at one of the temporary settlements located around the Alt mouth.

The footprints of adolescent and adult men are generally found running in an east–west direction, that is heading out to and then returning from the mud flats. Hints at the activity associated with this movement comes from rare occasions when male prints are directly associated with red and roe deer tracks. In particular, in one case the prints of two men are seen tracking a red deer at walking pace; their speed then increases as they close in on the animal and the tracks intercept (Gordon Roberts pers. comm.). Evidence for increased speed over the norm for activity on the soft mud, ~12–14 km hr⁻¹, together with a deeper indentation of the toes and metatarsus, could be interpreted as evidence of hunting, or at least some form of animal management.

This insight can be used to infer something of the attitudes of society to its constituent members and to the human life-cycle. It would suggest that particular roles were considered appropriate for certain members of society, particularly that hunting was an exclusively adult male activity. The only occasions when the prints of adult men are found with those of young women and children turn out to be when the man is suffering from some sort of disability, for instance in a case where arthritis was detected from a man's swollen foot and limping gait. Equally, the only times that mature adult female tracks are found, again with those of the young women and children, is when they are either suffering from physical abnormalities, or in one case, pregnant.

An adult woman, *c*.1.67m tall, moving at 3.24 km hr⁻¹, displays indications of ectrodactyly (split/claw foot) in both feet (Gordon Roberts pers. comm.; *31 & 32*). This is a serious condition that significantly impairs not only mobility but also manual dexterity as it may also be accompanied by a similar abnormality in the hands. The footprint trails of an adolescent woman, *c*.1.40m tall, perhaps with bursitis, are recorded on two occasions on the mud (Gordon Roberts pers. comm.). On the second occasion her gait could suggest that she was pregnant. She was walking awkwardly, weight firmly on her heels, feet arched and toes curled under, talon-like, striving to maintain her balance and posture as she slowly made her way across the slippery mud (*33*). She might alternatively have been gathering shell food in a heavy basket held across the front of her body, which could have affected her centre of gravity.

Young women were responsible for the collection of seafood but also had childcare responsibilities. At one site the frequency of a patch of tiny, sun-hardened footprints evokes the image of a small group of children stomping around in the mud while their elder sister foraged for shell-food nearby. Men and women whose physical condition prevented them from taking part in regular adult activity assisted them. In this sense the collection of shellfish can be seen as a form of light work considered outside the mainstream of adult occupations, yet enabling vulnerable adults to make a contribution to the group.

In many societies work undertaken by adults, particularly that of men, has more prestige attached to it than work undertaken by children and adult women. If this were so at Formby

32 Reconstruction of claw hand and foot based on footprints at Formby Point. *Illustration: Joanne Richards*

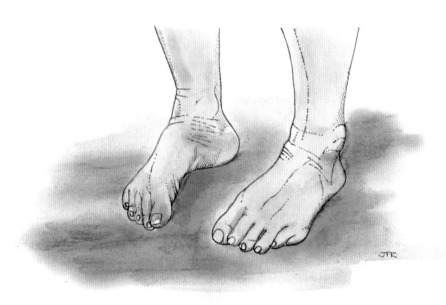

33 A reconstruction of the feet of a pregnant woman or someone carrying a heavy basket in front of them, derived from the shape of footprints found. *Illustration: Joanne Richards*

we should conclude that the gathering of shellfish was considered less prestigious than the hunting activity undertaken by men and the work undertaken by adult women, the details of which remain more obscure. By implication, those adults that also assisted in gathering shell fish might have been considered to have lost some status by having been 'demoted' to the gathering of food on the foreshore. Thus, physical abnormality and disease might be associated with negative connotations of loss of prestige, marginality and exclusion.

DISCUSSION

The people of the Mesolithic, although basically continuing an Upper Palaeolithic hunting and gathering way of life, had to adapt to changes in the environment which included the disappearance of large herds of elk to be replaced by widespread forest cover. The most visible of these changes was the development of new types of tool. By the Late Mesolithic much of Lancashire was covered in mixed deciduous forest. In the Pennines the continuous tree canopy gave way to scrub at around 335–360m, where it included hazel, grassland and occasional patches of peat. This habitat was attractive to red deer who could browse on the shrubs, and also to auroch, a type of wild cattle; hoof prints of both have been found in preserved silts on the beach at Formby. Wild pig would also have been present in the woodland. Fish may have been another important element in the diet as we have seen from the site of Marles Wood on the River Ribble where salmon and trout would have provided a seasonal variation to the diet. On the periphery of the Pennines surviving glacial lakes, as at Radcliffe and Ashton, would also have been a source of wild fowl, small mammals and fish. These would have been important sources of protein during the winter and early spring when plant food was at its scarcest. Grazing animals visiting sources of fresh water to drink would have provided the best hunting opportunities and may explain the sites of Dean Clough, March Hill, Warcock Hill and elsewhere.

Whilst a hunting group would probably choose a readily available natural shelter such as Mawdesley as a home base from which to exploit the resources of the surrounding area, the selection of a temporary location for a hunting camp would have been less influenced by environmental factors (Clark 1972). Even so certain locations were more attractive than others and may have been occupied on more than one occasion. Several locations in the Central Pennines and others on the coast may well fall into this category. People dependent on hunting and gathering normally range over a considerable area during the course of a year, exploiting the natural resources from season to season in different parts of their annual territory. During the winter they would have sheltered longest at one base, especially given that during the Mesolithic the climate was more extreme than now. Even in today's more moderate climate, red deer observe a seasonal rhythm in northern Britain, sheltering on low ground during the winter and moving to higher ground in the summer (Chaplin 1975, 41). The movements of individual herds would have followed the topography of the landscape, and this may account for the site of West Nab and the find spots in the Saddleworth-Marsden area of the Central Pennines where the uplands are at their narrowest (*24*). The occurrence of broad blade industries at sites like Warcock Hill, Windy Hill and Lominot, which lie above

380m and comprise no more than small round patches corresponding to tents or other flimsy structures, suggests hunting activities at the peak of the summer when the animals would be grazing the highest parts of their annual territories.

As we have seen for the discussion of the sites along the River Ribble and those in West Lancashire there is increasing evidence that groups wintered west of the Pennines. The evidence of the Highfurlong Elk find shows that during the Late Upper Palaeolithic hunting parties were active on the Fylde Coast (Hallam 1973; Barnes *et al* 1971). It died in the winter months suggesting that a winter camp must have existed within eight to ten kilometres of the find spot. During the Mesolithic rising sea level pushed deer and auroch populations inland into the developing mixed forest of the lowland coastal plains of the Fylde and West Lancashire making ideal hunting grounds (Evans 1975, 45).

Understanding of the Late Mesolithic occupation, based on the study of broad blade sites, shows that there were a variety of different sites. The presence of charcoal layers shows that the closed tree cover above 360m was suppressed by regular burning. Studies have described how burning improves both the quantity and quality of browsing for ungulates, presenting opportunities for easier hunting of herds and also imposing a degree of predictability on their movements (Mellars 1976a; Jacobi *et al* 1976, 315). People may have manipulated the woodland-edge habitat in this way, possibly reburning relatively small tracts of forest at 5–15 year intervals on a rotational basis (Jacobi *et al* 1976, 317). One effect of this burning would have been the encouragement of hazel (amongst other species), thus providing nuts for direct consumption. Besides those in the Pennines, others have been found at intermediate altitudes in the foothills, for example finds on sandy hillocks in the Manchester region (Hallam 1960, 84). Thus it can be demonstrated that alterations of the ecosystem started before the Neolithic period.

From the excavation of upland sites a basic chronology for the Mesolithic in Lancashire has been produced for the different flint types. This suggests that there is a distinctive flint technology for sites of the Early Mesolithic dated *c*.7500–6800 cal BC based on 'broad blade' characteristics and another, 'geometric' style for the subsequent Late Mesolithic up to *c*.3800 cal BC or possibly a little later (Jacobi 1976, 1987; Mellars 1976b). This broad division appears to hold, although many of the particular dates are less useful as they often have wide deviations and the contexts of the dated material in not always secure (Jacobi 1987).

In conclusion the Pennine assemblages differ markedly from assemblages from the Lancashire lowlands (Cowell and Innes 1994; Middleton *et al* 1995) having a higher percentage of microliths. This indicates that many of the Lancashire lowland sites appear to differ in function from the upland sites. The lithic evidence suggests that the lowlands might include both base camps and smaller specialised sites (Cowell and Innes 1994; Middleton *et al* 1995). The base camps were probably mainly in coastal areas, where larger groups may have congregated for longer periods of time, possibly in the winter (Bonsall 1981; Bonsall *et al* 1986). The specialised smaller sites may have included kill sites, butchery sites, hunting stands, and bivouac sites (Price 1978). Small-scale manipulation of the woodlands was also taking place in the lowlands, sometimes associated with evidence of burning suggesting fire-induced woodland clearance.

In the Early Mesolithic on the Wirral (Cowell 1992) and in eastern Yorkshire and in Lincolnshire (Jacobi 1978) the occurrence of flint and chert tools, many miles from the stone sources, suggests the movement of people and goods and provides the possibility of identifying the economic patterns behind this mobility. In the Late Mesolithic such patterns are harder to identify. Preliminary indications imply that different raw materials are used north and south of the Ribble, with areas to the north using a greater range of materials, most notably including various chert types, probably from the Pennines (Cowell and Innes 1994; Middleton *et al* 1995). It may be that raw material exploitation and subsequent use was carried out on a much smaller, more local scale during the Late Mesolithic in the region.

The transition from the Late Mesolithic to the Neolithic began during the fifth millennium BC when disturbed ground and associated small gaps in the woodland cover became more common across Lancashire. They occur both around the coastal areas and around the central mosslands, and even continued into the fourth millennium BC in Merseyside and Lancashire (Cowell and Innes 1994; Middleton *et al* 1995). At the coastal sites of Bidston Moss and Flea Moss Wood these phenomena are accompanied by cereal-type pollen at *c.*4900–4500 cal BC, mirrored at a number of other sites in north-west England and Northern Ireland (Edwards and Hirons 1984). If cereal type pollen, rather than positively identified cereal pollen, is taken as representing the introduction of domesticated plants into Lancashire, the implications are that Mesolithic communities were adopting aspects of an agricultural economy (Simmons and Innes 1987). The sites where this phenomenon is found lie along the western seaboard of Britain suggesting widespread contacts along the western coast (Edwards and Hirons 1984). The evidence suggests that small-scale agriculture may have gradually become part of the Mesolithic repertoire, in addition to the established lifestyle of gathering, hunting and fishing. It is notable that the occurrences of agriculture are found along the coast, where stronger evidence for the repeated use of the same locations is found (Bonsall 1981). The apparent lack of technological change between the flint assemblages of the later Mesolithic and Early Neolithic also demonstrates a gradual change, and suggests that many aspects of Neolithic lifestyle and economy were already in place by the fifth millennium BC.

CHAPTER 4

SHAPING THE WORLD WITH STONE: THE NEOLITHIC FARMERS

INTRODUCTION

Traditionally, narratives about the Neolithic, beginning around 4000 BC, have concentrated on the change from a transitory hunting and gathering lifestyle typical of Late Mesolithic groups to an increasingly settled agriculture. This change is marked by the appearance of a new artefact assemblage containing leaf-shaped arrowheads and pottery, together with ceremonial and funerary monuments. As was observed in the previous chapter, the cultivation of cereal has been seen during the Late Mesolithic, whilst it has been suggested that the Neolithic was less settled than had previously been proposed, and that people maintained a significant degree of seasonal or transitory movement, blurring the distinction between the two periods (e.g. Barrett 1989; 1994; Topping 1997; Whittle 1997). Contemporary interpretations also stress the regionality of this transition (Barrowclough 2007) with authors noting that whilst there are many shared elements of material culture and architecture across Britain, the manner and timing of the introduction of domesticated plants and animals, and the use of particular monumental forms may have varied considerably across different regions. Rather than a single model that explains 'the' British Neolithic we need to consider the variety of different ways in which a Neolithic package was adapted to local conditions. The Late Neolithic, 3000–2500 BC, is regarded as marking a phase of intensification of settlement, land-use and artefact production, and has been associated with the first indications for the existence of social hierarchies (Bradley and Edmonds 1993). There is evidence for long-distance communication and interaction, particularly in the realm of ritual and ceremony. In Lancashire, however, the period is also seen as one where distinctive regional characteristics become apparent (Piggott 1954; Bradley 1984; Harding *et al* 1996).

THE NEOLITHIC PACKAGE

The transition from the Mesolithic to Neolithic in Lancashire was a gradual process. Lithic scatters remain the most abundant source of evidence for human activity in the Early

Neolithic as they are in the Late Mesolithic. The shift from one to the other may be identified in the archaeological record by the introduction of a characteristic new technology, the leaf-shaped arrowhead, which replaced Late Mesolithic microliths. These arrowheads are most often found in isolation, perhaps as casual losses from hunting and related activities. It has also been suggested that there are some indications that the range of raw materials became more restricted – black Pendleside chert disappears from assemblages at the end of the Mesolithic (Middleton 1996, 36) – while better quality flint material was probably sourced from areas outside Lancashire, possibly arriving via networks of trade and exchange. Although many of the widely accepted typological or chronologically diagnostic forms for the Neolithic are represented, the most common of which is the scraper, assemblages are often characterised by informal or multi-use forms suggesting the expedient use of available raw materials. Mesolithic traits continue throughout a large part of the Neolithic, and in turn Neolithic types are found in Early Bronze Age assemblages.

Another characteristic of the Early Neolithic are polished stone axes, part of the economic changes associated with the adoption of agriculture and the domestication of animals. Most have been smoothed or 'polished' by rubbing or grinding on another stone. The rounded end of the axeheads would have been set in a wooden haft, with the wider end forming the cutting edge. Complete, or near complete, axes have been found throughout Lancashire in a range of different locations. A number have flattened sides, a typical feature of examples produced and found in the Lake District, and where thin-sectioning has been undertaken, the results confirm that most originated at Great Langdale in Cumbria (Clough and Cummins 1988, 219–221). Most of the axes date to the period c.2750–2000 BC, when agriculture was already established. From about this date the production of axes in upland areas such as the Lake District and North Wales was highly organised and products from these 'factories' travelled hundreds of miles into areas that do not contain such rocks. The other major new technological advance at the beginning of the Neolithic was the introduction of pottery, augmenting the earlier use of organic containers by Mesolithic communities. Pottery finds are, however, very poorly represented in Lancashire, perhaps as a consequence of the continued relative mobility of the population or perhaps because of the wet and humid climate which has an adverse effect on pottery production (Barrowclough 2007).

Despite the apparently enormous implications of the change to farming, the gradual incorporation of Neolithic elements into existing society means that much of the economy may have remained relatively unaltered. The extensive evidence for burning episodes from both upland and lowland situations suggests that there was substantial management and control of wild resources by Mesolithic people (Zvelebil 1994). These may represent the clearance of scrub and light woodland to attract animals to specific locations at which they could be culled (Jacobi *et al* 1976). There is now substantial evidence from the mosses of Lancashire that such episodes were taking place from the earliest Mesolithic through to the Bronze Age. It is not clear how much of this was caused by people, although its ubiquity suggests it may represent deliberate management of the environment (Hall *et al* 1995, ch. 6; Middleton *et al* 1995, ch. 8).

CHARACTERISTICS OF THE NEOLITHIC OCCUPATION

The character of Early Neolithic occupation has much in common with that of the Late Mesolithic. The evidence suggests that some places were visited repeatedly over relatively long periods of time, whilst small, less dense occupation evidence in other areas indicates short-term or transitory occupation. Excavations at Roose Quarry and Holbeck Park on the Furness Peninsula have produced assemblages including leaf-shaped arrowheads, flakes of polished volcanic tuff and Early Neolithic pottery (Jones 2001; Oxford Archaeology North 2002b). At Holbeck Park, deposits within a tree throw hollow contained 106 sherds of Early Neolithic pottery associated with rod microliths and two unpolished flakes of volcanic tuff (Oxford Archaeology North 2002b). Five radiocarbon dates, including one taken from a charred grain of wheat, have provided a date range of 4000–3700 cal BC for the assemblage (Huckerby in Hodgson and Brennand 2006, 32). Excavations of a sand dune occupation site at Walney North End on the Furness Peninsula revealed a substantial Late Neolithic and Early Bronze Age lithic assemblage together with hearths, middens and small amounts of Beaker pottery (Cross 1938; 1939; 1942; 1946; 1949; 1950; Barnes 1955; 1970). At Sandscale, 3km to the north-east of Walney, a small posthole structure and pits associated with a lithic assemblage of Late Neolithic and Early Bronze Age date were excavated (Evans and Coward 2004). The finds included characteristic Early Bronze Age barbed-and-tanged arrowheads and thumbnail scrapers, but the presence of a small polished axe of Langdale type suggests that the site was first occupied in the Neolithic. Polished stone axes generally have a coastal distribution and are particularly common in Furness and along the north coast of Morecambe Bay, the area of which accounts for approximately 50 examples, half of all the known axes in Cumbria. Of these, 60 per cent were found within 5km of the sea, a figure that rises to 90 per cent when rivers are included (Collingwood 1933, 163–200).

Elsewhere along the northern coast of Morecambe Bay polished stone axes have been discovered in small groups in fissures and gaps in out-cropping stone. At Skelmore Heads, near Ulverston, four flaked stone blades were found in 1959 in a limestone gryke (Barnes 1963). This pattern of deposition suggests a deliberate cache of axes, perhaps as part of a symbolic, possibly ritual activity, rather than an accidental loss (Bradley and Edmonds 1993). Studies undertaken at Foulshaw and Helsington mosses (Wimble *et al* 2000) indicate a small clearance episode during the Late Neolithic, *c*.2570–2140 cal BC (3870 ±70 BP; Hodgkinson *et al* 2000). This was followed by regeneration of the woodland until 2300–1890 cal BC (3690 ±70 BP) when the first significant *landnam*-type clearance in this area of Morecambe Bay took place (Wimble *et al* 2000), creating a number of scattered clearings, each occupied for a few years, before the inhabitants moved to a new area, allowing the recolonisation of the clearing by secondary woodland. This activity is associated with Beaker-style inhumation burials at Sizergh and Levens Park which mark the end of the Neolithic and the beginning of the Bronze Age (Turnbull and Walsh 1996). The possibility of a Neolithic round barrow tradition in Cumbria is suggested by the morphology of the excavated 'long' cairn at Skelmore Heads (Evans 2004; Clare 1979). The mound, which is more oval than long, was disturbed by an antiquarian group before being excavated by Powell (1963; 1972). Although the presence of some pottery and bones is recorded there is insufficient detail to comment on the details of the burial ritual.

Direct evidence for Neolithic occupation in the Lancaster area is less clear. A rare example of a Peterborough Ware vessel was found in the city centre (White 1974), although its context is unclear. North of Lancaster, at Borwick near Carnforth, the buried soil beneath an Early Bronze Age burial mound contained a quantity of lithic material including three kite-shaped arrowheads and one transverse, two scrapers, one borer, numerous blades and cores (Olivier 1987, 135). The kite-shaped arrowhead is a variety of leaf-shaped arrowhead more common in the north and west of Britain than the south and dated from the early fourth to the late third millennium BC (Green 1980, 97 and fig. 35). The examples from Borwick are thought to date toward the end of the period (Olivier 1987, 159) and have a parallel in the kite-shaped arrowheads found in the remains of a presumed ploughed-out barrow at Peel (below), suggesting that they relate to the early use of the funerary site (contra Olivier 1987, 159).

Most evidence of Neolithic occupation in the area comes from archaeobotanical studies of ancient pollen sampled from wetland sites. Studies of pollen from Hawes Water (Oldfield 1960) and Little Hawes Water (Taylor et al 1994), both near Silverdale, have tentatively identified the presence of cereal pollen, which may suggest that there was a limited amount of agricultural activity taking place nearby. The limited extent of the evidence suggests that cereal cultivation only played a small part in the economy of the Neolithic.

Cereal grains only seem to occur around the Elm Decline, which is dated regionally to c.3990–3640 cal BC (Hibbert et al 1971). There is little evidence for cereals either before or after. This pattern may represent an unsuccessful attempt to grow cereals early in the development of farming. One explanation for this is that the cooler and wetter climate of Lancashire made it impossible to sustain the farming of early varieties of cereal (see Kinnes 1979). Corroboration for this view is provided by the almost total absence of Early Neolithic serrated flakes, a diagnostic artefact associated with cereal cultivation, from the county's archaeological record (Middleton 1996, 39).

In the absence of cereals it is possible that the utilisation of wild resources continued. Given the coastal and riverine nature of the settlement pattern of Mesolithic sites along the Lune, Ribble, Mersey and Alt-Ditton valleys, a reliance on fishing and the hunting of deer may have continued. It is also assumed (Middleton 1996, 39), based on evidence from elsewhere in Britain, that the herding of domesticated animals, particularly cattle, gradually increased in importance, although direct evidence for this in the form of Neolithic and Early Bronze Age faunal assemblages is absent in the county.

The results of studies at what is now Leighton Moss nature reserve on Storrs Moss (Powell et al 1971) and at Little Haweswater (Taylor et al 1994), which have attempted to combine archaeological and palaeoecological work, suggest that Early Neolithic activity involved the creation of small clearances within a well-wooded environment. Excavation at Leighton Moss uncovered a possible Late Mesolithic and Early Neolithic site. A wooden platform and 'posthole' was excavated in an area where two polished stone axes had previously been found. The wood was dated to 3694–3384 cal BC although disturbance by the roots of reeds (Phragmites) made this a minimum age only; a true date on stratigraphic grounds was considered to be nearer 4333–4241 cal BC. The evidence suggests that settlement on the edge of the wetland had been associated with early attempts at cereal production. Identifiable structures were absent at Little

Haweswater where the main evidence for occupation was in the form of diffuse scatters of flint artefacts.

There are a number of Neolithic sites on and around the Fylde and Over Wyre mosses. A single sherd of undecorated bowl pottery similar to material excavated at Portfield Camp, Whalley (below) has been found on the floodplain of the River Wyre, immediately to the west of St Michael's-on-Wyre, in association with a leaf-shaped arrowhead and a small number of flint artefacts. The artefacts were found in a layer of peat, which also contained plant remains indicative of settlement. The context, which was sealed below two metres of alluvium, was dated to c.4330–3955 cal BC (5285 ±80 BP, GX-17293) placing it in the Early Neolithic (Middleton *et al* 1995, 58).

The North West Wetlands Survey also identified a number of Early Neolithic sites along the eastern edge of Pilling Moss. Within this poorly drained boulder-clay landscape are located occasional small hillocks or 'islands' of well-drained gravel, and it is on these islands that the sites are found (Middleton *et al* 1995, 56–60). A small lithic scatter was found on the north-western side of Friar's Hill and included a finely-made leaf arrowhead. Further finds included two small lithic scatters either side of the Eskham Gap, and a site on the south-eastern periphery of Pilling Moss consisting of a flake from a polished stone axe (Middleton *et al* 1995, 57). In addition to these sites there were a number of lithic scatters of similar appearance, but lacking diagnostic material, which seem to date to this period. For example, two sites located on adjacent patches of gravely boulder clay which formed low mounds at Island Farm, a scatter of debris on another gravel rise close by and another site, again on a small hummock of gravely boulder clay to the south of Bone Hill Farm (Middleton *et al* 1995, 58). The overall impression of Early Neolithic exploitation in the Over Wyre District is that it reflects its origins in the Mesolithic in the use of similar raw materials and flintworking technology. The sites also share similar locations with a preference for well-drained areas including both sand islands, such as Friar's Hill, and also mounds of gravely boulder clay. A cereal grain associated with limited evidence for clearance was recorded at Rawcliffe Moss in Over Wyre (Barnes 1975), and nearby at Fenton Cottage cereal pollen has been tentatively identified. This may suggest that, as with the sites at Silverdale, limited arable agriculture was being practised in the Over Wyre area (Middleton *et al* 1995, 141–152).

Nine polished stone axes have been found on Pilling Moss, in the Over Wyre District, five of which have come from below the peat. During the Early Neolithic this would have been a reed swamp environment (Middleton *et al* 1995, 195). The distribution of axes mainly seems to be concentrated in the northern part of Pilling Moss, and they appear to be associated with the ridge that separates the moss from Cockerham and Winmarleigh Mosses to the north-east. Most of the artefacts derive from a small area immediately south of Winmarleigh Moss. Two axes have been found on the western portion of the moss at Bradshaw Lane with a further example at Greengate Farm, Stalmine Moss. Two isolated examples are recorded from Staynall and one from Winmarliegh. The remainder of the axes, along with an adze and four polishers, come from Pilling Moss. An axe and an adze were found at Cogie Hill, whilst at Crookabreast Farm an axe was discovered with four polishers, used for the manufacture or re-sharpening of axes. One of the polishers was found pushed into a cavity in the roots of an oak tree (Sobee 1953, 14). The discovery of a polisher within the roots of what was presumably a 'moss stock', or bog oak, may suggest some measure of deliberate deposition rather than casual loss (Middleton *et al* 1995). Similar activity has already been described at Skelmore Heads and at Leighton Moss, whilst at Delph Reservoir on the Bolton Moors a pair of polished axes were also found in peat (Hallam 1970, 234). Recent work has established that these axe caches may have had a ritual significance, either related to the axe, or to the place of deposition (Bradley and Edmonds 1993). There is some evidence to suggest that rivers and wetlands were important places for deposition, and it is notable that the axes from Lancashire have a definite riverine and mossland distribution. It was thought that this reflected patterns of trade (Howard-Davis *et al* 1988, 17). We know that the axes had travelled to the area through studies of the rock from which they were made (Clough and Cummins 1988, 220–1; Coope *et al* 1988). Of eight axes studied four came from the Langdales in Cumbria, two from the southern Lake District and one from Penmaenmawr. The analysis of deposition, however, suggests that they were not accidental losses; it is now clear that many of the axes must have been deposited deliberately and that wet places, whether river or bog, had a specific significance. If that is the case it may be no coincidence that the same wetland locations were selected for the deposition of metal axes in the Early Bronze Age.

A further Neolithic site lies at Peel, near to Lytham. The site was first identified by the North West Wetlands Survey: field walking revealed a dense concentration of flints in the vicinity of Peel Hall Farm in an area measuring *c.* 100 x 150m, with the majority coming from a 'knoll of gravel' (Middelton *et al* 1995, 91). The lithic spread was dominated by cores and preparation flakes, and this was no different to other areas in the Peel and Ballam area. The assemblage was notable, however, for it included a number of finely made artefacts: six kite-shaped and one transverse arrowhead, a flake-knife and a serrated flake. Subsequently, field survey by the author recovered a fine leaf-shaped arrowhead (*34*), a ground stone axe (*35*) and a partially worked piece of amber (*36*). The arrowheads were fashioned out of a dark-grey mottled flint, which distinguished these artefacts from the majority of flint collected from the area. Middleton *et al* have argued that the distinctive quality of the flint, in terms of colour and grain size, and also the character of the artefacts made from it, are indicators that the flint was imported from outside the area (Middleton *et al* 1995, 96), and I see no reason to disagree with them. The raw material from which the artefacts were made is unlike anything found elsewhere in the Fylde and is comparable with the finest flint artefacts found in Britain.

The location of the site, combined with the nature of the finds, may suggest that it represents the remains of a ploughed-out barrow (*37*). A contour survey undertaken by the North West Wetlands Survey (Middleton *et al* 1995, 96 and fig. 52) hinted at the possibility of a barrow, as does aerial photography of the area (*colour plate 12*).

Observation on the ground confirms the suggestion of Middleton *et al* (1995, 96), based on aerial photography, that the site lies on a small promontory below which is a former river channel, a relic of an earlier landscape when sea levels were higher and the Lytham-Skippool valley in which Peel sits was flooded. During the Neolithic, Peel formed an island perhaps marking out the site as a special place in the landscape. Other burial mounds in the Fylde at nearby Weeton Heads Lane were similarly located on the edge of the valley, whilst the barrow at Stoney Hill Lodge, Blackpool (next chapter), was located on the coast, all associated with watery places. The artefacts, and the kite-shaped flints in particular, have parallels with the burial site at Borwick (Olivier 1987). There three kite-shaped arrowheads were found below the cairn, indicating that they were deposited before the construction of the monument, dated to 2278–1761 cal BC (3639

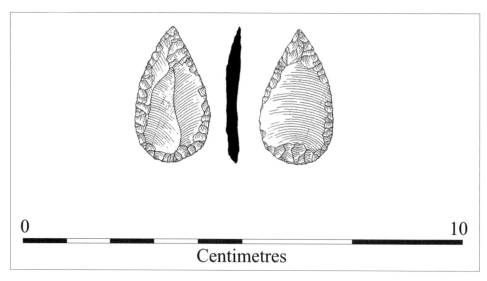

0   10

Centimetres

34 Leaf-shaped flint arrowhead from a ploughed-out barrow at Peel, Lytham

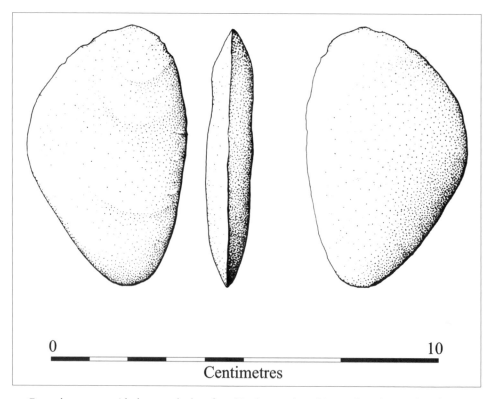

0   10

Centimetres

35 Ground stone axe with sharpened edges found in the remains of the earthwork at Peel, Lytham

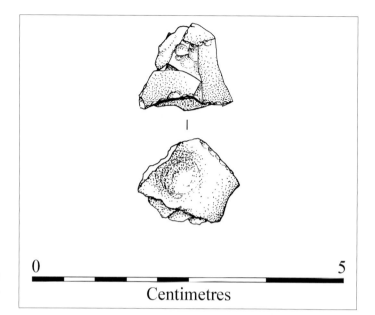

36 Worked amber found in the earthwork at Peel, Lytham. The amber exhibits evidence of having been drilled, as if being worked to form a bead

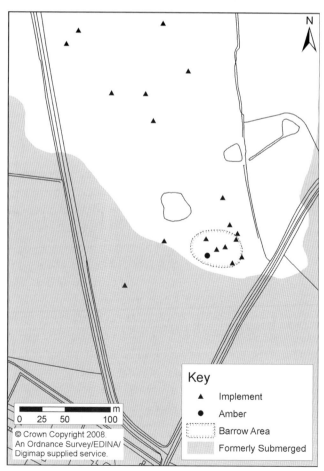

37 The location of implements found at Peel Hall Farm together with the conjectural location of the barrow based on contour survey, aerial photography and on site observation. *Map: Mary Chester-Kadwell after Middleton et al. 1995*

±80, HAR-5626). This is consistent with both the dates for the overlap between lozenge and transverse forms of 2500–2250 cal BC, and the funerary associations for these types of arrowheads (Green 1980; 1984). Elsewhere, Middleton *et al* (1995, 96) found parallels between the lithic assemblage and the Late Neolithic barrows of Derbyshire and Yorkshire where single burials under round barrows sometimes have similar artefact associations. The artefacts from Ayton East Field barrow are comparable with the arrowheads, as is the lithic assemblage from the barrow at Rudston (Cranswick 1) (Kinnes and Longworth 1985, 147–8, 74–6).

To the north of the barrow site the Wetlands Survey identified a thin spread of flint material. The assemblage was typical of a number of smaller contemporary sites found throughout the Peel and Ballam areas. The Wetlands Survey commented that it was noticeable that all of the fields surveyed in the area contained flints, either as isolated finds or in small clusters. This contrasted with the landscape to the north of the Fylde where the frequency of finds was far less (Middleton *et al* 1995, 91). There were a small number of implements, the majority of which were scrapers, and a predominance of waste material, including preparation flakes and pieces of irregular waste (Middleton *et al* 1995, 96). Most of the flakes retained a large proportion of cortex suggesting that much of the activity was aimed at the production of artefacts. On most of the sites, cores made up a relatively large part of the lithic assemblages, probably because the raw material was collected locally. Flint nodules had frequently split on planes of weakness and had then been abandoned, suggesting that flint nodules and pebbles were being worked in situ. The relative lack of implements suggests that few were discarded in the immediate area; instead they could have been used, re-sharpened and taken elsewhere to be used again. This may have been a particularly important strategy where the available raw materials were so poor (Middleton *et al* 1995, 91). Elsewhere on the Fylde Coast there is evidence for Neolithic exploitation at two sites identified in the sandhills at Starr Hills between St Annes-on-Sea and Blackpool (Middleton *et al* 1995, 90–91). The finds are poorly recorded but appear to have come from a hollow in the dunes, possibly associated with a hearth.

The pattern of exploitation revealed by these sites is one of the densest in Lancashire, in comparison to the Mesolithic and Early Neolithic pattern, which concentrated on areas of well-drained soil. In the Late Neolithic all areas of the landscape began to be exploited but there was a marked preference for the area around the Lytham-Skippool valley, the mosses and coast. There is also evidence from pollen samples taken from Peel of forest clearance and cereal cultivation at this time (Middleton *et al* 1995, ch. 7). The distribution of finds at Peel and Ballam suggests how the landscape might have been utilised. These sites could have been the result of groups repeatedly visiting the area in order to manufacture implements, which they then took away with them (Middleton *et al* 1995, 99). If that is the case it suggests a mobile community visiting favoured locations in the landscape with each visit represented by a discrete scatter. The exception to this appears to be the area of Peel Hall Farm where, north of the barrow, the Wetlands Survey identified a denser than usual concentration of lithic material. This was interpreted as evidence of repeated visits to the same spot (Middleton *et al* 1995, 99) and is interesting because it occurs in the vicinity of the barrow, indicating that this was a particularly favoured place.

South of the River Ribble there is a thin scatter of Neolithic lithic material along the Alt-Ditton valley, particularly around the estuary of the Alt. Generally it is difficult to identify Early Neolithic material from the majority of Mesolithic pieces. Only when stone axes and leaf arrowheads are found is it possible to distinguish the scatters (Cowell pers. comm.). The picture is one of continuity between Late Mesolithic and Early Neolithic. At Formby Point large numbers of prehistoric human and animal footprints and animal bones have been preserved in the beach sediments (Tooley 1970; Cowell *et al* 1993; Pye and Neal 1994; Roberts *et al* 1996; Gonzalez *et al* 1997; Huddart *et al* 1999a; 1999b). Gordon Roberts has systematically recorded human and animal footprints in compacted silts and muds for 4km along the coast (Roberts et al 1996). The exposure of sediments within a 100m-wide belt is due to the rapid erosion of the beach dunes, which can be up to three metres per year (Pye and Neal 1994). Although discussed in the context of the Mesolithic in the previous chapter the wide date ranges obtained from the print-bearing strata extend to cover the Neolithic and even later periods up to the Iron Age, suggesting a continued occupation. This evidence fits with the general picture for Lancashire, with a continuation of the Late Mesolithic subsistence practices into the Neolithic. The upper strata not only contained footprints but also a complete set of unshed antlers dated to 2570–2380 cal BC along with dog, red deer and auroch jawbones (Gonzalez and Huddart 2002). Close by at Hightown beach, Crosby, *c.*4km to the south, a short, two-metre, length of wooden track was excavated (*38*). The feature was 1.4m wide and made of branches laid longitudinally with, at one end, interwoven cross branches, and at the other a more haphazard arrangement (Cowell pers. comm.). Stakes had been driven into the underlying clay; perhaps to anchor the structure, one had been driven into the ground to a depth of one metre and two other branches had possible cut facets on them, two other pieces were charred (Cowell pers. comm.). This may have been part of a longer trackway, and has produced radiocarbon

38 Wooden track found off the coast at Hightown. *Photograph: Ron Cowell*

dates of 3960–3675 cal BC (5020 ±60 BP; Beta-119008) and 3795–3630 cal BC (4910 ±60 BP; Beta-119010; Cowell in Hodgson and Brennand 2006, 34). The existence of this Early Neolithic feature poses an interesting question concerning the degree of social organisation and sedentism in the area. The track established a route across the intertidal mud flats, perhaps to facilitate the collection of shellfish, and its construction suggests planning and co-ordination of activities designed to exploit the tidal reaches of the estuary. This would be consistent with a greater degree of sedantism than has previously been envisioned in Neolithic Lancashire. The presence of the track contrasts with the vast majority of the archaeological evidence which points to mobility within the population until at least the Late Neolithic.

To the east in the Sankey Valley at St Helens there is another concentration of Neolithic activity. The distribution is particularly strong at the southern end around its confluence with the Mersey and continues to some extent along the upper slopes of the River Weaver in north Cheshire (Cowell 1991a; 1995), whilst a small Late Neolithic flint site is recorded in the vicinity of Oakmere. In the area that now comprises Greater Manchester there are generally fewer Neolithic sites, perhaps due to the poor drainage of the Pennines. The few known sites produced small quantities of lithic material. A polished stone axe from the Lagdales was found at Crumpsall, eight flints came from Ashton Moss and worked flint and chert was found at Nook Farm on Chat Moss. These sites suggest a low level of activity, as does the palaeoecological record, which indicates small-scale clearings in the woodland (Hall *et al* 1995, 117). The Nook Farm site is a case in point, located on a ridge of glacial sand along the northern edge of Chat Moss, it comprises lithic material and carbonised wood. Pollen cores taken by the North West Wetlands Survey suggest that there was a small, *c.*50–100m diameter, clearing on the sand island during the Neolithic (Hall *et al* 1995, 58). This was probably the result of human activity, deliberately burning alder and birch woodland, so that the land could be cultivated. Charcoal from the site dated the event to 2853–2149 cal BC (3930 ±80 BP, GU-5325). The Nook Farm site may be used to recreate the pattern of occupation around the Manchester mosses during the Neolithic. In these lowland areas wetlands formed in shallow basins, the deeper parts of which were wetter and in them mires developed, whilst on the slightly higher sand ridges a small Neolithic population sporadically disturbed the alder and birch woodland using fire to create small clearings.

Across the south of the region, in addition to the distribution pattern of struck flint, polished stone axe finds are common. The north of the Wirral peninsula has the densest concentration of axes in Merseyside, focused around the former course of the Rivers Birket and Fender and particularly on the lower slopes of the sandstone ridges of Birkenhead and to a lesser extent Wallasey (Cowell and Innes 1994). There is a slight extension southwards onto the boulder clay areas of central Wirral around Barnston, possibly again connected with the valley of the former River Fender. The North Wirral also produced a rare faunal assemblage for the region. At Leasowe Bay the assemblage contained an auroch's skull, red deer antlers, dog and horse skulls and several vertebrae (Huddart *et al* 1999a, 569) dated to the third millennium BC (Kenna 1986, 5). The finds may relate to the exploitation of a now submerged forest off the north and west Wirral coast.

Generally in lowland Merseyside and Cheshire the lithic distribution pattern is biased towards single or near-single findspots (Cowell and Innes 1994; Leah *et al* 1997). In contrast to the usual pattern, whereby the bulk of total polished stone axe finds derive from non-local volcanic rocks

39 The earliest recorded illustration of the Calderstones Passage Grave, dated 11 October 1825. At that time only three stones were visible, the remainder being buried. The upright megaliths clearly depict the stones' decoration, including cup marks and sprials

that were exploited in the major production centres, Ron Cowell reported that a study of axes from the Merseyside area revealed that they appeared to be made from a local siltstone found in the Coal Measures between the Pennines and North Wales (Cowell 1995, 26).

A possible Neolithic hengiform monument has been identified from aerial photographs at Aighton in West Lancashire (Philpott in Hodgson and Brennand 2006, 39) but the only definite evidence for Neolithic burial practice on Merseyside comes from the site of the Calderstones, Liverpool (*39*). First mentioned in 1568 and described as a 'tumulus' (Stewart-Brown 1911) according to contemporary accounts, the covering mound was 'large' and 'very high and extensive' (Liverpool Daily Post 1896). The monument is a possible passage grave with parallels on Anglesey at Bryn Celli Ddu and Barclodiad y Gawres, which also have decorated stones. In 1765 the mound was disturbed and pottery and cremated bone were found (Baines 1825). Unfortunately the site was destroyed in the nineteenth century (Forde-Johnson 1957; Barrowclough 2007, 121). Although six stones, which are highly decorated with abstract cup, cup-and-ring, spiral motifs, and rare carvings of unshod feet, were saved by removing them for safe keeping, their archaeological context was lost (Forde-Johnson 1957; Cowell and Warhurst 1984; Barrowclough 2007, 121–124).

The exact form of the monument is not known but it is widely accepted that it should be placed in the general context of passage graves (*40*; Cowell 1991a, 35). In Ireland the earliest, very simple, undecorated passage graves date from the beginning of the third millennium BC in Ireland, with the most sophisticated decorated forms dating from the middle of that period (ApSimon 1985/6). It is suggested that Bryn Celli Ddu, Anglesey, was also a late second millennium BC construction as it is built on the site of a pre-existing henge monument (Lynch 1970, 55–65). If the Calderstones, as seems likely on the basis of the art style, was in this general

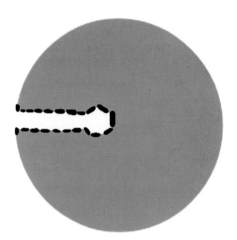

40 Conjectural illustration of the Calderstones based on the Boyne Valley tradition of passage graves

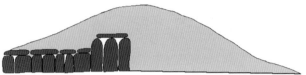

tradition it might therefore be placed after the middle of the third millennium BC when tombs in Ireland included very similar markings. Following Cowell it is perhaps safest to place the Calderstones, like the Anglesey examples, in the Late Neolithic (Forde-Johnson 1957; Cowell 1991a; Cowell and Warhurst 1984). It is likely, on the basis of some of the artistic motifs, including the halberd and footprints, that it remained open during the Early Bronze Age when these carvings were added to the stones in the chamber. The motifs may therefore have been executed both before and after the incorporation of the stones in the monument. Urns with burnt bone, presumably of Early Bronze Age date are also recorded as having come from within the mound and possibly the chamber.

The decoration includes a number of different motifs catalogued by Forde-Johnson (1957). These include markings of a type associated with the Boyne valley, Ireland: cup marks, cup-and-ring marks, concentric circles, spirals (some of which are joined so as to resemble a pair of eyes) chevrons, and a 'star-burst' motif (*41*A–F). There are also carvings whose origin lies outside the Boyne valley, namely the unshod footmarks and halberd (*41*D and *41*B). There are eight examples of spirals, a form that is characteristic of the Irish tombs, although the Calderstones and Welsh examples are less complex than Irish ones. Joined spirals, sometimes referred to as face-motifs, are another design associated with Irish passage graves, for example Newgrange (*42*). An interesting motif overlooked by Forde-Johnson, although illustrated, was what might be described as a star-burst. A similar motif is found in the central chamber inside Knowth (*43*). There are a number of references to comets and other astral objects in Celtic mythology which have recently been considered by Patrick McCafferty (2007, 229–233) these suggest a long-standing incorporation of cometery events into ritual and culture which may go some way to explaining the presence of these motifs at the Calderstones and Knowth.

Ten human foot markings are found on the Calderstones. They appear to have been pecked out of the stone and represent unshod feet. Several of them display genetic abnormalities, one has six toes and another four, which may be relevant to similar abnormalities found preserved in the prints at Formby Point close by at the mouth of the River Mersey (Barrowclough 2007, 121). There, several instances have been noted of feet with fused or missing toes,

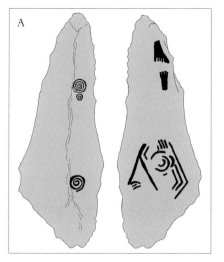

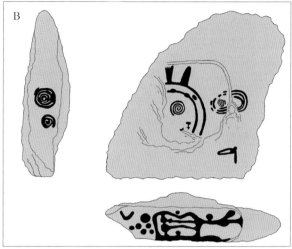

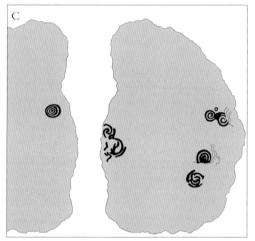

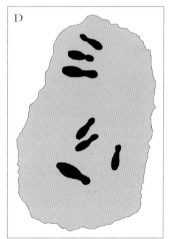

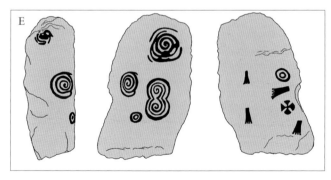

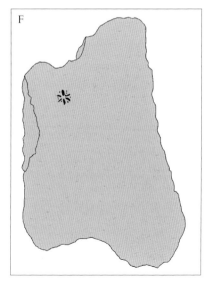

41 Carvings on the Calderstones, stones A–F

42 Double spiral motif from the kerb of Newgrange in the Boyne Valley

43 Starburst from within the central chamber at Knowth, Boyne Valley

discussed in the previous chapter. As already noted the prints span the period from the Mesolithic through to the Iron Age. Dating of the carved examples is difficult but they appear to post-date the suite of Irish influenced carvings as they are positioned in such a way as to respect what must have been pre-existing motifs (Forde-Johnson 1957, 36). If the earlier motifs date to the Late Neolithic this must place the foot carvings at the end of the period or in the Early Bronze Age, in which case the tomb remained open a little longer than might be expected. A suggestion that inurned cremations had been found in the chamber would be consistent with continued use into this period. An alternative explanation is that the tomb, once closed, had been re-opened in the Early Bronze Age; this cannot be ruled out.

No other examples of halberd carvings are known in Britain or Ireland although axes and daggers are known from a number of sites including Stonehenge. Forde-Johnson noted that the depiction was less like the English type and more like those found in Scandinavia and Ireland. Given the absence of such carvings in Ireland, and the presence of carved feet in Scandinavia this may hint at contact between Scandinavia and Lancashire as I have tentatively suggested elsewhere (Barrowclough 2007, 123–4).

The Calderstones provides the best evidence for Late Neolithic connections with Ireland and link it to the small number of monuments on Anglesey, suggesting that at this time the Mersey, North Wales and Anglesey shared cultural affinities. As we saw in the discussion of the sites around Morecambe Bay it seems that water was less of a barrier and more of an aid to communication in this period. Although the passage grave was derived from Ireland the motifs establish that there were other influences at work possibly from Scandinavia or Brittany (Barrowclough 2007, 121–124).

Stone axe concentrations are also associated with a thin distribution northwards on the Pennine slopes mainly at or above the 200m contour. General surveys of the distribution of Neolithic remains in the Lancashire part of the area have been made by Garstang (1906, 215–16), Jackson (1934–5, 72–6) and Leach (1951), and on the Yorkshire side of the Pennines by Petch (1924, 35–43), Cowling (1946, 31–60) and Watson (1952, 38–46), though there have been many subsequent reinterpretations of the significance of the finds. Polished stone axes concentrate around the peripheries of the uplands, often on the flanks of the major valleys. Over 100 examples are recorded, and of the 54 whose petrology has been identified 22 are of Cumbrian origin, four are from Graig Lwyd in North Wales, three are from Tievebulliagh in Northern Ireland, two are from the Whin Sill, while the south-west of England, the south-west of Wales and the Nuneaton area of the Midlands are each represented by a single example; in addition, there are around 20 flint axes. This distribution provides a marked contrast to those of the Mesolithic hunting camps and Neolithic leaf-shaped arrowheads.

Neolithic arrowheads often occur in conjunction with Mesolithic finds and have a thin distribution over all the upland areas, both in the Central Pennines proper and in the Rossendale uplands. They mostly consist of leaf-shaped arrowheads and to a lesser degree transverse types, whose distribution is also comparable with that of the later (and more frequently found) barbed-and-tanged arrowheads of Bronze Age times (*colour plate 5*).

A possible concentration might be discerned on the Marsden-Saddleworth moors. There does appear to be a predominance of earlier leaf-shaped forms over the later transverse types in the gritstone areas. The latter can be related to later Peterborough Ware and, more

44 Excavations at Portfield in 1967, Site 4 grid squares. *Photograph: John Hallam*

particularly, to Grooved Ware (Smith 1974, 121). Transverse arrowheads occur beyond the distributional range of Grooved Ware finds in the Pennines which are concentrated on the limestones of the Peak District and north-west Yorkshire (Manby 1974, fig. 1). Some of the other items usually associated with Grooved Ware, such as polished and flaked flint knives, Seamer axes and Duggleby adzes, also occur spasmodically in the Central Pennines; isolated examples have been picked up in the Central Pennines: an adze near Bacup and an axe at Keighley in the Aire valley (*40*; Manby 1974). In addition, flint chisels were found at Mellor near Stockport and at Torside Reservoir in the south of our area, while a flint 'axe' from Milnrow has many similarities with the Bacup adze. An interesting Late Neolithic adze has been discovered in the Medlock valley near Oldham, embedded in fluvial gravels.

The implications of the lithic evidence, so far as settlement is concerned, are tenuous. The best evidence for Neolithic settlement in the Central Pennines comes from the site of Portfield, Whalley (*44*). Excavations over a number of years revealed that below the Late Bronze Age hillfort was evidence for earlier occupation during the Neolithic (Beswick and Coombs 1986; Hallam pers. comm.). Previous publications omitted discussion of the excavations undertaken by John Hallam in 1967 (Beswick and Coombs 1986, 2); this was unfortunate as it excluded from debate consideration of an important aspect of the Neolithic site which is presented here courtesy of the excavator.

Excavations of an apparently undisturbed area close to the eastern escarpment, where no defence works were obvious, produced evidence for a chert chipping floor and postholes. The area, designated Site 4, measured 13.7 x 6.4m and was divided into eight grids each 2.7 metres square, of which Grids 1, 5 and 8 were excavated (*45*). In the south-west corner of Grid 1 two

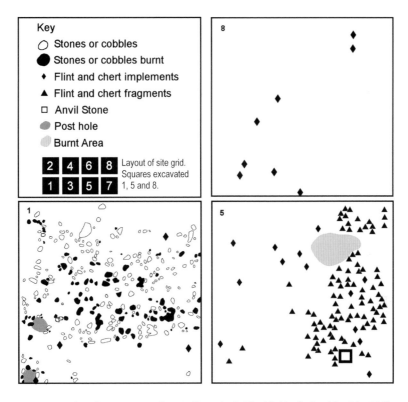

45 Excavated grid squares, numbers indicate individual lithic finds. *After John Hallam*

possible stake holes containing soft fill and flattish packing stones were discovered about one metre apart. No evidence of structures were observed in Grid 5 where 11 pieces of flint and chert were recorded in addition to approximately 100 pieces and fragments of local chert. An irregular-shaped block of sandstone, reddened on its upper surface by burning, may have been an anvil stone. The excavator considered that a chert leaf-shaped arrowhead discovered in Grid 8 could well have been one of the products made using it. In Grid 8 excavations produced several pieces of flint and chert. Irregular-shaped patches of brown compacted soil interspersed with spreads of protruding boulder clay, some of it compacted with occasional burnt stones, were noted. Fragments of charcoal were widely scattered throughout the sections, but were more concentrated in the sub-soil along with burnt stone and blackened cobbles. The indications of burning may be a consequence of the manufacturing process, chert that has been subjected to high temperatures being much easier to work than that which has not (Hallam pers. comm.). Taken together, the flint and chert remains and the chert leaf-shaped arrowhead indicate Neolithic activity in which local chert was being worked for implement manufacture.

Site 4 complements previously published accounts that have described finds of large quantities of Early Neolithic Grimston Ware and lithic material found deposited in pits (Beswick and Coombs 1986). Pit 1, 61cm in diameter, contained fragments of burnt bone and charcoal along with two chert blades, a single flake and nine sherds of pottery, including Grimstone Ware. Pit 2 was similar in size and also included two chert blades and a flake, and three sherds of Grimston

Ware. Although severely truncated, the pits have general similarities to features found in contemporary 'pit and posthole' settlements in southern and eastern England and form typical settlement evidence. Such sites are represented on the surface by diffuse scatters of worked flints and may be indicative of clearance and settlement, although the precise depositional circumstances of these deposits remain unclear. Neolithic features are generally very rare and the pits from Portfield hillfort are the exception in the Lancashire Pennines.

More limited excavations have taken place at the hillfort of Castercliffe, near Nelson, c.14km from Portfield (Coombs 1982). Although excavations of the ramparts by Coombs, which are discussed more fully in Chapter 7, failed to recover any evidence of Neolithic or Early Bronze Age activity, diagnostic lithics were found in the interior of the fort by Peter Whalley. It was the local custom for unemployed miners to search for surface coal during lean times and it appears that on one such occasion they dug pits into the hillfort. After they had left the scene Whalley inspected the pits that they had dug and found amongst the disturbed ground a number of worked flint and chert implements, including both a leaf and a barbed-and-tanged arrowhead (Hallam pers. comm.). These implements are diagnostic of activity during the Neolithic and Early Bronze Age on the site.

No other definite indications of Neolithic settlement have yet been identified on the Lancashire Pennines. A number of saddle querns and grain rubbers have been reported in the Rochdale and Burnley areas, but these are just as likely to be Bronze Age as Neolithic in date. The most promising indications of the location of Neolithic habitation would be provided by burial monuments, but here again the evidence is very slight so far as the Central Pennines and Lancashire in general are concerned.

Only two chambered tombs occur in the Central Pennine area, while another is located just beyond to the north-east; most of the chambered tombs in the Pennines are on the limestone of the Peak District where seven have been identified (Feather and Manby 1970). The Pikestones megalithic chambered tomb is located on the south-west facing slope of a lower terrace of the gritstone moorlands 275m above sea level on Anglezarke Moor near to Chorley. It is placed on top of a low ridge commanding extensive views overlooking the Lancashire Plain, which on a clear day include to the south-west the Welsh mountains and Anglesey, and to the north-west the Lake District mountains. It is aligned north–south and is of trapezoidal outline, being some 45.5m long, 19m wide at the northern end and 13.5m at the southern (*colour plate 13*). The monument is much disturbed and consists of the remains of a rectangular chamber which Lynch thought had probably been divided into two compartments set towards the northern end of an elongated cairn of small stones partly covered in peat and grass (Lynch 1966, 347). The site of the burial chamber at the northern end of the cairn is represented by five slabs, two still standing upright forming the eastern side, and it is at least 4.5m long (Manby 1967, 265). Two stones of the eastern side of the chamber remain upright and the west side-stone leans against them. Bu'Lock (1958, 143–5) postulated the existence of a forecourt, which Lynch disputed, arguing that the monument was too much robbed for this to be confirmed (Lynch 1966, 348). The poor state of the cairn allows something to be seen of the construction method of the builders. A line of pitched stones runs along the central axis forming a spine, otherwise the cairn is composed of small stones. The excavator compared it with Cotswold-Severn type barrows, of which the nearest example is in the Conway valley in North Wales (Bu'Lock 1958, 144). Whilst it shares a number of features in common with such tombs (including stone construction, a façade, a trapezoidal outline, and a burial chamber leading from a short passage with an opening in the middle of the façade) there must be some doubt as to whether it can be associated with morphologically similar monuments so far away, others seeing its affinities as lying in the Peak District (Lynch 1966). Lynch argued that it is best understood as a westward extension of the rather mixed group of megalithic tombs found in Derbyshire (Lynch 1966, 348).

A second chambered round cairn was identified through survey on the west-facing slope of the same moor. Although largely ruined, it appears to comprise a small, pear-shaped cairn with a chamber formed by unworked uprights. It bears some similarity to the Neolithic cairns of Cumbria and Northumbria, although no further work has been undertaken at the site since its discovery and so all conclusions must remain tentative at this stage (Howard-Davis 1996). Other fragmentary evidence of Neolithic occupation in the vicinity is related to stray finds of lithic character. It has also been pointed out that some of the local Bronze Age monuments, in particular the flat, circular, paved enclosures, which on excavation often yielded cremation burials, have superficially Neolithic traits (Bu'Lock 1958, 145).

The site of Round Loaf situated nearby on Anglezarke Moor has also been tentatively identified as a burial monument, possibly a round cairn or bowl barrow (Barnes 1982, 102). The site is a conspicuous feature on the moor standing 6m high with a diameter of 45–50m, and although it has the appearance of a burial monument it has been suggested that it is in fact a natural feature of glacial origin (Clare 1973, vol. 2). During the 1970s a group of amateur enthusiasts began to dig a hole into the mound from the summit. John Hallam reported coming across their activities and persuading them to lower him into the hole from which he gained the distinct impression that the mound may well have been an artificial construction (John Hallam pers. comm.).

The archaeological evidence suggests that, as in the lowlands, there was a continuum of occupation in the Central Pennine uplands from the Mesolithic into the Neolithic. This is confirmed by evidence from pollen analysis. For example, at Holcombe Hill there is very little evidence of any interference with the woodland during the Neolithic period (Tallis and McGuire 1972). Indeed an upward extension of the tree line at this time probably occurred throughout the Central and Southern Pennines generally (Tallis 1975). In the gritstone area of the Lancashire Pennines the pollen evidence consistently testifies to the lack of widespread forest clearances in the Neolithic. The Pennines here were still forested up to about 365m or more (Barnes 1982, 44). A similar pattern existed to the north of Lancashire and in the limestone area of North Yorkshire at Malham, where forest clearance did not occur until the Late Neolithic (Pigott and Pigott 1959, 97). Radley (1969) had also noted the archaeological evidence for a late survival of Mesolithic cultures in North Yorkshire. In one or two places, small-scale and localised agriculture had existed in small clearings over which the forest later regenerated itself (Spratt and Simmons 1976, 201). The exception to this is the evidence from buried soils beneath burial mounds at Winter Hill and Wind Hill where pollen indicated the existence of local heathland communities, suggesting to Barnes that there had been localised woodland clearance during the Neolithic. He postulated that the burial mounds had been constructed in long-established forest clearings (Barnes 1982, 46; Tallis and McGuire 1972, 729).

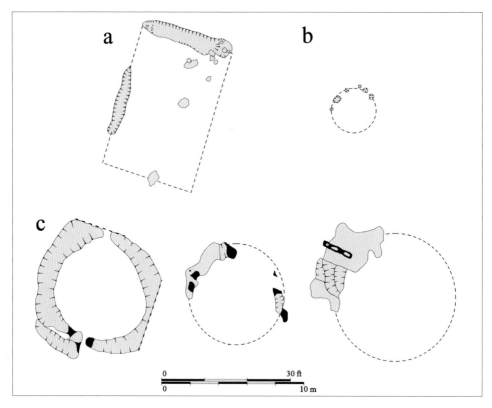

46 Site plans of excavated post built structures of Neolithic date. a) Oversley Farm. b) Tatton Park. c) Arthill. *Illustration: Mary Chester-Kadwell*

Further concentrations of stone axes are associated with the urban areas of the Manchester conurbation and the lowlands of Cheshire. A possible hengiform monument has been seen on aerial photographs near Radcliffe, Manchester (Redhead in Hodgson and Brennand 2006, 39). Neolithic monuments in Cheshire include a possible Late Neolithic/Early Bronze Age pit circle at New Farm, Henbury (Rowley 1975a, 1975b) and possible hengiform monuments identified from aerial photographs close to Sutton Weaver (Collens in Hodgson and Brennand 2006, 39). Once again the evidence for Neolithic burials is sparse. Cheshire has only a single Neolithic megalithic burial chamber, the Bridestones, which lies on its eastern boundary. The monument has parallels in south-west Scotland and Ireland (Clifford and Daniel 1940, 157; Powell *et al* 1969; Longley 1987, 44–6) and seems to fit within a general tradition of long cairns within the north-west of England. However, the burial deposit in the Bridestones appears to have been cremated bone, which is highly unusual in long cairns where the usual practice was to house large numbers of inhumations (Powell *et al* 1969). Cremation is more commonly practised in Irish Court Cairns, which suggests that the Bridestones may also share some affinities with the Irish tradition.

The area south of Manchester has produced the most stratigraphically secure excavated evidence for Neolithic houses. Apparently unenclosed Early Neolithic post-built structures have been excavated at Tatton Park, Cheshire, radiocarbon dated to 3500–2945 cal BC (*46b*; Higham and Crane 1999). The end of occupation of a second structure was dated to 2195–1680 cal BC (Higham and Crane 1999). A nearby pit containing oak charcoal, carbonised bone, fruit and seeds was radiocarbon dated to 3370–2925 cal BC (Higham and Crane 1999). At Arthill Heath Farm (*46c*) a probable later sub-rectangular enclosure has been excavated. Within an extensive ditch was a two-phase palisade with a number of buildings dated to 2790–2570 cal BC and 2210–2020 cal BC (Nevell 1988a).

Excavations at Oversley Farm revealed traces of a probable rectangular structure comprising linear construction trenches, postholes and a central hearth or cooking pit, dated to 3975–3675 cal BC (*46a*; Garner in Hodgson and Brennand 2006, 32). The pit or hearth contained a large assemblage of pottery with a high percentage of charcoal, fire-cracked stone and traces of naked barley and crop weed species. The presence of sheep or goat fats within possible cooking vessels was revealed by lipid analysis (Garner 2001). The rectangular building was subsequently overlain by a possible second rectangular structure with hearth deposits dated to 3015–2985 cal BC, possibly as a consequence of reoccupation and rebuilding on exactly the same location or less likely demonstrating a remarkable continuity of occupation.

The discovery of 162 fragments, representing at least 23 vessels, of Peterborough Ware in the mound of a round barrow at Woodhouse End is interpreted as marking a settlement (Rowley 1977). These small, highly weathered sherds comprise the largest assemblage of Peterborough Ware in the north-west of England. Another potential settlement site was uncovered during excavations at the medieval village of Norton, where pits containing Grimston Ware and flint flakes were excavated (Greene and Hough 1977, 80; Mullin 2002). Grimston Ware and leaf arrowheads have also been recovered from Beeston Castle suggesting a possible early occupation below the Late Bronze Age hillfort (Ellis 1993). If so there is a possible parallel with the Neolithic occupation of Portfield, and possibly Castercliffe and Mellor hillforts in Lancashire, that begins to confirm a pattern of long-term activity on these sites. It is not necessarily the case that this was a continuous uninterrupted occupation, but does confirm that the hillfort locations focus on ancient routeways that channelled people's movement through much of prehistory.

DISCUSSION

The region's broad topographical range and close juxtaposition of coastal, wetland and dry environments may have allowed gathering, hunting and fishing to remain of primary economic importance well into the Neolithic period, after which domesticated crops and animals became common (Cowell and Innes 1994; Middleton *et al* 1995; Hodgson and Brennand 2006, 31). It is also likely that there were variations between different parts of the region in the frequency of cereal use as an adjunct to wild resources. After an initial cereal phase in North Lancashire at the elm decline, dated at 3900–3640 cal BC at Red Moss (Hibbert *et al* 1971), subsequent woodland reduction episodes provide no hint of the presence of cereals (Middleton *et al* 1995), nor is there evidence for cereals in either the Pennine fringe areas or across most of the interior. It would perhaps be surprising if cereals played no part in these areas as the Neolithic progressed, but circumstantially it seems that they may have been characterised by a greater emphasis on animal management, either wild or husbanded. However, faunal assemblages are also rare, and details of diet and subsistence are still unclear.

The distribution of the lithic sites suggests that settlement was concentrated in the lowlands, mainly around the coast and in the river valleys, mirroring the Late Mesolithic pattern. The evidence from the lowland sites on Pilling Moss suggest that early farming communities preferred well-drained soils in a county where much of the landscape is covered by heavy clays or is relatively infertile. A number of explanations have been put forward for the distribution of axes seen across the region, mostly concerned with trade routes (Barnes 1982, 45; Cummins 1980). Bradley and Edmonds (1993) outline a more persuasive case for the distribution of axes through a network of social contacts and obligations. The local axes can therefore be seen as a vital element for interpreting the distribution of Neolithic settlement, whereby the axes were used locally for various woodworking tasks. They may also have had a wider use, particularly as gifts and for other types of exchange, which is likely to have been a central feature of social relations between the small groups of farmers who lived in the area. The distribution of axes is therefore held to be important evidence for the distribution of the earliest farmers in Lancashire as there is an absence of other indicators of settlement such as pottery, flint scatters and burial and ceremonial sites.

Barnes has argued that the relative absence of Neolithic material from the uplands, with the exception of arrowhead finds, is notable (Barnes 1982, 39–40). Only scattered Neolithic material within mixed assemblages has been recovered, for example from Worsthorne Moor (Leach 1951). The blurring of the Mesolithic into the Neolithic hinted at by the combination of artefact types means that the 'end' of the Mesolithic may be impossible to trace. In common with the Central Pennines, sites elsewhere in England have yielded Mesolithic flintwork associated with Neolithic artefacts (Ashbee 1978, 66) and it has been pointed out that it is no coincidence that the areas where Neolithic and Mesolithic equipment are found together are agriculturally marginal, areas which in all likelihood were used by farmers for hunting and not for agriculture (Bradley 1978, 101). The distribution of Neolithic arrowheads in the Central Pennines and elsewhere reflects this continuing use and disturbance of forest-edge habitats for hunting. The possibility that the Mesolithic mode of seasonal movement continued into Neolithic times must therefore be considered seriously. Neolithic clearings in the uplands may have been made in the course of hunting just as they were during the Mesolithic. Certainly it would appear, following Barnes (1982, 46), that there was a different approach to the Neolithic in this part of the north compared with southern England. Earlier, and possibly even later, Neolithic activities were not particularly different from Mesolithic practices, especially since pioneer agriculture may have been on too small a scale to register clearly in the pollen record. Again, the type of forest clearance in the gritstone areas of the Central Pennines differed from that of southern England, and probably also from that of the Peak District, in that small, temporary clearings were the rule compared with the widespread, longer lived deforestation on the Downs. No evidence exists about the techniques used, but it does appear that pastoralism was almost universal in the scattered clearings on the fringes of the uplands – possibly nomadic, or more accurately transhumant, in character, with an emphasis on hunting on the higher ground. Many of these clearings were short lived, and there is widespread evidence of forest regeneration. In Lancashire, besides the strong suggestion of continuity from the Mesolithic into the Neolithic period, there is also the likelihood of a further continuity into the Bronze Age period.

CHAPTER 5

IN MEMORY OF THE ANCESTORS: THE LATE NEOLITHIC AND EARLY BRONZE AGE BURIAL TRADITION

INTRODUCTION

Nationally the Early Bronze Age is marked by technological and ritual innovation. Archaeologically this is seen in the adoption of copper-alloy (bronze) metalwork, the introduction of new pottery styles and the construction of new forms of earthworks. In Lancashire and the neighbouring areas, the innovations that are seen at a national level in the latter half of the third millennium BC are reflected in changes in both social and religious practices. Equally there is considerable evidence for a continuity of practice between the Late Neolithic and Bronze Age. Many sites occupied in the Bronze Age had also been occupied during the Neolithic and continued to be occupied into the Early Iron Age. Stone utilised in the Late Neolithic continued to be exploitation for the production of axe hammers during the third millennium BC and there is a suggestion that the population retained a degree of mobility in their lifestyle.

The distinction between Late Neolithic and Early Bronze Age is therefore somewhat artificial, as others have pointed out (Burgess 1976a; Whittle 1980), and for this reason there will be an inevitable overlap between the two. During both the Neolithic and Early Bronze Age locally available flint sources appear to have been exploited extensively, whilst better quality flint material was sourced from areas outside Lancashire, presumably arriving via networks of trade and exchange. Although many of the widely accepted typological or chronologically diagnostic forms for the Early Bronze Age are represented, such as the barbed-and-tanged arrowhead, assemblages are often characterised by informal or multi-use forms which suggest the expedient use of available raw materials where these were easily available.

Many of the Late Neolithic and Early Bronze Age burial monuments were excavated in the nineteenth and early twentieth centuries but recent analysis and radiocarbon dating means there is secure dating evidence for a large number of them, so it is possible to begin to understand something of the fine-grained chronology of these sites (Barrowclough 2007). The transition from Neolithic to Bronze Age is marked in southern England by the Beaker period, but in Lancashire, as elsewhere in north-west England, Beaker burials are rare. None are known in the south of Lancashire, and only a single example is known from Cheshire (Mullin 2003, 13). North of Lancaster and in Cumbria the pottery becomes slightly more common with a handful of burials accompanied by Beakers recorded (Taylor 1881; Turnbull and Walsh 1996). Beaker sherds have been found in a variety of different contexts, sometimes implying curation of vessels, as at Carriers Croft, Pendleton (Barrowclough 2007). In place of the widespread adoption of Beaker-style burials, in Lancashire circular structures of wood and stone incorporating burials and later sealed by funerary or ring cairns appear to have been the common monumental form during the Late Neolithic and Early Bronze Age. Excavations have demonstrated the variety, complexity and longevity of these sites, and perhaps a long-term commitment to particular sites, by the communities who built and maintained them (Turnbull and Walsh 1997; Howard-Davis and Williams 2005; Barrowclough 2007). Continuity rather than innovation is once again a characteristic of prehistoric Lancashire.

EARLY BRONZE AGE TRADITION

In many areas of North Lancashire and Cumbria there is strong evidence for the deposition of artefacts and burials in natural features over the course of the Late Neolithic and Bronze Age. Cave sites and solution hollows such as Dog Holes cave at Warton, where a sherd of Beaker pot and flints were found (Jackson 1909, 1910, 1912), suggests that some of the remains may date to the Bronze Age. Other deposits in 'natural' places include Beaker sherds deposited in a limestone fissure and a polished stone axe placed in a gryke close by, both in the vicinity of the Sizergh funerary cairn (McKenny Hughes 1904a, b; Edmonds et al 2002; Evans and Edmonds 2003). This association suggests the articulation of a depositional practice whose origins lay in the Neolithic. The distribution of perforated stone axe hammers also resembles Neolithic distributions of polished stone axes. Perforated axe hammers are found in Furness, Cartmel and along the northern coast of Morecambe Bay but are rare elsewhere in Cumbria (Collingwood 1933, 181). The c.85 known examples are confined to low ground and the valleys leading up from them. The distribution resembles that of polished stone axes, the difference being that axes tend to be more coastal than the hammers whose distribution includes the valleys that run up from the coast into the interior. Collingwood interpreted this as evidence for the expansion of the population inland, extending the area of cultivation in response to population growth (Collingwood 1933, 181).

It is this most northerly point of Lancashire that contains some of the strongest evidence for artefacts of Beaker type. Beakers were recovered from domestic contexts on North Walney (Barnes 1970) whilst there are two concentrations of Beaker burials to the east of Morecambe Bay, at Sizergh and Levens Park (Turnbull and Walsh 1996). At Sizergh five inhumations were excavated from a cist and fragments of All Over Corded Beaker Ware were found nearby (McKenny Hughes 1904a; 1904b; Fell 1953, 1–5). The excavation of a funerary cairn at Levens Park (Sturdy 1976) revealed a large circle of boulders surrounding a central Beaker inhumation with Beaker pottery and a pair of flint knives (Turnbull and Walsh 1996). Two further inhumations and a covering barrow were added later. To the north at Allithwaite an Early Bronze Age cremation cemetery was excavated west of Levens producing dates of c.2023–1747 (3545 ± 50; Wild 2003).

The excavation of a large circular dished earthwork at Manor Farm, Borwick near Carnforth, revealed a substantial Early Bronze Age funerary monument (*colour plate 14*). The earliest structure

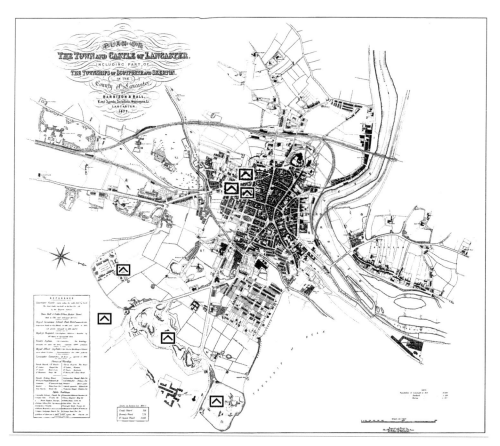

47 Harrison's 1877 Map of Lancaster showing the location of Early Bronze Age burials discovered
in the city, marked ⌂. The urns form two groups: first, a cluster in the city centre found at Queen's
Square (1847), St Thomas's Church (1840) and Penny St Bridge (1900). A second group found around
what is now Williamson Park is larger, comprising six urns from Lancaster Moor (186–35), six from
Bowerham Barracks, one found during quarrying (1872) and another in the cemetery (1894)

was a sub-rectangular enclosure of limestone boulders dated to *c.*1740–1640 cal BC (3270 ±80 BP,
HAR-5658), associated with parts of two poorly preserved inhumation burials lying on the
previously cleared ground surface (Olivier 1987, 129–186). Both burials were accompanied by
typologically early metalwork. The central inhumation was associated with a flat axe and dagger,
an extremely unusual trait, mirrored in few other instances in England (Hodgson and Brennand
2006, 42), suggesting to the excavator an individual of high status. The subsequent overlying cairn
of smaller stones included eleven fairly discrete concentrations of inhumed bone, and seven of
cremated bone and pottery whose date suggested that the monument was in use over several
generations. The excavation revealed not only the complexity of burial practice, but also the long
time over which monuments retained their importance as landscape features.

A significant number of burials in Collared Urns were found at Lancaster in the nineteenth
century (47). One was found in 1840 whilst digging the foundations of St Thomas's Church,
Penny Street, and Harker records six Collared Urns found at Bowerham Barracks in 1877

48 Urn from Bowerham Barracks at Lancaster and a wrist guard. *Photograph: John Hallam*

(Harker 1877, 125). Five of them were destroyed by workmen but the surviving Secondary Series North Western Style urn contained an archer's wrist guard (48). On Lancaster Moor, 275m away, a further six Collared Urns and an accessory vessel were found in 1865 and 1872 during quarrying operations at what is now Williamson Park. What makes the Lancaster finds noteworthy is that the urns were placed in pairs, buried c.60cm below the surface, in a long line at intervals of a metre or so, running in an east–west direction (Harker 1865, 159; 1877, 81).

The distribution of perforated axe hammers continues around the coastal area from the Lune south to Pilling Moss. Comparatively little is known about these implements, which seem too heavy and blunt to have been used as axes, whilst the suggestion that they were agricultural implements used for ploughing remains unproven. They appear to have a chronology that lasts throughout the Early Bronze Age, tailing off by c.1300 BC. The pattern of distribution points toward occupation around the shores of Morecambe Bay. Lithic finds suggest a large group of quite small sites, consisting often of only one or two pieces (Middleton *et al* 1995). This thin distribution of largely single finds is also found in the central Fylde and inland Merseyside, and may suggest that non-intensive or temporary occupation on a repeated or seasonal basis was the norm. The bay and its adjacent wetlands would have provided opportunities for the collection of shellfish, bird's eggs and the hunting of wildfowl, whilst the light soils of the coast would have been more easily ploughed than those further inland. Rather than a barrier the bay may have acted as a communication route connecting the people who lived around it. These people may have shared not only technology but also perhaps a common identity focused around the shared concerns and preoccupations of coastal communities.

In addition to the distribution of perforated axe hammers around Morecambe Bay there is a thin scattering of them in the Burnley, Rossendale and Macclesfield areas. In the Central Pennines over 70 stone implements with Bronze Age connections have been identified. The great majority of the larger stone artefacts occur as stray finds and are widely distributed.

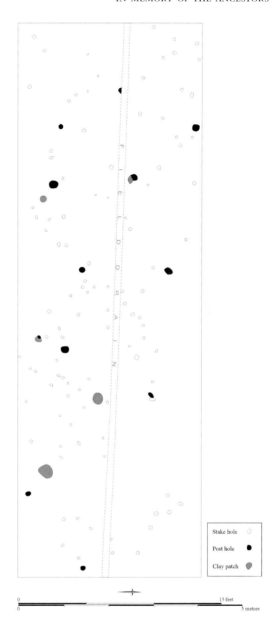

49 Excavation plan of Bond's Farm, Pilling. *After Edwards*

Stake hole
Post hole
Clay patch

0   15 feet
0   5 metres

One interpretation of this spread might relate it to the routeways through the uplands, especially when compared with the similar distribution of the metalwork. There is a notable concentration of these stone artefacts, and in particular of axe-hammers, the most numerous, along the southern flanks of the Rossendale Uplands and in the Manchester area, both in the Mersey–Irwell drainage basin, while another occurs in the Aire valley. Equally significant, however, is the possible relationship of this distribution to the areas of agricultural land on the periphery of marginal upland areas. Thus a study of the relative frequency of Neolithic axes and Early Bronze Age axe-hammers indicates much greater activity west of the Pennines than in Neolithic times (Cummins 1980, 50). The smaller flint implements, especially barbed-and-tanged arrowheads,

50 Wooden stake in situ at Bond's Farm.
Photograph: Ben Edwards

have a different distribution and are found almost entirely on the moors – a spread compatible with hunting. Many of them are found in the same localities as Neolithic arrowheads and Mesolithic flints. Axe hammers also dominate the perforated implement finds from Cheshire, with fewer battle axe and macehead finds than may be expected (Roe 1979, 26).

More certain evidence for Early Bronze Age exploitation of the Over Wyre area is provided by a site at Bonds Farm, Pilling (*49*). Excavations revealed stake structures together with coarse pottery, metalwork and an amber bead and spacer plate (*50*), with radiocarbon dates averaging 1445–1397 cal BC (Edwards 1978a; 1978b; 1992; 2007). The site had been truncated by ploughing, but nevertheless over 100 stake holes and a dozen postholes were identified in an area of 48 square metres (Edwards 1979). In total, 641 pottery sherds were excavated, mostly plain body sherds similar to those excavated at Walton-Le-Dale, Preston, discussed below. Of 345 pieces of flint recovered, 50 were implements, and the remainder were waste. The implements were mostly scrapers made of locally available beach flint, the exception being a barbed-and-tanged arrowhead (*51*). A stone measuring 20 x 10 x 10cm with scars on both surfaces was also found (*52*). According to the excavator it was an anvil, perhaps for crushing rock to act as temper in the manufacture of pottery. Finds of burnt clay and stones similar to those found crushed in pottery sherds on the site are consistent with this interpretation, as are areas of what looked like 'puddled clay'. Also found were two pieces of worked amber (*53* & *54*). Both are perforated as if to form a bead, and both attempts seem to have resulted in the shattering of the amber. This, again, points to this site being a specialist manufacturing

Above left 51 Barbed-and-tanged arrowhead. *Photograph: Ben Edwards*

Above right 52 Stone anvil from Bond's Farm. *Photograph: Ben Edwards*

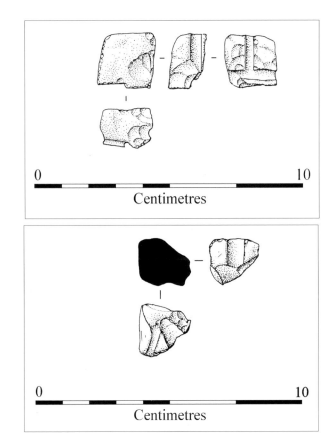

53 Amber spacer bead, and bead from Bonds Farm, Pilling

54 Reconstruction of the amber bead found at Bonds Farm showing how it may have been worn. *Illustration: Joanne Richards*

camp. The combination of post and stake holes is difficult to interpret. They seem not to represent a single structure and are perhaps best understood as the result of a number of light-weight temporary structures overlaying each other. Whatever the interpretation, this site provides the best chronological control for an associated flint assemblage in Lancashire.

The Over Wyre wetlands have also produced evidence of at least three wooden trackways in Stalmine Moss (Thornber 1837; Thornber 1851; Sobee 1953), which locally go under the generic name of Kate's Pad, one to the north of Friars' Hill and two, possibly three, to the south (*55*). Thornber (1851) records the track running from Hales Hall to Pilling Hall and says that by probing through the peat with a stick he was able to follow it for one and a half miles [*c*.2.4km]. He describes its construction which, rather like a railway track, consisted of a series of transverse planks pegged into the peat across which lengths of track were laid longitudinally. According to observations by Rev. Hoopell at Bull Foot Cottage recorded by McKay (1888) the track was wide enough for vehicles to travel over it. A second track, near to Friars' Hill, also known as Kate's Pad, was recorded by Sobee (1953) and a 65m length excavated. It was much simpler than the track recorded by Thornber comprising a series of large oak planks laid end-to-end without transverse 'sleepers'. However 17 of the planks had large mortice holes cut into one end (*56*). The trackways have been dated to the Early Bronze Age by stratigraphic association (Middleton *et al* 1995, 60–62).

Overlooking Pilling Moss, on higher ground at Bleasdale, there is a ceremonial burial site (Dawkins 1900; Varley 1938). Thomas Kelsall, a farmer, discovered the site during the summer of 1898 when he noticed a difference in the colour of the vegetation and in winter, after a

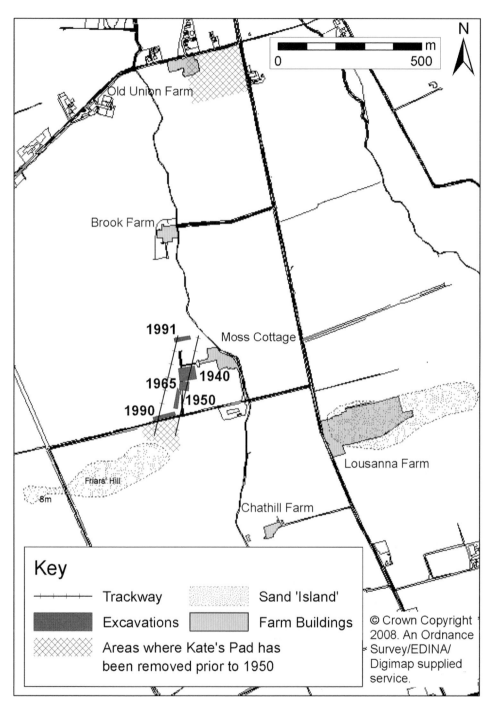

55 Location map showing the areas of excavation where parts of Kate's Pad trackway have been identified. *Mary Chester-Kadwell after Middleton et al 1995, Fig 35*

56 Timber from Kate's Pad track, Pilling Moss. *Photograph: John Hallam*

57 This photograph shows the excavations at Bleasdale Circle. Tom Kelsall (centre) is digging out the remains of the wooden timbers that he had discovered with Shadrach Jackson (left)

frost, the outline of a circle. He mentioned his observations to a local historian, Shadrach Jackson, and in 1898 they began excavating (57). The site consisted of a number of features and although each respects the other it remains unclear whether these were contemporary with one another or whether they represent a sequence of different phases. One possible interpretation sees the construction of a penannular ring ditch, the floor of which was boarded with oak branches, within which was set a circle of oak posts 11m in diameter. In turn this surrounded a central feature into which were deposited two inverted Collared Urns containing cremated human bone and an accessory cup. Charcoal from urn 1, Secondary Series North Western type, was dated to 1960–1750 cal BC (3535 ±35 BP, SUERC-6929) and from urn 2, a Primary Series type, to 2050–1880 cal BC (3615 ±35, SUERC-7286) (Barrowclough 2007). Subsequently the burial was covered by a barrow mound. The whole site was then encircled by an oak palisade approximately 46m in diameter (*colour plate 15*).

A sample from one of the timbers was subjected to radiocarbon assay and a date of 2462–1957 cal BC (3760 ±90, NPL-69) obtained. More recently a second sample was taken and dated to

2150–1950 (3675 ±35, SUERC-7154) by AMS radiocarbon assay (Barrowclough 2007). These dates place the structure in the Early Bronze Age, but they do not assist in determining the chronological relationship between the inner and outer elements because we cannot be certain which part of the structure the timbers came from. My personal opinion, having studied the surviving oaks, is that they probably relate to the floor of the penannular ring ditch. The timbers, although large, appear to belong to the branches of a substantial oak rather than the trunk, and are therefore probably insufficiently robust to have formed either the palisade or inner circle. If that is correct we can infer from the correspondence in date between the timbers and the burial that both were contemporary, but whether the palisade was later, or even earlier, is unknown.

On the Fylde Coast much of the archaeological evidence for burials was destroyed in the nineteenth century. On the coast at Blackpool there was a reported burial site at Stoney Hill Lodge, near to what is now Blackpool International Airport. Further inland, at Weeton Lane Heads, Weeton near Kirkham, a number of cairns have been recorded, at least one of which is still visible at the crossroads (58). Although the finds are lost the accounts seem clear that these were Early Bronze Age in date: 'A few years before 1851 Rev. W. Thornber came into possession of a rude thick half-baked urn marked perpendicularly with dots' (Thornber 1851). One appears to have been a stone cairn with 'many urns' and another find of 'urns' came from close by. A perforated stone hammer was also found in the vicinity. There are also records of a series of cairns, 'fire-burnt broken stones', in the vicinity (Middleton *et al* 1995, 111), which are as likely to have been burnt burial mounds (Hodgson and Brennand 2006, 43). A Late Neolithic burial site at Peel was also described in the previous chapter, all of which suggests that there may have been a more substantial Neolithic and Early Bronze Age presence in the area than we have been able to identify. It is noteworthy that there is a close association between these low-lying burial sites and water. During the Late Neolithic and Early Bronze Age sea levels were *c.*5m higher than at present and as a consequence the Lytham-Skippool valley was flooded (Tooley 1971; 1978). The effect was to create a series of off-shore islands, the largest of which containing what is today Blackpool. Around these flooded islands was reed swamp-type vegetation. The burials around Weeton and Peel were therefore sited at the time on hills and promontories overlooking water.

At Walton-Le-Dale, on the Ribble at Preston the surface below the Roman occupation layer produced evidence of Early Bronze Age settlement activity (Rachel Newman pers. comm.). Although inland today, during the Early Bronze Age this would have been a coastal or semi-coastal estuarine location. A pit, which measured 74 x 62 x 21cm, contained sherds of pottery, lumps of fired and unfired clay, charcoal and small fragments of heat-fractured stone. Environmental analysis identified a small amount of carbonised wheat and hulled barley. Fragments of coarse hand-made pottery and a thumbnail scraper dated the site to the Early Bronze Age, consistent with the discovery of a barbed-and-tanged arrowhead south of the site and of a scale-flaked knife to the north. A total of 31 fragments of pottery were recovered from the pit. Most were small and all derive from the same vessel. Although it proved impossible to reconstruct the vessel something can be said about its manufacture. The pottery was a softly fired, nearly completely oxidised, grog-tempered fabric. Analysis of the petrology by Dr Elaine Morris confirmed that this fabric was completely different to that of the Collared Urns that she had examined from Lancashire (Elaine Morris pers. comm.). Her interpretation was that the vessel incorporated three earlier vessels in the form of grog. The first pot had a

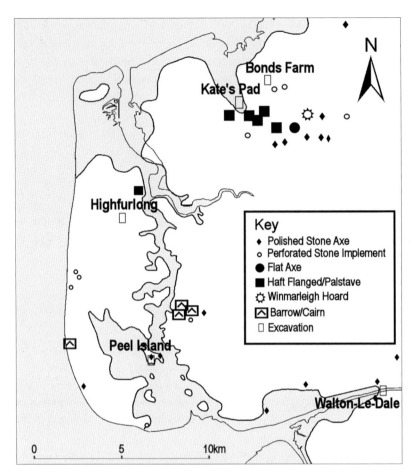

58 During the Late Neolithic and Early Bronze Age an increase in sea levels caused the Lytham-Skippool valley to flood, forming a number of off-shore islands separated from the mainland by reed swamp vegetation. A number of Late Neolithic and Early Bronze Age barrows are known in the area, indicated ⌂. Isolated examples occur at Stoney Hill Lodge, Blackpool, and at Peel Island in the Lytham-Skippool valley. On the mainland a small cluster has been located around Weeton, near Kirkham

sandy matrix and had been crushed to make grog A. The second was a very fine sand or silty fabric; again it had been crushed, to make grog B. The third vessel had used grog B from the second vessel as temper, before it had been crushed to make grog C. Finally, the potter of the vessel, the sherds of which had been found on site, had used both grog A and grog C as temper during its manufacture. This complex sequence of production involving several generations of vessels is something that has been observed elsewhere in the Early Bronze Age in Lancashire in the context of funerary assemblages and is discussed below.

South of the Ribble, excavation at Astley Hall Farm, Chorley, by John Hallam and the Chorley Archaeological Society revealed a penannular ditched enclosure (*59 & colour plate 16*) with two Collared Urns, a miniature Collared Urn and four deposits of cremated remains (Hallam pers. comm.). Urn 1, a Secondary Series North Western Style Collared Urn, was

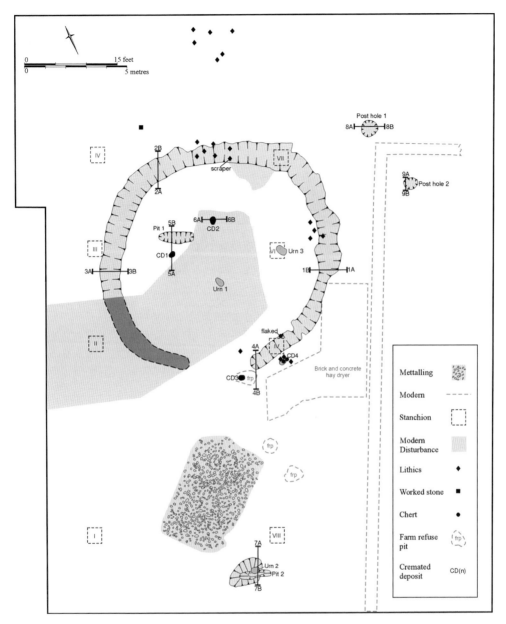

0 |————————————| **15 feet**
0 |————————————| **5 metres**

Post hole 1
8A ⊢●⊣ 8B

Post hole 2
9A ⊢●⊣
9B

IV

VII

2B
scraper
2A

Pit 1
5B
6A ⊢●⊣ 6B
CD2

CD1
5A
3A ⊢⊣ 3B

VI ● Urn 3

Urn 1

1B ⊢⊣ 1A

III

II

flaked
4A
V
CD4
CD3 ● frp
4B

Brick and concrete
hay dryer

frp

frp

I

VIII

7A
Urn 2
Pit 2
7B

Legend	
Mettalling	▦
Modern	- - - -
Stanchion	⬚
Modern Disturbance	▨
Lithics	◆
Worked stone	■
Chert	●
Farm refuse pit	⟨frp⟩
Cremated deposit	CD(n)

59 Site plan, Astley Hall Farm. Penannular ditch with a cobbled forecourt in front of the entrance. Primary urned cremation at the centre, and a second urned cremation in front of the entrance. Four other unurned cremations were excavated. Two post holes were found to the north-east of the monument. *After John Hallam*

placed centrally in the monument and was dated to 1960–1730 cal BC (3525 ±40 BP, SUERC-4454). It contained the cremated remains of an adult with indications that a second, younger person was also present. Grave goods consisted of a burnt plano-convex flint knife and an unburnt struck flake of igneous rock (*60*). Urn 2, a Secondary Series Collared Urn, was found

60 Urn 1, found among grave goods at Astley Hall. *Photograph: John Hallam*

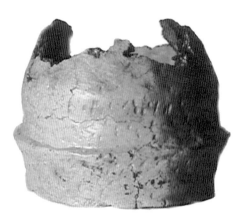

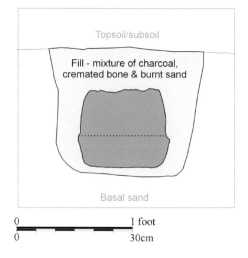

Topsoil/subsoil

Fill - mixture of charcoal, cremated bone & burnt sand

Basal sand

61 Urn 2 with section showing burial.
Photograph: John Hallam

0   1 foot
0   30cm

inverted in a pit 3m to the east of the first burial, outside the earthwork beyond a cobbled forecourt (61). It was dated to 1780–1520 cal BC (3390 ±40 BP, SUERC-4452) and contained the cremated remains of a child about seven years of age. Buried with the cremation was a miniature Collared Urn, fragments of a wooden bowl, three pieces of burnt flint and possibly a bronze dagger.

All four unurned cremations had been disturbed. Cremation 2, which appears to have been that of a child or adolescent (Hallam pers. comm.), is interesting as the plan view of the pit into which it was inserted has a definite squared profile; this is consistent with it being dug

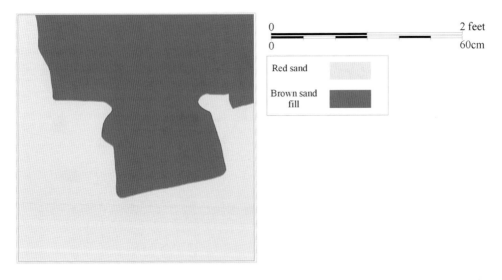

0 | 2 feet

0 | 60cm

Red sand

Brown sand
fill

62 Plan of Pit 2 showing the outline left by the use of a wooden shovel

with a shovel (*62*). Cremation 4 appears to be that of an adult and was dated to 1630–1410 cal BC (3250 ±45 BP, SUERC-4447).

Within the conurbation of Liverpool 'several urns' with cremations have been recovered from the sandstone hill overlooking West Kirby and from the eroding cliff. On the island of Middle Eye, close to the mainland, an inverted urn may represent another site. In Liverpool, the Wavertree burials consist of eight urns with burnt bones, of which only two Collared Urns have survived, with no record of an accompanying structure (Cowell 1991a). Late Neolithic traits may be seen in the multiple burials in 'ringwork'-type structures in this area and concentric circles of stake holes beneath the mound at Southworth (Bu'Lock 1961; Freke and Holgate 1988) with similarities to the inner ring at Bleasdale, to the posts found at Astley Hall and also Noon Hill.

The probable Neolithic passage grave site of the Calderstones, Liverpool, discussed in the previous chapter, may have been open in the Early Bronze Age when carvings which include concentric circles, spirals, chevrons, arcs, and feet, which have Neolithic and Bronze Age parallels elsewhere, were added to the stones in the chamber. The motifs may have been executed both before and after the incorporation of the stones in the monument. Urns with burnt bone are also recorded as having come from within the mound and chamber (Forde-Johnson 1957; Cowell 1991a; Cowell and Warhurst 1984).

Rock art is very rare in Lancashire. Beyond Calderstones a cup-and-ring decorated stone (*63*) was found at Rivington Reservoir. A similar sounding stone was excavated at Noon Hill but was stolen from the site before it could be recorded. It is possible that the stone found in the reservoir is one and the same, having been abandoned by the thieves, alternately this may be the second of two stones found on the Anglezarke uplands. The other candidates for consideration are the shod footprints at Craggs Farm, Pendleton (Hallam 1995), which given the presence of foot carvings at Calderstones are possibly late prehistoric, although close dating is not possible.

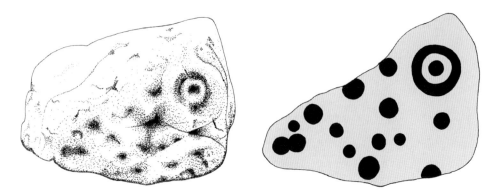

63 Cup and cup-and-ring decorated stone from Rivington Reservoir near Bolton. *Illustration: Mary Chester-Kadwell*

A small group of barrows is located in the Wirral. Examples include numerous finds of urns but few structures, suggesting some may actually represent deposition of urns in locations without funerary mounds, perhaps analogous to the burials on Lancaster Moor. In Merseyside and northern Cheshire there are three localities with Early Bronze Age lithic assemblages at Hale, Irby (Philpott and Cowell 1992) and Little Crosby (Cowell 1991b). A context for this type of site may be suggested close to Little Crosby at Mount Pleasant, north Liverpool, where cereal-type pollen is centred on *c.*1960 BC (Innes and Tooley 1993). A bone midden of wild animals dated to *c.*2030 BC from the north Wirral coast also provides a potential context for the activity represented by stone tools (Kenna 1978). The high tool ratio and lack of knapping debris in the Little Crosby assemblage, when compared against the flint evidence from a site such as Fengate (Pryor 1980), suggests that a wide range of heavy-duty tasks were undertaken. Cowell interpreted this pattern as one of mobility associated with temporary camps alongside places in the landscape which were occupied for longer periods (Cowell 2000a). This is an interpretation confirmed by small-scale excavation in the area.

At Brunt Boggart, Tarbock, Beaker pottery and fired clay, possibly from an oven, was recovered from a pit containing a large number of burnt pebbles dated 2120–1680 cal BC (3540 ±70 BP, Beta 118137). The pit had been cut into the primary fill of a 12m segment of a longer ditch. Very close by a short segment of shallow gully contained Late Neolithic and Early Bronze Age pottery with a few fragments of fired clay and burnt pebble (Philpott 2000, 120–122). On the slopes of a valley at Kirkby, north Liverpool, *c.*25m OD, two slightly curving sections of gully, representing two insubstantial structures, containing fragments of Collared Urn, were excavated and provided dates of 1910–1410 cal BC (3360 ±110 BP, Beta 9413) and 1945–1655 cal BC (3490 ±60 BP, Beta 94191) (Adams 1995). A third site, at Ditton Brook, lies in a similar location, at *c.*8m OD on the upper slope at the southern end of the same, relatively narrow, river channel. The traces of settlement were even less distinct than at Kirkby. Two small pits were found, one of which produced a small amount of pottery, dated to 1620–1130 cal BC (3140 ±90 BP, Oxa-3677). A small posthole several metres away was probably also of this approximate date (Cowell 2000b).

According to Cowell the excavated settlement evidence from east of the Mersey, when combined with the lithic distribution and palaeoenvironmental evidence, tends to suggest the existence of a combination of small, lightly used locations such as Ditton Brook and Kirkby, and more sedentary places, such as at Brunt Boggart. To the west, on the Wirral, there is less evidence for the period, however the implication is that the settlement pattern included a degree of mobility during the earlier Bronze Age that may have been maintained for some time within the central area of Merseyside and perhaps throughout the whole of lowland Lancashire. This may also suggest one element of land-use in the Wirral which Cowell associated with radiating pulses of economic or social activity tethered to a series of short-term sedentary sites.

The Early Bronze Age evidence from Greater Manchester and Cheshire is similarly dominated by funerary monuments. In Cheshire a total of 109 Bronze Age round barrows have been identified. Twenty-six of which are grouped within six cemeteries, the remainder occur in ones and twos. A group of five barrows lies around Winwick, to the north of Warrington. Two were recorded during the late nineteenth century (May 1904), while two have been excavated under modern conditions. One, badly disturbed, produced Beaker pottery. Another Beaker barrow at Southworth Hall Farm consisted of a two-phase monument with multiple cremations, a Food Vessel, two Collared Urns and an accessory cup. The radiocarbon dates for the two phases spanned about 400 years between approximately the eighteenth and fourteenth centuries BC (Freke and Holgate 1988; Cowell 1991a). A flint dagger of Beaker type has also been found in the area of the barrow group (Cowell 1995; Hall *et al* 1995). Another concentration lies around Withington and Joderell Bank, to the west of Oakmere and Macclesfield. Excavations at Fairy Brow, Little Bollington, revealed an unurned cremation with a bronze dagger dated to 1520–1450 cal BC (Tindall and Faulkner 1989).

Evidence of settlement was recovered from Oversley Farm on the site of the second runway at Manchester Airport (Thompson 1998; Garner 2001). Excavators found a Beaker pit and 'hollow way', as well as at least two circular buildings, associated with pits filled with 'midden' deposits (Garner 2001). The site appears to have continued in use throughout the Middle and Late Bronze Age, although the smaller number of features (mostly pits) and the ephemeral structural evidence might suggest less intensive occupation than earlier phases. Up to 2000 sherds of Bronze Age pottery were recovered, much of it Early Bronze Age, including Beakers, Cordoned and Collared Urns, incense/pygmy cups and Food Vessels. A small amount of Late Bronze Age pottery is also represented in the assemblage. Large quantities of lithic artefacts were recovered from Mesolithic and Bronze Age contexts including blades, scrapers and a barbed-and-tanged arrowhead.

Continuity was again found in Cheshire where the fill of a posthole from a possible roundhouse at Tatton provided a radiocarbon date of 2195–1680 cal BC, and was interpreted as the final occupation of a Neolithic structure (Higham and Cane 1999, 32). An undated roundhouse associated with stakeholes which probably represented fences was also excavated (Higham 1985, 78). At High Legh, Cheshire, a lithic scatter of possibly second millennium BC date was identified whilst two enclosures were identified from aerial survey (Nevell 1991, 18–19; 2003a). Two high-quality flint daggers have been found in Cheshire at Acton Bridge (Longley 1987, 79) and Basford. Flint daggers have predominantly Late Beaker associations and date typologically to the Early Bronze Age (Clark 1931; Grimes 1931); they are discussed

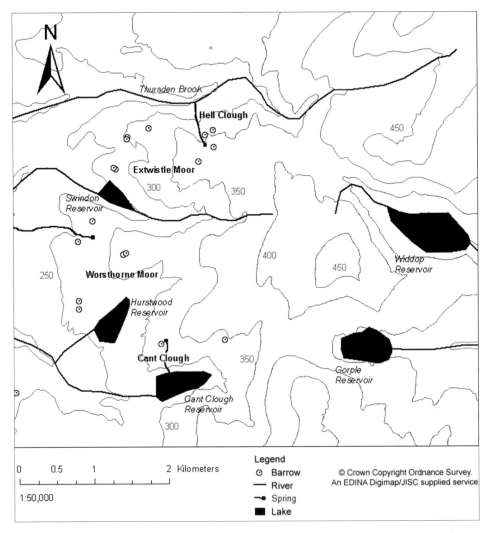

64 Distribution of Early Bronze Age burial monuments and earthworks on Extwistle and Worsthorne Moors, Burnley. *Map: Mary Chester-Kadwell*

more fully below. There are other excavated sites that may indicate a mobile element within the Early Bronze Age settlement pattern (Hodgson and Brennand 2006, 36). The site at Piethorn Brook, near Rochdale, produced a stake-built structure with a hearth, a small amount of flintwork, jet and shale ornaments, and Collared Urns and Beakers (Poole 1986). A further probable upland settlement context may be associated with four Beakers from Castleshaw, east of Manchester (Thompson 1974).

The largest concentration of burials comes from the Central Pennines. Most of these 78 sites are in the uplands, although several occur in the lower reaches of valleys, particularly around Bolton. The barrows on these gritstone areas are invariably cairns, built of local stone which occurs exclusively in the area. An exception to this is the moorland area east of Burnley where over c.25 square kilometres 14 stone circles, ring banks and small barrows have been

65 Excavation of the composite cairn at Noon Hill showing the large stones that formed the kerb

found (64). Bu'Lock (1961, 13) proposed the existence of two traditions: single grave burials with up to five bodies, and larger cemeteries, with twice as many cemeteries as single grave burials in Lancashire. Single grave burials include simple kerbed or revetted cairns covering inhumations, as at Haulgh and Walmsley, both near Bolton (Dawes 1851–2, 130–1), and Law House (Whitaker 1876, 195), near Burnley, as well as cremations as at Low House, Milnrow (Platt 1900, 95–7), and Noon Hill, Rivington (65). Some cairns in the Burnley area may have had free-standing peristaliths or this feature may represent the kerb of an outer earthen mound now disappeared (Bu'Lock 1961, 14). The composite cairn of earth and stone is a well-defined type: those at Noon Hill (*colour plate 17*), Winter Hill and Hades Hill (Sutcliffe 1899, 233–4), for example, had kerbs round earth and turf mounds over a central cairn, possibly suggesting modification and enlargement after the initial building.

Cremated human bone from Hades Hill was dated to 2040–1870 cal BC (3590 ±40 BP, SUERC-4424) and oak charcoal to 2470–2270 cal BC (3880 ±40 BP, SUERC-4425).

The Wind Hill cairn, near Heywood, was defined by a kerb of horizontal slabs up to three courses high, and on its eastern side the kerb had been heightened and straightened to focus on an opening two metres wide. A rectangular area outside this opening was defined by inward-leaning slabs, which were further enclosed by a satellite kerb. Both primary and satellite kerbs were finally concealed to give the cairn a squat pear shape. The excavator considered the burials here to be of Beaker date from the grave goods, and that the structural features of the cairn possessed elements characteristic of a mixed Neolithic ancestry (Tyson 1980).

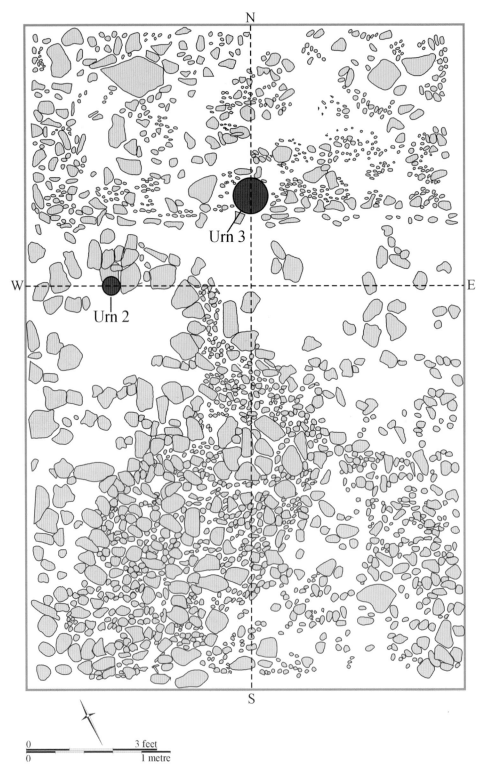

66 Site plan of Carrier's Croft, Pendleton, Lancashire. *After John Hallam*

67 Cobbled floor,
Pendleton. *Photograph:*
John Hallam

Twice as many burial monuments occur west of the Pennine watershed than to the east, though the former does include a greater proportion of the total area. While most of the actual barrows are on false crests, Barnes thought that a more interesting feature of the burials is provided by the contrast that emerges when the western and eastern flanks of the uplands are compared. To the west, most of the burials occur round the edges of the Pennines proper and the Rossendale uplands where there is a greater number at lower altitudes, all either on gravel terraces or on fluvio-glacial gravels, as at Bolton. The lowest are at Kenyon near Stonyhurst and at Pendleton: the former is the northern representative of a group on the low sandstone ridge which focuses on the ford at Warrington, whilst the barrows near Stonyhurst and at Pendleton are both near river crossings. The median altitude of the burials in the west is 240m, with the highest tending to occur on the far western fringes of the Rossendale Uplands. East of the Pennine watershed, however, the median height of the burials is higher, at 300m, and they occur especially on the south-facing flanks of Calderdale and the Aire valley. Only two are at 120m or lower, and even these are sited on gritstone terraces, well above the level of the River Calder (Barnes 1982, 56).

Burials also occur in flat cemeteries. At Carrier's Croft, Pendleton (*66*), excavations revealed a possible flat cemetery containing three Collared Urns with cremated remains beneath a cobbled floor (*67*). Urns 1 and 2 were Secondary Series North Western Style

68 Urn 2, Pendleton, containing an adult cremation. *Photograph: John Hallam*

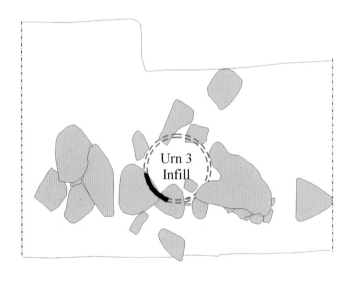

69 Urn 3, Pendleton, cremation of a child with grave offerings

Site	Diameter	Type
Broadbank, Burnley	45.5m	Earth circle
Delf Hill, Burnley	4m	Ring mound, 7 stones
Hell Clough 1, Burnley	7.5-9m	Ring mound
Hell Clough 2, Burnley	-	Ring mound, 7 stones
Hell Clough 3, Burnley	16.75-17.5m	Ring mound, 7 stones
Mosley Height, Burnley	13m	Embanked circle
Ringstone Hill, Burnley	-	Ring mound
Slipper Hill, Burnley	-	Ring mound, stone circle
Twist Hill, Burnley	8m	Earth circle
Wasnop Edge, Burnley	6.5m	Earth circle
Blackheath, Todmorden	30.5m	Embanked circle
Ringstone Hill 1, Nelson	-	Stone circle?
Standing Stones Hill, Anglezarke, Horwich	20-21m	Kerbed mound?
Chetham's Close 1, Turton, Bolton	16m	Stone circle
Chetham's Close 2, Turton, Bolton	22m	Ring mound
Whitelow, Ramsbottom	20.75m	Ring bank
Hill Top, Saddleworth	13.75m	Stone circle

70 'Ringworks' in the Central Pennines. *After Bernard Barnes 1982, table 3*

Collared Urns. Alder charcoal from urn 2 was dated to 1890–1680 cal BC (3450 ±40 BP, SUERC-4443), the urn being inverted over the cremated remains of an adult male (*68*). Urn 3 was a Secondary Series Collared Urn also found inverted over a cremation, this time of a child. Alder charcoal from the urn was dated to 1780–1600 cal BC (3400 ±35 BP, SUERC-4444), whilst cremated human bone from the urn was dated to 1920–1730 cal BC (3495 ±35 BP, SUERC-4445). The urn 3 burial (*69*) was associated with a few fragments of an accessory vessel, five sherds of re-fired Beaker Ware, a bone button, four quartz crystals and a gold object described as a 'bead', with Beaker affinities which will be discussed later (*colour plate 18*).

A further type of burial monument is the 'ringwork' (*70*), structures that range between two extremes: plain, earth-embanked circles with or without an entrance, made from scraping the soil from the outside or from the central area; and, secondly, free-standing stone circles (Radley 1966, 11). Between these are several variations: earth circles with a central mound, earth circles with standing stone circles inside or on the bank, and stone circles with a central mound, for example Hell Clough III (*71*; Bennett 1946). Where stones occur they are seldom more than one metre high, and most stand on low overgrown banks. The circles average about 10.5m in diameter and invariably enclose areas of multiple burials. A possible evolution occurred in these monuments during the second millennium, starting as free circles and concluding as tiny earthen enclosures (Burl 1976, 288). The only true stone circles in the Central and South Pennines are on the limestone of the Peak District, though in our area a 'plain ring', a circle consisting of 10 irregular stones, some 10.5m in diameter, with a circular structure in the centre, was recorded at Walshaw Dean in 1902 before the construction of the

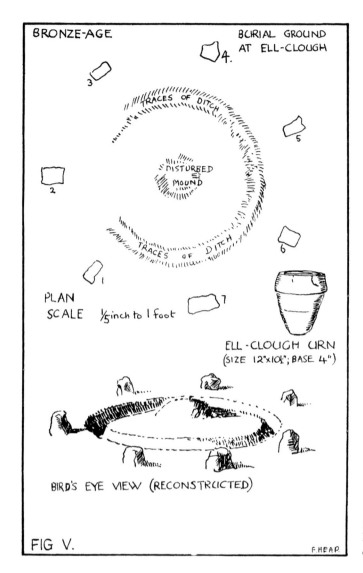

71 Ell or Hell Clough III, Early Bronze Age earthwork. *Bennett 1946, 20*

reservoirs. The two most spectacular examples are those at Blackheath (Roth 1906, 307–22) and Mosley Height (Bennett 1951, 204–8).

Blackheath is located on the south-facing slopes of the Calder valley, and is about 30.5m in diameter (*72*). An earthen circular bank enclosed an area with cairns containing cremations in association with Collared Urns. Sherds of several urns were found together with seven more-or-less complete urns and four accessory vessels. The central urn contained one of these accessory vessels, which in turn contained a bronze knife, a bronze and a bone pin. Two urns with cremations were probably covered by other vessels, one of them also containing an accessory vessel and various beads, which will be discussed later. A fourth urn had a cremation and a bone pin. The vessels were all upright and some were surrounded by numerous thin, flat stones placed on edge. One urn was found in the bank. Some parts of the floor were

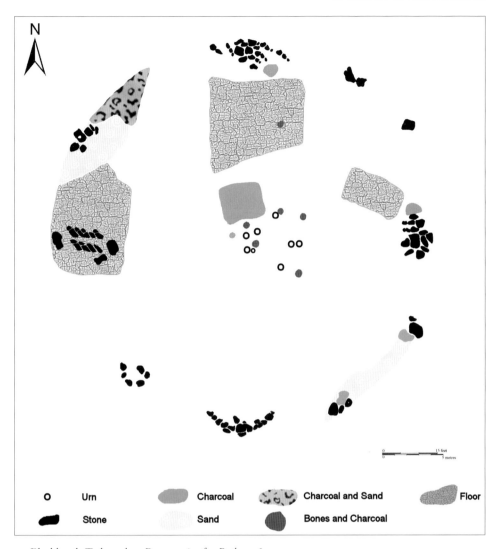

72 Blackheath, Todmorden. *Barnes 1982 after Roth 1906*

baked by great heat, and the excavator suggested that the pots may have been made here, and where possibly the bodies were cremated. Clay for the urns was seemingly dug from two deep holes found within the circle, and it was tempered with pounded gritstone of which great quantities lay in part of the enclosure. There was the suggestion of at least one rudimentary 'furnace', a cist-like structure surrounded by baked soil. Some of the cremations were found in hollows without urns, while other finds scattered about the site included flint scrapers and knives, a burnt leaf-shaped arrowhead near the centre, a whetstone and grain rubbers (Roth 1906, 307–22).

The Mosley Height circle was likewise situated on a hillside, overlooking the northern entrance to the Cliviger gorge. A circle of 18 large boulders, irregularly spaced, stood on a stony bank enclosing a paved space 13m across (73). Three bowl-shaped holes were found in

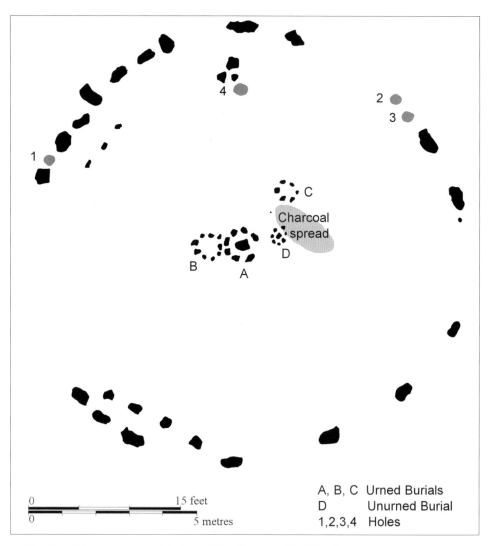

73 Site plan of the excavations at Mosley Heights, Burnley. *After Walter Bennett 1951*

the bank and a fourth just outside (*74*). A small central cist contained an inverted Primary Series Collared Urn 'A' with the cremated remains of an adult female, the urn being crudely decorated with four rows of twisted cord. Oak charcoal found in the urn was dated to 1960–1730 cal BC (3525 ±40 BP, SUERC-4427) and cremated human bone to 1920–1730 cal BC (3490 ±40 BP, SUERC-4431). In pits set about this primary burial were other cremated burials (*75*). An inverted Secondary Series South Eastern Style Urn 'B' was found in a cist adjoining 'A' and to the north-east a Primary Series Collared Urn 'C' was found badly broken. Oak charcoal from urn 'C' was dated to 1960–1740 cal BC (3540 ±35 BP, SUERC-4437) and cremated human bone to 1880–1610 cal BC (3420 ±40 BP, SUERC-4426). Oak charcoal from unurned cremation 'D' was dated to 1960–1740 cal BC (3540 ±35 BP, SUERC-4434) and human bone 1780–1600 cal BC (3410 ±40 BP, SUERC-4432). There is a suggestion that the

74 Excavations at Mosley Heights in 1950. *Photograph: Walter Bennett*

75 Urns A and B (left to right), found during the excavation of the funerary monument, Mosley Heights. *Photograph: John Hallam*

pottery was made from local clay within the ring bank itself (Hallam 1970, 235). Grave goods included several flint implements, including scrapers, arrowheads and knives, two pieces of Kimmeridge shale, two grain rubbing stones, pieces of quartz, calcite and galena. Burl suggests that this site in particular has demonstrable affinities with enclosed cremation cemeteries and with stone circles, while there are several other smaller ringworks with stone settings in the same neighbourhood, about which far less is known.

It has been suggested that in addition to burial places circles were the site of ritual activity (Fleming 1971, 23ff). This would go some way to explaining the 'ritual pits' found at some of them. It is possible that ringworks developed from an earlier phase in the ritual, which culminated in the erection of a barrow. Many excavation reports mention that barrows contained internal perimeter pre-barrow enclosures which stood while the primary and satellite burials were being made. The reason why they were never completed may be due to a decline in the size of the population which meant that labour could not be spared to cart the stone needed to build the cairn.

Both inhumation and cremation were practised in the area during the Bronze Age, though the latter was far more numerous: only six inhumations have been definitely recorded. A possible continuance of Neolithic traditions is seen in the re-use of barrows for more than one inhumation as at Wind Hill, Heywood, and at Ferry Fryston, just outside the area, though in each case the earlier burial was destroyed in the process. At only two Pennine sites, Pule Hill and Stonyhurst, were the two burial rites found together, two inhumations and at least two cremations at Pule Hill, a pattern also seen outside the Pennines as at Borwick. Multiple burials, however, are common. At Darwen the Whitehall barrow or 'cemetery mound' (Abram 1877, 23–4; Jewitt 1886, 137–8; Jackson 1935, 88; Bu'Lock 1961, 17) contained ten cremations, nine in urns, which in each case were covered by a flat stone, one being accompanied by an accessory vessel and bronze dagger (76). Charcoal from a Secondary Series North Western Style Collared Urn (WH4, U8) dated to 1940–1740 cal BC (3520 ±35 BP, SUERC-4463) and that from a similar style urn (WH8, U12) to 1980–1770 cal BC (3560 ±35 BP, SUERC-4464). Cremated human bone from the latter urn dated to 1890–1730 cal BC (3480 ±35 BP, SUERC-4465). The burial mound at Noon Hill, Rivington, contained six or seven groups of cremated bones, one under an inverted Food Vessel in a stone cist consisting of three individuals, a man, woman and child. Both the burial mounds near Ramsbottom at Whitelow and Bank Lane contained multiple cremations as did the Cliviger Laithe cairn near Burnley. At Whitelow five Collared Urns were excavated, one Secondary Series and four Secondary Series North Western Style urns. Radiocarbon dates for Secondary Series North Western Style urn burials 'G' and 'L' were 1890–1680 cal BC (3470 ±40 BP, SUERC-4457) and 1920–1730 cal BC (3495 ±40 BP, SUERC-4455) respectively, and for burial 'H' 1940–1730 cal BC (3515 ±35 BP, SUERC-4456). Cremated human bone from Cliviger Laithe, where the burnt remains of up to five persons were accompanied by three urns, was dated to 1880–1680 cal BC (3455 ±35 BP, SUERC-4436). At nearby Hell Clough, an urn contained the cremated remains of two people, an adult and a child. As mentioned earlier, some of the ring monuments contained a considerable number of burials: Blackheath, Todmorden, at least ten; Mosley Height, Burnley, four; and in Calderdale at Ringstone Edge, five. It has also been described how some sites were possibly flat cemeteries: thus at Rastrick some 20 urns were unearthed; at Breightmet 12; at Warley at least 5; and just

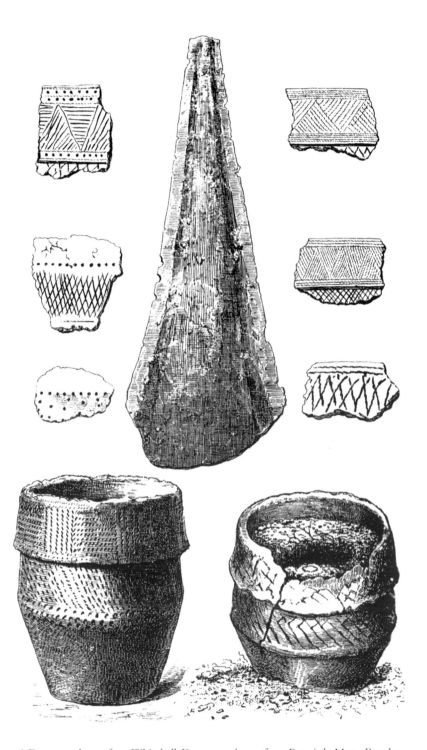

76 Dagger and urns from Whitehall, Darwen and urns from Extwistle Moor, Burnley

outside our area at Skircoat 3. These cremation cemeteries of the Early Bronze Age can be seen to continue Neolithic ideas of multiple burial (Burgess 1970, 210).

Inhumation burials in barrows occur on the natural surface or in a pit, and in the latter case they may be in a cist, roughly enclosed by stones, or laid on a pavement. Cremation burials, too, may be in a pit, cist, below a pavement, or roughly enclosed by stones. The simplest form of grave pit is commonly associated with Beaker burials, illustrated by Beaker inhumations in the Peak District (Lewis 1970, 52). Beaker burials are poorly recorded in Lancashire, but at Ferry Fryston just to the east a Beaker was accompanied by a crouched inhumation in a pit (Pacitto 1968, 297). The possible Beaker burial at Wind Hill, Heywood, occurred as a surface inhumation below a barrow (Tyson 1980). The cairn at Walmsley, Bolton, contained an inhumation in a cist accompanied by a possible Food Vessel, while at Noon Hill, Rivington, an enlarged Food Vessel occurred in a secondary position in the cairn. The Pule Hill Food Vessel burials were in cavities in the rock about 45cm deep, 91cm long and 61cm wide, while at Ferry Fryston a crouched inhumation accompanied by a Food Vessel occurred in a secondary position to that of the Beaker interment (Pacitto 1968, 297).

In Lancashire the cremation pits commonly connected with Collared Urn burials were usually shallow, though the structures varied enormously. Some occurred in cists. Inhumations were found in cists at Law House, Burnley, and at Walmsley and Haulgh, both near Bolton; in the latter the structure measured 1.4m in length and 30cm in depth. At Hell Clough 'A', two cremations in an urn were in a cist of 45 square centimetres, built of 'unhewn' stones, which was covered by a triangular slab of grit (March 1886), the whole being enclosed in a circle monument. The urned burial at Lowhouse, near Milnrow, was also placed in a rough cist, while the burial at Snoddle Hill, Littleborough, had probably been placed in a similar rough structure. Finally, at Wasnop Edge II, Burnley, in a cairn excavated in 1886, no burial was found but the centre was 'arranged like a long sarcophagus' (Harrison 1892). The main grave in the Bank Lane, Ramsbottom, cairn was a stone-lined pit two metres long and half a metre wide, and this, too, was empty when opened. Like the Wind Hill cairn, several of the other cairns and circles in the area had no pits or cists, namely Hades Hill, Rochdale, Cliviger Laithe, Burnley, and possibly Darwen. The settings of the urns at Blackheath, Todmorden, have already been described, and they too were on the surface. The urn in the Rose Hill cairn at Bolton was inverted and sunk about 15cm into the earth. When a mixture of grave traditions are considered together with the nature of the burial structures and the pottery, many survivals from the Neolithic can be discerned. It is suggested that this is entirely in keeping with the other aspects of continuity seen in Lancashire.

Thus we may determine two features of the urned cremations. Firstly, that a decision was made whether to invert the urn or place it upright (77). Analysis of urns where their position has been recorded reveals that equal numbers were placed upright to those inverted, and the dual practices of inversion continued from the Primary Series through to the Secondary Series (Barrowclough 2007, 104–6). Secondly, that they were often capped by placing a flat stone over the mouth of the urn (78). The practice of capping is first seen in the Secondary Series North Western Style urns and is mostly a feature of those urns placed upright in pits, as at Wavertree, rather than cists (79). Presumably for those urns inverted, the base of the pit, or cist, was often considered sufficient to seal the urn, removing the need for a cap, although

		Upright	Inverted
	Food Vessel	3	3
Collared Urn Series	Primary Series	4	6
	Secondary Series	2	9
	Secondary Series North Western Style	22	16
	Secondary Series South Eastern Style		2
	Unclassified Collared Urn	5	4
	Cordoned Urn		2
	Urns Unclassified	6	
	TOTAL	42	42

77 Number of urns upright-inverted by type N=84

		Upright		Inverted	
		Pit	Cist	Pit	Cist
Collared Urn Series	Primary Series				
	Secondary Series			2	
	Secondary Series North Western Style	11	2	4	3
	Secondary Series South Eastern Style	1			1
	Unclassified Collared Urn	4	3		
	Urns unclassified	3	6		
TOTALS		19	11	6	4
		30		10	

78 Number of funerary urns covered by single slabs or placed in stone cists by type. N=40

examples do occur where the urn was inverted over a flagstone placed at the bottom of a pit. In several other cases, for example Bleasdale Circle, coarse cloth has been recovered from the mouth of urns, suggesting that it had been tied round the urn neck, sealing it off.

Whatever the method, containment was important. It may be understood that the corpse was considered unclean, and therefore polluting, and perhaps socially dangerous. A considerable body of literature exists around the binary concept of pollution and purity first developed by the anthropologist Mary Douglas (1966). The period following death, but before burial, when the corpse is 'betwixt and between' is a particularly unsettling time for society (Douglas 1966; also Leach 1976; 1977, 171–3). The living are confronted by the danger

79 Collared urns from Wavertree, Liverpool, upright covered with stone and inverted. *Source: Ecroyd Smith 1868, 130*

brought about by death of a torn social fabric, a time when long-standing social relations have to be renegotiated. They also have to confront the physical contamination of a decaying body. It is this liminal stage of the final rite of passage in the human life cycle that is most dangerous and must be contained.

Containing the corpse is a preoccupation of many cultures and what we see in the cremated remains of the funerary urns may be just the final stage in a process of containment that began when the deceased first passed away. The requirement to prepare the corpse, including some form of purification, is almost universal among contemporary cultures. There is slight evidence that the Early Bronze Age was no different. Excavations at Astley Hall, a penannular ringwork, revealed in the ditch a worked stone which has been interpreted as a plug similar in shape to ones used in hospitals today for stoppering the anal orifice of the dead to prevent post mortem bowl movement (Mr Owen Edwards, Consultant Surgeon, Addenbrooks Hospital, Cambridge pers. comm.). It is possible that the plug was placed in the body, only being removed immediately prior to cremation.

Edmund Leach (1977) argued that all humans are interested in what distinguishes the outside from the inside of their bodies, especially with orifices which connect the two: anus, urethra, penis, vagina, nipples, mouth, eyes, nose and ears. These orifices have major symbolic significance (Leach 1977, 171) and require careful control. In corpses these boundaries begin to break down; the bowls, for example, generally move once after death unless action is taken to prevent it. As transgressors of boundaries, corpses are sites of power and danger (Kristeva 1982). This idea echoes that of Mary Douglas that 'interest in [the body's] apertures depends on the preoccupation with social exits and entrances, escape routes and invasion' (Douglas 1973).

Further evidence of preparation of the body prior to cremation comes from the site of Carrier's Croft, Pendleton. Excavation of a cremation from this platform cairn uncovered a delicate double-perforated, diamond-shaped, bone button (*80*). It was burnt and found within the urn mixed with the cremated human bone, suggesting that it had fastened a light garment the corpse had been wearing when cremated. Wrapping the corpse in textile is another common form of containment, which may be imbued with symbolic meaning (Schneider

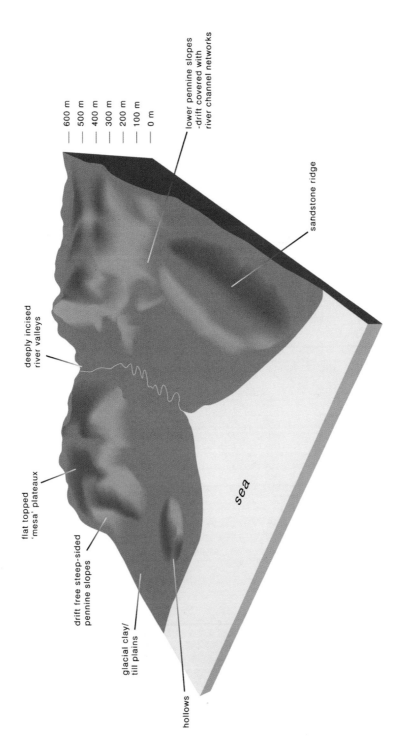

— 600 m
— 500 m
— 400 m
— 300 m
— 200 m
— 100 m
— 0 m

lower pennine slopes
-drift covered with
river channel networks

sandstone ridge

deeply incised
river valleys

flat topped
'mesa' plateaux

drift free steep-sided
pennine slopes

glacial clay/
till plains

hollows

sea

1 Model of regional morphology indicating major features of significance

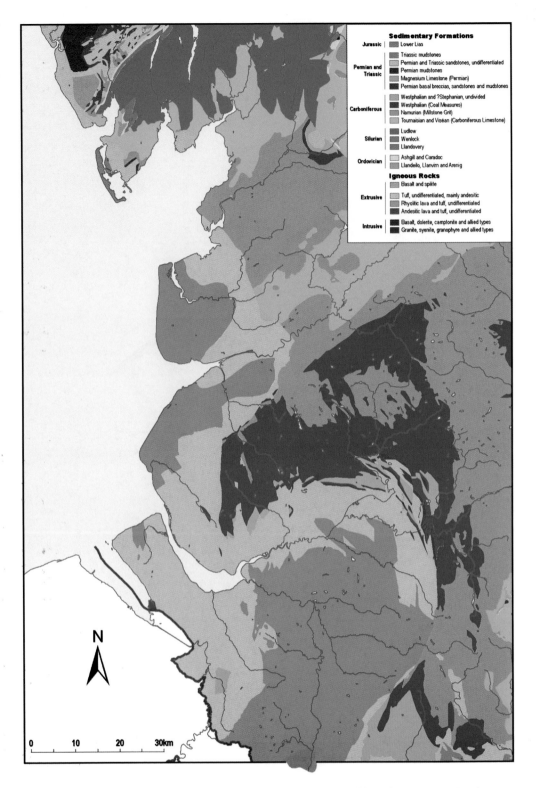

2 Map of the solid geology of the study region. The north is dominated by volcanic (igneous) and limestone rocks, the Pennines by Coal Measures and Millstone Grit, the coastal plain mudstone (Mercia Mudstone Group) and sandstone (Sherwood Sandstone Group). *After British Geological Survey*

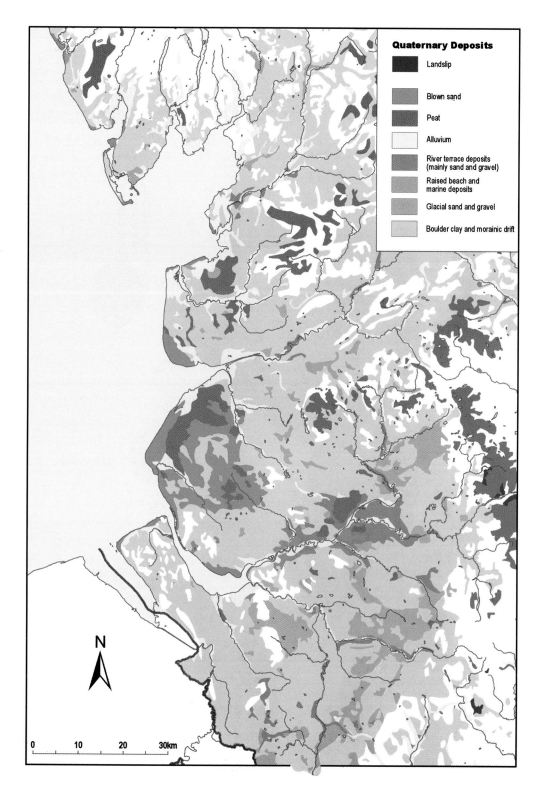

3 Superficial geology of the region. Lowland areas are dominated by boulder clay (blue) with significant wetland deposits of peat (brown) also found on upland moors. *After Soil Survey*

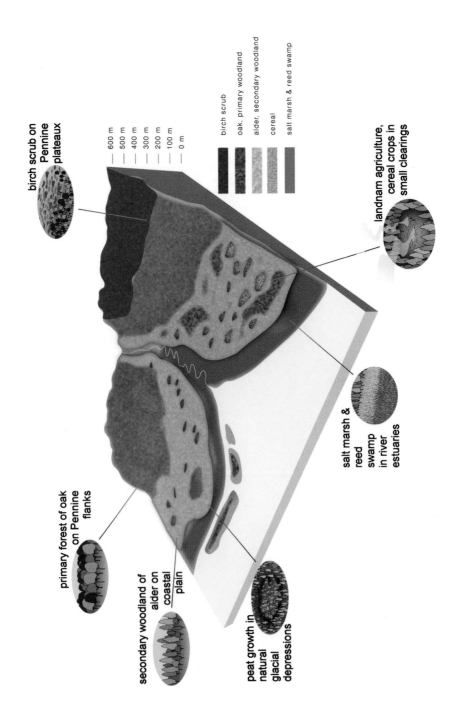

birch scrub on Pennine plateaux

—— 600 m
—— 500 m
—— 400 m
—— 300 m
—— 200 m
—— 100 m
—— 0 m

birch scrub

oak, primary woodland

alder, secondary woodland

cereal

salt marsh & reed swamp

landnam agriculture, cereal crops in small clearings

primary forest of oak on Pennine flanks

secondary woodland of alder on coastal plain

peat growth in natural glacial depressions

salt marsh & reed swamp in river estuaries

4 Neolithic, 4500–2350 cal BC, environmental reconstruction

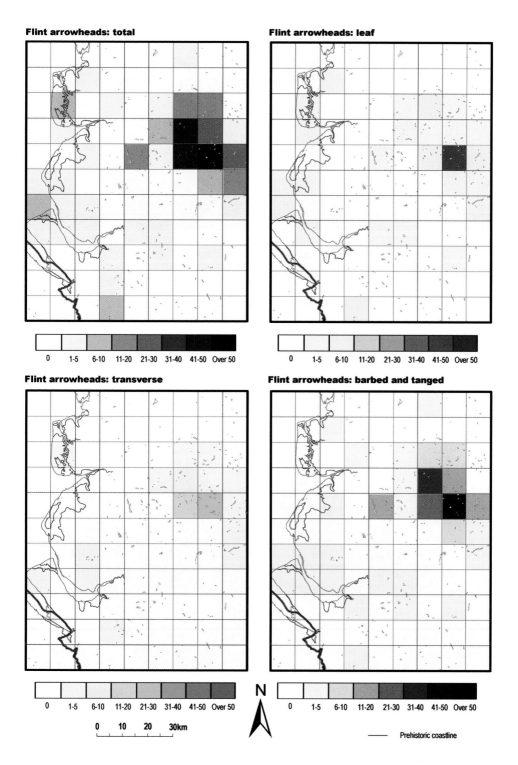

5 Density plot of the distribution of all flint arrowheads, together with plots for each type

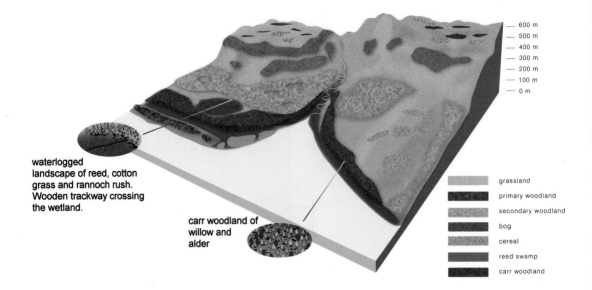

waterlogged
landscape of reed, cotton
grass and rannoch rush.
Wooden trackway crossing
the wetland.

carr woodland of
willow and
alder

	grassland
	primary woodland
	secondary woodland
	bog
	cereal
	reed swamp
	carr woodland

— 600 m
— 500 m
— 400 m
— 300 m
— 200 m
— 100 m
— 0 m

6 Early Bronze Age *c.*2350–1400 cal BC environmental reconstruction

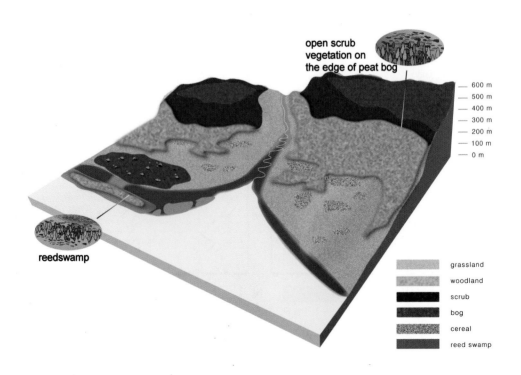

open scrub
vegetation on
the edge of peat bog

reedswamp

	grassland
	woodland
	scrub
	bog
	cereal
	reed swamp

— 600 m
— 500 m
— 400 m
— 300 m
— 200 m
— 100 m
— 0 m

7 Later Bronze Age *c.*1400–600 cal BC environmental reconstruction

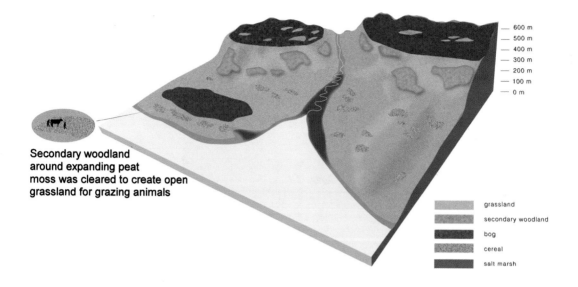

Secondary woodland
around expanding peat
moss was cleared to create open
grassland for grazing animals

— 600 m
— 500 m
— 400 m
— 300 m
— 200 m
— 100 m
— 0 m

grassland

secondary woodland

bog

cereal

salt marsh

8 Iron Age *c.*600 cal BC–cal AD 43 environmental reconstruction

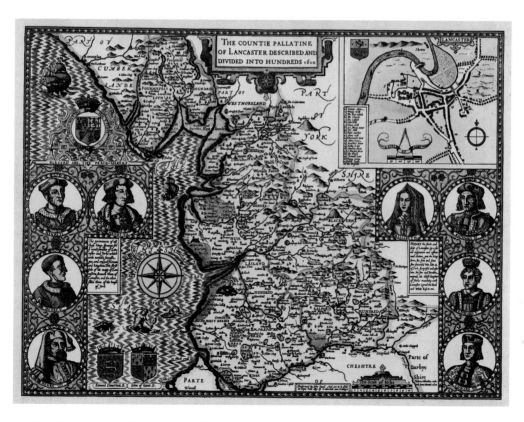

9 John Speed's map of Lancashire dated 1610

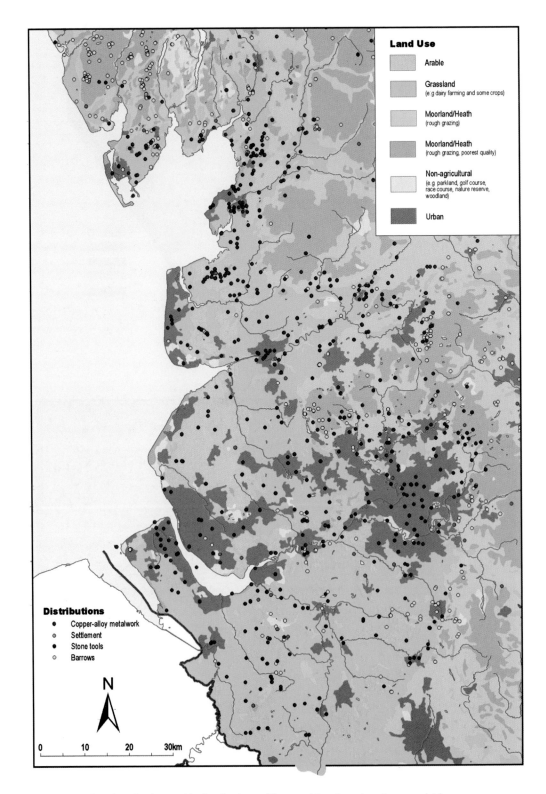

Land Use

Arable

Grassland
(e.g dairy farming and some crops)

Moorland/Heath
(rough grazing)

Moorland/Heath
(rough grazing, poorest quality)

Non-agricultural
(e.g. parkland, golf course,
race course, nature reserve,
woodland)

Urban

Distributions

- Copper-alloy metalwork
- Settlement
- Stone tools
- Barrows

N

0   10   20   30km

10 Map of modern land-use with distributions of later prehistoric archaeology overlaid

11 Charles Towneley in his Sculpture Gallery 1782 by Johann Zoffany. Oil on canvas, 127 x 102cm.
Seated, centre, Charles Towneley, with Charles Greville, a politician, Thomas Astle, conservator of the
British Museum, and also seated Pierre d'Hancarville, French antiquarian in Rococo costume. *Towneley
Hall Art Gallery and Museum, Burnley, Lancashire*

12 The location of the Peel barrow site, indicated by the pale-coloured spread at the centre of the photograph

13 Reconstruction of Pikestones Chambered Tomb, Anglezarke

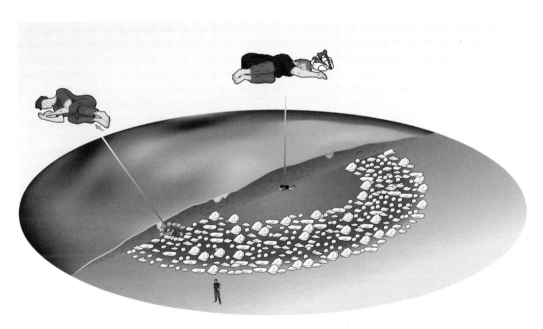

14 Reconstruction of a round barrow at Borwick, Lancashire. Primary central burial was an inhumation with an earth barrow covering. A second inhumation was placed in a stone cist on the edge of the original barrow, which was extended to cover it. Subsequently, several unurned cremations were dug into the barrow

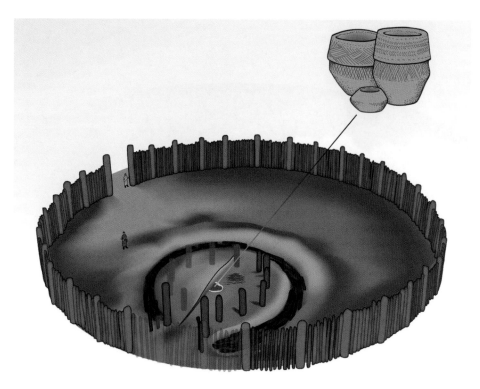

15 Reconstruction of Bleasdale timber circle.: a palisaded enclosure containing a second timber circle and timber-lined ditch, within which was a barrow containing two urned cremations and an accessory vessel. Radiocarbon dates have been obtained from both timber and charcoal

16 Reconstruction of Astley Hall Farm. *Illustration: Nicholas Dooley*

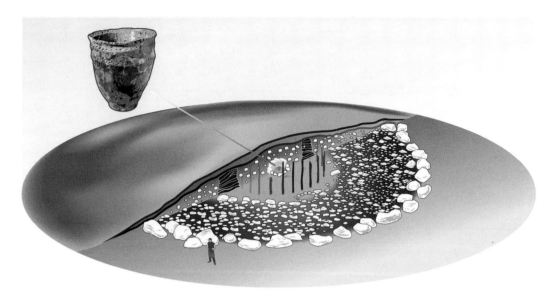

17 Reconstruction of composite stone and earth cairn, Noon Hill, Lancashire. A central stone cist contained an urned cremation in a Food Vessel Urn. Post holes were found beyond the cist, suggesting that there had been a wooden circle of posts at some time before the mound was constructed. Beyond the posts was a cobbled area bounded by a stone kerb. The composite mound was formed by a circular 'wall' of stacked turf positioned inside the cobbled area, either side of which was a filling of earth and stone

18 Urn 3 grave offerings placed with cremation of a child

19 Thin section of urn from Pleasington Cemetery. Igneous rock and grog with grog inclusion. *Photograph Elaine Morris*

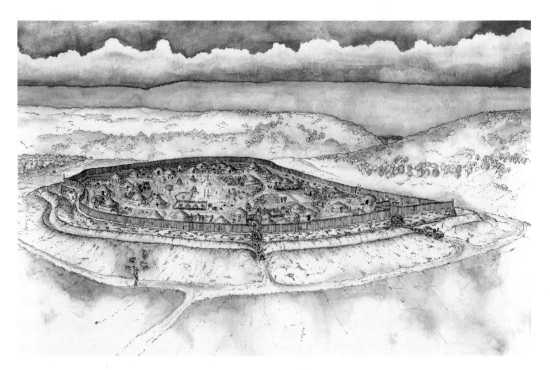

20 Reconstruction of Portfield hillfort. *Illustration: Nick Dooley*

21 Section through Box Rampart 2, Castercliffe hillfort. A continuous bedding trench can be seen running through the front of the picture terminating in a post hole which formerly housed the timber from which the enclosing box was constructed. A second post hole can be seen on the outside of the rampart, marked by the surveying pole where a second continuous bedding trench runs. *Photograph: John Hallam*

22 Aerial photograph of High Park, Leck. The photograph shows a number of settlement features, significant among which is the site of Castlehill, a curvilinear feature in the bottom left of the picture. *Lancashire County Council*

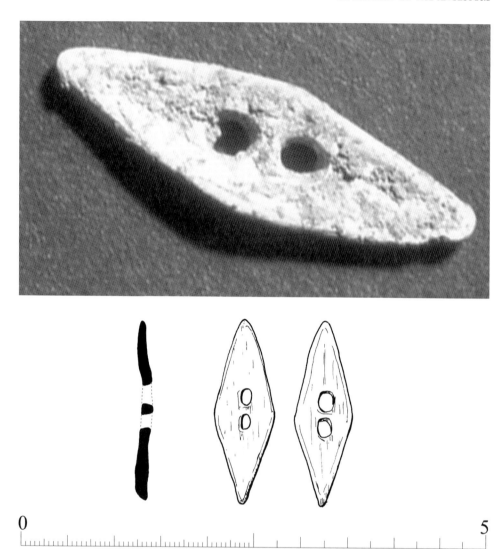

0

5

centimetres

80 Bone button, Pendleton

and Weiner 1989). For example, Feeley-Harnik's (1989) study of the *lamba mena*, the funerary shawl used for wrapping and enclosing corpses in Madagascar, explores the symbolism of how kin relations are represented through these fine cloths (Parker-Pearson 1999). At this distance, and with so little to go on, it is impossible to reconstruct the symbolism attached to the shroud from Pendleton. However, it highlights the need to be aware that the act of containment involved several stages beginning with the moment of death.

The inversion of urns may also have a specific ritual significance because the performance of actions backwards, and of things being inverted or turned inside out, are common ritual elements in funerary practices. Ucko considers the case of Zulu ceremonies in which the coffin bearers walk backwards, a hole in the house wall is used instead of the door, 'yes' is used to mean 'no' and vice versa (Ucko 1969). The eschatology is that of a world of the dead inverted to that of the living. Turning inside-out the clothing on the corpse is a common practice in many societies; among the Lo Dagaa the smock worn by the corpse was turned inside out. Reversal reinforces the normality and naturalness of everyday practices by defining their opposite in ritual time. It also serves to separate the dead and their realm from the living.

Turning to the pottery at Castleshaw, Beaker sherds were discovered during the excavation of the Roman fort, in a 'domestic storage pit' (Thompson 1967). Five distinct Beakers were identified, 75 of the 122 sherds, which Clarke described as a small but characteristic selection from the Late Southern Beaker domestic array, comprising a giant storage Beaker with rusticated decoration and a two-tier neck, a small rusticated Beaker, two incised and stamped Beakers, and a comb-impressed Beaker (Clarke 1970, 227). Longworth has pointed out that the linear-incised decoration on vessel 1 was of particular significance in the history of Bronze Age ceramics in north-western England for it displayed the linear incision that became a technique typical of the Collared Urn tradition of the area. Furthermore, vessel 5 was not far from the general form of the cordoned urn, providing evidence that cordoned vessels were being made as domestic ware by Late Beaker potters (Longworth in Thompson 1967, 16–17). The Neolithic ancestry of such so-called 'Beaker Domestic Ware' has been discussed (Burgess 1976a, ii), and this occurrence may be regarded as yet another link between the Early Bronze Age and earlier periods in Lancashire. Burgess has gone on to argue that while Food Vessels and urns are entirely associated with burial/ritual purposes, everyday pottery may be represented by these 'Beaker Domestic Wares' (Burgess 1976b, 320). It is of possible significance that, in the same general area of the gritstone Pennines, flint daggers of the same period have been recorded at Ragstone near Denshaw, Rocher Moss and Warlow. A discoidal flint knife from Slatepit Moor may also be of this age, and these flint artefacts together with the numerous barbed-and-tanged arrowheads provide further evidence for not inconsiderable activity along these western slopes of the Pennines.

Less information is available about the other Beakers found in the Central Pennines, all apparently in funerary contexts. The lower part of a Beaker was found in 1882 on Extwistle Moor near Burnley and contained burnt remnants of bone (Manby 1968). At Portfield near Whalley a Beaker was found beneath Iron Age fortifications. These examples are in close proximity to the Aire–Ribble crossing of the Pennines, as is another Beaker found in a barrow at Ferry Fryston (Pacitto 1968). The latter was also described as belonging to the Developed stage of Clarke's Southern Beaker Tradition and was associated with a crouched burial, a bronze awl and evidence of a previous inhumation. Another possible link with Beaker settlement in the area is provided by the assemblage associated with an inhumation in a barrow at Wind Hill, Heywood, where a triangular flint knife, a pebble hammer, a V-perforated jet button and a flint scraper were found (Tyson 1980). Just outside our area, a large flint point was found alongside a skeleton at Otley, and this too may represent a Beaker burial (Cowling 1946, 62). Other flint knives have been reported in the Central Pennines, and a flint axe of Beaker date at Cullingworth.

The pattern of distribution of Beaker pottery is reinforced by that of flint daggers which are associated with Beaker assemblages and typologically dated to the Early Bronze Age (*81*).

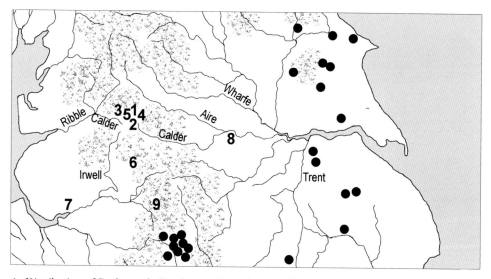

81 Distribution of Beaker-style flint daggers throughout northern England. 1) Cant Clough 1.
2) Cant Clough 2. 3) Roggerham. 4) Upper Gorple Reservoir. 5) Hurstwood Reservoir, Worsthorne.
6) Ragstone Clough, Denshaw. 7) Southworth-with-Croft, Winwick. 8) Ferry Fryston, S. Yorkshire.
9) Mellor, Stockport

82 Beaker-type flint dagger, Cant
Clough 2 found close to the location
of flint dagger Cant Clough 1 (not
illustrated). Jet beads and ring also found
close to the location of Cant Clough;
formerly a river valley it is now a
reservoir. *Photograph: John Hallam*

83 Food Vessel urn found at Noon Hill containing a cremation and barbed-and-tanged arrowhead. *Photograph: John Hallam*

Five daggers are known from the moors around Burnley and seem to reflect the western extension of activity in the upland area around the Calder valley, which may have been an important communication route (*82*). The same may be said of the Denshaw dagger on the Castleshaw pass. The Winwick example is no doubt associated with the well-evidenced Early Bronze Age community living on the River Mersey, which again may have been an important route for communication between the Irish Sea and the trans-Pennine valley passes. A dagger found at Mellor, near Stockport, is best interpreted as a northern extension of the large cluster of daggers that occurs in the Peak District of Derbyshire. Although geographically close they are part of a system of rivers that generally looks towards the south-east rather than Lancashire. Contact with the Irish Sea coast via rivers draining to the Mersey was likely, perhaps bringing them into contact with the population living around Winwick.

The Beakers in the Central Pennines, therefore, all belong to the latest periods of the British Beaker tradition, overlapping the span of radiocarbon dates for Collared Urns (see below), and a distribution which contrasts markedly with that of flint arrowheads. There are similarly few Food Vessels in the Central Pennines: only eight possibilities have been identified, all of them 'Yorkshire Vase' type (Barnes 1982, 50). Four Food Vessels, together with a pygmy vessel, were discovered on the summit of Pule Hill, near the watershed between Saddleworth and Marsden. Excavation in 1899 (Clark 1902) showed no signs of a mound, where in 1896 a burial group of two crouched inhumations, at least two cremations with vessels and two further pots had been found. The site was possibly a flat cemetery, though erosion might have removed the mound. As was the case with the Beaker finds in the Central Pennines, this Food Vessel burial site occurred to the north of the high moors which separate the area from the Peak District to the south, and the affinities of these vessels lie to the east rather than the south, one of them resembling a Food Vessel found at Ferry Fryston (Pacitto 1968), another, a footed bowl belonging to a small group of vessels whose distribution is concentrated in East Yorkshire, while the accessory cup is described as belonging to the contracted-mouth group concentrated in north-east Yorkshire and the Central Pennines (Manby 1969, 275). The Food Vessel series belongs, by analogy to a vessel on Harland Edge in North Derbyshire, to the period 1490 ± 150 BC (BM 178).

The other Food Vessels reported in Lancashire are mainly from the fringes of the uplands: Noon Hill, Rivington; Walmsley near Bolton; Bank Lane, Ramsbottom; Twist Hill, Burnley; and two possibilities outside Lancashire on Baildon Moor to the north-east. Some of these references are very vague, with little information available about the vessels. The Twist Hill example was found in a stone circle while that at Walmsley, a doubtful example, was in a cairn over an inhumation. The Noon Hill Urn (*83*) was an enlarged Food Vessel and contained a cremation, and was also associated with a barbed-and-tanged arrowhead. Oak charcoal from the urn was dated to 2210–2020 cal BC (3725 ±35 BP, SUERC-4446).

The Bank Lane Food Vessel was found in a cairn with sherds from a Collared Urn. Food Vessels were associated with Collared Urns and cremation deposits within four Cheshire round barrows. At Grappenhall 2 a Food Vessel contained cremated remains while at Church Lawton 2, two Food Vessels were placed in pits in the mound of the barrow, but not apparently associated with cremated remains (Mullin 2003, 14). Food Vessels date to *c.*1920–1800 cal BC with a focus on the period 1900–2100 cal BC (Barrowclough 2007). Food Vessel sherds from an apparent non-funerary context are known from Oversley Farm, dated to the centuries either side of 2000 cal BC.

Collared Urns (*84*) are descended ultimately from Neolithic pottery, and thus from a heritage which included multiple cremation burials within enclosures. In Lancashire, Collared Urns are much more widespread than both Beakers and Food Vessels, with 140 examples. Generally they occur on the fringes of the higher areas or in valleys. Primary urns occur in the area but in small numbers (Longworth 1961, 300–1). They are best represented in East Yorkshire, while 25 per cent of the Peak District urns fall into this category (Lewis 1970, 86). Primary Series North Western Style urns fall within the date range 1710–2050 cal BC, concentrating on 1750–2040 cal BC (Barrowclough 2007). Most of the Central Pennine urns belong to Longworth's Secondary Series, characterised by relatively deep collars and pronounced lower collar lips, and range in date from *c.*1700–2000 cal BC with a focus on 1750–1950 cal BC (Barrowclough 2007, 103).

Radiocarbon evidence (Appendix 1) suggests an overlapping sequence of urn usage from Food Vessels to Primary then Secondary Series Collared Urns (Barrowclough 2007). This evidence also suggests that even the latest examples were evidently deposited within the Early Bronze Age (Challis and Harding 1975, 31). The term 'Secondary Series North Western Urn' is somewhat misleading as these vessels are not contemporaneous with the Secondary Series, which are somewhat later. Analysis of the position of urns in funerary monuments confirms this (*85*). The position of various types of ceramic vessel in the monument reveals a sequence that coincides with the radiocarbon assay. Beaker Vessels were always found in primary positions, invariably with inhumations, but not exclusively. Food Vessels are also associated with primary positions in the monument, but this time generally cremations rather than inhumations, although there were rare finds in secondary positions. Collared Urns are always

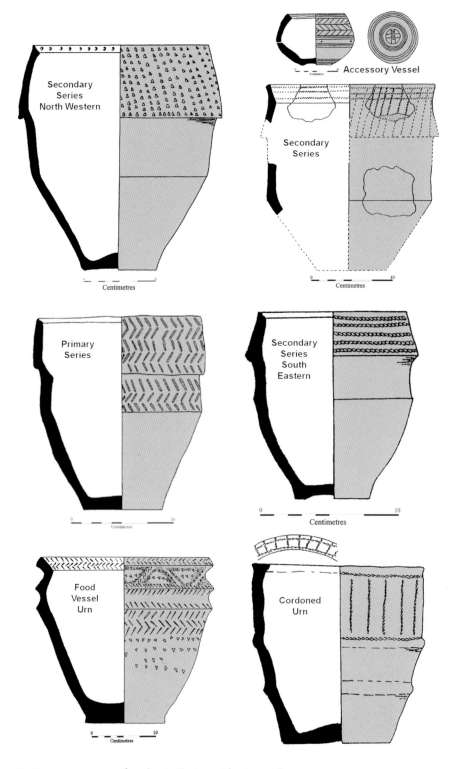

84 Key pottery types referred to in the text. *After Ann Hallam*

		Primary inhumation	Primary cremation	Secondary inhumation	Secondary cremation	Outside monument, in ditch or in upper layer of mound
	Beaker Vessel	8	1			
	Food Vessel	2	5	2	2	
Collared Urn Series	Primary Series		5		2	2
	Secondary Series				1	7
	Secondary Series North Western Style		6		7	2
	Secondary Series South Eastern Style					1
	Unclassified Collared Urn					5
	Cordoned Urn					2

85 Urn position in funerary monument. N=60

associated with cremations, never with inhumations; Primary Series, largely in primary positions; and Secondary Series, in secondary positions in the monument and also in ditches or outside the monument. The distribution pattern of Secondary Series North Western Style urns is more closely related to the Primary Series than the Secondary after which it is named. It is found in primary and secondary positions in almost equal numbers, with a small number outside the monument or in ditches. Secondary Series South Eastern Style and Cordoned Urns are both restricted to locations outside the monument or in ditches.

A further piece of evidence that supports the argument that Primary and Secondary Series North Western Style urns are contemporaneous was provided by the excavation of a Primary Series urn and Secondary Series North Western Style urn, one within the other, at Ribchester, and of a Primary and Secondary Series North Western Style urn together in the primary pit at Bleasdale.

Different types of pottery were associated with particular burial rites. Having established the chronology for different pottery types it is possible to use this information to construct a sequence for changing burial rites (*86*). The earliest pottery, Beaker Vessels of Step 1–2, is associated with inhumations placed in natural caves. The practice of cave burial was replaced during the Late Beaker period, when crouched inhumation burials were placed in stone cists and covered over by a cairn. At the same time the first cremation burials began to appear, with late Beaker pottery placed with the cremation, and a round barrow built over them. The coexistence of cremation and inhumation continued in the next ceramic phase, when Food Vessels replaced Beakers. At this time both inhumations and cremations were placed in stone cists under cairns and barrows respectively. Primary Series Collared Urns gradually replaced Food Vessels marking the end of the practice of inhumation. From this point burials were all cremated. The consolidation of cremation as the preferred way of disposing of the dead coincided with an increase in the variety of burial monuments.

Secondary Series North Western Style urns replace those of the Primary Series. These urns begin by being placed in primary positions in the centre of earthworks, although the tradition of placing unurned cremations in stone cists comes to an end in this period, when cists are

2800	2700	2600	2500	2400	2300	2200	2100	2000	1900	1800	1700	1600	1500	1400	calBC

Late Neolithic	Metal Using Neolithic	Early Bronze Age	Mid B A
	Period 1	Period 2	Period 3	Period 4	Period 5
Mount Pleasant	Overton	Bedd Branwen

Inhumation in Cave, Beaker Vessel

Crouched Inhumation in cist in Cairn, with Beaker Vessel

Inhumation in cist in cairn, with Food Vessel

Unaccompanied primary inhumation in cist in cairn

Cremation in Round Barrow, with Beaker Vessel

Cremation in cist in Barrow, with Food Vessel

Cremation primary position in Kerbed Barrow, with Food Vessel

Cremation in Round Barrow, Primary Series Collared Urn

Cremation in Ringwork: embanked circle, primary position, Primary Series Collared Urn

Cremation in cist in Flat Linear Cemetery, Primary Series Collared Urn

Cremation in primary position in Flat Cemetery, Primary Series Collared Urn

Cremation in Flat Grave, Primary Series Collared Urn

Cremation in Round Barrow, primary position, Secondary Series North West Style

Cremation in pit in Flat Linear Cemetery, secondary position, Secondary Series North West Style

Cremation in Ringwork, secondary position, Primary Series Collared Urn

Cremation in Round Barrow, secondary position, Secondary Series Collared Urn

Cremation secondary position in Barrow ditch, Secondary Series Collared Urn

Cremation ururned in cairn, secondary position

Cremation unurned in pit, secondary position

86 Sequence of burial rites showing the transformation from cave through urn to unurned deposit

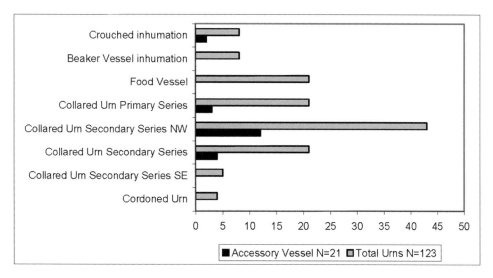

87 Urn and accessory vessel associations

replaced by pits, but then shift to secondary positions under earthworks and then to the ditches that bound the monument. Flat cemeteries appear for the first time whilst barrows and cairns take on a variety of forms. Cremations in urns continue to be placed in stone cists under cairns, but are also placed in cists in linear cemeteries. Secondary Series Urns succeed them; these are never found in primary positions in urns, always in secondary locations on the edges of field monuments. Contemporaneously, unurned cremations placed in some sort of organic container, leather or cloth bag, begin to appear, again in secondary positions. This unurned tradition continues after the use of urns ceases, marking the end of the earthwork sequence.

The Collared Urn from Harland Edge is comparable with the two 'Pennine' urns from Tower Hill, Warley. Inside one of these urns was an accessory vessel decorated with lines of twisted cord. Two urns, decorated on collar and neck with a twisted cord pattern, were found at Brownhill, Saddleworth, one containing a pebble macehead. Longworth demonstrated that certain traits such as whipped and twisted cord, and grooved decoration found on his Primary Series of Collared Urns had their origin in the Neolithic ceramic traditions of Peterborough Ware (Longworth 1961). Another interesting group occurs in the burial circle at Mosley Height, Burnley (73). There were four pits: the primary burial in the centre had a cremation in a twisted cord decorated Collared Urn, a second pit contained an inverted Collared Urn, another contained badly broken urns while the fourth contained an unurned cremation. Other remains here included two polished grain rubbers, three fragments of querns, three polished hand hammers and one pestle, together with flint scrapers, arrowheads, knives and pieces of quartz, calcite and Kimmeridge shale. Four accessory vessels, various kinds of beads, a bronze dagger and an awl were found in direct association with at least six cremation burials in 'Pennine' urns at Blackheath, Todmorden, which like the Mosley Height burials was near the Long Causeway.

There are some 42 occurrences of urns in the Central Pennines, some of these with considerable numbers. Besides those mentioned above, 12 urns were found in a flat cemetery at Breightmet, Bolton, 9 at Darwen, about 20 at Rastrick with cremations, 3 inverted urns at Skircoat and 4 at Warley with an accessory vessel. At Whitelow, Ramsbottom urns were associated with a bronze awl, whilst an accessory vessel and a flat riveted bronze dagger were found with an inhumation burial in a cist at Haulgh, Bolton (Bu'Lock 1961, fig. 111, 1). Another accessory vessel, this time associated with an inhumation, occurred at Clifton in the Irwell valley, north of Manchester. The evidence suggests that the accessory vessel was current during the richest phase of urn burial, if the number of grave goods is any criterion (*87*). Thus several examples of continuity involving Beakers, Food Vessels and urns can be suggested. The urns imply a growing population in the Central Pennines during the earlier part of the Bronze Age.

In burials where accessory vessels were not present, sherds of Beaker Vessel, or less frequently Collared Urn, accompanied the cinerary urn. Visual inspection of the ceramic accessory vessels revealed a grog-tempered fabric which ranged from fine 'Beaker-like' vessels to crude 'thumb pots'. In order to understand more about their construction a sample was taken from one of them, a miniature Collared Urn from Astley Hall, and subjected to thin-section petrological examination, undertaken by Dr Elaine Morris of Southampton University (Morris 2005). Microscopic examination revealed a grog-tempered fabric (*colour plate 19*). The grog appeared to come from a Beaker Vessel. A hypothesis was proposed that the grog was made from a Beaker Vessel, which had been made in the vicinity of the accessory vessel, but that the accessory vessel fabric recipe also contained added rock temper. This suggests a possible link between burials, accessory vessels and sherds of pottery placed in burials.

A number of Collared Urn vessels were also examined and they revealed a similar constitution – grog derived from crushing an original vessel. The sequence of events can be reconstructed as follows based on analysis of a Collared Urn from Pleasington Cemetery, Blackburn, oak charcoal from which was dated to 1950–1740 cal BC (3530 ±35 BP, SUERC-4441) and cremated human bone to 1940–1740 cal BC (3520 ±35 BP, SUERC-4442) (Barrowclough 2007):

1. Pot 1 constructed using a rhyolite-tempered fabric;
2. Pot 1 crushed to make grog;
3. Pot 1 grog added to crushed rhyolite to make temper for the fabric of Pot 2;
4. Pot 2 constructed and used as a cremation urn.

In this scenario there is likely to have been some connection between the person cremated and buried in Pot 2 and the original Pot 1. Suggestions include that Pot 1 belonged to the deceased and that upon their death relatives crushed up their personal pot in order to make grog temper for the cremation urn Pot 2, or Pot 1 belonged to an ancestor of the cremated person found in Pot 2, and this is a representation of the past in the present for the relatives and respect for ancestors. By extension this hypothesis can be extended to the sherds of Beaker Ware found with cremations, for example at Pendleton. In this instance after relatives broke the original pot instead of crushing it and incorporating it into the new urn they simply placed a sherd with the burial. Again the original pot may have belonged to the deceased or an ancestor. The key idea here is that objects are reproduced rather than produced. This implies that there is a personal contribution to the value of an object, which is closely related to the value of the person involved. The exchange of inalienable objects means that an indissoluble link exists between all owners or users of an artefact and the artefact with its distinctive biography.

The burial assemblages contain other examples of fragmentation. Beads are found, but never as entire necklaces. Instead single or small numbers occur, as at Whitehall, Blackheath and Shuttleworth. Ear plugs occur, for example, at Whitelow, but again singly rather than in pairs. It could be that only one ear had been pierced, or that the ear plugs were misidentified, that they were, for example, lower-lip plugs. There is a sense that sets were being broken and perhaps redistributed, as part of the symbolism of regeneration. Fragments of Beaker pottery from the time of the ancestors were incorporated into the burial of the deceased, while some of the possessions of the deceased were divided amongst their living descendents or friends. In exchanging objects people are also exchanging themselves. The exchange of ceramics and beads establishes a chain of personal relations, which Chapman terms 'enchainment' (Chapman 2000). Enchained relationships are established through fragmentation. To establish a social relationship, a specific artefact is broken in two or more pieces, each party keeping one or more parts as a token of the relationship. In turn each fragment can be broken further so that new relations with a third party can be entered into. These fragments are kept until the reconstitution of the relationship, which may occur at death, with parts brought together and deposited in a structured way. This may account for the incorporation of ancestral Beaker sherds into the burial in one way or another.

The process of enchainment operates at different levels – at one, between fragments and the complete vessel, that is between entire vessels and sherds placed in the burial; and at another, between complete objects and sets of objects, that is, single beads and necklaces. The interaction between parts, wholes and sets provides part of the dynamic of prehistoric communities.

Funerary urns should not be considered in isolation, but as part of the assemblage that accompanies the dead. This includes metal and stone implements, exotic materials, accessory vessels, animal parts and personal ornaments. The sacrifice of possessions, whether living or not, may be a means of communication with the other world. They may be viewed as gifts, tribute or even fines to be paid to the supernatural as expressions of a reciprocal relationship, rather than a material exchange. These gifts do not necessarily force a repayment from the supernatural but link the living to that realm. Grave goods should not be seen just as personal trappings, whether or not polluted by association with the corpse, but as items bound up in gift exchanges with the dead, as in the case of personal equipment which was definitely never used, but instead made specifically for the deceased. Heirlooms may be placed in the grave, possibly because there was no successor to inherit them. An example is the placing of jet necklaces in British Early Bronze Age burials. From the wear on the beads and the evidence for multiple repairs and replacements of beads, many of these necklaces were clearly very old by the time they went into the grave (Sheridan and Davis 1998).

Artefacts found in burials include: bone pins and buttons; flint implements; gold, jet, amber, shale and clay ornaments; and galena and quartz crystals. In one of the urns in the cremation cemetery at Blackheath, Todmorden, were four segmented faïence beads, all with eight

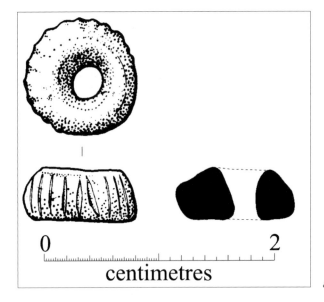

88 Ceramic bead, Darwen

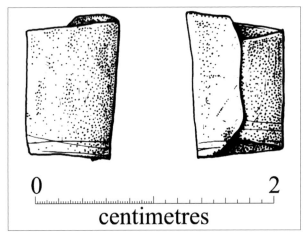

89 Gold tress, Pendleton

segments, three spherical beads ornamented with grooves, some large amber beads, nine beads of jet or shale, two bone pins, a pygmy cup, flint flakes and a leaf-shaped arrowhead. The urn was sealed by another inverted over it (Stone and Thomas 1956, 80). Another segmented faïence bead has been found in the cairn at Bank Lane, Ramsbottom, where it might have been associated with either a Food Vessel or an urn. It is interesting that only eight faïence beads have been found in the Peak District (Lewis 1970, 150), where, with the area's trading connections, one might have expected a greater number. A ceramic bead was found at Darwen (88) whilst at Carrier's Croft a gold bead or possibly a hair tress with Beaker affinities was found in urn 3 (89).

Only five, possibly six, larger stone implements were found associated with burials. At Lowhouse, Milnrow, an axe-hammer was found with an unurned cremation in a composite cairn, while a flint 'battle-axe' is reputed to have been found in a ring mound at Hell Clough

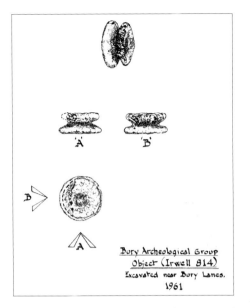

90 Ear plug and reconstruction of how it may have been worn. *Illustration: Joanna Richards*

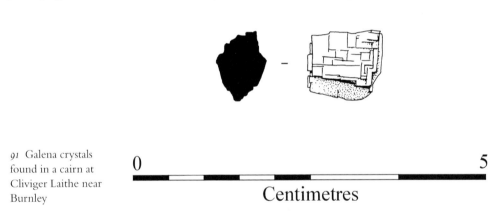

91 Galena crystals found in a cairn at Cliviger Laithe near Burnley

0   5

Centimetres

II, Burnley. A pebble macehead was found inside an urn at Brownhill, Saddleworth, and a second 'celt' is said to have been found later on the same site. In the Mosley Height burial circle near Burnley, loosely associated with several urned burials, were a number of stone implements including two polished grain rubbing stones, parts of three querns, three polished 'hand hammers' and a 'pestle', together with numerous flint scrapers, arrowheads and knives and two pieces of Kimmeridge shale. All the other associated finds consist of smaller objects. Flint knives were found in cairns at Walmsley, Bolton and Wind Hill, Heywood, at the latter with a pebble hammer, while flint arrowheads, scrapers and pieces of flint occur widely in burial mounds and circle monuments, such as those at Astley Hall Farm, Blackheath, Todmorden, Wind Hill, Heywood, Snoddle Hill, Littleborough, Pule Hill and Wadsworth, and sometimes they are burnt as at Hades Hill, near Rochdale. At Whitelow, Ramsbottom, a clay stud, possibly an ear plug (*90*) was found with flints in secondary burial 'E' (Tyson 1962, 5), and at Noon Hill, Rivington, a wide variety of flint implements was found with the several burials,

Burial Type		Worked flint	Stone tool	Copper alloy tool	Worked bone	Accessory vessel	Pot sherds	Personal ornament	Mineral	Wooden vessel	Cloth	Unworked bone
Crouched Inhumation				flat axe flat dagger knife dagger								
Beaker	Step 1/2				antler comb							
	Step 5							jet ear plug				
	Step 6	knife										
	unclassified	2 knives										
Food Vessel		2 knives flakes B&T arrowhead		fragments copper				faience bead				
Collared Urn	Primary Series	Leaf arrowhead B&T arrowhead		awl riveted knife	pin x4 perf cheek piece	3	beaker sherd	4 faience 8 jet 6 amber & 1 clay beads	galena		cloth frag	
	Secondary NW	B&T arrowhead blade knife x3 flake scraper	perf macehead wrist guard hexagonal slate x2	pin tanged knife dagger	pin x2 dia button needle	12	beaker sherd	gold tress clay bead x2	galena coal x2 quartz		sacking cloth	fish head bird knuckle
	Secondary	worked x2 scraper multiple flakes		razor fragment stain	pin toggle	2	min collared urn			bowl		boar's tusk
	unclassified	flint axe 3 flints flint knives x2	battleaxe	pin/awl x2 dagger riveted tanged spear-head tanged riveted knife metal binding	perf pin x4 pommel		6 sherds coll urn					animal bones
Cordoned Urn		leaf & B&T arrowhead										
Unurned		knife multiple flints						clay ear plug	galena & 'onyx'		cloth	berry fish vertebrae Animal bone

92 Burial assemblages according to burial type. N=230

including burnt barbed-and-tanged arrowheads, a transverse arrowhead and scrapers, together with a sandstone 'ball' and a flint knife. A jet stud, again a possible ear plug, is said to have been associated with a barrow on Rishworth Moor. Other finds of jet in the Central Pennines are at Blackheath, Todmorden, and Wind Hill, Heywood. Pieces of galena were found in the cairn at Cliviger Laithe, near Burnley (91), together with a bone pin, and such pins also occurred with the burials at Blackheath, Todmorden, Revidge, Blackburn and Breightmet, Bolton.

Besides the flint knives found in the barrows mentioned above, they have also been found widely scattered, though comparatively few in number, on the moors, where they are of rather uncertain age, as at Ragstone and Rocher Moss, both in Saddleworth, West Nab, Meltham, two on Rishworth Moor and at least two from Worsthorne, near Burnley.

A useful way to study grave goods is to consider the types that are found with particular types of urns, as that way the ceramic typology can be used to help us study changes in preferences of grave goods through time (92). Generally the idea of placing some sort of object with the dead can be seen throughout the Early Bronze Age. However, the type and number of objects deposited varied through time, with an increase during the Collared Urn phase, starting with the Primary Series, and reaching its maximum during the Secondary Series North Western Style Collared Urns, after which it went into decline. This pattern reflects that already described in the case of the field monuments whose most active and varied forms occur during the same period.

93 Burial from Darwen including copper-alloy dagger

Looking at the table of grave goods (*92*) reveals that certain limited types of object recur throughout the period; this suggests that objects were being selected to fulfil specific cultural requirements. Consideration of the objects might usefully reveal something about society in the Early Bronze Age. One of the most frequent objects deposited in graves is the knife or dagger. This can be made of flint, 12 examples, or metal, 6 examples (*93*). Interpretation of the significance of these items is difficult. They may have been possessions of the deceased, or they might be mourners' gifts to the dead. They may have been placed with the burial to serve to equip the dead for the world of the afterlife, or to prevent the dead coming back to haunt the living. Parallels drawn from anthropology may assist us to explore the range of possibilities, without excluding others. What is interesting about the selection of knives and daggers is that they are artefacts associated with the act of cutting, with separation of one thing from another. One possibility is that the placing of a knife or dagger on or in their grave by their survivors may represent the dead's severance from the living. The aim of placing the object with the burial may serve to prevent the deceased from remaining in the world of the living. For example among the Iban of Borneo a knife may be included in burials to symbolise the cutting of those ties (Uchibori 1978).

Hunting equipment such as leaf and barbed-and-tanged flint arrowheads, flint blades and scrapers, animal parts including unworked bones from salmon fish, red deer, boar and birds, and 18 accessory vessels, mostly ceramic, although also of wood, for example a bowl from Astley Hall Farm (*94*), often accompany the dead. These could be accoutrements to feed the dead in the afterlife, or complex symbols, which express the values, aims, and attitudes of mourners. For example the presence of fish placed with a burial may have cosmological

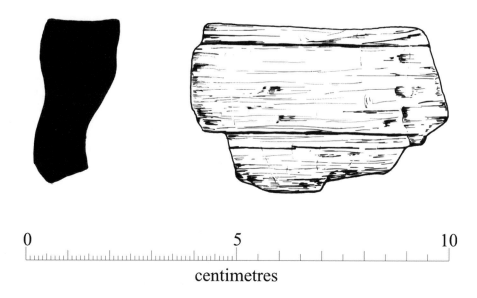

0   5   10

centimetres

94 Fragment of wooden bowl, Astley Hall Farm

significance according to Kaul's reconstruction of prehistoric cosmology, as evidenced by the decorated metalwork of Bronze Age Denmark (Kaul 1997).

In his interpretation of the cosmology a ship draws the sun across the sky. At different stages in the cycle, a horse, a snake and perhaps significantly, a fish assist it. The passage of the sun during the night, its absence from the world, in a symbolic sense its death, is associated with a fish (Kaul 1997). If we accept that this interpretation has some validity for the prehistory of Scandinavia and by extension for the North West of England (Barrowclough 2007, 123–4) then we can begin to understand some of the rationale behind the choice of objects placed in the grave.

The fish recalls the association between water, in general, and the sea, in particular, that is a characteristic of northern mythology and the Early Bronze Age funerary monuments. In one case, Lancaster Moor, the fish was identified as that of the genus *Salmonidae* and in another, Shuttleworth, from the class *Osteichthyes* (bony fish), which include the *Salmonidae*. This may be significant because the life-cycle of the salmon involves cyclical movement from rivers down to the sea, and then back to the river to spawn before its death. We saw in the discussion of monuments on the Fylde Coast and the moors outside Burnley (*64*) that funerary monuments are often separated from the world of the living by flowing water and it may be that this choice of location had further symbolic significance, linking the world of the living to that of the dead through flowing water.

In the case of 88 cremations, there was sufficient data to establish age and/or sex (*95*). Of these, 59 were determined to be adult and 29 children. It is not possible to reliably determine the biological sex of children morphologically and so no attempt was made to do so. In the case of 59 adults 12 were identified as male, 15 female and 32 could not be sexed reliably. The total number of male and female burials is roughly equal, 12 and 15 respectively, suggesting that men and women were equal in death, whilst the number of children present is

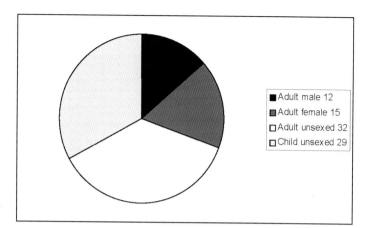

95 Age/sex of cremated human bones from burial monuments. N=88

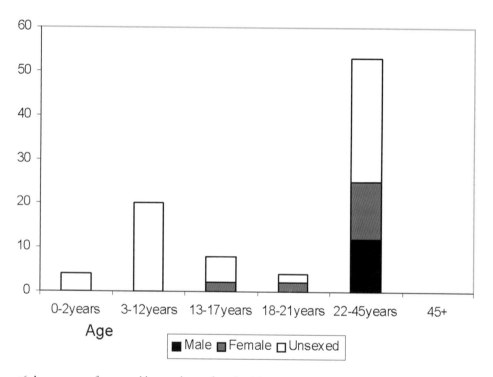

96 Age-groups of cremated human bones from burial monuments. N=88

comparatively large, 29 out of 88. The explanation of this lies in the breakdown of the burials (96). Focusing on the age at which individuals died reveals that although the total number of male and female burials is roughly equal, the age distribution is different. The age of death range for women is much wider than that of men. Women are found in both the 13–17 and 18–21 year-old ranges, where men are absent. There therefore seems to be a difference based on biological sex. A possible explanation for this is that the risks inherent in childbirth lead to premature death in women. This fits with the footprint data in Chapter 3 where the height distribution of women favoured the young. We have also seen, in the case of footprints on Formby foreshore, possible evidence for pregnancy in an adolescent female, c.1.40m tall, confirming that adolescent women of 13 and upward were falling pregnant. This explanation is therefore entirely feasible.

Deaths amongst children are also high, accounting for 29 out of 88 burials. This represents a relatively high rate of childhood mortality, the years between 3–12 being more dangerous than those of infancy, perhaps because breast milk offers protection for diseases, which is lost once the child is weaned. This is consistent with estimates of rates of at least 50 per cent for childhood mortality in prehistoric populations (Chamberlain 1997). Alternatively, the very small number of neonate (one example) and young children found in barrows contrasts with general estimates of 15–30 per cent mortality for children under one year of age in prehistoric populations (Rega 1997). This may suggest that burial in barrows was thought inappropriate for the very young and that they were dealt with in some alternative way that is not archaeologically visible.

Another feature of the data is that there are no adult burials over the age of 45 years. This finding must be treated with caution. Ageing cremated skeletal material is difficult once a person reaches maturity; it is therefore possible that within the sample population there were some adults over the age of 45. The data does indicate that life was short, because there were no clear examples of either men or women suffering from what would be considered diseases of old age in modern populations.

The association between adult and child burials may be informative. Lucy (1994; 1997) cautions that children were buried by adults, so we never experience the world of children, only the experiences of adults coming to terms with, and ascribing meaning to, their brief lives and premature deaths. Although she was writing in the context of early medieval cemeteries the point is relevant to the prehistoric period. What we see in the archaeological record is to some extent an idealised version of adult-child relationships.

Of 79 burials where detailed data was available (97) it was found that the vast majority of adults were buried on their own (53 examples). Only two instances were recorded where an adult was buried with another. For the majority of children burial on their own was inappropriate and they were buried with adults: 16 with an adult and only 8 alone. This is particularly striking as we have already seen that the peak age for childhood deaths was in the range 3–12 years. In other words, these were not the result of death during childbirth in which mother and baby passed away. They are instead most likely those children dying of childhood diseases, and so it is unlikely that the adult they were buried with had died at the same time, of the same disease. This suggests that the decision to bury a child with an adult was one dictated by social rules rather than expediency. There are a number of alternative possibilities. One is that the child was buried with a close family member, perhaps a parent. Analysis of this group of burials reveals instances where children were found buried with both female and adult males. It appears that burial was not restricted to a mother, or mother figure, but could include a father, or father figure. If the child were being buried with a parent it would suggest that a considerable period of time might have elapsed between the death of the child and the death of a parent. During this time the child, who presumably had been already cremated, must have been stored above ground awaiting the death of the parent.

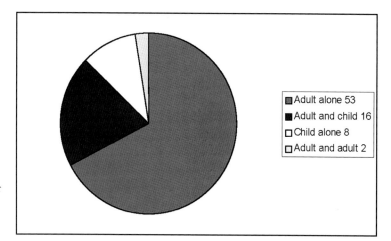

Adult alone 53
Adult and child 16
Child alone 8
Adult and adult 2

97 Burial associations: number of cremations and their associations. N=79

An alternative explanation is that the adult is not a parent, but is some other adult from the group who may, or may not have been related in a more distant way. Given the evidence for genetic abnormalities seen at Formby, it is likely that most members of the community were related in some way. If the rite required that the child was buried with an adult who was not necessarily a family member, it would mean that it was less likely that the child's body would have to be stored above ground awaiting interment for an extended period of time. Although the majority of children are buried with adults, they are not all. There are eight instances, one third of the known examples, of children being buried alone. Interestingly these burials account for some of the richest and most elaborate burials in the series, for example a burial at Pendleton, which contained the only known gold object of the Early Bronze Age in Lancashire. Perhaps exotic grave goods were placed with the child as a substitute for the missing adult, the preferred accompaniment.

A possibility that arises from this data is that we can attempt to understand something of the attitude of Early Bronze Age society toward personhood. First, there was a notion of the category of child. The distinction between childhood and adulthood is in part a function of physical maturity, but equally, is a social construct varying from one society to the next. The fact that burials of those under the age of 12 are treated differently from those of adults suggests that the category of child existed with a transition at that age. Further, the fact that the main, or preferred, treatment of child burials was to place them with an adult suggests an attitude of adults toward the young that saw them as in some way vulnerable and in need of the protection of adult members of society. At this stage of life (*98*) a person may not have been considered to be an individual with his or her own personality and identity, but may have still been part of the parent. If this were the case it would explain why dead children were kept unburied and close to the adult parent until such time as a parent died when the two were re-incorporated in burial.

At some point around the age of puberty the person moves from the state of childhood to that of adult, a transition associated with the achievement of an individual identity of their own. For a boy this would mean leaving the other children, young women and disabled

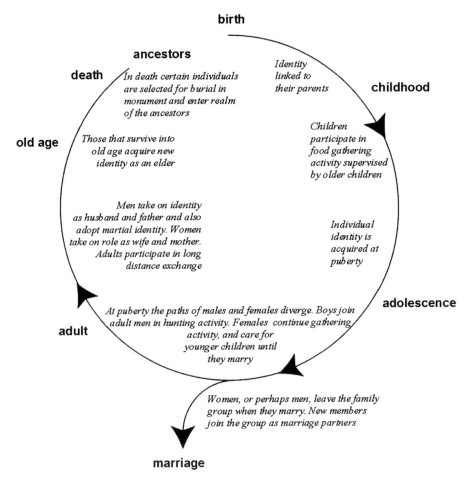

birth

ancestors

death *In death certain individuals are selected for burial in monument and enter realm of the ancestors*

Identity linked to their parents

childhood

Children participate in food gathering activity supervised by older children

old age *Those that survive into old age acquire new identity as an elder*

Men take on identity as husband and father and also adopt martial identity. Women take on role as wife and mother. Adults participate in long distance exchange

Individual identity is acquired at puberty

At puberty the paths of males and females diverge. Boys join adult men in hunting activity. Females continue gathering activity, and care for younger children until they marry

adolescence

adult

Women, or perhaps men, leave the family group when they marry. New members join the group as marriage partners

marriage

98 Reconstruction of the human life-cycle, indicating the range of potential identities that may be acquired in the course of a person's lifespan

adults, whom they had previously accompanied on the shellfish-gathering expeditions, and joining the adult men in their hunting activities. For girls the change took a different form. In the first instance, they continued to collect shellfish on the foreshore, taking on further responsibility for care of younger children. But it is likely that soon after puberty they would be 'married', and nature allowing, they would then begin to have children. It is at the point at which they become mothers that they cease to be visible on the foreshore having joined the realm of adult women who presumably took responsibility for home-based activity and perhaps the tending of garden plots.

If this model is correct it would tend to point toward a rite of passage that represents the shift in identity from child to adult. This rite occurs at different times, and most probably takes a different form for men than for women. In the case of the boy-man transition it occurs at a given age, about 12, perhaps triggered by puberty, and is associated with a dramatic shift in activity and social relations, from mixed male/female gathering activity to male-only hunting.

For women the change seems to occur not with the onset of puberty but with either marriage or the birth of their first child. An individual's identity as a woman therefore seems to be constructed in part through biology but in part socially out of their changing relationships with men as either wife or mother. At the moment of change they lose the freedom to roam widely and instead are brought physically closer to home and socially closer to other adult women. This separation of adult men from women and restriction on adult female activity may have reflected a concern to control the fertility of women of child-rearing age.

For both it suggests that as children they lacked both individual identity and also perhaps sexuality. The social category 'child' was that of a dependent, inseparable from the parent, even though in practice children had considerable independence and were expected to assist with food procurement activity.

CONCLUSION

A Neolithic to Early Bronze Age continuity is clearly demonstrated in Lancashire's archaeological record. Evidence for Early Bronze Age occupation consists mainly of burial monuments, their associated grave goods and lithic implements – the same classes of evidence as were used to construct an understanding of the Neolithic. The origins of the practices that have been identified in the Early Bronze Age may likewise be traced back to the Neolithic. In particular surviving Neolithic traits in urns demonstrate a close relationship between the two periods. The Early Bronze Age was also a time of increasing diversity, seen in the variety of burial monuments, interments and grave assemblages, accelerating a pattern that began in the Late Neolithic.

In the lowlands, particularly around the coast, but increasingly moving onto heavier soils further inland, indications are of a largely pastoral economy supplemented by some cereal cultivation. Pollen evidence suggests widespread but irregular and spasmodic forest clearances during the period, although generally small scale in character. From this it may be inferred that there was a larger population in the Early Bronze Age than in the Neolithic period. The presence of many barbed-and-tanged arrowheads on the upland Pennine moors, including the highest ground, presumably means that hunting remained a means of food gathering, reflecting the continuing disturbance of the forest cover on the higher ground. This was possibly a seasonal activity carried on from settlements of more lasting status on the lower ground.

CHAPTER 6

LAND AND WATER: THE DEPOSITION OF BRONZE AGE METALWORK

INTRODUCTION

At a national scale the Bronze Age is associated with the introduction of copper-alloy (bronze) metalwork. In the previous chapters we have seen how aspects of the occupation of Lancashire exhibited considerable continuity across traditional period divisions. This continuity can likewise be traced in practices of metalwork deposition. Collingwood (1933, 184), for example, noted an association between the distribution of bronze implements and perforated stone axe hammers in Furness. The distribution follows an earlier pattern established in the Neolithic. Half the known examples of polished stone axes in Cumbria come from Furness and the area along the northern coast of Morecambe Bay; similarly, of *c.*66 bronze implements known from Cumbria half come from Furness and Cartmel. We have also seen in the previous chapter how some aspects of culture fail to respect traditional period boundaries, the barrow-building tradition for example begins in the Late Neolithic and continues to the end of the Early Bronze Age. What gives meaning to the 'Bronze Age' in Lancashire is metalwork, it is the one category of data that crosses boundaries between the Early, Middle and Late Bronze Age, giving coherence to the period.

The metalwork of the British Bronze Age has been extensively researched, by for example Lort (1779), Evans (1881) and Burgess (1979; 1980; 1988). As a result there exists a number of chronological sequences for the different types of metalwork. Needham (Needham 1996; Needham *et al* 1997) divides the metalwork of the British Bronze Age into eight time periods (*1*) with different types associated with particular periods (*99*). The extent to which the types identified by contemporary archaeologists reflect prehistoric reality is open to question. The typological approach is, however, often the only available tool when dealing with unassociated and undated 'stray-finds' and is applied here for that very reason.

INTERPRETING CHANGE THROUGH TIME

Locally Bronze Age metalwork has been catalogued (Davey and Forster 1975; Barrowclough 2006) and its distribution considered (Davey 1976; Barrowclough 2007). Davey (1976) identified

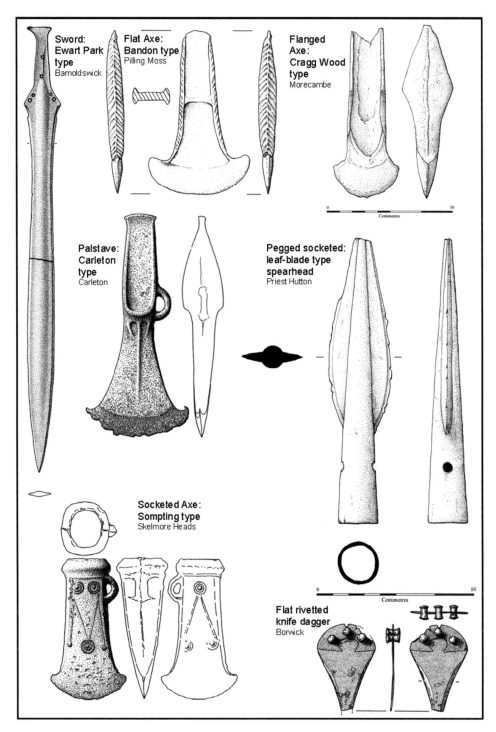

99 Key bronze artefact types referred to in the text

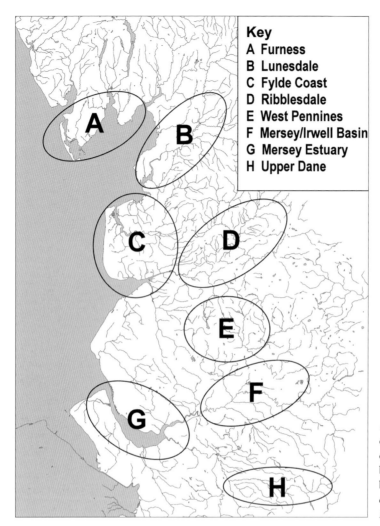

Key
A Furness
B Lunesdale
C Fylde Coast
D Ribblesdale
E West Pennines
F Mersey/Irwell Basin
G Mersey Estuary
H Upper Dane

100 Eight areas of Late Bronze Age occupation identified by Peter Davey on the basis of metalwork distributions. *After Davey 1976, fig. 4*

eight areas with statistically significant concentrations of artefacts (*100*) based on the finds up to 1975. The areas were Furness, Lunesdale, the Over Wyre District and Fylde Coast, Ribblesdale, the Rossendale uplands, the Mersey and Irwell river basins, the Mersey estuary and to the south of Lancashire the Upper Dane. Since that date additional material has come to light, partly as a consequence of metal detecting, which has largely confirmed the existence of the areas identified by Davey (Barrowclough 2007). The Furness area has been identified in previous chapters as an important area of human activity throughout prehistory. Lunesdale further around Morecambe Bay has a less dense concentration of finds with numbers increasing in the Late Bronze Age. The area of the Over Wyre mosses has also been identified as an important area of settlement in previous periods, something that is born out by the metalwork distribution through the Early, Middle and Late Bronze Age. In the Late Bronze Age the upper reaches of the River Ribble valley form an important low-lying zone between the two major upland moors of Bowland and Rossendale corresponding to possible trans-Pennine routes

(Davey 1976, 7). The majority of finds are either from the river itself, or from the well-drained river terraces. The uplands of Rossendale form a westward extension of the Pennines dissected by deep valleys, such as at Edgeworth, where a palstave was found, and the valleys cut by the Darwen and Calder rivers. The concentration of Middle Bronze Age finds from this area suggested to Davey that its south-west facing shelves with access to upland pastures would have lent themselves to settlement and agriculture during this period. One of the largest single groupings of finds is that from the Mersey and Irwell valleys. Davey identified two regions within the area of particular significance: the crossing point of the Irwell at Manchester and the Mersey at Warrington, which may have provided a focal point for overland movement round the Mersey estuary. The density of metalwork and evidence for settlement on the river terrace gravels around Warrington fits with evidence discussed in the last chapter for burials around Winwick. The combination of river crossing and agricultural land would have made this a favoured location for settlement. Once again there is evidence of a shift toward the higher reaches of the river in the Late Bronze Age, a probable response to wetter conditions. The Mersey Estuary around the Wirral and south-west Lancashire has a distinct distribution of mainly Middle Bronze Age finds that separate it from the higher reaches of the river. They may represent the presence of a coastal and estuarine fisher-farmer community consistent with the pattern of land-use described by Ron Cowell for the area (1991a).

Of 382 bronze objects known for Lancashire and the surrounding areas (Barrowclough 2007) the most numerous single type represented is the socketed axe of which 73 are recorded, followed by spearheads, 72, palstaves, 59, flat axes, 51, and flanged axes, 37, with other types making up the remainder. Chronologically 159 objects can be ascribed to Period 5, the Middle Bronze Age Acton/Taunton/Penard (Wallington) phase of activity dated c.1500–1150 cal BC. The preceding periods 1 and 2, 3 and 4 reflect a consistent level of activity. After a brief relapse in Period 6, Period 7 represents a further fluorescence of activity in the Late Bronze Age, Blackmoor/Ewart phase dated c.900–750 cal BC (*101*).

The earliest evidence for the use of metalwork in Lancashire comes from artefacts deposited with burials in the so-called 'metal-using' Neolithic, Periods 1 and 2, c.2500–2050 cal BC (*102*). Evidence for the early use of metalwork in a non-funerary context comes from the Over Wyre area where axe marks on the Kate's Pad trackway suggest that metal implements may have been in use by 2345 cal BC (Middleton *et al* 1995, 60–65). There were hints that a bronze object had once formed part of the burial assemblage at Astley Hall Farm near Chorley. When excavated, although no bronze artefacts were present, there was a green residue suggestive of copper-alloy on the bones of one of the cremations (Hallam pers. comm.). In the Central Pennines 10 bronze artefacts, out of more than 120, have been found in definite association with burials (Barnes 1982, 61). At Revidge, Blackburn, a bronze pin head was found associated with a cremation in an urn together with a bone pin and at Darwen, a dagger was found in one of the nine urned cremations. Also worthy of note is the burial site at Pendleton as, although no bronze artefacts were excavated at the site, one of the burials did include a gold bead or hair tress. At Hell Clough, on the moors at Burnley, the embanked circle had a cist containing an urn with two cremations and a bronze pin or awl 10cm long (Barnes 1982, 61) whilst in West Yorkshire the central burial in the embanked circle at Blackheath, Todmorden, contained a bronze knife and awl together with a bone pin and clay beads. At Whitelow,

Period Year cal BC	Metalwork Types	Total
1 and 2 2500–2050	Armlet 2, Flat Axe 30, Knife Dagger 4, Tanged Dagger 2	38
3 2050–1700	Awl 4, Dagger 2, Flat Axe 21, Knife Dagger 6	33
4 1700–1500	Chisel 5, Dagger 5, Flanged Axe 15, Razor 2, Spearhead 3	30
5 1500–1150	Adze 2, Armlet 1, Dirk 8, Flanged Axe 18, Palstave 57, Rapier 9, Socketed Axe 16, Spearhead 43, Spear Ferrule 1, Sword 4	159
6 1150–920	Harness Fitting 2, Socketed Axe 3, Spearhead 8, Spear Ferrule 1, Sword 3	17
7 920–750	Casting Waste 4, Socketed Hammer 3, Socketed Axe 31, Socketed Gouge 5, Socketed Knife 1, Spearhead 4, Spear Ferrule 1, Sword 1	52
8 750–510	Socketed Axe 12	12
		341

101 Metalwork types found in Lancashire according to chronological period

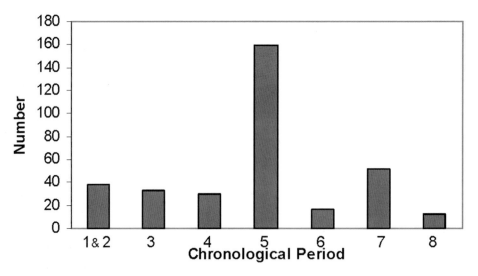

102 Number of bronze objects according to time period. N = 341

Ramsbottom, a bronze awl was found with the primary cremation burial in a pit, and in the cairn at Haulgh, Bolton, a dagger with three rivet holes, broadly contemporary with the sparse, late insular Beaker tradition, was found in a cist with a contracted inhumation. The dagger had been placed on one side of the head while on the other lay an inverted accessory vessel. Also present within the county are 15 early flanged axes, such as one from Radcliffe,

Greater Manchester, four awls, three tanged spearheads from Nelson, Burnley, and Boggart Hole Clough, Manchester and two tanged daggers.

The geographical distribution of Early Bronze Age metalwork in the Central Pennine area is restricted largely to the valleys and valley sides, and to the foothills of the Pennines. It is particularly associated with the better drained areas, and possibly with routeways through the hills following the Ribble-Aire Gap (Elgee and Elgee 1933; Raistrick 1929; Watson 1952; Manby 1964, 346). Bronze axes show a concentration extending from East Yorkshire, via York and Tadcaster (Radley 1974, 11) to Leeds, and then through the Aire Gap to the Ribble valley. Another minor concentration of finds occurs along the Yorkshire Calder valley possibly connecting either with the Ribble valley via the Cliviger gorge in the Burnley area, or with the Mersey basin to the south-west via the Manchester district. They include examples of flat axes from Blacko Tower, Great Harwood, three from Read and one from Ickornshaw Moor, all on the southern flanks of Ribblesdale. Examples of flanged axes include the Rishworth and Radcliffe axes, and from West Yorkshire, axes found at Keighley and Bradford, together with one from Silsden to the north of our area.

Metalwork forms the main evidence for the Late Bronze Age in Lancashire as elsewhere. By far the largest number of metal objects of Middle Bronze Age date, 1500–1000 cal BC, Periods 5 and 6, are palstaves, of which 57 are known. Also present are 18 haft flanged axes, 29 looped spearheads, and 9 rapiers. During the Middle Bronze Age, deposition shifted away from burials toward 'ritual' wet places. This is reflected in the distribution pattern of bronze artefacts according to underlying superficial geology, elevation, aspect and proximity to water (Barrowclough 2007) all of which indicate strong preferences for 'wet' lowland locations (*103, 104*). In particular Period 5, the Acton/Taunton/Penard (Wallington) phases, was a time of intense activity associated with unprecedented amounts of metalwork (159 objects), significantly larger than that which came before and was to come after, and was a time of different types.

A common feature of the metalwork distribution in the British Late Bronze Age period is its bias towards wetland areas and rivers, particularly in the form of hoards (Bradley 1984). This is seen as occurring at, or shortly before, a time of climatic deterioration, which is a possible cause for the changes seen at the end of the Early Bronze Age (Burgess 1974). In Lancashire, as generally in the north-west of England, hoards are rare, the pattern being dominated by single finds (Barrowclough 2007; Davey 1976). Where they do occur, for example at Skelmore Heads, Urswick; Winmarleigh in the Over Wyre area; and at Congleton in Cheshire, they are considerably smaller than those in the south of England. At Skelmore Heads six socketed axes were discovered in a limestone fissure. They include three exceptionally fine examples of Sompting type (*99*). The Winmarleigh hoard is important regionally, it was found at Cogie Hill inside a large oak box fastened with oak pins. The hoard consisted of a lunate spearhead, a socketed and riveted spearhead with leaf-shaped blade, five socketed axes with three vertical ribs on the faces, a leaf-shaped dagger, a facetted socketed axe and two three-ribbed socketed axes (*115*). It is the largest hoard yet found in Lancashire and the only one in which the objects were contained in a wooden box. At New Street, Congleton, a barbed spearhead, lunate spearhead, two spearshaft ferrules and a three ribbed socketed axe were found when workmen were digging foundations for a new school (Davey and Forster 1975, No. 125–9). Swords

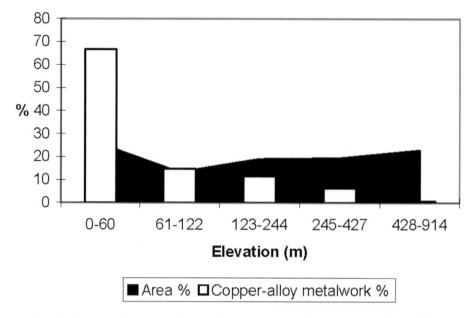

103 The distribution of bronze metalwork, plotted against elevation during Period 5, establishes a significant relationship between deposition and low-lying ground, confirming anecdotal evidence that wetlands and rivers were favoured locations

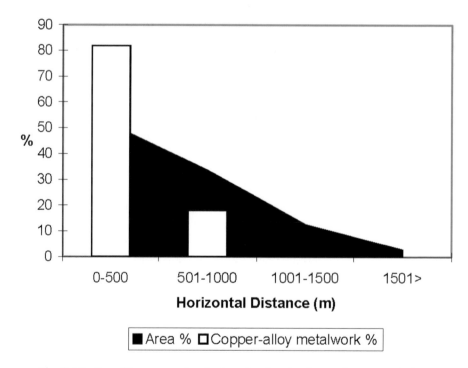

104 The distribution of bronze metalwork, plotted against the distance from water during Period 6, establishes a close link between deposition and wet places

although present are comparatively rare, not only in Lancashire but throughout the north-west of England, with only eight examples recorded from the region. There are, however, some early types with solid cast hilts in the Ambleside hoard, which are rare in Britain (Barrowclough 2007; Needham 1982).

Generally, metalwork deposition tends to be located in the middle to upper reaches of the main rivers in the region, in contrast to the Early Bronze Age pattern which is associated more with the lower reaches of rivers (Davey 1976; Barrowclough 2007). For example a small hoard consisting of two socketed axes was found in the upper reaches of the River Ribble at Clitheroe (Davey and Forster 1975, No. 120). This dislocation of the pattern of metalwork finds eastwards into the Pennines has been interpreted as a response to a worsening of conditions on the lower ground (Davey 1976; Nevell 1997). The palaeoenvironmental evidence suggests that areas around the wetlands were the focus of relatively concerted farming activity during the first millennium BC (Cowell and Innes 1994).

The Late Bronze Age and Early Iron Age Periods 7 and 8, 920–750 and 750–810 cal BC, are dominated by socketed axes of which there are 62. This period marks the end of metalwork deposition in watery places. Analyses of metalwork distributions reveal a resurgence in activity on the northern coast of Morecambe Bay, the location of a series of hillforts, extending from the Irish Sea coast through North Lancashire to Warton Crag, and into North Yorkshire at Ingleborough. Generally finds of metalwork in this area are in dry places and favour south-facing slopes, which are associated with favoured locations for settlement (Barrowclough 2007). At Portfield hillfort near Whalley a dry land hoard comprised two socketed axes, part of a socketed gouge, parts of the hilt and blade of a tanged knife, part of another possible knife blade, and a tanged stud, all of which had been damaged in antiquity. There was also a lock-ring and bracelet with outwardly expanded terminals, both made of gold and in good condition (*105*). The association of different designs and types of gold and bronze objects gives a firm date within the Heathery Burn phase of the Late Bronze Age. The hoard is considered to reflect contacts with the Irish metal industry and possible trans-Pennine routes (Blundell and Longworth 1967–8, 13). Bu'Lock (1965) suggested it was the property of a trader, bartering from a small stock of new gold ornaments for scrap bronze, but equally it may support the view that hillforts were centres of metalworking during the period (Barrowclough 2007 and below).

The changing relationship between metalwork deposition and wet-dry locations is unsurprising given the substantial body of literature that exists describing Bronze Age practices of deposition elsewhere in Britain and Northern Europe (Bradley 1990). In this sense Lancashire can be seen as part of the wider European Bronze Age. However, the detail of practices in the region are worthy of closer scrutiny as they show differences with practices elsewhere that give the region a unique identity. This may lead to a reconsideration of Bu'Lock's suggestion that a 'North Western Culture' existed (Bu'Lock 1961, 36–8).

Closer analysis of the particular contexts of deposition reveals the nature of the practice. 'Wet' locations have already been separated from 'dry' locations, but each can be further subdivided into particular types of wet or dry places (*106*). Three major types of wet location can be distinguished: major rivers, streams and peat bogs. Four major types of dry location may be distinguished: burials, settlements, dry hoards and caves. Cave sites are somewhat

105 Gold lock ring,
Portfield Hoard.
Photograph: John Hallam

ambiguous: although located in the dry limestone uplands they are also associated with drainage of water and therefore can be described as wet locations. This ambiguity may have been part of their attraction. For the present purposes they are placed in the dry category, and cognisance will be taken of their potential 'wet status' in the discussion that follows.

It was possible to determine the context for 270 artefacts, 178 for wet and 92 for dry (*106*). From this a number of patterns are discernable. First, in a number of instances particular types of object are only ever found in dry and some only ever in wet contexts. Thus, armlets/ bracelets, awls, casting waste, knives and knife daggers are confined to dry locations. Adzes, harness fittings, rapiers, spearshaft ferrules and tanged daggers are always found in wet locations. These are the exceptions, however. In most cases objects can be found in either wet or dry locations, but what is significant is the relative proportions in each. Although dry land examples exist, by far the majority of each type are found in wet locations: flat axes 5 dry and 28 wet; flanged axes, 3 dry and 22 wet; and spearheads, 5 dry and 42 wet. The distribution mostly favours wet locations, but this is not universal – both daggers, 5 dry and 1 wet, and swords, 12 dry and 4 wet, are most often found in dry places.

In order to begin to understand these distributions it is helpful to look at the particular type of wet or dry context. For example, not only is casting waste never found in wet locations,

	WET							DRY		
Object	Major River	Stream Valley	Peat Bog	'Wet'	'Dry'	Dry Hoard	Burial	Settl.	Cave	Not known
Adze			1		2					1
Armlet/Bracelet						2	3	1	3	1
Awl					1		3			1
Casting Waste					3			4		1
Chisel					2				2	
Dagger		1			2		3			2
Dirk		5	1	1	3					2
Flanged Axe	3	1	14	4						12
Flat Axe	2	4	15	7	4		1			17
Hammer										3
Harness Fitting	1			1						1
Knife					1			1		2
Knife Dagger							7			3
Palstave	4	2	9	12	9			1		20
Ornament	1		1					2		
Pin	1									
Rapier	1		2	3					1	3
Razor										2
Socketed Axe	12	3	6	8	8	6		9		21
Socketed Gouge	1	1		1				1		1
Socketed Knife								1		
Spearhead	14	5	16	7	1	1		2		25
Spearshaft Ferrule			1							3
Sword	1		3					2		4
Tanged Dagger			1							
Tanged Copper Dagger				1						1
Total	41	22	70	45	36	9	17	24	6	126

106 Analysis of bronze deposition according to context

it is also only found in one type of dry context: settlement, Late Bronze Age defended hillfort sites. The single example of casting waste from an unattributed 'dry' context refers to a metal-detected find, possibly the location of a hitherto unknown settlement, highlighting a potential use of this new source of data. Similarly, when swords are found in dry locations they are always found in settlement contexts. Other types are associated with Early Bronze Age burials, awls and daggers in particular. What I want to focus on is the distribution of metalwork in different wet contexts. The analysis of depositional practices may offer insights into continuity and change in belief during the Middle and Late Bronze Age, a period for which we lack burial data, the usual source of information on such questions.

Within wet conditions particular types favour particular contexts, thus bogs are the focus of deposits of flat axes (bogs 15, streams 4, rivers 2), flanged axes (bogs 14, streams 1, rivers 3) and palstaves (bogs 9, rivers 4, streams 2); stream valleys, the focus of dirks (streams 5, bog 1, river 0); and major rivers, the favoured location for socketed axes (rivers 12, streams 3, bogs 6). This distribution suggests a diachronic pattern. Artefacts found in bogs tend to date to the metal-using Neolithic and Early Bronze Age, Periods 1, 2 and 3, with further deposition in Period 5, the Middle Bronze Age. Those found in stream valleys are restricted in type to dirks, and to Period 5, whilst major rivers were the focus of activity in Period 7, the Late Bronze Age. Spearheads represent an exception to this pattern of distribution; they are found in all three wet contexts: 16 in bogs, 14 in rivers, and 5 in streams. This distribution is interesting, as the spearheads found in these contexts date, in the main, to Period 5. The Middle Bronze Age has already been identified as representing a peak in depositional activity, and it may be this intensity of deposition that first motivated the deposition of objects outside bog contexts, which, up until Period 5, had been the only site of wet deposition.

The deposition of metalwork in wet places has been widely interpreted as one aspect of Bronze Age ritual practices, the majority of which are lost to us. Many key aspects of people's lives and social personas are embedded within, framed by and organised around forms of ritual practice that we may broadly term 'religion'. At one end of a continuum are the relatively intangible structuring principles of social life, the *habitus* embedded in, and reproducing, habitual forms of social existence (Comaroff and Comaroff 1989, 272). At the other, and more visible, we can see in the deposition of metalwork the end product of highly elaborated, structured and overt practices and displays. These practices may have been integral elements of a political project that maintained religious identities so as to construct and manipulate, either inclusively or exclusively, both community affiliation and social boundaries.

Identity, at the level of the regional group, is created in opposition to other group identities, as part of an ongoing historical relationship. This view of cultural identity as an aspect of relationships contains the idea that the group has to be constantly maintained. In its maintenance over time, it will be subject to small changes, which will lead to its gradual transformation. The interest lies in how that reproduction of feelings of solidarity happens in society through time.

One of the most powerful ways to reproduce feelings of cultural identity and belonging is to make use of symbolic resources, especially material culture and everyday practices. The role of dress and bodily adornment is a good example that has received attention in previous

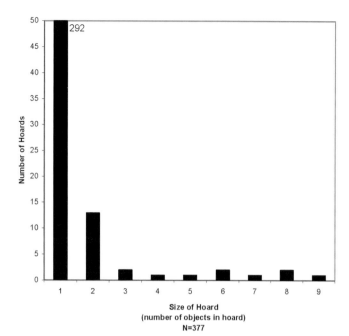

107 Analysis of bronze deposition in Lancashire according to the number of artefacts contained within hoards

studies of the Bronze Age (Treherne 1995; Sørensen 1997). While rarely consciously articulated, the ways in which people dress are subject to a range of culturally informed ideas and expectations. Cultural differences in dress are one resource that can be seized upon in the articulation of difference, as can be seen with national or regional costumes, or differences in military dress. The same may be true of the articulation of ritual among, and between, different groups, which when expressed through practices of deposition, are rendered visible to archaeological analysis.

The symbolic resources drawn on in the construction of group identity are not arbitrary. The cultural practices and representations that become objectified as symbols of the group have to resonate with people's usual practices and experiences (Jones 1997: 90). It is pre-existing differences that are drawn upon in the creation of shared feelings; it is interaction with others of a different cultural tradition that makes people think about the observed differences in a conscious way (Eriksen 1993, 34; Jenkins 1997, 76–7; Jones 1997, 95). A study of metalwork deposition therefore has the potential to inform our understanding of regional identity.

To those familiar with the pattern of metalwork deposition in Britain throughout the Bronze Age what may be most striking about the preceding analysis of the Lancastrian metalwork is the relatively small quantity. The point is reinforced by examination of hoards (*107*). A defining practice of the British Middle Bronze Age is the deposition of large amounts of metalwork together in wet places as hoards, and yet this is a practice rarely encountered in Lancashire. Of 377 artefacts where data are available only 85 were deposited in hoards (defined as two or more objects placed together), and of those, most were placed in pairs. Only occasionally were multiple objects deposited. I feel that the absence of hoards defines Lancashire in this period substantially contributing to a sense of regional identity. Understanding why hoarding apparently played such a small part in ritual practice is central to the formation of a model for social organisation within the region, and yet, although widely recognised, it has received comparatively little attention.

The most common, and tacitly accepted, explanation is functional. Following Cyril Fox (1932) it has been argued that the north-west of England, along with other areas of the highland zone, was peripheral, both economically and socially, to the south. A characteristic of the highland zone was that it was a 'difficult' area to live in. A cooler, wetter climate led to a shorter growing season, and lower yields than lowland areas. As a consequence, the population was characterised as stressed, struggling to survive, with little time for either cultural or technological pursuits. People relied upon technological advances imported from 'core' areas. According to this model, the relatively small amount of metalwork, and the almost complete absence of large hoards, was easily explained. For a 'marginal' population, reliant on expensive imports, metal was simply too scarce and valuable a commodity to 'waste' by throwing it away.

This account does not bare close examination. First, Lancashire straddles both highland and lowland zones, from the Pennines to the coastal plain. Environmental conditions alone cannot explain the different distribution. Second, the notion of marginality does not fit with aspects of the evidence that show that contacts between the region, and the rest of Britain, were widespread. The Langdale axe trade, for example, located immediately to the north of the study area, flourished during the Neolithic. Widespread trading links established contact across Britain and these appear to have continued into the Bronze Age as evidenced by the presence of a wide range of different metalwork types, although in low numbers.

In order to understand the absence of hoarding as a widespread activity we need first to investigate the nature of those hoards that do exist. It is possible to date each hoard using the known typo-chronological sequence, taking the date of the youngest artefact as the date for the deposit (*108*). The temporal sequence of 22 known hoards follows the pattern that has already been described for individual objects. There were low numbers during the Early Bronze Age, followed by a peak of activity in the Middle Bronze Age, Period 5, which tails off toward the Early Iron Age.

We have already seen that many of the hoards are small, comprising just a pair of objects. Although the number are too few to justify statistical analysis, some patterns do appear noteworthy (*109*). Objects were not deposited arbitrarily, only certain pairings were considered appropriate. In particular it was appropriate to place two objects of the same sort together. As in the case of two bracelets and two socketed axes, there are two instances of a pair of palstaves being deposited together. Another association worthy of note is that between socketed axe and socketed gouge, of which three examples exist (*110*). In each instance the gouge had been rammed into the axe socket so firmly that it proved impossible to remove one from the other without damage. In order to do this the axe handle had been removed. The performance associated with the deposit therefore required the decommissioning of the tool and then its removal from circulation.

The composition of the larger hoards, three or more objects, also reveals repeated deposition of a restricted range of objects. Objects appropriate for placing in hoards were swords, rapiers, spearheads and, in particular, socketed axes. To understand why this might be is to understand that communal identity is an aspect of social practice. Identity has to be

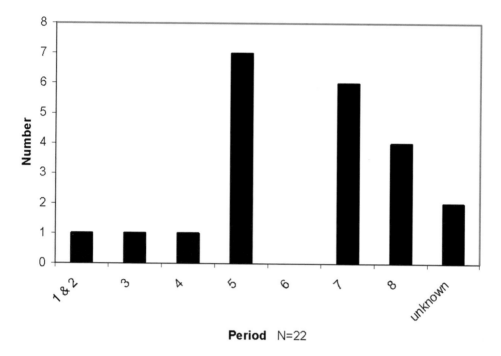

108 Analysis of hoards by period. Deposition begins in Periods 1/2 (dry hoards) and peaks in Period 5 (mainly wet hoards)

	Bracelet	Casting Waste	Chisel	Dirk	Flat Axe	Knife Dagger	Palstave	Ring	Sock'd Axe	Sock'd Gouge	Sock'd Spearhead
Bracelet	O										
Casting Waste Chisel					O				O		
Dirk					O						
Flat Axe Knife Dagger						O					
Palstave							□				
Ring							O				
Sock'd Axe									O		
Sock'd Gouge									✧		
Sock'd Spearhead			O								

109 Hoard associations. Paired objects: O = single instance, □ = two instances, ✧ = three instances continually constructed and generated and this is most effectively done through shared ways of doing things. Studying group identity involves paying attention to the uses of material culture in social interactions. One approach has been to investigate material culture in respect of style, attempting to read this as if it were a text. The problem with that approach was that little consideration was given to the role of living human beings in the interactions made possible by those artefacts (Boast 1997, 181–2). As a consequence, interpretations 'overlooked the contexts within which the variation arose, how the artefacts in question were used, and that they were a part of the production of meaning to prehistoric peoples.' (Conkey 1990, 10).

SOCIAL IDENTITY: A BIOGRAPHICAL APPROACH

There is more potential in biographical approaches (Kopytoff 1986) that take account of all the stages of production and use of artefacts, the *chaînes opératoires* (operational sequences), including deposition (see Mauss 1979 [1950]; Conkey 1990, 12–13; Lemonnier 1993, 2–3; Dietler and Herbich 1998). Within this perspective the knowledge drawn on in the creation and use of artefacts, and ways of doing things, such as deposition, is constituted in social and historical worlds. This knowledge is generally context-specific and not necessarily explicitly discussed (Edmonds 1990).

This idea has implications for discussing group identity in Lancashire. Previously it was thought that group identity could be inferred from artefacts by looking at static features, for example, axe decoration, which defines the various types and sub-types, and then plotting distributions of the various sub-types to map material culture groups. Taking his lead from Childe this was the approach adopted by Bu'Lock, which led him to posit the existence of a 'North Western Culture'. The life-history perspective is somewhat different: 'not only decorative patterns or secondary aspects of shape are used to define one's status or ethnic identity but also the use of given artefacts or entire processes of production' (Lemonnier 1993, 20). Material culture is actively involved in social practice, and social practice cannot exist without material culture. Social practice involving material culture is how the idea of the group, whether social, familial, ethnic or other, becomes articulated: it is not something that can be 'read off' from the artefactual evidence without regard for its contexts of use and production.

An important distinction that should be made for the present study is that between 'specific' object biographies and 'generalised' biographies (Gosden and Marshall 1999, 170–1). Specific biographies are about the idiosyncratic histories of objects, whilst generalised biographies describe the characteristics of widely shared features of an object's life-path. In this study of object deposition I am referring to generalised biographies. Archaeologically, it is much more difficult to come to terms with specific biographies, since they are outside established patterns.

Every biography commences with production. In making an object the smith is both constrained by practical factors, such as availability of materials and skill, and cultural factors such as, which objects were considered appropriate to produce and what they should look like. The best known evidence for early mining in the region is that from Alderley Edge,

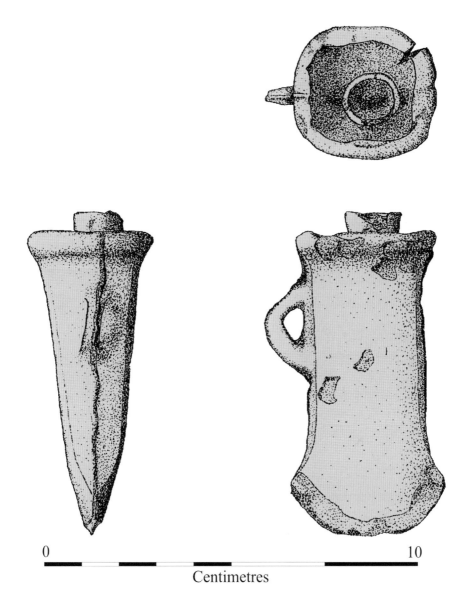

110 Socketed axe found by a metal detectorist at Twiston Brook, a tributary of the upper reaches of the River Ribble. The axe was found with a socketed chisel lodged inside it. *Illustration: Iona Robinson*

Cheshire. Excavation at Bryndlow Levels recovered 100 grooved stone hammers (Dawkins 1875) and an oak shovel found in early copper workings was dated to the Bronze Age (2025–1536 cal BC) (Garner 1994). Metal from the Alderley Edge source has been traced within bronze artefacts of the Ewart Park Periods 6 and 7, *c.*1020–800 BC (Rohl and Needham 1998, 107–8). These are dated considerably later than the current evidence for ore extraction.

Lead mining in the Pennine region has a long history (Ford and Rieuwerts 1983) and was particularly intensive during the eighteenth and nineteenth centuries, but the presence of galena crystals in Early Bronze Age burials suggests that it may have its origins in later prehistory. The presence of galena in burials at Cliviger Laithe discussed in the previous chapter suggests that sources of lead in the Pennines may have been utilized in the production of early copper-alloy metalwork, although 'lead bronze' is usually associated with the Late Bronze Age. The question of whether lead was extracted in the Bronze Age is relevant to our understanding of metal production. However, no mine workings of such an early date have been recovered. This may be because later intensive mining activity on the ore seam destroyed the earlier evidence, in which case it might be that recovery of archaeological evidence of early ore extraction is impossible. The earliest phases of metalworking within the region are therefore poorly understood.

An approach that offers the possibility that we might be able to find evidence for mining activity in the prehistoric period comes from the techniques of Magnetic Measurement and Heavy Metal (lead) Assay. Both analyses rest upon the theory that particulate matter, settling out from the atmosphere onto developing peat deposits, will be incorporated into the sedimentary record, provided that they are not subsequently removed by erosional processes (Oldfield 1963; 1969). The technique of Magnetic Measurement rests upon the fact that the combustion of fossil fuel releases into the atmosphere ferromagnetic particles, 'magnetic spherules', composed mainly of magnetite, Fe_3O_4 (Oldfield *et al* 1981). Oldfield *et al* (1978) demonstrated that peat horizons produce records of magnetic spherule deposition, the concentration of which can be determined by measuring the Saturation Isothermal Remanent Magnetisation (SIRM) in a sample by magnetometer (Oldfield *et al* 1979). The techniques of lead assay and magnetic analysis may be applied to samples from the prehistoric period, when combined with radiocarbon dating of peat horizons (Barrowclough 2007; Malcolm Bain pers. comm.).

Samples were removed from peat taken from the prehistoric sites of Winter Hill and Round Loaf, both located on the Central Pennine moors and assayed for lead content by Dr Malcolm Bain (*111* & *112*). At Round Loaf there was an isolated peak in lead deposition at 1.35m (560 µg g⁻¹), which is a significant indication that lead mining may have occurred in the Bronze Age. The estimated date for the record is about 1770 cal BC. Also noteworthy are increases in lead deposition at cal AD 680 (HAR 6416, 0.35 m), which extend to *c*.cal AD 880. Increasing SIRM values dated to the late Saxon/Norse Period cal AD 680 coincide with lead increases and may also be linked with mining. This coincides with the periods of Saxon and Norse activity in Lancashire, and may relate to greater local demand for lead at that time. At Winter Hill the analysis is presented from cal AD 680 back to *c*.2000 cal BC. Minor increases noted at 1.35–1.25m are of Bronze Age provenance, 1800 cal BC to 1545 cal BC. The values are not high, but may represent mining activity in this period. The Bronze Age increase accords with the prominent value recorded at Round Loaf dated to *c*.1750 cal BC. The increased SIRM value at 1.35m underlies a charcoal prominence at 1.33m and may reflect local burning in the prehistoric period. Increases in the lead record at these levels supports a view that mining may have contributed to this SIRM elevation in the period 1800–1545 cal BC (Bain pers. comm.). Minor SIRM increases are similarly recorded in a charcoaliferous phase of the stratigraphy between 1.20–1.05m. This charcoal abundance is associated with fluctuations in arboreal pollen proportion, suggestive of interference episodes in peripheral woodlands

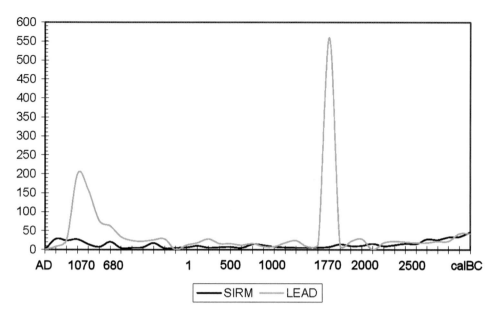

111 Anglezarke uplands (Round Loaf), Lancashire. Lead values at 1700 cal BC indicate possible extractive activity. *Barrowclough 2007*

between 1200 cal BC and 840 cal BC (Bain 1991). The isolated increase at 0.40m, cal AD 680, again coincides with charcoaliferous evidence for local burning. Increased SIRM values are also noted at Round Loaf at this time, and with the Winter Hill fluctuation, this may well represent evidence of metalworking during the Early Bronze Age.

Moulds are the most certain evidence for metal production. The earliest metal artefacts were made using open stone moulds, none of which have been found in Lancashire. The closest examples are stone moulds from Croglin in Cumbria (Anon 1884, 279) which would have made twin-looped, leaf-shaped spearheads (Burgess 1968, 25) of Period 5. A ceramic object accompanied cremated remains within the secondary phase of a barrow at Gawsworth, Cheshire, which may have been a mouth bellows associated with metalworking (Mullin 2003, 15). But within the region it is not until the Late Bronze Age that we have direct evidence for metalwork production. Five clay crucible sherds and 20 fragments of moulds were found at Beeston Castle within the Late Bronze Age enclosure (Ellis 1993, 25). The mould fragments were generally poorly preserved, but seem to have been for casting swords and a ferrule, and probably dated to Period 6 or 7 (Ellis 1993, 55). A local source of copper was available, located at Bickerton, although no firm evidence that this source was exploited has been found (S. Timberlake pers. comm. in Hodgson and Brennand 2006). In Lancashire, at Portfield hillfort, near Whalley, casting waste was found and at Mellor near Stockport, seven sherds of crucible, a possible mould fragment and a number of pieces of slag were found (*113*). Analysis using fluorescence detected copper, tin, zinc and lead and points to them having been used for melting Bronzes (Dungworth 2000). The crucible fragments show the continued use of bronze into the Iron Age, probably in specialist centres, making

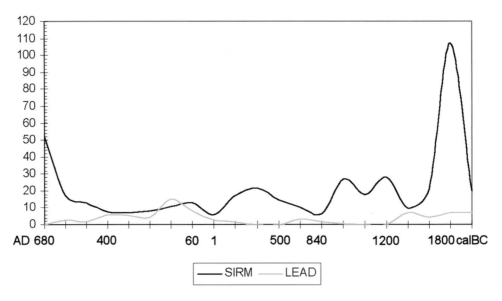

112 Winter Hill, Lancashire. SIRM values at 1800 and also 1200 and 1000 cal BC indicate human activity, possibly associated with extraction. *Barrowclough 2007*

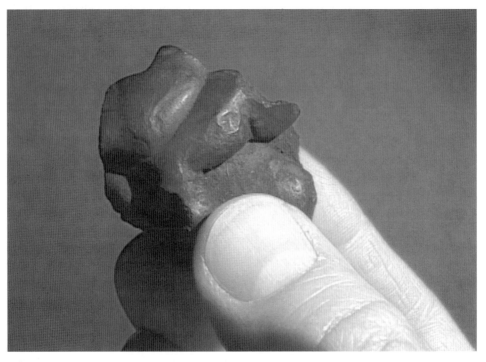

113 Iron slag found at Mellor indicating that metalworking was practiced on the site. *Mellor Archaeological Trust*

smaller more intricate items than the larger tools. It is possible that the raw material was acquired through trade in the form of currency bars. These have been found in numerous locations in the south of England but have been less common in the north. Fragments of crucible used in bronze casting have been found in some similar sites but are not common. This indicates an element of prestige at the Mellor Settlement and possibly other hillforts (Beswick and Coombs 1986; Dungworth 2000).

The elaboration of Late Bronze Age settlements, discussed in the following chapter, compared to what had gone before, suggests the emergence of social hierarchies. Architecture and the structuring of space can be used to emphasise communal similarity and difference at both conscious and unconscious levels. The association between metalworking and these hilltop sites suggests that metal production during the Late Bronze Age may have been tightly controlled, with smiths working under the protection of an emerging elite. With metal production controlled, the distribution of metalwork was at the discretion of those in power. This leads to consideration of the next stage in the biography, use-life.

Consumption of metalwork is one of the factors that emphasise communal similarity and difference. The ownership of metalwork and activities such as deposition which went along with it were social markers used in group affiliation. Deliberate deposition of particular objects suggests that they had specific meaning; this meaning came about during the life of the object (Munn 1986; Rowlands 1993, 147, 149). This implies that during its life an object is likely to undergo transformations of meaning. In order to become valuable and earn the right to be ritually deposited artefacts must fulfil specific expectations. If they do not fulfil the expectations, and follow the life-path considered appropriate, they may lose their significance. This is something which has been recorded for several ethnographic case studies on the use of valuables (Weiner 1992). In the case of metalwork it is unclear whether objects began their lives as commodities, later transforming their status to that of valuable, or whether they always existed as valuables. It is likely that bronze objects may have been both gifts and commodities (Bradley 1990, 144–8) with different spheres of exchange co-existing (Bloch and Parry 1989, 15; Kopytoff 1986, 71–2). As Mauss (1993 [1923/1924]) has shown, during gift exchange an object is to some extent seen as imbued with the presence of the former owner, hence the inalienability of the object. It becomes to an extent personified. Godelier (1999) has argued that in the case of valuables perceived as very special, objects are not only seen as signalling the presence of former owners, but of very special persons, and even ancestors or gods.

The transactions themselves are hard to recognise archaeologically. One way that we may identify the existence of spheres of exchange is to examine objects in hoards. Valuables are likely to have passed through several hands in order to accumulate complex biographies before being deposited (see Malinowski 1922 for discussion of the *kula*). They are therefore likely to have achieved considerable age and to bear the marks of circulation at the point of deposition. When objects of different types, and therefore different ages, are found together in hoards it is possible to estimate the time that some of the objects were in circulation. This is because the older objects could not have been deposited until at least the date that the younger objects were manufactured.

Taking data from seven hoards (*114*) for which the typology of the contents could be determined it was possible to determine the age range of the contents. In the case of the

Winmarleigh hoard (*115*) the oldest objects, peg-socketed leaf-shaped spearheads, were dated to the Middle Bronze Age, Penard Phase of Period 5, 1300–1150 cal BC and the youngest, for example the Yorkshire-type socketed axes, to the Late Bronze Age, Period 7, Ewart Park phase 1000–800 cal BC; thus the oldest objects were between 150 and 500 years old at the time they were deposited. Although the dating is approximate it is clear that even using the most conservative estimate of age, the oldest object must have passed through several generations before it was deposited. Similarly lengthy periods of circulation were found amongst objects deposited in hoards at Congleton, Beeston Castle and in the River Ribble.

Support for the hypothesis that objects, which circulated over long periods of time, acquired extensive biographies prior to deposition is provided by analysis of use-wear. Repeated resharpening of the edges of objects has been noted elsewhere in the European Bronze Age (for example Vandkilde 1996, 32). In Lancashire a number of instances of resharpening can be identified in spears (for example a side-looped spear from Prestwich, Manchester). Objects can also be modified: Bridgeford (1997, fig. 1) cites an example of a sword that ended up as a dagger. A Group II dirk of Period 5, Acton phase, found at Foulshaw/Helsington Peat Moss, Cumbria, has had its butt reworked to form a broad tang with a secondary hole drilled through it for rehafting (Barrowclough 2007, fig. 6.29). With each event the artefact acquired additional meaning imbuing it with individual character.

The discussion, so far, has rested upon a combination of typology and relative dating, tied to a relatively small number of absolute radiocarbon dates, used to construct a sequence for Bronze Age metalwork. A potential problem is that the sequence rests in large part on material from outside the region (*1*). Burgess (1968, 1) noted the difficulty of relating finds from northern England to chronologies based on southern traditions and developed a typology of northern and Scottish forms. Burgess' proposal of a northern Britain Wallington tradition (Burgess 1968), the partner to the southern Willburton, *c.* 1150–1000 cal BC, was severely undermined by Needham (Needham 1996) and is no longer widely supported; instead the Wallington material is placed in the Penard phase. The need for regional chronologies is still important and is exemplified by the socketed axe. On the basis of the Petters, Surrey axe finds Needham (1990, 28–43) grouped axes into types A to D, however following the find of axes at Beeston Castle in Cheshire he had to adjust his typology to include a new type E (Needham 1993, 41). The subsequent discovery of a socketed axe at Twiston (*110*) has cast further doubt on the applicability of Needham's classification. The Twiston axe does not fit into the ribbed classes B, C or E, nor into the octagonally sectioned, faceted class D. With its plain, sub-rectangular body, it bears the closest resemblance to class A, the south-eastern type. However, south-eastern axes are more slender than the Twiston axe, and are characterised by a double, rather than single, moulding at the mouth. Thus the classification devised by Needham, based on examples from the south of England, has proved unhelpful in describing the material from the north-west of England. Within the county an absence of large hoards leaves little scope for the construction of a regional chronology based upon metalwork associations. An alternative way forward for an understanding of metalworking in Lancashire is to construct a regional suite of radiocarbon dates. In one instance a metal-detected find of a pegged socketed leaf-blade spearhead came to light

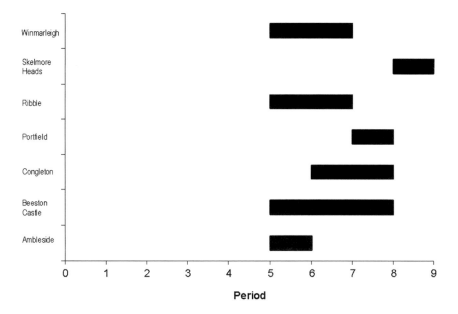

114 Length of circulation of metalwork prior to deposition in hoards. N=46

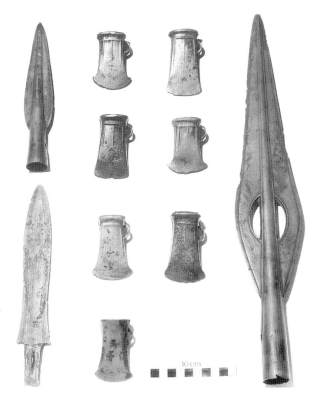

115 Bronze hoard from Cogie Hill Farm, Winmarleigh, Over Wyre, Lancashire. Illustrated: pegged socketed spearhead (top left), lunate spearhead (right), socketed axes, Yorkshire type (centre), dagger. Found in 'a strong, rude, oaken box' (Garstang 1906, 236). *Courtesy of Warrington Museum*

complete with a portion of the shaft in situ (*99*). Radiocarbon assay of the *Fraxinus* shaft produced a date in the range 1080–890 cal BC (2820 ±35 BP, SUERC-4466). On typological grounds alone the spearhead dates to Period 5, Penard phase, 1300–1150 cal BC. The difference between the two dates, which corresponds to similar use-lives found in hoarded objects (above) suggests that the spear was in circulation, perhaps even re-hafted, for a period between 70 and 410 years.

Exchange takes place between people and also between people and supernatural forces, ancestors, spirits and gods (Godelier 1999), and it is this that leads to consideration of the final stage in the life-cycle of metalwork – deposition. For the purposes of the discussion that follows, a distinction must be made between objects that were placed in the ground with the intention of leaving them there forever, and those that were only temporarily stored but never retrieved. The former marks the intentional end of an object's biography, from the point of view of those making the deposit, the latter the unintentional interruption of a biography. Objects that were lost are another example of an unintended interruption of an object's life.

When objects are deposited they are taken out of circulation. It is this economic aspect of hoarding that has often received greatest attention. In this study I wish to emphasise another aspect, that of the relationship between the people making the deposit and the location in which it is made. The act of deposition brings together histories of people, of objects and of places. This aspect of deposition is generally neglected in studies (Bradley 2000), perhaps because detailed palaeoecological reconstructions are rarely possible. In the case of lowland Lancashire it has been possible to reconstruct the Bronze Age landscape in some detail (see Chapter 1) making this approach possible.

Pilling Moss, in the Over Wyre district of Lancashire, lies on the southern edge of Morecambe Bay (*58*). During the Late Neolithic it was inundated with water, but as sea levels fell, as they did throughout the Bronze Age, a substantial area of wetland 'moss' was created. Human activity in this area is evidenced by the presence of stone tools, wooden trackways and in particular by a concentration of metal artefacts. In all, 24 bronze artefacts have been found in this location, more than anywhere else in the study region (*116*). They include the Winmarleigh hoard already considered as part of this discussion. The density of deposited objects and the period of time that they represent, from Periods 2–7, 2300–750 cal BC, suggest that this location was held to have particular meaning over a long span of time, making it particularly appropriate to the deposition of metalwork (*117*). This case makes the point that significance may reside not in a single event but in the repetition of events, each of which contributes to the construction of a cultural landscape.

Within this long time-span depositional activity concentrated on certain types of object, in particular axes and spears. Deposition was clearly selective as, for example, all of the flat axes deposited in Period 3, Overton Phase, were of the same type, Bandon (*99*): of five flanged axes, three were of type Lissett, whilst all of the socketed axes were of Yorkshire-type (*115*). This strongly suggests that selection was taking place, arguably as a means of maintaining group identity through material culture.

The increase in Late Bronze Age material deposited in the Over Wyre area and also in the Ribble and wetlands of the Fylde may suggest that strong socio-political control was

Period	Phase	Type	Sub-type
Late 2	Mount Pleasant	Flat Axe	Migdale, decorated variant
3	Overton	Flat Axe	Bandon
3	Overton	Flat Axe	Bandon
3	Overton	Flat Axe	Bandon
3	Overton	Flat Axe	Bandon
4/5	Bedd Branwen	Flanged Axe	Uncertain
5	Acton	Flanged Axe	Balcarry
5	Acton	Flanged Axe	Callander
5	Acton	Flanged Axe	Lissett
5	Acton	Flanged Axe	Lissett
5	Acton	Flanged Axe	Lissett
5	Acton/Taunton	Palstave	Primary Shield Pattern
5	Taunton	Spearhead	Side looped
5	Taunton	Spearhead	Side looped
5	Penard	Spearhead	Pegged socketed, leaf blade
5	Penard	Spearhead	Pegged socketed, leaf blade
5	Penard	Sword	Limehouse, Mugdrum variant
6	Wilburton	Spearhead	Pegged socketed, lunate
7	Ewart Park	Socketed Axe	Yorkshire
7	Ewart Park	Socketed Axe	Yorkshire
7	Ewart Park	Socketed Axe	Yorkshire
7	Ewart Park	Socketed Axe	Yorkshire
-	-	Spearhead	-
-	-	Tanged Dagger	-

116 Metal artefacts found in Pilling Moss, Lancashire, classified according to Period and Type. N=24

established across the landscape, an interpretation consistent with the rise of the defended hilltop settlements seen at Warton Crag and also in the Pennines at Portfield.

The nature of the objects deposited may be a clue to the people involved in the act of deposition (Treherne 1995; Ehrenreich 1997; Sørensen 1998, 262; Bradley 2000, 56). In line with the general evidence on prehistoric weapon graves, it is assumed that activity around Pilling Moss was primarily masculine. I would not want to place too much emphasis on attempts to identify the people involved in the act of deposition, but I feel safer in asserting that the choice of depositional location appears to have been steered by cultural considerations. Given the combination of selected location and selective deposition, rules and perhaps taboos may well have existed which stated that a particular type of object should only be deposited in a particular place.

The act of deposition brings about change to the people, the object and the place involved. The object is removed from society, and with it the biography of its past owners; the people, who no longer possess the object, are perhaps transformed in status, especially if the object was associated with illustrious owners; and the place itself, in the memory of the participants, will be linked to the act of deposition. The setting in which the act took place, a wetland environment prone to seasonal flooding, may also be perceived as symbolically changed by the act. As a result the location, already redolent with communal memories of earlier acts of deposition, can have added resonance in the memories of the

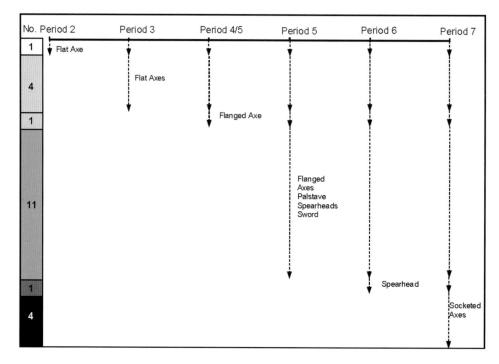

117 The cumulative effect of a series of acts of deposition, Pilling Moss, Lancashire. Repetition of practices constructs and maintains a cultural landscape. N=22

participants. Although knowledge of the ceremony may be transferred from generation to generation the exact details will fade, be reinvented, and embellished. With no permanent marker, so far as we are aware, the narrative is open to 're-writing' and manipulation by future generations.

We have seen that deposits were placed cumulatively in Pilling Moss over a period of several centuries. The mechanism that triggered these acts of sacrifice is unclear. One interpretation of metal deposited in natural places would be to see the deposits as funeral hoards. This is an explanation offered by Warmenbol (1996) with regard to deposits in Belgium, but based on the earlier ideas of Wegner (1976) and Bradley (1990, 102). They observed that weapon sets first deposited in graves were, at later stages of the Bronze Age, placed in hoards. I favour this mechanism as it fits the pattern of activity found in Lancashire.

In Early Bronze Age burials, for example Borwick, single or occasionally a pair of axes were deposited. Later, in the Middle Bronze Age, deposits of axes, again often singly or in pairs, formed the basis of deposits in natural places. Stronger evidence for the link between death and hoarding comes from a rare Late Bronze Age burial at Butts Beck Quarry, Dalton-in-Furness, where a pegged socketed leaf-blade spearhead was found with a Ewart Park, Northern Step 1 sword and human bones in a stone cist along with the bones of a horse (Gaythorpe 1899, 164–66).

Hoards in natural, 'wet' locations may be interpreted as hoards of personal equipment, deposited at the moment of death, but buried separate from the body. The implication is that weapon deposits are related to the conceptualisation of the deceased, but in a skewed manner. Blok (1994, 34 cited in Fontijn 2002, 231) argues that using violence against others is a polluting action, since it transgresses the boundary between the category of life and death. As such it may have repercussions for the way in which people deal with weapons, both in daily life and in ritual. For this reason, the use of violence is often related to rituals (Blok 1994, 34). In the case of the Butts Beck burial the sword had been deliberately bent, perhaps as an act of decommissioning, and similar acts of deformation have been observed in swords and rapier deposits in watery locations in Lancashire, for example a rapier found bent in the River Ribble at Ribchester.

The separation of certain classes of artefact – bronze spears, axes, and also swords – implies that they represent an ambiguous category in material culture. Weapons are often seen as ambiguous, even dangerous in ethnographic studies. Politically, weapons are dangerous because their presence in a social group implies 'haves' and 'have-nots', and thus potentially a group who can impose their will upon others (Claessen 1988, 7–8). In small-scale society where there was previously no authority with an effective monopoly of force (Roymans 1996, 14), the presence of weaponry may have threatened established social cohesion. Thus, ideologies are reflected and constructed in the practices and lifestyles of people. In the evidence from metal deposition we can see at least a glimpse of the connection between ideological values and real life.

CONCLUSIONS

The analysis of the landscape context of metalwork during the periods of the Bronze Age leads to the following conclusions. First, deposition was selective, both in terms of artefacts selected, and of places in the landscape chosen for deposition. Secondly, deposition was also cumulative, with repeated acts of deposition occurring in the same place, and other places therefore being repeatedly ignored. Thirdly, deposition was ideological, it was used to construct and maintain identities, elements of which were regional.

This discussion has demonstrated that when we start to examine the detailed local contexts of use and deposition of artefacts, that previously would have been interpreted as evidence for 'migration' or 'invasion' (or centre and periphery), we will start to identify subtle local variations pointing to the appropriation of items of material culture for particular purposes. It is at the local scale that we may be able to identify certain patterns of use that point to the deliberate articulation of cultural differences. It is also in the historical depth that archaeology provides that we may be able to trace the formation of new types of identities through the use of material culture. Such patterning may be due to different types of communal identity such as familial lineages or territorial groupings.

CHAPTER 7

ENCLOSING THE LAND:
LATER PREHISTORIC SETTLEMENT

INTRODUCTION

It has been argued here and elsewhere (Cowell 2000b) that until the end of the Early Bronze Age, social organisation and economy in Lancashire and the north-west of England generally were based on a system that involved a high degree of mobility. In the Early Bronze Age there was a shift away from mobility towards the creation of fixed places in the landscape, where land was owned and exploited by individual families, inhabiting traditional farmsteads. The shift is therefore a crucial development in economic and possibly social change. To say that farmsteads did not exist in the Early Bronze Age in Lancashire would be an oversimplification as recent evidence has shown (Adams forthcoming; Thompson 1998), but the general trend in the evidence is that farmsteads were probably only a minor component in the landscape, much of which was exploited in an occasional and non-intensive way. By the Late Iron Age, the creation of farmstead enclosures involving the investment of much more labour and time in their construction and upkeep suggests that in some parts of Lancashire land-use and settlement patterns had changed drastically. The pace and process by which this came about is of great significance and the changes seen at the end of the Early Bronze Age provide the most likely context for subsequent developments. The Late Bronze Age is therefore a key period in this debate.

MIDDLE BRONZE AGE SETTLEMENT

Evidence of Middle Bronze Age, *c.*1500–1000 BC, settlement is limited. South of the River Ribble two small pits containing Middle Bronze Age pottery excavated at Ditton Brook, Tarbock, produced a radiocarbon date of 1620–1130 cal BC (Cowell 2000a). More reliable settlement evidence was recovered from Oversley Farm on the site of the Second Runway at Manchester Airport (Thompson 1998; Garner 2001). The site has already been discussed in the context of the Early Bronze Age, however occupation appears to have continued in use throughout the Middle and Late Bronze Age. Features, mostly pits, the ephemeral structural

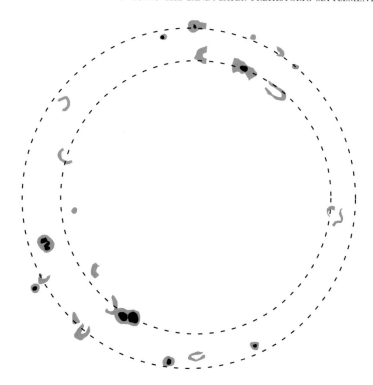

118 Middle Bronze
Age domestic
structure, Irby,
Wirral. *After Cowell*

evidence and the small amount of Late Bronze Age pottery, represented in the assemblage,
suggested to the excavator less intensive occupation than earlier phases (Thompson 1998;
Garner 2001).

The most comprehensive evidence for a Middle Bronze Age domestic settlement in the
north-west of England was found at Irby, Wirral (*118*). A circular structure with pottery,
possible oven fragments, bronze-working debris and evidence for the farming of cereals, dated
to 1620–1130 cal BC, was excavated (Philpott and Adams forthcoming). Most settlements of
the Middle Bronze Age are found in southern England and have features in common with
the site of Irby. Settlements consist of moderately sized rectilinear enclosures associated with
scatters of pits and rather fragmentary post-built buildings (Barrett *et al* 1991). On the
chalklands, farmsteads were integrated into a system of fields, trackways, ponds and associated
burial grounds (Drewett 1980). The south-west has fewer long-lived, intermittently occupied
farmsteads with associated fields (Nowakowski 1991), whilst at Fengate in East Anglia, ditched
field systems laid out on the edge of a wetland have occasional buildings dispersed amongst
them (Pryor 1980).

Irby shares with Middle Bronze Age houses elsewhere a repeated ordering of internal
space. Cowell (pers. comm.) identified a number of common Middle Bronze Age features
found elsewhere and at Irby these include circular or oval double ring post construction; a
south-south-westerly entrance, compared to a mainly south-easterly or southerly aspect found
elsewhere; and a potential porch which includes pottery and clay artefacts in the post-sockets,
similar to many other houses with differentiated, structurally embellished entrances which
often contain special deposits in the postholes or slots (Brück 1999, 155; Parker-Pearson 1996).

In other respects Irby represents a regional variation differing in some respects from the pattern found in the south. This difference is represented in the size of the house. It has an external diameter of 14.8m and inner diameter of 12m for the posts, making it somewhat larger than houses of the same period in the south, which fall within the range 7 to 9m. The house also differs in its lack of symmetry. Elsewhere Middle Bronze Age houses exhibit symmetry in the equal spacing of posts either side of the main axis, suggesting a degree of formality in their construction. Irby lacks the regular spacing of its posts. A feature of Middle Bronze Age settlement elsewhere in England, which according to the radiocarbon dates is shared by Irby, is short-lived, single phase occupation. Estimates for the length of time that such settlements might be occupied range between a few decades and 50–100 years (Cowell pers. comm.). Assuming that a household was established at marriage and lasted until the partners died, a single phase of occupation may span 20 to 40 years (Brück 1999, 149).

Finds consisted of locally made decorated and plain pottery, three struck flints, two spherical clay weights, potential oven clay, emmer wheat and naked barley suggesting that the building was associated with the storage and preparation of food and the manufacture of clothing. The evidence from Irby is of a small farmstead occupied for a limited time sometime during the fourteenth century BC. It must have been associated with fields or plots where wheat and barley were cultivated, although no evidence has been found of such enclosures (Cowell pers. comm.). The structure is larger than the typical Middle Bronze Age farm found in southern England. It may, following Cowell, have potentially served a larger group, perhaps in some communal form of living, suggesting that the mobile element within land-use patterns, identified as characterising the Early Bronze Age in lowland north-west England, continued into the Middle Bronze Age period.

LATE BRONZE AGE AND EARLY IRON AGE

Four main farmstead enclosures with Late Bronze Age occupation have been excavated in Lancashire, all in the Mersey Basin (Cowell pers. comm.). At Brook House Farm (Cowell 2000a, 48), a wooden plinth which came from the inner enclosure ditch has produced a Late Bronze Age radiocarbon date of 1000–800 cal BC (2720 ±50 BP; Beta-117717), although this date should be younger by c.10–55 years to allow for the loss of sapwood (Cowell 2000a, 59). This intriguing object consists of a square (c.50cm) pyramid, 5–6cm high, of carved oak with a central circular perforation, c.75mm in diameter (119). Close examination of the object revealed that it had been fashioned using a metal axe and gouge and the overall impression given its unweathered condition and generally very good state of preservation was that it was 'viewed rather than used' (Darrah in Cowell 2000a, 49). It is uncertain what the object was used for; one suggestion is that it acted as a plinth upon which sat some sort of statue, but this can only be speculation. The object seems to have been in use for a long time, being deposited in the Middle Iron Age, some c.500 years after it was made (Cowell 2000a, 60). This may be a hint of Late Bronze Age activity on the site (119).

At Irby, Wirral, evidence for bronze working and also pottery are dated to the Late Bronze Age (Adams and Philpott forthcoming) whilst evidence for Late Bronze Age structures was

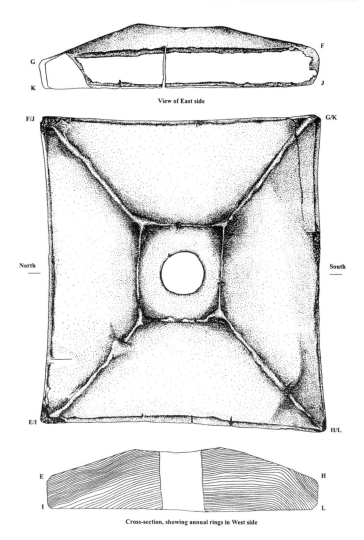

119 Carved
wooden plinth from
Brookhouse Farm.
Cowell 2000, fig. 3.16

120 Warton Crag Hillfort, Carnforth

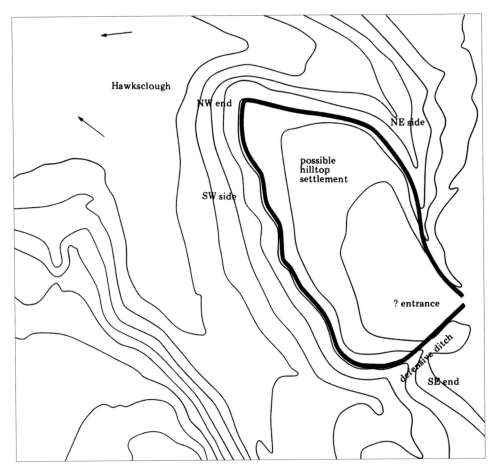

Hawksclough

NW end

NE side

possible
hilltop
settlement

SW side

? entrance

defensive ditch

SE end

121 Possible defended site at Hawksclough. *Map John Hallam*

excavated at Brook House Farm, Bruen Stapleford. Two roundhouses were dated to 920–780 cal BC and 800–350 cal BC (Fairburn *et al* 2003, 25), although the presence of earlier features might suggest that this represents a continuation of settlement from the Middle Bronze Age.

Settlement activity for the Late Bronze Age is best known from excavation of defended hill-enclosures. By default these hillforts were once assumed to be classic Iron Age monuments – large, heavily defended sites, each acting as the focus of a clan or the seat of a tribal chief, exerting considerable land control on the immediate hinterland – but more recent research has placed many of these sites in earlier periods. North Lancashire is predominantly upland and the evidence for settlement is dominated by defended sites, typically univallate and small in size (Forde-Johnson 1962). At Skelmore Heads, near Ulverston, for example, a palisaded defence was succeeded by a dump rampart (Powell 1963). Datable material from the site included a *La Tène* decorated bronze fragment. North of Lancaster, Warton Crag, near Carnforth (*120*), combines the natural defences afforded by cliffs with three widely spaced ramparts to enclose an area of 6.2ha. A smaller site, also on a promontory, lies 10km to the north-west at Castle Head. This hillfort was protected by a single north-facing rampart,

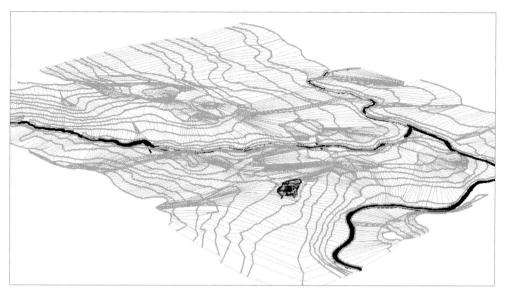

122 Digital terrain model of Portfield Hillfort and its surrounding landscape. The fort is situated on a promontory giving extensive views over both the Ribble and Calder rivers

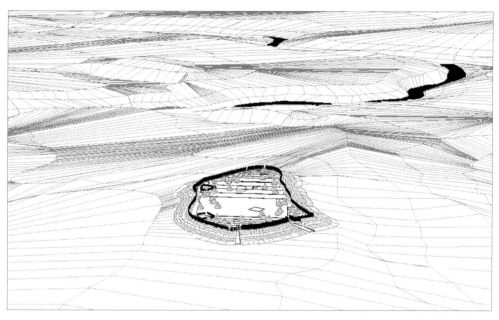

123 The promontory on which the fort is situated is relatively sheltered with a spring nearby and land suitable for mixed agriculture. The hill itself is capped by a thin boulder clay layer overlying Middle Sands

revetted in front by dry-stone walling. Outside the area, but still worthy of note is Ingleborough hillfort, which may have acted as a regional centre for an area including part of North Lancashire (Challis and Harding 1975).

124 View of the eastern side of Portfield showing natural defences. *Photograph: John Hallam*

So-called hillforts south of the Ribble are scarce and so far appear to be confined to the upland fringes of the Ribble valley, the western Pennine foothills and the central Cheshire Ridge. Possible exceptions are Hawksclough (*121*) and Dovecote on the east side of the River Lostock, Clayton-Le-Woods, both of which are possible hilltop defended settlements (Hallam 1988, 31).

Further up the Ribble valley in the western part of the Central Pennines are two hillforts, Portfield and Castercliffe. Portfield is strategically located at 121m OD on a south-facing promontory, 90m above the River Calder *c.*4km from its confluence with the River Ribble (*122*). At this point the Calder valley is at its narrowest, forming what is called the Whalley Gap, and the promontory gives access to extensive views across the floodplains of both the Ribble and Calder Rivers (*123*). In the vicinity of these confluences Late Bronze Age finds have been discovered and one certain and three possible Early Bronze Age barrows occur on the floodplain. These finds, along with others, suggest that the Whalley Gap was an important gateway in prehistoric times, as it is today, linking north-east Lancashire and the West Riding of Yorkshire with the Lancashire coast and the Irish Sea. The fort itself is relatively sheltered and would be difficult to see from the rivers.

The hillfort is 1.4ha in area and was defended by a series of earthwork ramparts which were altered and extended during the life of the site. To the west a steep natural scarp runs down to the River Calder affording a natural defence (*124*), but to the south, where the natural slope is less steep, defences had to be constructed. Enclosing the site was a continuous outer bank and ditch system within which was an inner rampart (*colour plate 20*). The rampart was up to six metres wide and faced with vertical slabs of stone, which

125 Excavations of the stone-faced rampart, Portfield hillfort. *Photograph: John Hallam*

may have been topped by a wooden palisade (Forde-Johnston 1962). The slab revetment of the inner rampart is interpreted as the earliest rampart on the site (Tyson and Bu'Lock 1957), later replaced by a clay-cored, stone-revetted rampart (*125*). The use of vertical stone slabs in these types of defences is known from other sites in the Pennines, for example in the earlier phases at Almondbury (Challis and Harding, 1975; Varley, 1976) and Ingleborough.

Excavation revealed that there were two entrances both in the northern wall with cobbled metalled surfaces. Inside the fort limited excavation revealed post and stake holes together with traces of shallow earth-filled rectilinear features associated with coarse prehistoric pottery and hearths. The pattern of postholes, together with stone packing, suggests that there had been a number of circular huts within the hillfort (*126*). Consistent with this was a find of daub. The most significant find from the site was a Late Bronze Age hoard, discussed in the previous chapter. Other finds included sherds of late prehistoric pottery confirming the dating of the site in the Late Bronze Age and Early Iron Age (Longworth 1967; Davey and Forster 1975; Beswick and Coombs 1986). Also found were a number of stone balls interpreted as sling stones by the excavator (*127*) (John Hallam pers. comm.). Sling stones might represent part of the defensive function of the fort, but this interpretation is not as straightforward as it may seem as they were found in an earlier, Neolithic, context (see earlier chapter). It may be that in a site that is much disturbed they had been redeposited amongst Neolithic material; this is certainly a possibility (John Hallam pers. comm.).

126 A series of three post holes with stone packing, Portfield Hillfort. *Photograph: John Hallam*

127 Stone balls found at Portfield Hillfort and interpreted as slingstones. *Photograph: John Hallam*

128 Intaglio of Ceres. She faces right holding a plate of fruit in her upper hand and a sheaf of corn in the other. Around her head appears to be a sombrero which should depict a diadem. The work is crude and suggests the hand of a British rather than Roman craftworker. *Photograph: John Hallam*

129 View of Castercliffe Hillfort, Lancashire. *Photograph: John Hallam*

Although the site is associated with Late Bronze Age and Early Iron Age activity there was slight evidence for occupation in the Roman period. Dr Martin Henig identified an oval intaglio measuring 18 x 13.5mm and made of glass paste dated to the second century AD (*128*). The subject is Ceres, a deity concerned with agricultural prosperity and plenty, standing to the right, holding corn ears in her right hand and a dish of fruit in her left. She wears a chiton and over it a peplos, while around her head is a diadem. The piece is poorly executed suggesting that it might be the work of a native British craftworker (Martin Henig pers. comm.).

The hillfort of Castercliffe, near Nelson, stands on a small hilltop 150m above Pendle Water, a tributary of the Calder (*129*). Like Portfield it is placed in a strategic position at the convergence of two important routes: one from the Aire Gap to the east, the other from the Huddersfield area to the south-east. The Aire Gap linked Lancashire with the populated limestone country to the north, dominated by the hillfort on the summit of Ingleborough, and the Ilkley Moor and Rombalds Moor area to the south, with what may be a defended settlement site at Horse Close Farm, to the immediate south of Skipton. The importance of the Huddersfield area is witnessed by the presence of a large hillfort at Almondbury and traces of other settlements in the vicinity.

The hilltop site measures 107 x 75m and encloses *c.*1.7ha. There is no clear evidence of an original entrance, but three defensive ramparts have been identified. Excavations produced evidence of an inner rampart 1 that is stone built with timber lacing, and an outer rampart 2 that is of the narrow timber box type with evidence of abandonment before completion (Coombs 1982). Radiocarbon dates of 510 ±70 BC and 510 ±60 BC respectively were obtained for these ramparts. There is also evidence of a free-standing palisade outside the ditch.

130 Section through Rampart 2, Castercliffe. The construction of the box rampart can be determined. Part of the continuous bedding trench is shown, terminating in a post hole (bottom left) which housed a substantial timber used to construct the box. Inside, the box was filled with rubble forming the rampart. Two layers of fill were observed: grey clay rubble above yellow clay rubble. The uppermost layer consists of a modern thin soil and turf cover. *Photograph: John Hallam*

Rampart 1 can be classed as a partly vitrified rampart (Coombs 1982). Originally it consisted of upright timbers set in two lines *c.*2m apart with a spacing of 2m and longitudinal timbers set within the framework. The bulk of the rampart was constructed from stone and earth and may have had a stone facing similar to the rampart at Portfield. At some time the timbers had been burnt causing some of the stones to shatter and the vitrification of material. Ramparts with no accompanying ditch are not an uncommon feature, especially in the hillforts of Lancashire and Cheshire where six other hillforts are also without ditches. Rampart 2 is a narrow box rampart (*130, colour plate 21*). However, when the building technique is analysed in detail it appears to be unique in this class (Coombs 1982). The commonest arrangement is to have individual postholes at the front and back of the revetment as at Ivinghoe Beacon, Buckinghamshire (Frere and Cotton 1968), and Grimthorpe, Yorkshire (Stead 1968). Castercliffe is the only fort to have continuous bedding trenches at the front and back. Where bedding trenches occur in other forts they are always placed at the front associated with individual postholes at the back: Breedon on the Hill, Leicestershire (Wacher 1964), Bindon Hill, Dorset (Wheeler 1953) and Dinorben, Denbighshire (Gardner and Savory 1964). In this respect the construction of Rampart 2 at Castercliffe can be compared with the double-palisaded enclosures of the north of England and Scotland, which also have continuous bedding trenches. Coombes (1982) argued that this comparison could be taken further in that the distance between the palisades is comparable to the distance between the revetment in the narrow box ramparts and the size of the enclosed area is often comparable to Castercliffe. If left uncovered, the timbers set into the bedding trench would have left the fort vulnerable to fire. Avery (1967) has suggested that although the timbers would have projected through the rampart the lower parts would have been covered by a turf or earth dump. This seems to have been the case at Castercliffe (Coombs 1982), where the final effect would have been of a rampart rising out of the ditch, surmounted by a timber wall formed by the projecting timbers.

An interesting point that arises from the excavation of the site is the virtual absence of cultural material, something found elsewhere in Lancashire and the surrounding area that makes any discussion regarding chronology or cultural affinity extremely difficult. The scattered distribution of the hillforts compared with other areas in England and Wales is notable, however where they do occur they form small clusters, one of which is along the northern coast of Morecambe Bay and includes Skelmore Heads, Castle Head and Warton Crag and another which consists of Portfield and Castercliffe, and focuses on the valleys of the tributaries of the River Ribble. Excavations at Castercliffe, Lancashire; Mellor, Greater Manchester; Beeston Castle, Cheshire; and Maiden Castle, Cheshire, have all produced Early to Middle Iron Age radiocarbon dates (Matthews 2002; Nevell 1999a). Radiocarbon dating suggests that the earliest sites are of a Late Bronze Age date, perhaps even before 1000 BC at Beeston Castle, and that they were abandoned during the Middle Iron Age (Nevell 1999a). Evidence for continued occupation during the Late Iron Age or at the time of the Roman conquest is weak (Matthews 2002), although there is artefactual evidence from Portfield and Mellor for a re-occupation in the later first century AD (Nevell 2001; Redhead and Roberts 2003). Excavations within hillforts have tended to concentrate on ramparts and entrances although there is evidence from Portfield, Ingleborough and Mellor that the interiors were inhabited. South of Lancashire in Cheshire at Castle Hill, Eddisbury, roundhouses with stone footings were built over the slighted ramparts, whilst interior excavations at Portfield, Mellor and Beeston have revealed post-built roundhouses.

Mellor, near Stockport, lies at the western end of a promontory c.220m OD. To the south, west and north it slopes sharply, whilst to the east it rises gently over 900m to a summit at 278m OD. The site is c.23ha in area and enclosed by two ditches. There is a deep inner defensive ditch and an outer, shallower, boundary ditch. Initially the excavators described the site as a hillfort, however as excavations continued and the extent of the site became apparent they felt it more appropriate to describe the site as a 'Hilltop Settlement'. However, the depth, indications of a palisade, and size of the area enclosed by the inner ditch suggest that it was at least partly defensive.

Within the defences were a number of roundhouses. Excavations revealed a complex system of intercutting gullies and postholes representing at least four phases of construction. Roundhouse gullies were in the region of 10–12m in diameter and entrances were oriented toward the north-west. Postholes were packed with small stones in a manner very similar to that found at Portfield, above. The excavators thought that it was quite possible that timber uprights could have been supported on pads of stone or wood or that the walls of some structures might have been entirely constructed of stone but leaving no record as they were reused during a later period. Unlike the excavations at other hillforts in Lancashire work at

Mellor has been able to address how the site may have changed through time. Archaeologists from the Greater Manchester Archaeological Unit have identified numerous changes, from domestic or industrial use, to partly enclosed and divided areas of stock control. Iron Age cooking pits were found, as were pits containing possible evidence of industrial waste dated 190–50 cal BC (Beta-209510). These hint at possible industrial processes occurring within the roundhouses or in their immediate vicinity. Two parallel lines of stake holes running up to the roundhouse gullies provided evidence for a possible fenced-off animal enclosure.

Finds from within the enclosure include sherds of Iron Age pottery, which are generally very rare in Lancashire (as in the whole of north-west England). In one instance excavations inside the hillfort recovered 125 sherds of pottery from the same handmade vessel. The fabric was light to dark brown in colour and had been smoothed on the outside to give a roughly burnished appearance. Although much of the vessel was missing, particularly around the rim and central body area, it was possible to reconstruct a basic profile of what is known as the Mellor Pot.

A total of 21 sherds of briquetage, salt-drying and transporting containers, from Cheshire, were identified in the ceramic assemblage by Dr Elaine Morris. This particular type of briquetage, originally named Stony VCP or a stone-gritted Very Coarse Pottery, is quite distinctive due to the oxidised firing condition, resulting in an orange-coloured clay matrix and the presence of large angular fragments of igneous and sedimentary rock in the fabric. Middlewich is thought likely to be the source of this Iron Age salt production given the presence of Roman salt working there. The earliest, well-dated deposits indicate that this material was not in use at the site during the Late Bronze Age but was present during the aceramic Early Iron Age. The latest use of these containers for salt transportation appears to be in the Early Roman period (Morris www.mellorarchaeology.org.uk accessed 20 March 2008). The distribution of salt in distinctive containers demonstrates the extensive networks of exchange present during the second half of the first millenium BC in Britain. Salt would have been required for a variety of preservation uses, such as in salting meat, making cheese and preserving hides. Morris suggests that there is always the possibility that its value may have been similar to a type of early currency, in the absence of coinage, and it could have been employed as a form of bridewealth amongst Iron Age tribal groups. In addition seven sherds of crucible, a possible mould fragment and a number of pieces of slag have been found on the site; these were the subject of discussion in the previous chapter. Fragments of crucible used in bronze casting have been found in some similar sites but are not common.

It is noticeable how many of these sites, together with the other fortified farmsteads mentioned below, are on the drier eastern side of the Pennine watershed, particularly on the more pliable soils of the Coal Measures. Barnes (1982, 72–83) suggested that the idea of a series of small fortified centres is probably more realistic than the picture of a line of forts which, together with Man Tor and Almondbury, supposedly defended the southern end of the Brigantian territories (Preston 1954, 18).

South of the Mersey at Beeston Castle (Ellis 1993), there is a Late Bronze Age bank, possibly timber-laced, and on-site bronze working dated to 1290–830 cal BC (2860 ±80 BP; HAR-4405). Excavations at Beeston Castle revealed evidence for an enclosure formed by a sand-dump rampart, which was probably timber-laced, with a scatter of pits and postholes representing contemporary settlement to the rear. Timber from the rampart was radiocarbon dated to 1270–830 cal BC and a deliberate deposit of two Ewart-phase socketed axes, placed 4m apart, was recovered from under the rampart (Ellis 1993, 47). A total of seven circular buildings were assigned a Late Bronze Age or Iron Age date (Ellis 1993, 39). The settlement may have been a specialist Late Bronze Age metalworking site as crucibles, moulds and refractory debris were recovered from the site and, although the evidence is equivocal, swords and ferrules seem to have been amongst the objects manufactured.

Metalwork, which has been discussed in the previous chapter, is difficult to interpret in terms of settlement distribution, consisting in the main of single finds dominated by socketed axes. In social terms, Cowell (2000b), following Ehrenberg (1989, 86) saw areas with low densities of finds and a lack of clear-cut regional types as representing a low or a less wealthy population. In addition, with the incidence of relatively few weapons, which Ehrenberg links to social elites, she suggests that social stratification may not have been as marked as in other areas. Hoards are few, although they are more frequent in the Late Bronze Age than in earlier periods in the region. The hoard at Portfield, Whalley (Longworth 1967; Davey and Forster 1975) is perhaps a smith's hoard, while that at Winmarliegh (Davey and Forster 1975) contains a proportion of weapons. The hillforts may have been associated with either the manufacture of metalwork, as in the cases of Mellor and Beeston Castle, and/or been involved in its control or consumption, as in the site at Portfield. All these locations might suggest sites associated with a social elite.

Defended hilltop sites may have lain at the head of a hierarchy of sites during this period but, if so, such a system has not yet been recognised. This may be due either to the restricted work on enclosures in the region or a lack of visibility of certain other types of Late Bronze Age permanent settlement site on the lower ground. An alternative view might see the Early Bronze Age pattern of mobility continuing into the early part of the first millennium BC. For the earlier part of the Bronze Age, patterns of flintwork distribution have been used here and elsewhere to suggest differences in land-use (Cowell 2000b). With the apparent disappearance of worked flint from the archaeology of the Late Bronze Age, it is almost impossible to identify by archaeological means a settlement pattern based on activity loci associated with an essentially mobile pattern of extensive land-use. Neither is the palaeoenvironmental record sensitive enough to identify such patterns. The beginning of the first millennium cal BC is regarded as heralding a decline in the climate in the north-west. This involved increased rainfall and a fall in temperature of $c.2°$ C, giving a summer average $c.0.5°$ C lower than that of today (Lamb 1981).

Raised bog became prevalent during the middle to later part of the first millennium cal BC (Bain 1991; Oldfield et al 1981; Godwin and Switsur 1966). It is recorded in the major lowland valleys of North Lancashire and the Mersey Basin, particularly the middle Mersey (Birks 1964), in the uplands (Bain 1991, Tallis and Switsur 1973) and in lowland inland mires such as at the Over Wyre, Simonswood and Parr Mosses, (Cowell and Innes 1994). This suggests that within a period of general climatic deterioration during the first millennium cal BC, which led to the expansion of areas of low agricultural productivity, more rapid and extreme pressure on land-use might have been encountered for several centuries around the Early to Middle Iron Age.

In the west of the county, pollen sequences from several mosses show that, in some cases for the first time, the still heavily wooded areas around these wetlands were the focus of limited but relatively concerted intensification of land-use during the early to mid first millennium cal BC, in contrast to earlier periods at the same sites. This is signified by the first relatively intense clearance of woodland associated with the first indications of arable farming at, for example, Simonswood Moss B in a Late Bronze Age/Early Iron Age context. At Parr Moss, a similar event is seen in a Late Bronze Age/Early Iron Age context. Here the significance of the clearance is only marginally greater than any comparable Early Bronze Age episode at the same site but it does include the first indications of cereal farming at this site. The Parr site may be important because it lies on the boulder clay plain of West Lancashire, which produces the traditional 'heavy' soils that had seen little exploitation in earlier prehistory. At Knowsley Park Moss, a concerted phase of activity is evident in a Late Bronze Age context, without cereals, although here there had been similar episodes in the Early Bronze Age (Cowell and Innes 1994).

At Beeston Castle, Cheshire, large amounts of charred cereals, with a possible Late Bronze Age/Early Iron Age date, were recovered from pits that might suggest storage on a scale greater than the purely domestic, possibly for redistribution (Ellis 1993, 82). There are hints that intensity in land-use may have occurred some time around the Late Bronze Age/Iron Age boundary. This may have been through maintaining clearances for longer, through larger areas being cleared, or through a greater reliance on cereals. Intensification of land-use in certain areas might be a more expected response to the deterioration of other resources than widespread abandonment of the area, as has been interpreted from the metalwork evidence.

It might be suggested that an intensification of land-use, with a greater investment in cereals could provide a context for the construction of large farmstead enclosures. Either pattern, or a combination of the two, could have existed within a context of special, fortified, possibly central-place sites, as exemplified by some hillforts. This situation echoes that of the Early Bronze Age, where burial grounds may have formed the focus for special, elite-associated activities rather than reflecting the locations of adjacent farms and fields (Cowell 2000b). In the Late Bronze Age, such practices had died out and such social distinctions may have been expressed in the growth of defended enclosures, which may have had some connections with the control of metalwork. This might be one reflection of the political and social changes that had taken place during the early part of the millennium.

EARLY IRON AGE

By the Early Iron Age, lowland settlements, different in scale and character from earlier periods, were part of the landscape. At Irby, Wirral, there are pits with probable Early Iron Age pottery, although there is no evidence that the settlement was enclosed at this time (Adams and Philpott forthcoming). At Brook House Farm, the radiocarbon dates for the enclosure ditch and for some structural activity suggest it was in existence in this form by the Middle Iron Age. There is a hint that by the Early Iron Age land-use intensification may have been underway. The intensification appeared slightly earlier in the west of the county than in the east, and the effects on the landscape are somewhat different in each area. In the eastern parts of the Mersey Basin, there are few reliably dated pollen sites, which provide only a general later first millennium cal BC estimate for trends seen in the pollen record (Howard-Davis *et al* 1988). The better dated evidence tends to suggest that intensification of land-use in the east belongs to a Middle to Late Iron Age horizon. However, when it happened it appears that the effects were more concerted than in the west. In the lowlands, at Lindow Moss, bog stratigraphy and a radiocarbon date of 790–390 cal BC (2430 ±60 BP) mark the beginning of a major phase of tree reduction, burning and cereal farming which persisted for some centuries (Oldfield *et al* 1986).

In the west, a more mixed response to intensification may have been possible, with cereals present at an earlier date. The proximity of the warm coastal waters would have allowed a slightly longer growing season and less harsh winters, while average rainfall today is less than to the east, lying as it does in the rainshadow of the Welsh mountains. In the western part of the basin, however, it is less clear what happened in the period after the approximate Early Iron Age intensification horizon. Pollen diagrams show clearance activity with some cereal evidence, but none of the sites are dated absolutely (Cowell and Innes 1994) making it difficult to identify the nature of Late Iron Age land-use here.

The environmental evidence, with less evidence for anthropogenic disturbance within the pollen record, along with a lack of identifiable sites, have led some to suggest there was a lower population density within Lancashire during the Early Iron Age, and even abandonment of the uplands (Nevell 1992a; 1999a; 2004; Wimble *et al* 2000, 28) even though localised clearance has been identified (Dunmaye 1995, 27; Wimble *et al* 2000, 27).

The poor visibility of the Iron Age in the archaeological record has meant that it has been difficult to recognise open settlements. The ones that we know are the result of accidental discoveries, for example during pipeline construction, as at Lathom and Bruen Stapleford (Nevell 2001; Matthews 2002; Cowell 2003; Fairburn *et al* 2003). There is evidence that middle Iron Age activity at Irby was set within an enclosure, but the scale of the excavations would not confirm this (Philpott and Adams 1999). While the large double-ditched curvilinear enclosures, where examined, have Iron Age origins, such as Brook House Farm, Halewood or Great Woolden Hall near to Manchester, the majority of Iron Age sites are represented by single banked or ditch enclosures, and morphology has frequently been considered as an unreliable guide to chronology (Bewley 1994, 32–34; Matthews 2002, 9). The form of the settlement is generally considered to have more to do with its function than its date. Although aerial photography has revealed several potential promontory sites in the Irwell and Roch valleys and hilltop enclosures in the uplands, it may be unsafe to date sites to this period on morphological grounds or on the basis of field-walking finds alone. The form of the middle Iron Age settlement site at Mill Hill Road, Irby, is difficult to define, but the site had a long occupation sequence dating from the Late Bronze Age to the medieval period (Philpott and Adams 1999, 66), although it may be dangerous to regard it as typical.

The lowland enclosures fall into a number of types including promontory enclosures, oval enclosures and sub-rectangular enclosures. Some are univallate and some are bivallate, and social ranking has been proposed as a factor behind this difference (Matthews 1994, 53; Nevell 1992b; 1999b; 2004). It has also been proposed that the limited variations in size of enclosures is evidence for limited social differentiation and therefore for a lack of social (and settlement) hierarchy (Nevell 1999b, 63). This has been challenged on other grounds, notably the distribution of exotic material culture, as well as site location and social formation (Matthews 2002, 33), although the restricted range of settlement types and sizes is not disputed (Nevell 2004). It has been suggested that during the Early Iron Age the smaller lowland promontory enclosures, such as Peckforton Mere or Oakmere, were closely connected with nearby hillforts in some form of settlement hierarchy (Matthews 1994, 53) although these sites remain undated. There is little information about the interior of any of these sites, and the nature, scale and duration of occupation is unclear. It might be suggested that the hillforts were home to rather larger populations than the lowland promontory enclosures, and given the close geographical association between the two types, it has been proposed that the latter may have been the residences of elites (Matthews 1994, 53; Nevell 1992b; 1999a). There are also hints that some of the single-ditched curvilinear enclosures, such as Legh Oaks I (Nevell 2003a), belong to this early period, while some open sites, such as Brookhouse Farm, Bruen Stapleford, are certainly Early Iron Age, and in this case, occupation begins during the Late Bronze Age.

LATE IRON AGE

Evidence for Late Iron Age activity in Lancashire comes mainly from the lowlands of Merseyside and Greater Manchester. The radiocarbon dates for the Great Woolden site provide a Late Iron Age/Romano-British date (50 cal BC – cal AD 80; 1990 ±25 BP; GrN-16849 and 210 cal BC – cal AD 320; 1970 ±100 BP; GrN-16850) for occupation at the site (Nevell 1988b; 1999b). The enclosure at Mellor contained a roundhouse radiocarbon dated to 520–380 cal BC, although an extensive assemblage of Romano-British finds from the inner enclosure ditch attest to continued occupation throughout the Roman Period. The Brook House Farm site was also active during the mid to Late Iron Age although the details are unclear. A pit, probably associated with an enclosure, at Rainsough, has also produced potential late first-century BC pottery (Nevell 1994b). At Tatton Park, Cheshire, although the structures are most probably associated with the Early Romano-British period, some limited activity is represented at the site dated 800–110 cal BC (2340 ±120 BP; HAR-5147) (Higham 1983; Higham and Cane 1999, 46). The multi-period site at Meols on the northern tip of the Wirral peninsula is best known as a source of unstratified material although timber structures were reported during the nineteenth century and included both rectangular and circular forms, which may be pre-Roman in date.

The most detailed evidence comes from the farmstead site at Lathom in West Lancashire. Excavation revealed four adjacent roundhouses, with the last in the sequence being associated with Romano-British pottery (Cowell and Adams 2000). The largest house had a diameter of 10.5m, with a central posthole and a double entrance on an east-to-west axis. The outer eves drip gully of the house produced radiocarbon dates of 195–5 cal BC (2090 ±40 BP; Beta 153894) and 170 cal BC to cal AD 410 (1890 ±120 BP; Beta 153893). The only Iron Age pottery from the site consisted of two rim sherds from the terminal of the gully marking the eastern entrance, which tends to support a first- or second-century BC date for the structure.

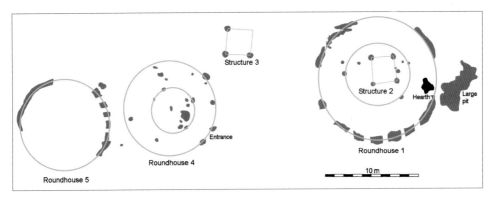

131 Roundhouse structures, Lathom, West Lancashire. *After Cowell 2001*

The earliest structure within the enclosure (structure 2, *131*) is of four posts and has been dated to the second or first century BC. A second four-post structure, 3, is also associated with the late prehistoric settlement (Cowell 2002). Four-post structures are usually associated with the storage of grain (Gent 1983) and the thick, deeply set posts are thought to have carried a raised floor perhaps to keep damp at bay. They are found on many late prehistoric and Early Romano-British sites (Musson 1991) including high-status hillforts, as well as smaller farmsteads. This is the second site to include them in the region, after an example from a double-ditched enclosure at Brook House Farm, Halewood, which was associated with Middle to Late Iron Age Cheshire Very Coarse Pottery (Cowell 2000a).

Structure 2 was probably dismantled and replaced by roundhouse 1 which was in use sometime during the period 170–5 cal BC (Beta 153893, Beta 153894) (Cowell 2002). This falls within the period covered by the use of beehive querns (Buckley 1979; Welfare 1985), one of which was found adjacent to the house made from Central Pennine Millstone Grit, probably from near Sheffield (Brooks 1999). The excavators record that the circular gully had an internal floor diameter of 10.3m, with two entrances, one on each side, on an east–west axis, with the eastern one slightly the wider; the western entrance may have had a porch attached. The size of roundhouses in Lancashire and Cheshire varies, examples range from over 11m in diameter, as at Mellor, Great Woolden Hall Farm and Brookhouse Farm, Bruen Stapleford, to 4m at Tatton Park. The dominance of south-east-facing entrances, noted on sites elsewhere in Britain is also evident in these examples (Fitzpatrick 1997, 77). The frame of the wall may have been set in the outer gully, although gullies are usually interpreted as drainage features, with the wall set several metres inside. The roundhouse 1 gully may have had posts set at *c.*2m intervals along its internal edge. Cowell felt that there was reasonable confidence that the posts could have helped support the rafters of the roof (Cowell 2002a). There was also evidence for a wattle-and-daub wall around the structure. Small fragments of daub along with hazel, willow and blackthorn charcoal were found in the gully, suggesting that some stakes may have been burnt in situ.

The rafters of the roof may also have been supported by a central post *c.*0.3m wide. This is an unusual feature in Iron Age houses, but Cowell thought that extra support was needed because of the soft sandy subsoil at this site (Cowell 2002). This might also help explain the posts on the edge of the gully, another rare feature, which acted as wall and roof

Lathom
Trench IX

132 Plan of cart ruts, Duttons Farm, Lathom, West Lancashire. *After Cowell 2002*

supports. Alternatively the central post may have supported a mezzanine floor creating a storage area in the roof (Reynolds 1979, 35–6). Within the building several small pits or postholes were excavated, some of which could have belonged to an internal ring of posts *c*.5.8m in diameter. This would have served to both help support the roof and divide the floor area into different zones, around which different kinds of activities could have been structured (Cowell 2002). Unusually, the hearth was on the edge of the floor area inside the east entrance, whilst the majority of houses of this period have hearths in their centre. Another unusual feature were two sherds of late prehistoric pottery found in the northern ditch terminal of the eastern entrance. They may represent a special deposit associated with the disuse of the house. Hints that this was in some way a special structure come from its single phase construction, *c*.40–60 years, followed by disuse during which other structures were constructed respecting its location.

The group of roundhouses to the west consisted of three secure examples and potentially a further three (Cowell 2002). The successive phases of building and rebuilding on the same spot make it difficult to conclusively identify the individual houses, 5, 6 and 7. If we assume that each house belonged to one generation this suggests a minimum of three generations of people living on this spot. To the west of the site there is evidence for an agricultural landscape associated with the farmstead. This consists of a number of trackways and field boundaries (*132*). The trackways consist of short lengths of hollows, many of them with distinctive linear depressions between *c*.0.3m and 0.6m wide, running along the base, interpreted as the ruts left by carts, for example at the locations numbered 422, 449 and 437 on the plan. The tracks run diagonally converging on a boggy area, 483, where they have not been preserved. A number of cropmark sites in the Mersey Basin show some evidence for field systems associated with rectilinear enclosures. What little excavation there has been of these enclosures (Philpott *et al* 1993; ch. 4) suggests that these are Romano-British. This is broadly consistent with the pollen evidence for the wider North West, which demonstrates a major increase in clearance and in cereal pollen by the Romano-British period.

The evidence suggests that animal husbandry dominated the economy of Lancashire in the late prehistoric period. This is largely interpreted from the climatic evidence, with annual precipitation well over the preferred rate for barley and wheat (Haselgrove 1996). Although it has been argued that potential cereal farming in the west was a feature at the beginning of this period, it does not appear to have been on a large scale, nor was it accompanied by large-scale woodland clearance. Animals were being butchered on the site at Brook House Farm from the Middle Iron Age. The heavily wooded nature of the landscape around the site is surprising but it may be that the banks of the ditch were heavily wooded therefore screening the pollen catchment area from pollen beyond, which might be expected to have included cleared land. The east–west boundary ditch between the two enclosure circuits continued beyond the enclosure, where it may have functioned as part of a field system or droveway. Such field systems have not been identified for Iron Age sites yet. From the little evidence there is, it is tentatively suggested that the Brook House Farm example was in use by the end of the first millennium cal BC.

The Great Woolden enclosure is very similar in form to that at Brook House Farm, being double-ditched, although the area between the ditches is about a third less and it is the outer ditch which seems the more substantial (Nevell 1988b; 1999a). The original size of the Brook House Farm enclosure might have covered a little over 1.5ha compared to a slightly smaller area at Great Woolden. It might be suggested that for these types of site there was a large investment in stock, with the area between the two ditch circuits being used to corral cattle. One possibility is that in the Mersey-Dee area, in broad terms at least, there was a functional change over time away from bivallate curvilinear enclosures. This might be associated with a decline in the importance of herding livestock and a greater emphasis on arable farming, which tended to employ rectilinear enclosures (Philpott in Cowell and Philpott 2000). If it is correct to see the space between widely set ditches as intended for corralling, sorting and penning livestock close to the farmstead, a change in farming practice may account for the reduction in size of enclosure boundaries. A shift from a largely pastoral to arable economy might have reduced the need for corralling large herds at the farmstead itself. On the other hand, the change may reflect the breakdown of a tribal or clan system of herding, where communal herds or flocks were held and sorted collectively at important local centres. This may have been replaced by a landholding pattern of smaller land units farmed from a larger number of individual settlements, to each of which separate herds were attached. The larger double-ditched enclosures were constructed with slighter boundaries adequate to contain smaller herds (Philpott in Cowell and Philpott 2000).

It is argued that some upland hillforts, including Castercliffe, Lancashire, went out of use about the beginning of the Middle Iron Age, in accordance with the climatic deterioration of

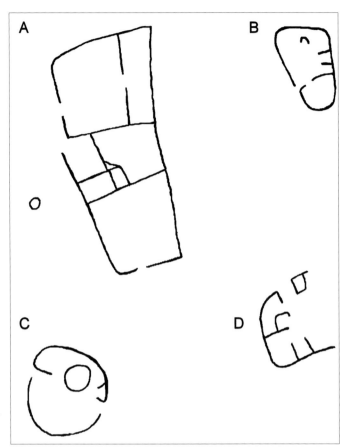

133 Iron Age sites in the Lune valley, near Kirkby Lonsdale. A) Eller Beck C. B) Eller Beck D. C) Borrans. D) Eller Beck E. *After Haselgrove 1996*

this period (Nevell 1992a, 50). Beeston Castle, however, continued to play a role in the Iron Age landscape being fortified with ramparts in the Middle to Late Iron Age (Ellis 1993, 89). It is part of a string of defended hill top settlements, which lie along the central Cheshire ridge, although none of these are adequately dated.

In North Lancashire known non-hillfort settlement sites of Iron Age date are at present rare, perhaps because pasture, which dominates the land-use, is not conducive to revealing sites by aerial photography. Where aerial photography is possible sites do occur, the best known of which is Eller Beck in the Lune valley (Lowndes 1964). This site has been interpreted as an Iron Age settlement with subsequent Roman occupation (Marriott 1991, 9). Settlement consists of rectangular, sub-rectangular, circular and oval settlements (*133*). Also present are unenclosed hut circles (Marriott 1991, 16–18). The curvilinear site of Castle Hill, Leck (*colour plate 22*) is undated but has counterparts east of the Pennines, for example at Cockfield Fell, County Durham, which would normally be ascribed an Iron Age date (Haselgrove 1996, 65).

In the whole of Lancashire, Iron Age metalwork finds are very small in number, with only about six or seven items in all, mostly bronze, having been recovered. A bronze dagger sheath was found at Pilling Moss (*134*), at Manchester a small bronze ox-head ornament was found, and on the hill slopes north of Littleborough at Mowroad a heavy, beaded torque necklace

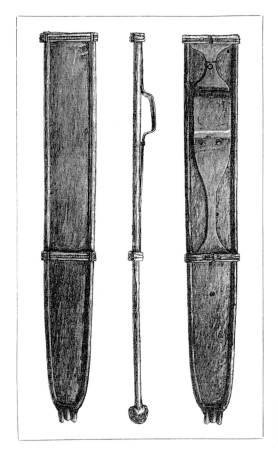

134 Bronze dagger or sword sheath found in Pilling Moss in 1859. It was said to have been found 'in deep clay under the bog' at Hackensall measuring 30 x 4.5cm

with iron securing pins was unearthed early in the nineteenth century. Just inside the Lancashire boundary on Blackstone Edge, to the east of Littleborough, an iron spearhead was found in close proximity to an ox's horn. Further north, near the River Ribble at Billington, iron spearheads were uncovered in a tumulus: this is the only suggestion so far of an Iron Age burial in the Central Pennine area. Evidence for metalwork production in the Iron Age is limited to excavations at Mellor hillfort already discussed.

Among the other items, a fine shale armlet was found on Flint Hill just to the east of Blackstone Edge, which closely resembles the Kimmeridge shale armlets found at Glastonbury (Bulleid 1968, Plate XIV, 9); fragments of another armlet were found on Snoddle Hill near Littleborough in the same area and these too may be of Iron Age date, while parts of a similar Kimmeridge shale armlet were discovered south of our area in Harborough Cave in the Peak District (Jackson 1929–31). The thinly scattered nature of these Iron Age artefacts bears a close relationship to the major river valleys of the eastern flanks of the hills, and there is also a minor cluster in the Littleborough–Blackstone Edge area, a district subsequently crossed by a Roman road.

In the uplands, heather and sphagnum moss spread during the Iron Age, gradually reducing the area available for summer pasture, while a decline in temperature and increase in rainfall would also have steadily reduced the upper limit for cereal cultivation up to the second century cal BC (Nevell 1992a). A number of upland sites, however, show a similar pattern of concerted vegetation changes from approximately the Middle Iron Age into the Romano-British period. At Rishworth Moor, near Oldham, substantial woodland reduction occurs between 800–21 cal BC (2420 ±100 BP; GaK-2824) and 100 cal BC – cal AD 320 (1920 ±80 BP; GaK-2825) (Bartley 1975). Deep Clough in Rossendale, at 340m OD, has substantial clearance from c.350 BC to AD 290 (c.2220–1750 BP) (Tallis and McGuire 1972; Nevell 1992a, 52). At Featherbed Moss in the southern Pennines, the same is found between 400 and 170 cal BC (2251 ±50 BP; Q-854) and from 170 cal BC to cal AD 80 (2028 ±50 BP; Q-853) (Tallis and Switsur 1973).

It is perhaps a little unsafe to try to interpret the pattern of clearance in the vicinity of these upland sites from the pollen record alone, but it seems that natural conditions would not have favoured cereal farming in many areas during the middle to later part of the millennium. The upland sites mentioned above show that cereal farming may have become a feature only late in the sequence, i.e. Towards the end of the Iron Age or in the Romano-British period. One reason may be a growth in the demand for cereals in the Roman period to feed the army. Temperatures improved after c.150 cal BC (Lamb 1981) and perhaps facilitated such a development.

The larger hillforts, such as Ingleboroguh in the north, Almondbury on the Yorkshire side of the Central Pennines and Eddisbury and Kelsbarrow in Cheshire, are of a size and form to suggest they may have functioned as tribal centres, with an assumption that they are at the head of a settlement hierarchy. Matthews (1994) suggests that some of the defended hill sites may have acted as central places for the redistribution of goods. Jones and Moss (in Ellis 1993, 82) make the tentative suggestion that Beeston may have had a cereal surplus on the site which could have been used for such a purpose, although the dating is no more precise than the pre-Romano-British period and could even be Late Bronze Age. The areas north and south of the Mersey, including North Wales, are different in character in relation to the presence of defended hill-enclosures. Large areas of the lowlands between the Ribble and the Mersey are distant from such sites. The Mersey appears to have marked the boundary between the late prehistoric tribes of the Brigantes to the north and the Cornovii to the south, while the Deceangli lay to the south-west of the Dee. Direct social or political influence from hillforts in the latter areas, therefore, might be assumed to have been minimal on settlements in the area north of the Mersey.

Embanked enclosures exist on land above c.60m OD at Woolton in Liverpool (Forde-Johnston 1962), at Werneth Low in Manchester (Nevell 1992a, 51–2; 1992b) and Walmersley, Bury (Fletcher 1986), the latter two at 240m and c.100m OD respectively. However, they are very poorly understood and cannot really contribute to the debate at the moment. In the area north of the Mersey other types of site in different topographical positions perhaps represent the higher status sites. It has been suggested (Matthews 1997) that in the north-west livestock may have been more than of purely economic importance and that they could have been indicators of prestige. The form of Brook House Farm may have been dictated by animal husbandry, however the deep inner enclosure ditch appears too large for a purely stock management function. The size of the ditch and the area of the enclosure at c.1.5ha is comparable to many of the Cheshire or Lancashire hillforts. This site, and by analogy Great Woolden, may have exerted a similar influence in the lowlands to some of the defended hill enclosures elsewhere in the region. If so, the lower-status fixed settlements of the Iron Age in the region still have to be found. Until more work has been done it cannot be clear to what extent this is an archaeological visibility problem. The class of curvilinear cropmark recognised in the region (Nevell 1988a; Collens 1994; Philpott in Cowell and Philpott 2000) may represent such a type of site.

Material evidence of a native elite is hard to find in the north-west. So far, there is only one possible instance of elite goods of Roman type of this period at a settlement, in the shape of an unstratified pottery assemblage at an earthwork site at Rainsough, Greater Manchester. There are some reservations over the origin of the material, which includes eight first-century vessels including a *terra nigra* bowl and a bowl of Gallo-Belgic type (Nevell 1994b, 14). This could imply some contact between a native elite in the north and either Romanised or Roman groups in the south of England, even if the mechanisms for such an exchange are unclear (Philpott in Cowell and Philpott 2000). Meols, south Wirral, may have been associated with this kind of exchange. It was probably a centre of organised trade in the Late Iron Age and the presence of Armorican coins has been seen as indicative either of the presence of foreign traders there or of the trade in curios (Matthews 1996, 19–20).

All the above-mentioned sites, except for Tatton Park and Meols, have Cheshire Very Coarse Pottery (VCP) as their almost exclusive form of pottery. Other types of pottery are rare. There is some probable Early Iron Age material from Irby (Woodward in Adams and Philpott forthcoming) and a few sherds of potentially imported ware from Beeston Castle (Royle and Woodward in Ellis 1993, 74), while Great Woolden has two Gallo-Belgic forms (Nevell 1994a). Otherwise the most significant find of a domestic ware was that from Mellor mentioned above where sherds of VCP was also excavated, representing the northernmost distribution of this fabric so far found. Cheshire VCP has been linked to the drying and transportation of salt throughout the region in the second half of the first millennium BC, potentially from brine springs in the area around Northwich, Middlewich and Nantwich. Brook House Farm, along with Great Woolden Hall *c.*20 km to the east, and Mellor in the Pennines identifies the northern end of its distribution pattern, which reaches as far south as Hereford and Worcestershire and as far east as Leicestershire (Morris 1985). During the Middle Iron Age, it has been suggested that sites in the Mersey Basin may have been largely aceramic except for the use of the VCP (Royle and Woodward in Ellis 1993, 74).

The three major Iron Age lowland settlement sites in the region, Irby, Great Woolden and Brook House Farm, were all occupied during the Romano-British period. The other sites have more evidence than Brook House Farm, where the phase 4 structure, and possibly either the phase 5B arrangement of postholes or the undated post-built rectilinear Structure 1 of phase 5C, represent the Romano-British occupation. It is interesting to speculate whether in the Romano-British period these sites retained a different status in relation to the new settlements that were created in the late first and early second century AD, based on their ancestry.

There is some limited evidence of a break in the Late Iron Age at Brook House Farm. Such evidence is slight at the moment and even if it were more convincing, there might be many reasons for abandonment.

TRIBES

The overall picture in the Iron Age is one of a society living in relatively small, dispersed settlements with little evidence for non-organic material culture. This in turn has been taken as evidence for a relatively shallow settlement hierarchy, perhaps reflecting an egalitarian society (Nevell 1992a; 1999a). Although this view has been challenged as an over-simplified interpretation of the evidence (Haselgrove 1996, 69; Matthews 2002) despite 20 years of active research, the region remains characterised by a lack of large settlement sites and an absence of extensive ceramic assemblages (Hodgson and Brennand 2006).

Lancashire, along with Cumbria lies within the so-called territory of the Brigantes, while Cheshire has been presumed to be part of the territory of the Cornovii. However, evidence for the extent of Cornovian territory is late second century AD and refers to Romano-British, not Iron Age, administrative arrangements. There is no evidence that a people known as the Cornovii even existed during the Iron Age (Wigley 2001, 9). Likewise, the probable late first-century source used by the historian Ptolemy in compiling his *Geography* implies that Cumbria and Lancashire belonged to the Brigantes, but we cannot know whether this territorial arrangement was ancient or an innovation of Roman provincial government. Three tribes in northern England seem to have been favoured by the Romans, the Brigantes, Parisi and Carvetii, resulting in their formation into *civitatas* (Shotter 2004, 5). The Brigantes, a name that refers either to 'upland locations' or to 'overlordship', suggests a possible Pennine location (Shotter 2004, 2). They are generally associated with the whole of northern England during the Roman period and were described by the historian Tacitus as 'the most populous in Britain' suggesting that to some extent the Roman administration created a 'Greater Brigantia' which subsumed a number of smaller tribes, including the Carvetii and, outside our area in East Yorkshire, the Parisi. The Carvetii territory extended from at least the Solway Plain in the north through the Eden valley to perhaps as far south as the Lune valley.

Ptolemy also refers to a site named *Portus Setantiorum*, 'Harbour of the Setantii', in the north-west of England. There are several possible locations for the port according to Shotter (2004, 6–7). These range from the Mersey in the south, to the north coast of Morecambe Bay. Shotter seems to favour a location on the coast at the southern end of Lake Windermere. He argues that the existence of the hillforts at Skelmore Heads, Castle Head and Warton Crag suggest that this had been an important area in the pre-Roman Iron Age compatible with an important trading port. Whilst this is true there is no direct archaeological evidence to link the hillforts to a port. There has been a long-held local tradition that the *Portus Setantiorum*, now lost to coastal erosion, was located near the mouth of the River Wyre at Fleetwood (Harris and Hughes 2005, 64–70). Over the years a number of stray finds of pre-Roman date (22 BC) and Roman coins have been found in the town, including a hoard of 400 denarii discovered in a brickfield near to Rossall Point. During the construction of the seawall

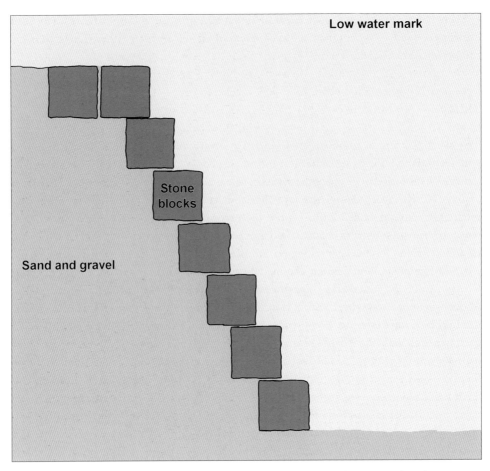

Low water mark

Stone blocks

Sand and gravel

135 Illustration of a submerged wall found off the coast of Fleetwood. *After Harris and Hughes 2005*

workmen uncovered, beneath wind-blown sand, what appeared to be a Roman road heading out under Morecambe Bay (Porter 1876). In the same general area farmers had been reported removing the foundations of several large buildings, which had hindered the cultivation of their fields (Thornber 1837). Archaeologically a possible harbour wall about 4.5m high and at least 12m long, faced with dressed stone blocks measuring 60cm square was recorded by divers 60cm below the surface of the sea at low tide off the coast of Fleetwood (*135*; Robert Long pers. comm. in Harris and Hughes 2005, 69). Further investigation is required to ascertain the date of this structure without which a Roman provenance cannot be claimed. It does, however, keep open the possibility that the tradition of a Roman port off the modern coast of Fleetwood bears some truth.

The name *Seteia* appears to have been linked to the River Mersey, which is believed to have formed the boundary between the Cornovii in Cheshire and another tribe to the north that may have been the Setantii. If this is correct then the Setantii may have occupied the area of Lancashire from the Mersey up perhaps as far as the Lune where they met with the Carvetii in North Lancashire. To the east the territory may have extended into the Pennines where they met with the Brigantes, whose name as has already been noted may refer to 'upland locations', but who may also have assumed 'overlordship' of the Setantii and Carvetii during, and perhaps with the assistance of, Roman rule. It is noteworthy that the possible boundaries for the Setantii territory are all locations marked by the presence of hillforts, in the north by the line running along the north coast of Morecambe Bay to Warton Crag and into North Yorkshire, and by those running down the Central Pennines such as Castercliffe, Portfield and Castle Hill at Almondbury. Finally numerous hillforts are known in Cheshire whilst there was a possible hillfort in Liverpool.

In Ireland it has been argued that so-called 'bog bodies', the remains of victims killed in circumstances that have suggested some sort of ritual sacrifice, were often placed on tribal boundaries (Kelly pers. comm.). Eammon Kelly noted 40 locations in Ireland where bog bodies were found in proximity to important boundaries, mainly barony boundaries. Furthermore, he found that most of the provenanced metalwork of the later prehistoric period found in Irish bogs was deposited in close proximity to important boundaries, especially barony boundaries, but also including parish boundaries. In Lancashire a number of bog burials have been recorded in the wetlands and rivers, these are discussed more fully below. For the present purposes it is noteworthy that bodies have been found in bogs and mosses that may have formed the boundary of the Setantii territory. Heads found at Pilling in the Over Wyre District, Briarfield near Poulton-le-Fylde and at Birkdale near to Southport may all mark out the coastal limit of the territory, whilst those found around Manchester at Red Moss, Ashton Moss and Lindow Moss may mark an inhospitable liminal area between the Setantii and the Cornovii territory that is marked elsewhere by the River Mersey. If that is the case the deposits of metalwork discussed in the previous chapter that were placed in similar locations may suggest the origin of tribal affiliations lays in the Middle and Late Bronze Age when people first came together in order to participate in acts of ritual affiliation.

BURIAL EVIDENCE

Substantial areas of the north of the region appear to have been cleared, and were grazed by stock or cultivated with cereals prior to the arrival of the Roman military. There are likely to have been both enclosed and unenclosed settlements as identified in South Lancashire and Cheshire, but few large and strongly defended sites. Metalwork is relatively rare although horse fittings have been found at Grange-over-Sands and Walton-Le-Dale and fine gold metalwork is present in the hoard from Portfield hillfort. Evidence for burial or funerary practice is extremely rare. At Butts Beck Quarry, Dalton-in-Furness a Late Bronze Age 'warrior' burial was found in 1873 (Gaythorpe 1899, 161, 164–166). A stone cist *c*.1.8 x 1.2 x 1.2m was found to contain a single adult inhumation together with the bones of a horse and an assemblage of weapons. The latter included a sword which had been deliberately bent in the middle and a peg-socketed leaf-shaped spear.

An Iron Age inhumation cemetery was excavated at Nelson Square, Levens in what is now Cumbria but was formerly North Lancashire (Parsons 2004; Rachel Newman pers.

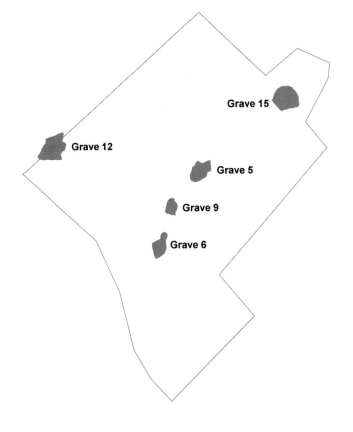

136 Late Iron Age
inhumation cemetery,
Nelson Square, Levens.
After Parsons 2004

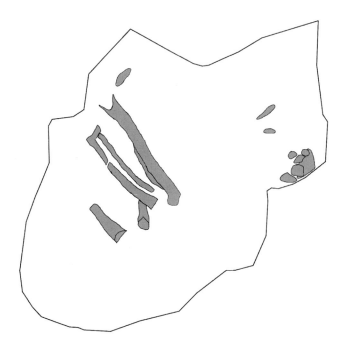

137 Late Iron Age burial.
Grave 5, Nelson Square,
Levens. *After Parsons 2004*

comm.). An area of 140 square metres was stripped of topsoil revealing five Late Iron Age graves containing five, or possibly six, inhumation burials, all cutting into the limestone bedrock (*136*). Grave 5 measured 1.35 x 0.85m, with the long axis aligned north-east to south-west (*137*). A skeleton was found within the grave in a crouched position lying on its left side. Grave 6 measured 1.35 x 0.76m, was hourglass in shape and aligned north to south. An inhumation lay in a semi-crouched position on its left side. Grave 9 measured 0.85 x 0.55m aligned north to south. The skeleton was poorly preserved. Grave 12 measured 1.06 x 1.77m aligned north-east to south-west. The skeleton was again poorly preserved. Grave 15 measured 1.1 x 1.15m and irregular in shape, it contained the mandible from a second skeleton and there is a possibility given the 'unnatural' placing of the limb bones of the main interment that they had been disarticulated prior to burial (Parsons 2004, 17). No dateable finds were recovered from the graves but radiocarbon assay of Grave 5 skeletal material placed the burial in the Late Iron Age at 172–44 cal BC (2089 ±24 BP, KIA-24385).

Inhumation cemeteries of Iron Age date are very rare in Britain with only *c.*30 examples recorded in England, the majority of which are in Cornwall and Dorset (English Heritage 1990). They first appear in the fourth century BC, in the Middle Iron Age, and continue into the Roman period. Most articulated inhumations occur as isolated burials within pits and ditches, as in the case of the Butts Beck Quarry burial. Nelson Square is an exception to this and has parallels with the larger cemetery at Worton Rectory Farm, Yarnton in Oxfordshire, where nine of the 35 crouched, north to south orientated burials were radiocarbon dated to the Middle Iron Age (Hey *et al* 1999). Most prehistoric inhumation cemeteries have been located on relatively low-lying land, the majority under 120m OD, and many are near to rivers, with Iron Age examples showing a preference for burial in a crouched position with the head to the north. The Nelson Square site fits this trend as it lies at approximately 45m OD and overlooks the Rivers Kent and Gilpin (Parsons 2004). Where bone preservation was sufficient to establish orientation and position, all the burials were crouched with the head to the north. Tightly crouched burials, often suggestive of the binding of the corpse after death, are a common feature in the treatment of the corpse in the prehistoric periods. Iron Age regional variations in funerary rituals, such as the Arras culture and Durotrigan warrior burials, also predominantly involve positioning the corpse on its side in a crouched position (Taylor 2001, 73–5), as do most Iron Age pit burials (Cunliffe 1978, 312; Whimster 1981, 211; Wait 1985, 83). The rather unnatural positioning of skeleton in grave 15 and the presence of the mandible of another individual within the same grave are suggestive of excarnation before burial (Parsons 2004, 28). These 'bag' or 'sack' burials, where largely disarticulated bones were interred, are known from other Iron Age sites, such as that at Fengate, Peterborough (Pryor 1991, 369).

Beyond Nelson Square the evidence for burial in the Iron Age consists of so-called bog bodies and heads, the most well known of which is a body found at Lindow Moss, south of Manchester (Stead *et al* 1986). Lindow Man probably died during the first century AD. The careful manicuring of his fingernails would be consistent with this date, since toilet sets are frequent finds in Iron Age settlements and burials in southern England. On the Fylde Coast the head of a man aged *c.*25–35 years was found at Briarfield close to Poulton-Le-Fylde (Wells and Hodgkinson 2001). The skull was dated to the Late Bronze Age, 1260–840 cal BC

(2845 ±65, AA-28733). To the north of the find, *c.* 10km away, the head of a woman with long plaited auburn hair was found in Pilling Moss in the Over Wyre District in 1864 (Edwards 1969; Middleton *et al* 1995, 66). The head was reportedly wrapped in a piece of coarse woollen cloth and with it were two strings of cylindrical jet beads, with one string having a large amber bead at the centre. The association with jet beads suggested that it should be dated to the Early Bronze Age (Edwards 1969), although there is no independent evidence for this date. Other finds of female heads come from Red Moss, Bolton, again with plaited hair, but undated (Hall *et al* 1995, 86) and from Lindow Moss dated to the early centuries AD. A female head with a large hole in the back of the skull was amongst 23 heads found in the River Ribble (Gonzalez and Cowell forthcoming). The head was dated to the Neolithic, 3110–2900 cal BC (4370 ±45 BP, OxA-71416). A number of heads, *c.*23, were found in the River Ribble during the excavation of Preston Docks (Dickson 1888). Other artefacts found included wooden dug-out canoes and a possible brushwood platform. In a study undertaken by Silvia Gonzalez she found that some skulls showed signs of violence including cut marks and holes, particularly on the back of the skull, suggesting a violent death and the possibility of deliberate decapitation. Dates for the skulls show that they were not all deposited at the same time. Five of the human crania were Neolithic, one was Bronze Age 1780–1600 cal BC (3380 ±40 BP, OxA-71418), one Late Iron Age or Romano British 60 cal BC – cal AD 130 (1980 ±40, OxA-9291) and one Saxon cal AD 680–890 (1244 ±30 BP, OxA-9292). The heads do not show the sort of damage that would have been caused if they had been transported large distances by the river, suggesting that they had been placed in the river near to Preston after decapitation. Six of the heads examined bore evidence of trauma, three with perforations, one a depressed fracture and four cut marks (Gonzalez and Cowell forthcoming). Another dated head burial from Worsley, Greater Manchester (Hall *et al* 1995, 19) indicated a Late Iron Age to Romano British date cal AD 66–400 (1800 ±70 BP, Garland 1987; 1995; Turner 1995, 13). Little is known about the context of heads found at Birkdale, near Southport, in the late nineteenth century (Busk 1874), but more may be said about a male skull found at Ashton Moss, Tameside (Duckworth and Shore 1911; Nevell 1992a). The Ashton Moss example has close parallels with the Briarfield find (Wells and Hodgkinson 2001, 170). In both cases death had occurred before the age of 50 and both date to the Late Bronze Age, the Ashton Moss head dating to *c.*1320–980 cal BC (2950 ±60 BP, Beta-97721; Robinson and Shimwell 1996).

Deposition of bodies, and of heads in particular, belong to a wider northern European tradition of disposing of the dead in wet places. The tradition seems to be long lived, spanning several millennia from the Neolithic to the early historic period, the height of which was during the first millennia BC and AD, suggesting that the severed head represents a discrete category of bog deposit, which appears to be particularly well represented in Lancashire (Stead *et al* 1986). Further evidence for a possible 'Cult of the Head' comes from a number of carved stone heads that have been recorded, in which a stone head perhaps substitutes for the real thing. Given the difficulties in dating heads, many of which were found in disturbed contexts, it is uncertain how many examples of Iron Age date occur in Lancashire. In the north of the county at Lancaster a stone head with characteristic Celtic moustache was found at De Vitre Street (*138*). At Preston a stone head in the Harris Museum, Preston, bears a label stating that it was found in the River Ribble, perhaps emulating the practice of placing human

138 Celtic stone head with distinctive moustache found at De Vitre Street, Lancaster

heads in rivers and bogs. Another, found in a field at Hollinshead Hall, Tockholes near Blackburn is unusually large, standing about 1m tall and made of local gritstone (Hallam pers. comm.). The only mention of a stone head from Lancashire in Anne Ross' survey (1967) was found at the site of the Roman fort in Hulme, Manchester and seems to reflect the Iron Age tradition (*139*). The features, treatment of the hair and general appearance combined with its find context suggest an Iron Age or Romano-British date. Another stone, which consisted of a stone pillar engraved with three human faces, was described by Thompson Watkin as having been found in 'Roman Lancashire' (Watkin 1883, 98). To the south-west of the county a 'Celtic' carved head was found near Lydiate and another similar statue possibly of Iron Age origin was found at Blundellsands.

Human skulls have been found in bogs and rivers in other parts of Britain, with several hundred having come from the River Thames, and have usually been understood to be physical evidence of ritual activity, although the exact nature of this has been poorly

139 Stone head found at Hulme, Manchester. The head is now lost. *Anne Ross 1967*

understood (Bradley and Gordon 1988; Knüsel and Carr 1995; 1996). Although care must be taken when reading classical texts, they are of assistance in forming an understanding of the cult of the head. Strabo described the activity, basing his account on the writing of Poseidonius who visited southern Gaul in *c.*90 BC and appears to have witnessed the act:

> In addition to their witlessness they [the Celts] possess a trait of barbarous savagery which is especially peculiar to the northern peoples, for when they leave the battlefield they fasten to the necks of their horses the heads of their enemies, and on arriving home they nail up this spectacle at the entrances to their houses … they embalmed the heads of distinguished enemies with cedar oil, and used to make a display of them to strangers, and were unwilling to let them be redeemed even for their weight in gold.
>
> Strabo *Geographia* IV, 4, 5; trans. Tierney 1960

The head was clearly thought to hold particular symbolic importance and the deposition of bodies has been linked with ritual and ceremonial activity, which included sacrificial killing and the ultimate deposition of heads or whole bodies in bogs and rivers. In this regard the association of bog burials with hazel may be significant. Following Wells and Hodgkinson (2001, 170) the Briarfield head was found with abundant remains of hazel; the last meal of Lindow Man had also included hazelnuts (Holden 1995); whilst in Cumbria a body found at Seascale Moss was associated with a hazel 'walking stick' (Turner 1989; 1995, 113, 209). Aldhouse Green has reported similar associations in Denmark and Ireland and links the practice to an East Anglian lead curse tablet that describes sacrifice to the water god Neptune (Aldhouse Green 1998a; 1998b).

Strabo's text refers to an observation in Gaul not Britain, but there is archaeological evidence from this country consistent with the curation of heads (Ralph 2007, 305–12). At the Late Bronze Age and Early Iron Age settlement of All Cannings Cross in Wiltshire, Cunnington (1923, 40) interpreted the dispersed remains of 32 skull fragments in a midden deposit as evidence of head hunting. A decapitated individual was excavated at Stanwick, Yorkshire, (Wheeler 1954) whilst a re-analysis of human remains from Danebury revealed the presence of weapon-related injuries, suggesting that the remains were the result of violent deaths and the exhibition of the dead (Craig *et al* 2005). Sarah Ralph argued that it is conceivable that some part of the soul, essence or spirit of a deceased individual can be captured by the removal and retention of the head. If this is so it may explain why the Briarfield head was apparently deposited in a defleshed state without the mandible (Wells and Hodgkinson 2001, 169). Four defleshed skulls, all male and dating to the Late Bronze Age, were recovered from the Thames (Bradley and Gordon 1988). These finds suggest that excarnation had taken place and I think it is possible that they had been curated for a period of time before they had been deposited. The separation of the mandible may have been deliberate given the find at Nelson Square, and suggests that it represented a battle trophy embued with symbolic meaning. This meaning is described by Jacobsthal:

> Amongst the Celts the human head was venerated above all else, since the head was to the Celt the soul, centre of the emotions as well as of life itself, a symbol of divinity and of the power of the other-world.
>
> Jacobsthal 1944

This goes some way to understanding the deposition of heads. The appropriation of the head would therefore hinder or prevent the incorporation of the deceased into the spirit world or realm of ancestors. As such decapitation could be a final punishment. Possession of the head may also act to transfer control or ownership of the deceased's spiritual force from one person to another, perhaps protecting the possessor (Ralph 2007, 310).

CONCLUSION

The perceived lack of artefacts within the Iron Age archaeological record of Lancashire has often been interpreted as evidence of an impoverished culture, whilst the lack of an extensive settlement hierarchy has led to reconstructions of a society with little social stratification. However, the small number of high-status and traded artefacts may suggest this is an oversimplification, at least in parts of the county. Although the archaeological remains do not directly relate to the economy of Iron Age people, they do suggest an emphasis on pastoral activities with some arable agriculture. In the lowlands preserved footprints of cattle have been found in horizons dated to the Iron Age on the beach at Formby whilst the horn cores of *Bos longifrons*, the so-called 'Celtic shorthorn', have been found from time to time within the upland peats as at Cowpe, near Waterfoot in Rossendale, and on the site of the Ashworth Reservoir, north of Heywood (Baldwin 1903, 109).

Two hillforts west of the Pennines occur in the vicinity of the River Ribble. It was argued by Barnes (1982, 81) that it was in this area that the traditional concept of Iron Age pastoralism would be fulfilled, supplemented by small scale cereal cultivation. The general picture in the Central Pennines at the later Bronze Age/Iron Age transition period was one of small communities of herders moving their livestock between summer and winter pastures. On the lowlands of West Lancashire a number of settlements have emerged during the last ten years suggesting that the area was more densely populated than had been thought even as recently as the 1980s (Barnes 1982, 81). The economy like that of the uplands seems to have been based on pastoralism to the extent that cattle may have been the common currency locally (Matthews 1997). It was during this period that fully fledged tribal systems emerged. References, dated to the Roman period, giving the names of tribes require archaeological evidence to confirm their relevance to Iron Age political organisation and other aspects of regional cultural identity. Nonetheless they hint at the possible division and affiliation of the county's population. Those living in the Pennines, the Brigantian heartland, may have had more in common with their neighbours living in the uplands of West Yorkshire than with the population inhabiting the coastal lowlands who formed the Setantii.

CHAPTER 8

CONCLUSION:
THE PREHISTORIC LEGACY

PREHISTORY IN THE PAST

The earthworks and monuments constructed during the Late Neolithic and Bronze Age periods became fixtures in the landscape of future generations. Many of the monuments remained visible from the time of their construction to the recent present, and some are even visible to this day. As a result, over the millennia they have variously attracted veneration, fear and curiosity. The study of the life-histories of monuments, how monuments were reused by future generations, is the subject of academic debate and discussion (Kopytoff 1986; Thomas 1996; Tilley 1996; Jones 2002). Cornelius Holtorf has persuasively argued that life-histories relate not only to prehistoric monuments and landscapes, but also to objects (Holtorf 2005, 80; Holtorf 2002). The point he makes is that 'the meanings of archaeological sites and artefacts have always been changing and cannot be fixed' (Holtorf 2005, 80). Life-histories therefore trace the history of cultural memories and *Geschichtskulturen*. The latter is Rüsen's notion of history, which may be translated as the 'culture of history' (Rüsen 1994). The implication of this approach for our study of the prehistoric archaeology of Lancashire is that history not only includes what really happened in the past, but also how it is remembered, perceived and even how it is imagined.

In Chapter 6 the role of bronze metalwork in Late Bronze Age society was considered. The practice of ritual deposition in wet places was discussed and conclusions concerning the life-cycle of metalwork presented. From the perspective adopted here the life histories of these objects does not end with deposition but continues until the present day. The discovery, recovery, analysis, interpretation, archiving, exhibiting and storage are also part of the life of the artefact (Holtorf 2005, 80). For most of Lancashire's metalwork their histories of discovery are uneventful, often emerging as the result of plough action or metal detection. But for a small number the circumstances of their discovery hint at events during their long lives that say something about the attitudes of past people toward prehistoric objects.

A palstave was found in Chester. A label on the axe states that it was found within the Priory wall, Northgate Street, in 1840. The find was unusual not just because it was found in a medieval context, overlying earlier Roman occupation, but also because it was of a north

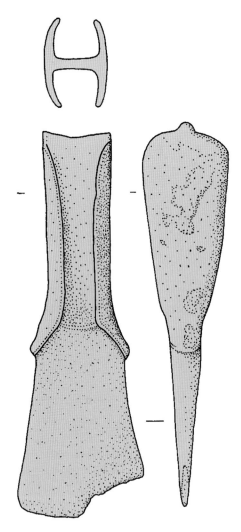

140 North Italian type palstave found in Northgate Street, Chester, in 1840. *Davey and Forster 1975, No 168*

Italian type (*140*). No other examples of this type of palstave are known from the north-west of England. The combination of its location, and its origin, in Italy, suggest that a member of the Roman military may have brought it to Chester. If so it is putative evidence of a classical awareness and interest in prehistory. We may only speculate as to why it was brought such a long way. One possible answer may be that the axe was thought to be imbued with some sort of mystical or magical properties that protected the owner from harm. Its subsequent deposition inside the priory may suggest that similar motives may be attached to the medieval builders of the wall in which it was found.

Similar motives may have been behind the actions of the medieval builders of Piel Castle, Barrow-in-Furness, on the northern flank of Morecambe Bay. When constructing the walls of the castle, *c.*1324, a Late Bronze Age peg-socketed spearhead was incorporated. This was not an isolated practice because at Gleaston Castle, also on the north side of Morecambe Bay, a socketed axe was found incorporated into the structure. The utilisation of ancient metalwork as foundation deposits in medieval castles suggests that these objects were appreciated as talismans capable of offering protection for future generations. Such a belief does not depend upon any knowledge of the original Bronze Age context of these artefacts only that the medieval masons imagined that the original owners were powerful and perhaps possessed of supernatural powers.

Elsewhere in England the reuse of Late Neolithic and Early Bronze Age burial monuments during the early medieval period, first millennium AD, has been noted. Williams (1998, 94–5) demonstrated that monument reuse was a widespread and frequent practice in early Anglo-Saxon England. In southern England in Wessex, in the Peak District and over the Pennines in East Yorkshire, Anglo-Saxon graves were found in secondary contexts (Meaney 1964; Mortimer 1905). A recent regional study of Norfolk by Mary Chester-Kadwell (2008) demonstrates that monumental re-use of this sort was highly selective and related closely to the context of other local landscape features. One of the first to recognise its importance was Richard Bradley who noted the positioning and alignment of burial sites, and also timber halls, at Yeavering and Millfield, which may have sought deliberately to reuse long abandoned prehistoric monuments (Bradley 1987, 1993; Hope Taylor 1977). Bradley discussed the ways in which the character of the rituals conducted may have linked the present with a mythical past, suggesting that the rulers of Bernicia reused barrows as a source of power during the seventh century AD. His approach focuses on the ways in which ritual may be used to manipulate the perception of time and the past, so serving to legitimise the inequalities of early medieval society (Bloch 1977; Bradley 1987). Bradley's study has proved influential, guiding the interpretation of monument reuse at other early Anglo-Saxon burial sites in England (Blair 1995; Härke 1994; Lucy 1992).

In North Lancashire radiocarbon dates for secondary inhumation burials inserted into the Early Bronze Age barrow at Borwick revealed that although most were prehistoric there were also two concentrations of medieval human bone. The first burial was dated to cal AD 425–640 (1530 ±90, HAR-7012) and consisted of an adult human, probably female, together with a foetus and animal bone (Olivier 1987, 162), suggesting a high-status early medieval burial. A second scatter, c.2m long by 1.2m wide from a disturbed area, may have originally been buried next to the cairn, only later being combined with the monument as a result of disturbance (Olivier 1987, 145). This burial was dated cal AD 670–940 (1220 ±90 BP, HAR-7013) and was identified as a young adult (Olivier 1987, 162). At Southworth Hall Farm, Winwick near Warrington an Early Bronze Age ditched barrow had been constructed from sand; underneath was a large pit and two cremations (*141*). That mound had been levelled in prehistory and a second turf mound constructed in its place containing 10 cremations (Freke and Holgate 1988, 9–30). There is evidence that the site was subsequently re-used and elaborated as an inhumation cemetery for at least 800 individuals in the first millennium AD (Freke and Thacker 1988). Over 1200 square metres and 800 grave slots were excavated, although the boundary was not found suggesting to the excavators that there may have been as many as 1200 burials. It is highly probable that the cemetery was Christian given that a large number of burials were placed with the head facing west and the lack of grave goods, although neither can be taken as conclusive evidence.

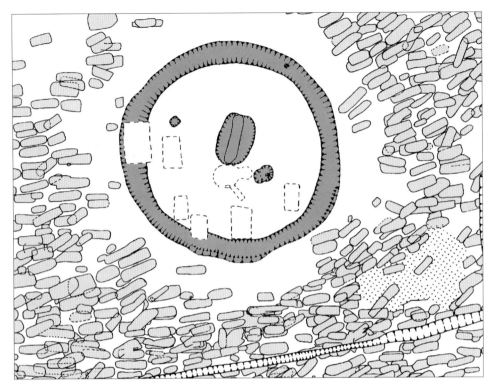

141 Southworth Hall Farm Early Bronze Age barrow surrounded by a ditch beyond, and possibly over, which is a first-millennium inhumation cemetery containing over 800 burials. *After Freke & Holgate and Freke & Thacker 1988v*

The graves at Winwick were deliberately placed close to the barrow, strongly suggesting Germanic influence. No burials were found on top of the mound itself (Freke and Thacker 1988, 31), which may indicate that the prehistoric barrow was 'respected' or given a different, archaeologically invisible role in the funeral. Ellis speculated that monuments served as stages for ritual performances involving the laying out of the dead or perhaps the cremation of the body (Ellis 1943, 105–11). Care should be taken in reading too much into this at Winwick as the absence of burials on the mound may be the result of plough damage. It seems there was a deliberate ordering in the organisation of mortuary practices with reference to ancient monuments. According to the excavators the majority of grave alignments varied around the east–west axis, sometimes following the contours of the mound. However in some areas burials were arranged radially in relation to the mound (Freke and Thacker 1988, 32).

In order to begin to understand something of the motives of the early medieval population we need, following Sarah Semple (1998, 109–126), to consider the literary evidence. Most famous is the Anglo-Saxon poem *Beowulf*, in which we are given an account of the death, cremation and burial of a migration period ruler in southern Scandinavia (Williams 1998, 90). Beowulf's death occurs whilst fighting the dragon at what appears to have been a Neolithic chambered tomb. This monument is described as a construction of ancient people, containing a hoard of treasure guarded by a dragon (Alexander 1973, lines 2213–40). Beowulf's body was first cremated before a barrow was raised over the pyre, presumably close to the prehistoric tomb (Alexander 1973, lines 31137–49; Hills 1997, 301). *Beowulf* is not the only literary evidence that suggests ancient monuments were invested with ancestral and supernatural associations. In Felix's *Life of St Guthlac*, an ancient mound was presented in a similar light to that in *Beowulf*. Guthlac lived as a hermit upon a prehistoric mound and, when he died, he was buried beneath it. According to Williams (1998) the earthwork symbolised the distant past and the burial place of an individual who could contact the supernatural.

During the seventh century an emerging elite began to transform and manipulate the ideology of burial. This was a period of religious change throughout England; in the north the formation of kingdoms took place under the hegemony of the powerful rulers of Northumbria (Higham 1992, 1995). Whilst communal cemeteries continued to focus upon ancient monuments, a new form of elite reuse began that was exclusive to single graves (Williams 1998). In Lancashire a late first millennium burial came from Quernmore north of Lancaster, where a coffin burial was excavated complete with shroud (Edwards 1973, 298–301). The coffin was formed of two pieces of oak, from the same tree and erroneously published in *Antiquity* as a Bronze Age burial on the basis of superficial similarities with coffin burials found in Denmark, despite clear indications that the textile was of Anglo-Scandinavian type. Subsequently radiocarbon dates were obtained which placed the burial to the period between the sixth and tenth centuries AD. At Claughton, near Garstang a tenth-century AD Scandinavian burial was recovered from an Early Bronze Age barrow. The burial was accompanied by a pair of tenth-century tortoise brooches, a brooch made from a silver gilt Carolingian baldric mount, and an Early Bronze Age stone hammer (Garstang 1906, 261). The circumstances of the find are not sufficiently well recorded to determine for certain whether this was a secondary burial inside a Bronze Age barrow, which is perhaps most likely, or a first millennium barrow in which the interment was accompanied by a prehistoric axe. In the latter case the axe must have presumably been found locally, and curated, before deposition.

Whatever the explanation, what is significant about the burial is the association between a richly furnished first-millennium grave and a prehistoric artefact contained within a barrow. So-called 'high status' burials with prehistoric and elaborate artefacts may have signified the graves of an elite. It has been suggested that the symbolic act of burying such valuable objects with the dead may have contributed to establishing relationships with a supernatural past. This could also have been emphasized through the reuse of ancient artefacts and the burial of objects such as axes with possible cosmological significance (Andren 1993; Meaney 1981; White 1990; Wilson 1992). It seems possible that the discovery of ancient implements may have encouraged mythical and supernatural interpretations of ancient monuments. The importance of artefact discovery is hinted at in the description of the dragon's treasure in *Beowulf* (Ellis 1943, 35–6):

> The ravager of the night,
> the burner who has sought out barrows from old,
> then found this hoard of undefended joy.
> The smooth evil dragon swims through the gloom
> enfolded in flame; the folk of this country

hold him in dread. He is doomed to seek out

hoards in the ground, and guard for an age there

the heathen gold: much good does it do him!

Trans. Alexander 1973, 122–3

The exploration of older monuments may therefore have been more than simple grave robbing. The complex symbolism of the grave goods at Sutton Hoo in Suffolk and elsewhere may have acted as metaphors for mythological narratives as well as the status symbols of an elite (Andren 1993). Where new barrows were constructed, including possibly at Claughton, they were no longer smaller than ancient monuments, and became the exclusive domain of elite individuals, rather than the material embodiment of a communal concept of ancestry and the past. The central placing of high-status graves may represent attempts to transform the dead into the original builders of the barrows. Williams suggested that the people who were buried with so many valuables in these graves were not venerating the ancient past, but were going one step further and trying to become the ancestors and deities that other groups had celebrated (Williams 1998). By situating their dead at ancient monuments and also building new barrows, elite groups were symbolising their exclusive links to divine ancestry and supernatural power (Chaney 1970; Wolfram 1994). This symbolism worked because it involved the appropriation and alteration of existing attitudes towards prehistoric monuments (Bradley 1987). Their association with powerful forces and a distant past may have served to legitimise political strategies in the present.

As we move further forward in time popular perceptions of the past and their interpretations of prehistory are still largely lost to us. Often all that remain are place names. Some of these names are tantalising reminders of the narratives that may have explained their presence, narratives that are often lost because they were transmitted orally. Occasionally, folklore exists that hints at past attitudes to prehistory. One of these is the legend of 'The Devil's Footprints on Pendle and the Stones dropped by him on Apronfull Hill' (Fielding 1905; Self Weeks 1917), otherwise abbreviated to 'The Pendleton Legend' (Hallam 1970). Folklore has it that footprints found cut in stone near to the Lancashire village of Pendleton were created by the Devil, a giant who strode across the Lancashire moors, on his way to destroy Clitheroe Castle. The legend, which may have medieval or earlier origin, was passed down orally until it was first published by John T. Fielding in 1905, following a visit to Pendleton by the Darwen Rambling Club. It runs as follows:

It would be impolitic to pass this village without reference to one of its legends. Near the church, until recently, stood some huge stones, like the one we noticed spanning the brook. These were said to have been thrown by the Devil; one especially was said to still bear the impress of his fingers.

The story continues,

… and they say that the Devil was coming with an apronful of stones for the purpose of knocking down Clitheroe Castle. Coming from Accrington way, he stepped from Hambledon to a large block of sandstone lying on Cragg's Farm, above Sabden. From here he stepped to the Apronful Hill, above Wellsprings, leaving foot-prints on the stones at Cragg's Farm. Being now in sight of Clitheroe Castle, he took one of the stones he was carrying, and threw it towards the Castle, but just then his brat string broke and all the remaining stones fell to the ground, where they still lie just as they fell. The stones he threw fell short of the Castle and landed near the church in Pendleton.

Fielding 1905, 14

A second version was published by Self Weeks in 1917:

… On Craggs Farm, near Sabden, on the sloping side of Pendle, is a mass of sandstone rocks that have fallen down from the scar above. On one of these big stones are two marks, side by side, about 2ft 6ins long and about 6ins wide.

They certainly resemble gigantic footmarks, and are said to be the Devil's. 'Old Scrat', however, when he alighted upon this stone, he must have crossed his legs, as the left footprint is on the right side. The outline of one foot is perfect, but the other is ill-formed, which is, however, easily explained, as it is well known the Devil has a club foot.

The legend is that the Devil was one day coming with an apronful of stones for the purpose of knocking down Clitheroe Castle. He stepped from Hambeldon Hill to Craggs, where he left the footprints before referred to. His next step was to 'The Apronful'. Here, being in view of the castle, he took one of the stones and threw it at the castle, but as he was in the act of throwing his 'brat string' broke, and all the stones he was carrying were tumbled on the ground. The stone which he threw fell short of the mark, and may still be seen lying on the ground just above Pendleton, with some marks upon it, which are said to be the print of his fingers.

Self Weeks 1917, 86

The legend may have medieval or earlier origins (Hallam 1995, 141). One interpretation is that it possibly hints at local animosity toward outside authority as represented by the castle. Alternatively, following Jacqueline Simpson (1983) who discusses the many parallel legends in which the Devil or a giant tries to destroy a prominent building by throwing a stone at it, or a town by dropping a mass of earth on it, a better explanation is that this is an instance of the malevolence of supernatural beings towards humanity. In this context it is likely that Clitheroe Castle is mentioned as the target because it is a prominent landmark, far enough from the place where the Devil is said to have stood to make his throw a spectacular feat. The legend was offered as a popular explanation for a series of archaeological features in the area: a panel of rock art depicting carved feet, a ringwork/platform cairn and a possible cup-marked stone. Mention of giants and association with the Devil in the context of prehistoric archaeological features in Lancashire occur at the Early Bronze Age burial sites of 'Giant's Grave', 'Hell Clough' and 'Hades Hill' although we no longer have the folklore to explain how these earthworks came to acquire their names. The stone circles still to be seen at Heathwaite in north Furness are said to mark the burial-places of the giants of the 'earliest ages', and a legend states that the last of them was mortally wounded in combat on the hill of Bawithknott (Langley Roberts 1931, 72).

Clitheroe Castle, the object of the Devil's attack, occupies the summit of a limestone knoll in the centre of Clitheroe, Lancashire. Built in the eleventh century it was deliberately damaged after its capture by Parliamentary forces during the Civil War in 1644. The part of the legend telling of the Devil throwing stones at the castle could be regarded as the interpretation of this event. That the legend had earlier antecedents dating at least to the construction of the castle is possible (Hallam 1995, 141). It could be imagined that the legend expressed the hatred of local people towards the original building of the castle in 1186 and those who had ordered it, or conversely, that the castle had divine protection from evil aggressors.

Apronful Hill, Pendle, is a slight prominence on Pendleton Moor lying to the east of the Nick of Pendle. To the north and east it commands a splendid view of the Ribble valley; to the south, it looks across East Lancashire. On a clear day the coast and the estuary of the Ribble to the south-west are visible. Just off the summit, overlooking the village of Pendleton, a circular spread of stones represents the traditional spot where the Devil dropped his bratful of stones. Whilst this site has yet to be excavated, it is typical of Early Bronze Age burial cairns found elsewhere in Lancashire. The location of Apronful Hill is recorded by the first edition of the Ordnance Survey 1848. In northern Britain, Wales, Ireland and Scandinavia the terms 'apronfuls of stones' and 'broken apron strings' recall traditions of giants carrying apronfuls of stones for building or throwing as missiles in battle (Self Weeks 1917, 87). Supernatural beings who could build a cairn in such a way would no doubt gain the respect of the local population. 'Brat' is a common Lancashire dialect word meaning 'apron'; in Old Irish it means 'cloth', 'plaid' or 'cloak'. The nearest example of the name 'Apronful' to Pendle Hill is a round cairn at Thornton-in-Lonsdale named 'Apronful of Stones'. Self Weeks quotes:

> The Devil (giant) was building a bridge at Kirkby Lonsdale. He was leaping over the hills from the Yorkshire side to the Lancashire side, carrying an apronful of stones, when his apron string broke, letting his burden fall, and the rocks still lie in the valley where they fell...
>
> 1917, 86–7

A letter to George Godwin on the subject of 'Remains ascribed to the era of the Druids in Furness, north of Lancashire' by Charles Jopling includes the following account reported to him by an 86 year-old man:

> The Devil had contracted with a certain king of the north country, to build a bridge over one of the Lakes. For the purpose he put on a leather apron, and went to the adjoining Duddon Valley to procure the necessary material, which as he gathered he put into his apron. Having got one good load he essayed to return, and had crossed the highest part of the hill and descended partly into the valley, when the apron strings broke and the stones fell into a heap at his feet ...(for some reason or other) he then threw up the contract.
>
> Jopling 1846, 451–2

Other examples are: a long barrow in Cumbria known as 'Sampson's Bratful' and a mound in Radnorshire that carries the name: 'Devil's Apronful of Stones'. The above-mentioned chambered tomb on Anglesey bears the name '*Barclodiad-y-Gawres*' which means 'Apronful of the Giantess' and in Flintshire the name '*Arffedogiad-y-Wrach*', meaning 'Apronful of the Hag'. In northern England, associated with ritual sites are the names 'Old Wife's Howes' in North Yorkshire; 'Skirtfull of Stones' in West Yorkshire and 'Auld Wife's Apronful of Stones' in Northumberland.

Place-names and legends referring to 'stone-carrying women' or giantesses have evolved around outcrops of stones and cairns. The best known of these is the Irish legend associated with the cemetery of cairns at Loughcrew, County Meath. In the eighteenth century Jonathan Swift visited the place and hearing the legend from a local gardener put it to verse:

> Determined now her tomb to build
> Her ample skirts with stones she filled
> And dropped a heap on Carnmore
> Then stepped one thousand yards, to toar[?]
> And dropped another goodly heap;
> And then with one prodigious leap
> Gained Carnbeg; and on its height
> Displayed the wonders of her might
> And when approached death's awful doom
> Her chair was placed within the womb
> Of hills whose tops with heather bloom.
>
> Attrib. Jonathan Swift in McMann 1993

The Hag's Chair stands by the side of the largest of the Loughcrew cairns, hewn out of a solid block of stone three metres long and two metres high (Shee Twohig 1996, 78).

The village of Pendleton lies at the foot of Pendle Hill. As discussed in Chapter 5, a burial urn was discovered behind a cottage at the western end of the village. Subsequent archaeological excavation led to the discovery of two more urn burials containing cremated bone and ceremonial offerings in a stone circle or cairn dating to the Early Bronze Age.

What is most interesting is the reference to footprints left by the Devil in the rock. As mentioned in Chapter 4 in the context of the Calderstones, engraved footprints, or natural marks resembling footprints, although rare, have a wide geographic distribution across Brittany, Britain and Scandinavia, and are generally described in folklore as representing visitations by gods or symbols made to invoke their presence conferring magical fertility upon the earth. In north-western Europe, particularly Scandinavia, representations of human feet are found amongst other symbols of prehistoric art such as axes, swords and ships, or alongside circles or figures denoting gods, dating to the Bronze Age. These symbols carved or engraved on boulders, rock outcrops and slabs forming megalithic graves are obviously of some significance, and were perhaps involved in ritual ceremonies and worship.

The Craggs Farm footprints lie less than a kilometre north-east of the ruins of Craggs Farm at the Deerstones rocks, which lie below a steep-sided ridge to the north. The two depressions

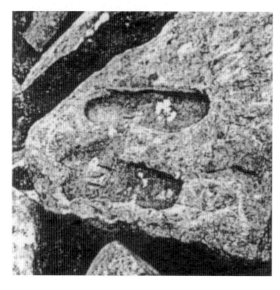

142 Rock-cut carvings of human feet, Craggs Farm, Pendleton. *Photograph: John Hallam*

are easily visible amongst the tumbled mass of landslip rocks. They occur on the flat upper surface of an angular-shaped block of stone and face towards Hambledon Hill 17km to the south. The two impressions, side-by-side, are *c.*75cm long and 15cm wide at their broadest and seem to have changed little since they were described by Weeks (*142*). Viewed from the south, the left-hand footprint has the shape of a large right foot. The other is more irregular in shape, perhaps a result of differential weathering or of subsequent vandalism.

There is some doubt as to the antiquity of these carvings, rock art being notoriously difficult to accurately date. Although prehistoric foot carvings are known from the Calderstones, those carvings were of unshod feet, whilst those at Craggs Farm are shod. Shod carvings do occur in prehistoric art, but there is also a local nineteenth-century Lancastrian tradition of carving

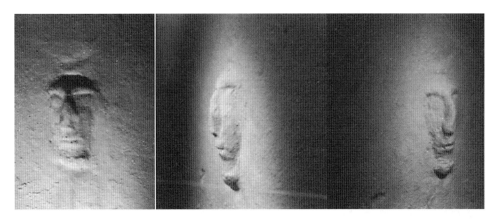

143 Seventeenth-century relief carving at Stanley Farm House, Bickerstaffe, nr. Ormskirk. *Photograph: Ann Ross*

that makes dating more difficult. One of the Calderstones is decorated with seven carvings of shod prints that date to the nineteenth century (43D). A similar problem occurs with the dating of carved stone heads. In the previous chapter the notion of an Iron Age 'Cult of the Head' was introduced and linked to the carving of stone heads. In some instances the context of finds in Roman forts at Lancaster and Manchester suggested a Late Iron Age or Romano-British date, but in others there is evidence that the heads are much younger and that the tradition of stone head carving has continued up to the present. At Stanley Farm House, Bickerstaffe, near Ormskirk, dated to the seventeenth century there is a small head in relief outside the door of a small room in the cellars (*143*). In its early days, according to present hereditary tenant, it was the local manor house and miscreants were locked up in this room awaiting the magistrate. Other heads, some of which may be medieval or younger were photographed on a farm in the Todmorden area by John Hallam (*144*). The farmer had reportedly collected them from the local area (John Hallam pers. comm.). The tradition has continued up to the present day and as this anecdote recounts care must be taken in provenancing them:

> The tour of the museum led to a display of Iron Age archaeology. Taking pride of place were two recently donated Celtic heads. The guide paused to explain what archaeologists had inferred about ancient Lancashire's ritual beliefs and practices, from these precious objects. At the back of the small crowd an elderly man strained to look at the carvings. As the guide finished her talk, he worked his way to the front, so as to have a better view. 'Ah,' he exclaimed, his face lighting up. The guide looked pleased at his evident interest. 'Aren't they nice?' she asked.
> 'Aye,' came the retort. 'Wondered what had happened to 'em.'
> 'Yes, wondered what had 'appened to them after t' war 'ad ended.'
> 'I'm sorry I don't understand?'
> 'After m' brother was called-up in t' war we lost track of what 'ad happened to 'em.'
> 'You mean you've seen them before?'
> 'Seen um? It was m' brother what carved them.'

144 A collection of stone heads from the Todmorden area, some of which appear to be younger examples of the Late Iron Age tradition. The one pictured bottom right has a decidedly Tudor look about it. *Photograph:Ann Ross*

The crowd began to shuffle uneasily and the tour guide appeared not to know what to say.

'Surely you're mistaken? These heads are two thousand years old.'

'No, m' brother carved 'em in t' war, and we used to push 'em about in a wheel barrow, to raise money for t' war effort. Can't you see? That one's Hitler and t'other one's Mussolini!'

Barrowclough 2004, 3–4

CONCLUSION: UNDERSTANDING SOCIAL REPRODUCTION IN LANCASHIRE

Throughout the chapters of this book we have seen how the relationship between long-term continuity across archaeological periods on the one hand and technological innovation on the other was articulated. Continuity was particularly clear between the Late Upper Palaeolithic, Mesolithic and Early Neolithic when a high degree of mobility characterised the population. In Chapter 2 the notion of a particular North Western Culture was introduced (Bu'Lock 1961), it is now time to revisit the notion in the context of the identity of the later prehistoric inhabitants of Lancashire, and to propose a new, diachronic, model for this small-scale society. In the preceding chapters we have seen that a feature of the archaeological record, as elsewhere in Britain and beyond, was the burial of individuals in funerary monuments and the deposition of metalwork in natural places. It was through those acts that the identity of places in the landscape was constructed. We also saw that the particular form of burials, and the particular metalwork types selected for deposition had a distinctly regional flavour. It was in the selection and performance of those acts that the participants defined themselves, through practices, as a community with its own identity. This is how the small-scale prehistoric society of Lancashire reproduced itself as a community with a distinct regional identity whilst at the same time being recognisable as part of the wider Neolithic, Bronze and Iron Ages.

A number of recent archaeological studies (see papers in Canuto and Yaeger 2000; Chester-Kadwell 2008) have demonstrated that an individual can be, simultaneously, a member of different communities: a household, an age group spanning several households, a burial community, and a sacrificial community. This is because a community is a symbolic construction: it is about differentiating between 'us' and 'them'. Membership is based on practices, knowledge and symbols, by which a group distinguishes itself from others (Yeager and Canuto 2000, 1–15). In a study of later prehistoric society in the southern Netherlands, Gerritsen (2001) showed how different practices, carried out in the landscape, were related to the construction of communities. Similarly, in the case of Lancashire, the siting of particular practices in the landscape can be linked to the construction and maintenance of communal identities.

Burials of the Late Neolithic and Early Bronze Age are one example. In life individual households were dispersed across the landscape. In death individuals were brought together in funerary monuments, which perhaps represented the household, at least symbolically, of the dead. These monuments tend to cluster in groups, for example around what is now Lancaster; in the Lytham-Skippool valley on the Fylde Coast; on Worsthorne Moor near Burnley; around Bolton and also Winwick. They bring together several households in a community of the dead. By burying the dead of several households within the same barrow cemetery, a sense of community was expressed that did not come to the fore in other aspects of culture. Funerary monuments are therefore a symbolic resource, through which people defined themselves as a community, for example 'the people who bury their dead on Worsthorne Moor'.

In the Middle and Late Bronze Age a different type of community was constructed, a sacrificial community centred on bronze deposition in natural places. In this case special practices of deposition were performed in specific, often wet, places in the landscape. These too, may have resulted in the construction and maintenance of community affiliation.

Although there are stark differences between burial and sacrificial communities, particularly in the types of places selected as significant locations, there are also important similarities. Whilst expressing wider, national, cultural traits, both articulate these in a distinctive manner. This gives the assemblages of material culture a regional identity, implying the existence of a community, not just of people who co-existed but also of shared ideology. This is rendered visible to archaeologists in the selection and adoption of particular local forms of burial urn, the North Western Style Collared Urn, and the choice of some metalwork types, spears and axes, and not of others, particularly swords. Regional identity in Lancashire was therefore constructed in opposition to supra-regional Bronze Age identities.

UNDERSTANDING REGIONAL IDENTITY

The difference between local and non-local identity mattered in Lancashire and had implications for the way in which objects were treated. Regionality was important, and as one of the 'ties that bind', was inextricably linked to the diachronic reproduction of society. The reality of a community firmly rooted in a specific environment, and the ensuing sense of belonging, seems to have been at odds with another reality, that of participation in long-distance, supra-regional, exchange networks. These were not just about acquiring access to non-local materials, but also about sharing cultural knowledge of the supra-regionally acknowledged categories that give each archaeological period its distinct character.

In Chapter 6 we saw that although the region contains raw materials, copper and lead, which were to some extent exploited, the inhabitants of Lancashire chose, in the main, to import their bronze from elsewhere. In this sense it was, to adopt Fontijn's terminology, an 'importing community' (Fontijn 2002, 273). In Chapter 5 we saw that this was true, but to a lesser extent, during the Late Neolithic and Early Bronze Age. Flint, for example Beaker-style flint daggers, were imported from beyond the region. Thus, the necessity to participate in exchange networks spanning vast areas must have been an essential characteristic of the *longue durée* of prehistoric communities in Lancashire.

This point has consequences for the way Lancastrians perceived themselves as part of the wider world. Helms (1988, 22) showed that all social groups recognise spatial and cosmological frames, within which they occupy the central position. However, such frames were conceptualised, they are essentially about the identity of the group as constructed in opposition to the world beyond. We know that Lancastrians systematically derived vital items via long-distance contact networks, so it may be assumed that there must always have been a tension between two different kinds of social reality. First, the reality of the 'regional' community rooted in a sense of belonging to a specific locality. This is the reality of daily life and feelings of belonging. It is also about feeling attached to the area in which one lives: the specific environment, the buildings, the monuments and its idiosyncratic local history (Gerritsen 2001). For the small-scale society that we are studying this local identity must have been the most important and pervasive social reality (Chapman 1998, 110).

Secondly, there is also a reality that is detached from locality. This is the reality of the 'importing' society, in which one's own group is perceived as being part of a wider social network (Barth 1992, 29). Here people saw themselves as necessarily linked to a more encompassing social world, acknowledging that the cycles by which a social unit reproduces itself draws upon resources derived from a wider geographical and social world (see Barrett 1998, 19).

These two realities need to co-exist. For a local group to reproduce itself, the world beyond that group is vital, if only for the exchange of marriage partners and of crucial non-local materials, for example bronze. At the same time, the outside world is potentially ambiguous and dangerous. A sense of belonging to a wider social world denotes the dependency of the local group on others for the reproduction of the local group. It emphasises dependency on factors beyond one's own control. Crucial is the realisation that what effectively links both realities is the imported object or material or individual (marriage partner). Helms shows how foreign things for that reason alone tend to be seen as imbued with meaning. They are the objectification of the reach of the local group upon resources beyond their existence as determined locally (Helms 1993, 99).

THE SIGNIFICANCE OF NON-LOCAL IDENTITY

Non-local materials were of importance, for example, even when a local industry existed bronze continued to be imported. Bradley has shown that one of the characteristic features of the European Bronze Age is the enormous distance travelled by some types of artefacts. He makes the argument that it must have been the foreignness of the metal itself which mattered. There must have been a cultural preference for non-local material (Bradley 1990, 131–5). Such a preference has wider implications than just the objects themselves. By adopting supra-regional artefacts, membership was claimed of distant non-local communities. Following Isbell (2000, 243–66), we may perhaps speak of membership of 'imagined' communities.

The point is that within Lancashire there was a concern with concepts of identity in which the links with the world beyond were emphasised. As Barrett (1998, 23) puts it: 'In such cases the biographical histories of objects and of the body itself may have converged in such a way as to ensure that the body's identity was expressed in terms of distances travelled and of absent origins'. The significance of adopting such non-local identities seems to have been considerable. When local bronze industries emerged there never seem to have been attempts to make tools or ornaments that primarily emphasised locally or regionally specific identities.

Inherent in this situation, where the world beyond daily existence mattered considerably, was a tension between the significance of local and non-local identities, which had to be managed and resolved. It is argued that practices of deposition, associated with burial and also with metalwork, were related to this.

The deliberate giving up of apparently valuable objects was a culturally prescribed and meaningful way to deal with objects in the Late Neolithic and Bronze Age (Fontijn 2002, 275). Whether placed in a grave, singly or in hoards, we are dealing with biographies of objects in which a life of circulation ended in deliberate deposition, where a useable object was sacrificed.

TIME AND CONTINUITY OF DEPOSITION

Metalwork deposits of the Middle Bronze Age were structured; specific object types ended up in specific places (Chapter 6). There appears to have been general agreement amongst the population that the landscape was structured in such a way that certain kinds of places were appropriate for depositing particular types of object. This implies that other environmental elements, for example clay soils, were not considered the right place to deposit objects. The system of selective deposition seems to have been based on a shared, cultural understanding of the landscape. Every new deposit reproduced this understanding. The system must therefore have been profoundly traditional. People repeatedly visited specific types of places in the landscape in order to carry out specific types of deposition. Throwing a spear into a bog leaves nothing but a memory in the mind of the observer. In the absence of permanent markers, for which there is no archaeological evidence, there existed a collective memory for the traditional location of deposition. To an outsider there would be nothing to indicate the long-term history of deposition in a moss or river. Yet particular locations were selected time after time for such actions, in the case of Pilling Moss from the Neolithic through to the end of the Bronze Age. The repeated use of the same places must have been deliberate: such places were meaningful and historical, and imbued with memory.

It is impossible to recapture archaeologically what it was that made some places culturally appropriate locations for deposition. But, we may attempt to understand the mechanism by which knowledge was transmitted through the generations within the community by way of ethnographic analogy. These sources confirm the existence of comparable natural sacrificial sites, with usage over equally large spans of time as those in prehistory (Mulk 1997). Key to the transmission of such knowledge in non-literate society is myth and folk tale. We saw a hint of this in the discussion of the Pendleton Legend. Küchler (1987) and Rowlands (1993) both make the point that in the transmission of cultural knowledge there is a tension between continuity and change. In order to memorise particular mosses and rivers as historical locations for deposition people must have drawn upon mental templates to create a mental map (Rowlands 1993, 141; see also Gell 1992, 190–205).

In the case of bronze deposition in Lancashire we see evidence for the interplay between continuity and change. At Pilling Moss, in the Over Wyre region of Lancashire deposition of metalwork took place throughout the whole of the Bronze Age Period. The historical practice of deposition defines this context as a particular zone in the landscape. This continuity is set against changes that took place during the period. In particular one can point to the shift from burial deposition to metal deposition in natural places, dated to the Middle Bronze Age. This seems to have been associated with the acquisition of new forms of martial identity. In Pilling Moss the response was seen in the increased number of artefacts deposited during this period.

Continuity and change were in tension. In this context the Winmarleigh hoard may be re-interpreted as an attempt to break with the past. It reflects, in both its structure and components, a deliberate attempt to differentiate past from present as a way of claiming new status positions. These went hand in hand with attempts at naturalising these new positions by claiming bonds with former occupiers of the land. This is most clear at Pilling Moss where the large quantity of Middle Bronze Age metalwork continues an earlier tradition of deposition begun in the Late Neolithic.

THE REPRODUCTION OF LANCASTRIAN SOCIETY THROUGH DEPOSITION

We have seen that depositional practices were conceptually linked to imported objects. The strangeness and foreignness of the import is something that required a response among the people who acquired it; the object needed to be recontextualised. This required practices suppressing strangeness, relocating the artefact within Lancastrian society enabling its comprehension (see Barrett 1999, 23). These might involve practices that ignored the dependency to which the imported object testified, and realigned the object with the moral order at home (Bloch and Parry 1989). Metal artefacts, as carriers of histories of long-distance exchange, so often ended up in deposition, that we may assume that deposition was one way to achieve this.

The particular way in which deposition achieved this is unclear from the archaeology. The local landscape is the most conspicuous environment from which local communities can derive a sense of belonging (Gerritsen 2001, 125–6). Placing imported objects in this landscape might therefore be considered a compelling way to realign a foreign idea, symbolised by the object selected for deposition, with the local order at home. Bloch and Parry (1989) state that such practices are widespread. On the basis of ethnographic examples they point out how sacrifice, or transformation, of some representative item was a way to make alien, ambiguous items derived from beyond, morally acceptable at home.

Deposition was about much more than simply recontextualising foreign items. Rather it was about the recontextualisation or ordering of specific ideas and values. Many of the objects deposited have far more meanings and qualities than just being exotic. They are about personal statuses and identities, related to life-cycles, social power and special activity (such as participating in long-distance exchange and warfare). They are about communal practices and identities: cutting down forest, building barrows, or highly specific ideas and values celebrated in ceremonial items, for example the lunate spearheads found in both the Winmarleigh and Congleton hoards.

Many of the identities are charged, ambiguous and dangerous. Evidence for warrior identity is provided by the conspicuous ritual deposits of weapons. It is argued that this is in line with situations in which small-scale warfare is endemic, taking place as part of the life-cycle of individuals. Warfare is therefore primarily of ideological importance. In such circumstances, aggression is something that requires a ritually transformed self. Following the anthropologist Harrison (1995, 87, 91) martial identities are essentially temporary ones. They are something on the outer surface that can be worn or shed by wearing or laying down the appropriate paraphernalia in ritualised circumstances.

It is argued, following Fontijn (2002, ch. 11), that the practice of weapon deposition in special places and circumstances may well be understood as the reflection of the ritual laying down of such roles. Supra-regional personas that were constructed through foreign, or foreign-styled, objects may also have been charged, confined ones, at odds with the reality of the local group, who defined itself as belonging to the people they live and work with on a daily basis and their attachment to the local environment.

Deposition by its very nature has the quality of coping with ambiguous and circumscribed identities and the values they represent. The meanings of the objects are celebrated and magnified in front of onlookers but deconstructed as well. The ritual ends up in their definite disappearance. Particularly in the case of weapons, the paraphernalia signalling it are laid down, making the elements of deconstruction almost tangible. It may be no coincidence that depositional locations were themselves often ambiguous in nature as were the objects which were placed in them.

Selective deposition, whether in burials or more clearly so in the case of metalwork deposition, is a system of maintaining regional identity whilst articulating change. As such it is a system for resolving ideological and political tensions stemming from different ideas and values that exist within every society. It is through this mechanism that we can see, in part at least, how small-scale society in Lancashire was reproduced throughout the prehistoric period.

Individual and social identities are fluid and learnt and they cross-cut gender, age and status identity. They are dependent on constant reiteration through both everyday actions and discursive practice that continually recreate and define the boundaries of those groups. Archaeologists should no longer see a direct link between the artefacts that people use, the way they dress, the monuments they bury their dead in, and their 'identity'. Nor should they see 'societies' or 'cultures' as static, isolated and homogenous, when they are in reality constantly in flux, characterised by ambiguity and complexity. Society in general, and identity in particular, are much more complex phenomena and have to be studied with greater subtlety, and with a greater regard for issues of action, interaction and practice. In order to study aspects of communal, *regional*, identity, archaeologists need to pay more attention to the diachronic contexts in which things are used and the ways in which people use them across different scales of analysis. It is these differences in practice that may serve as the locus for emphasising communal distinctions.

APPENDIX

TABLES OF RADIOCARBON DATES

AMS radiocarbon dates from the Lancashire Radiocarbon Dating Programme undertaken by the author and Dr Gordon Cook of SUERC

EARLY BRONZE AGE BURIALS

Site name and No.	Sample	Laboratory Code	¹⁴C Age (years BP ± 1σ)	Date cal BC (95.4 per cent confidence)
Astley Hall, urn 1	Bone, cremated	SUERC 4454	3525 ± 40	1960–1730
Astley Hall, urn 2	Bone, cremated	SUERC 4452	3390 ± 40	1780–1520
Astley Hall, urn 2	*Quercus*, charcoal	SUERC 4451	3575 ± 35	2030–1870
Astley Hall, pit C4	Bone, cremated	SUERC 4447	3250 ± 45	1630–1410
Bleasdale, urn 1	*Quercus* charcoal	SUERC 6929	3535 ± 35	1960–1750
Bleasdale, urn 2	*Quercus* charcoal	SUERC 7286	3615 ± 35	2050–1880
Bleasdale, timber	*Quercus* post	SUERC 7154	3675 ± 35	2150–1950
Carrier's Croft, urn 2	*Alnus*, charcoal	SUERC 4443	3450 ± 40	1890–1680
Carrier's Croft, urn 3	*Alnus*, charcoal	SUERC 4444	3400 ± 35	1780–1600
Carrier's Croft, urn 3	Bone, cremated	SUERC 4445	3495 ± 35	1920–1730
Cliviger Laithe	Bone, cremated	SUERC 4436	3455 ± 35	1880–1680
Hades Hill	Bone, cremated	SUERC 4424	3590 ± 40	2040–1870
Hades Hill	*Quercus*, charcoal	SUERC 4425	3880 ± 40	2470–2270
Mereclough	Bone, cremated	SUERC 4435	3510 ± 35	1930–1730
Mosely Height, urn A	*Quercus*, charcoal	SUERC 4427	3525 ± 40	1960–1730
Mosely Height, urn A	Bone, cremated	SUERC 4431	3490 ± 40	1920–1730
Mosely Height, urn C	Bone, cremated	SUERC 4426	3420 ± 40	1880–1610
Mosely Height, unurned D	Bone, cremated	SUERC 4432	3410 ± 40	1780–1600
Mosely Height, unurned D	*Quercus*, charcoal	SUERC 4434	3540 ± 35	1960–1740
Mosely Height, urn C	*Quercus*, charcoal	SUERC 4437	3540 ± 35	1960–1740
Noon Hill	*Quercus*, charcoal	SUERC 4446	3725 ± 35	2210–2020
Pleasington	*Quercus*, charcoal	SUERC 4441	3530 ± 35	1950–1740
Pleasington	Bone, cremated	SUERC 4442	3520 ± 35	1940–1740

Shuttleworth	Bone, cremated	SUERC 4461	3635 ± 35	2050-1880
Shuttleworth	Bone, cremated	SUERC 4462	3480 ± 35	1890-1730
Whitehall, WH4 U8	Charcoal	SUERC 4463	3520 ± 35	1940-1740
Whitehall, WH8 U12	*Betula*, charcoal	SUERC 4464	3560 ± 35	1980-1770
Whitehall, WH8 U12	Bone, cremated	SUERC 4465	3480 ± 35	1890-1730
Whitelow H	*Quercus*, charcoal	SUERC 4456	3515 ± 35	1940-1730
Whitelow G	*Quercus*, charcoal	SUERC 4457	3470 ± 40	1890-1680
Whitelow L	Bone, cremated	SUERC 4455	3495 ± 40	1920-1730

LATER BRONZE AGE SPEARS

Site name and Type	Sample	Laboratory Code	^{14}C Age (years ±1 BP)	Date cal BC (95.4 per cent confidence)
Brogden Lane Pegged-socketed spear	*Fraxinus,* wood	Beta 243685	2950 ±40	1300-1020
Priest Hutton Basal-looped spear	*Fraxinus*, wood	SUERC 4466	2820 ±35	1080-890

BIBLIOGRAPHY

Abram, W.A. 1877. *A History of Blackburn, Town and Parish*. Blackburn

Adams, M.H. 1995. *An Archaeological Evaluation at St Chad's Church, Kirkby, Knowsley, Merseyside*. Liverpool Museum unpublished report

Adams, M.H. Forthcoming. *An Early-Middle Bronze Age Settlement Site at St Chad's Vicarage, Kirkby, Merseyside*. Liverpool Museum

Adams, M.H. and Philpott, R. Forthcoming. *Excavations on a Prehistoric and Romano-British Site at Irby, Wirral*. Liverpool: Liverpool Museum

Aldhouse-Green, M. 1998a. Human sacrifice in Iron Age Europe. *British Archaeology* 38, 8–9

Aldhouse-Green, M. 1998b. Humans as ritual victims in the later prehistory of western Europe. *Oxford Journal of Archaeology* 17, 169–90

Alexander, M. (ed.) 1973. *Beowulf: A Verse Translation*. London: Penguin

Andren, A. 1993. Doors to other worlds: Scandinavian death rituals in Gotlandic perspective. *Journal of European Archaeology,* 1: 33–56

Anon. 1884. *TCWAAS* VII, 279

Anon. 1893. Extwistle Moor, Burnley. *TLCAS* 11, 156–61

ApSimon, A.M. 1985/6. Chronological contexts for Irish megalithic tombs. *Journal of Irish Archaeology* 3, 5–15

Ashbee, P. 1978. *The Ancient British*. Norwich

Ashmead, P. and Wood, R. 1974. Second report on the archaeological excavations at Kirkhead Cavern. *North-West Speleology* 2, 24–33

Avery, M. 1967. Excavations at Meare East 1966. *Somerset Archaeological and Natural History Society* vol. 112, 1967/68, 21–39

Bain, M.G. 1991. *Palaeoecological Studies on the Rivington Anglezarke Uplands, Lancashire*. Salford: University of Salford

Baines, E. 1825. *History, Directory and Gazetteer of the County Palatine of Lancaster*, vol. II, 698–99

Baldwin, W. 1903. Some prehistoric finds from Ashworth Moor and neighbourhood. *Transactions of the Manchester Geological Society* 28, 108–13

Barnes, B. 1975. *Palaeoecologial Studies of the Late Quaternary Period in the North West Lancashire Lowlands*. Lancaster: University of Lancaster

Barnes, B. 1982. *Man and the Changing Landscape*. Liverpool: University of Liverpool, Department of Prehistoric Archaeology, Work Notes 3

Barnes, B., Edwards, B.J.N., Hallam, J.S., and Stuart, A.J. 1971. The skeleton of a Late-Glacial elk associated with barbed points from Poulton-le-Fylde, Lancashire. *Nature* 232, 488–9

Barnes, F. 1955. Pottery from Prehistoric sites, North End, Walney, *TCWAAS* 55, 1–16

Barnes, F. 1963. Discovery of four roughed-out stone axes at Skelmore Heads, July 1959, *TCWAAS* 63, 27–30

Barnes, F., 1970. Prehistoric pottery from Furness, *TCWAAS* 70, 1–8

Barrett, J. 1989. Time and Tradition: The Rituals of Everyday Life, in H.A. Nordsorm and A. Knape (eds) *Bronze Age Studies*, Stockholm 113–126

Barrett, J.C. 1994. *Fragments from Antiquity: an archaeology of social life in Britain, 2900–1200 BC*. Oxford: Blackwell

Barrett, J.C. 1998. The politics of scale and the experience of distance: the Bronze Age world system, in L. Larsson and B. Stjernquist (eds) *The World View of Prehistoric Man*. Stockholm: KVHAA Konferenser 40, 13–25

Barrett, J.C. 1999. The mythical landscapes of the British Iron Age, in W. Ashmore and A. B. Knapp (eds) *Archaeologies of Landscape: Contemporary Perspectives*. Oxford: Blackwell, 253–65

Barrett, J.C., Bradley, R, and Green, M. 1991. *Landscape, Monuments and Society, the Prehistory of Cambourne Chase*. Cambridge: Cambridge University Press

Barrowclough, D.A. 2004. Introduction: our precious past, in D.A. Barrowclough (ed.) *Our Precious Past, sharing responsibility for our archaeological heritage*. Cambridge: Red Dagger Press, 1–15

Barrowclough, D.A. 2005. Dancing in time: activating the prehistoric landscape, in M.E. Chester-Kadwell (ed.) Active landscapes, *Archaeological Review from Cambridge* 20.1: 39–54

Barrowclough, D.A. 2006. *Multi-Temporality and Material Culture: An Investigation of Continuity and Change in Later-Prehistoric Lancashire*. Doctoral thesis. Department of Archaeology, University of Cambridge

Barrowclough, D.A. 2007. *Multi-Temporality and Material Culture: An Investigation of Continuity and Change in Later Prehistoric Lancashire*. Oxford: BAR British Series 436

Barth, F. 1992. Towards greater naturalism in conceptualising societies, in A. Kuper (ed.) *Conceptualising Society*. London, 17–33

Bartley, D.D. 1975. Pollen analytical evidence for prehistoric forest clearance in the upland area of Rishworth, West Yorkshire. *New Phytologist* 74, 375–81

Bennett, W. 1946. *The History of Burnley to 1400*. Burnley: Burnley Corporation

Bennett, W. 1951. Report on excavations near Burnley. *TLCAS* 62, 204–08

Beswick, P. and Coombs, D.G. 1986. Excavations at Portfield Hillfort, 1960, 1970 and 1972, in T.G. Manby and P. Turnbull (eds) *Archaeology in the Pennines: studies in honour of Arthur Raistrick*. Oxford: BAR British Series 158, 137–79

Bewley, R.H. 1994. *Prehistoric and Romano-British Settlement in the Solway Plain, Cumbria*. Oxford: Oxbow Monograph 36

Birks, H.J.B. 1964–65. Chat Moss, Lancashire, *Memoirs and Proceedings of the Manchester Literary and Philosophical Society* 106, 24–43

Blair, J. 1995. Anglo-Saxon pagan shrines and their prototypes, in D. Griffiths, *Anglo-Saxon Studies in Archaeology and History* vol. 8. Oxford: Oxford University Committee for Archaeology, 1–28

Bloch, M. 1977. The past and the present in the present. *Man* 12: 278–92

Bloch, M. and Parry, J. 1989. Introduction: money and the morality of exchange, in J. Parry and M. Bloch (eds) *Money and the Morality of Exchange*. Cambridge: Cambridge University Press, 1–31

Blok, A. 1994. Zinloos en zinvol geweld, in H. Driessen and H. de Jonge (eds) *In de Ban van Betekenis. Proeven van Symbolische antropologie*. Nijmegen, 27–45

Blundell, J.D. and Longworth, I.H. 1967–8. A Bronze Age Hoard from Portfield Farm, Whalley, Lancs. *Brit. Mus. Quart.* 32, 8–14

Boast, R. 1997. A small company of actors: a critique of style. *Journal of Material Culture* 2(2): 181–2

Bonsall, C. 1981. The coastal factor in the Mesolithic settlement of North West England, in B. Gramsch, (ed.). *The Mesolithic in Europe*. Second International Symposium, Potsdam, April 1978, Report, Veröffentlichungen des Museums für Ur- und Frühgeschichte Potsdam Band 14/15. Berlin: Deutscher Verlag der Wissenschaften, 451–72

Bonsall, C., Sunderland, D., Tipping, R. and Cherry, J. 1986. The Eskmeals Project 1981–5: an interim report. *Northern Archaeology* 7 (1), 1–30

Bradley, R. 1978. *The Prehistoric Settlement of Britain*. London

Bradley, R. 1984. *The Social Foundations of Prehistoric Britain*. London: Longman

Bradley, R. 1987. Against objectivity: an overview, in C.F. Gaffney and V.L. Gaffney (eds) *Pragmatic Archaeology: theory in crisis?* Oxford: BAR British Series 167, 115–19

Bradley, R. 1990. *The Passage of Arms: an archaeological analysis of prehistoric hoard and votive deposits*. Cambridge: Cambridge University Press

Bradley, R. 1993. *Altering the Earth: The Origins of Monuments in Britain and Continental Europe.* Edinburgh: Society of Antiquaries of Scotland

Bradley, R. 2000. *An Archaeology of Natural Places.* London: Routledge

Bradley, R. 2007. *The Prehistory of Britain and Ireland.* Cambridge: Cambridge University Press

Bradley, R. and Edmonds, M. 1993. *Interpreting the Axe Trade.* Cambridge: Cambridge University Press

Bradley, R. and Gordon, K. 1988. Human skulls from the River Thames, their dating and significance. *Antiquity* 62, 503–509

Bridgeford, S.D. 1997. Mightier than the pen? (an edgewise look at Irish Bronze Age swords), in J. Carman (ed.) *Material Harm: Archaeological Studies of War and Violence.* Glasgow: Cruithne Press, 95–115

Broadhurst, F.M. 1985. The geological evolution of North-West England, in R.H. Johnson (ed.) *The Geomorphology of North-West England.* Manchester: Manchester University Press, 26–58

Bronk Ramsey, C. 2001. Development of the Radiocarbon Program OxCal. *Radiocarbon,* 43: 355–63

Brooks, I.P. 1999. *Treales to Burscough gas pipeline: Watching Brief.* Engineering Archaeological Services unpublished report

Brück, J. 1999. Houses, lifecycles and deposition on Middle Bronze Age settlements in southern England. *Proceedings of the Prehistoric Society,* 65, 145–166

Brück, J. (ed.) 2001. *Bronze Age Landscapes, Tradition and Transformation.* Oxford: Oxbow Books

Buckland, P.C. and Dolby, M.J. 1973. Mesolithic and later material from Misterton Carr: an interim report. *Transactions of the Thoroton Society Nottinghamshire* 77, 5–33

Buckley, D.G. 1979. The Stone, in G.J. Wainwright, *Gussage All Saints: an Iron Age Settlement in Dorset.* London: HMSO, 89–97

Buckley, F.M.S. 1920–48. *Notebooks* and *Drawing Books.* Tolson Memorial Museum, Huddersfield

Buckley, F. 1921. *A Microlithic Industry, Marsden, Yorkshire.* Privately Printed

Buckley, F. 1922. Yorkshire gravers. *Proceedings of the Prehistoric Society* 3, 542–7

Buckley, F. 1923. Some recent discoveries in our local flints. *Oldham Chronicle,* December 15

Buckley, F. 1924. *A Microlithic Industry of the Pennine Chain.* Privately Printed

Bulleid, A. 1968 (6th ed). *The Lake-Villages of Somerset.* Street

Bu'Lock, J.D. 1958. The Pikestones: a chambered long cairn of Neolithic type on Anglezarke Moor, Lancashire, *TLCAS* 68, 143–6

Bu'Lock, J.D. 1961. The Bronze Age in the North-West. *TLCAS* 71, 1–42

Bu'Lock, J.D. 1965. Some Notes on the Planeswood Hoard of Gold and Bronze Objects of the Late Bronze Age. *TLCAS* 76, 218–21

Burgess, C.B. 1968. *Bronze Age Metalwork in Northern England c.1000 to 700 B.C.* Newcastle-upon-Tyne: Oriel Press

Burgess, C.B. 1970. The Bronze Age. *Current Archaeology* 19, 208–15

Burgess, C.B. 1974. The Bronze Age, in C. Renfrew (ed.) *British Prehistory: a New Outline.* London, 165–232

Burgess, C.B. 1976a. Britain and Ireland in the Third and Second Millenia B.C.: a Preface, in C. Burgess, and R. Miket (eds) *Settlement and Economy in the Third and Second Millenia B.C.* Oxford: BAR 33

Burgess, C.B. 1976b. The Beaker Phenomenon: Some Suggestions, in C. Burgess and R. Miket (eds) *Settlement and Economy in the Third and Second Millenia B.C.* Oxford: BAR 33, 309–23

Burgess, C.B. 1979. The background of early metalworking in Ireland and Britain, in M. Ryan (ed.) *The Origins of Metallurgy in Atlantic Europe: proceedings of the fifth Atlantic Colloquium.* Dublin: Stationery Office, 207–14

Burgess, C.B. 1980. *The Age of Stonehenge.* London: Dent

Burgess, C.B. 1988. Britain at the time of the Rhine-Swiss group, in P. Brun and C. Mordant (eds) *Le Groupe Rhin-Suisse-France-Orientale et la Notion de Civilisation des Champs d'Urnes.* Nemours: Mémoires du Musée de Préhistoire d'Ile-de-France No. 1, 559–73

Burl, A. 1976. *The Stone Circles of the British Isles.* New Haven: Yale University Press

Busk, G. 1874. Human skull and bones of the Red Deer etc found at Birkdale, near Southport, Lancashire. *Journal of the Anthropological Institute* 3, 104–5

Camden, W. 1971 [1586]. *Britannia: or, a chorographical description of the flourishing kingdoms of England, Scotland, and Ireland, and the islands adjacent; from the earliest antiquity.* Newton Abbott: David and Charles

Canuto, M.A. and Yaeger, J. 2000. *The Archaeology of Communities, a New World Perspective*. London: Routledge

Challis, A. and Harding, D.W. 1975. *Later Prehistory from the Trent to the Tyne*. Oxford: BAR British Series 20

Chamberlain, A.T. 1997. Commentary: missing stages of life – towards the perception of children in archaeology, in J. Moore and E. Scott (eds) *Invisible People and Processes: writing gender and childhood into European archaeology*. Leicester: Leicester University Press, 248–50

Chambers, F.M. and Elliott, L. 1989. Spread and expansion of Alnus Mill. In the British Isles: timing, agencies and possible vectors. *Journal of Biogeography* 16, 541–50

Chaney, W.A. 1970. *The Cult of Kingship in Anglo-Saxon England*. Manchester: Manchester University Press

Chaplin, R.R. 1975. The ecology and behaviour of deer in relation to their impact on the environment of prehistoric Britain, in J.G. Evans, S. Limbrey and H. Cleere (eds) *The Effect of Man on the Landscape: the Highland Zone*. CBA Research Report 11, 40–2

Chapman, J. 1998. Objectification, embodiment and the value of places and things, in D. Bailey and S. Mills (eds) *The Archaeology of Value, Essays on prestige and the process of valuation*. Oxford: BAR International Series 730, 106–30

Chapman, J. 2000. *Fragmentation in Archaeology: people, places and broken objects in the prehistory of south-eastern Europe*. London: Routledge

Cherry, P.J. and Cherry, J. 2000. A Late Mesolithic assemblage from Levens Park. *TCWAAS* 100, 25–32

Chester-Kadwell, M.E. 2008. *Early Anglo-Saxon Communities in the Landscape of Norfolk: Cemeteries and Metal-detector Finds in Context*. Unpublished doctoral thesis. Department of Archaeology, University of Cambridge

Claessen, H.J.M. 1988. *Over de politiek denkende en handelende mens. Een inleiding tot de politieke antropologie*. Assen/Maastricht

Clare, T. 1973. *Aspects of the Stone Circles and Kindred Monuments of North West England*. Unpublished M.A. Thesis, University of Liverpool, 2 vols

Clare, T. 1979. Rayset Pike long cairn in the Matchell mss., *TCWAAS* 79, 144–6

Clark, E.K. 1902. Excavations at Pule Hill, near Marsden. *Yorkshire Archaeological Journal* 16, 38–42

Clark, J. 1931. Note on some flint daggers of Scandinavian type in the British Isles. *Man* XXXII, 186–190

Clark, J.G.D. 1932. *The Mesolithic Age in Britain*. Cambridge: Cambridge University Press

Clark, J.G.D. and Rankine, W. F. 1939. Excavations at Farnham, Surrey (1937–8): the Horsham Culture and the question of Mesolithic dwellings. *Proceedings of the Prehistoric Society* 5, 61–118

Clark, J.G.D. 1972. *Starr Carr: a case study in bio-archaeology*. Reading, Mass

Clarke, D.L. 1970. *Beaker Pottery of Great Britain and Ireland*. Cambridge: Cambridge University Press

Clarke, D.L. 1973. Archaeology: the loss of innocence. *Antiquity* 47, 6–18

Clifford, E. and Daniel, G. 1940. The Rodmarton and Avering portholes. *Proceedings of the Prehistoric Society* 6, 133–165

Clough T. and Cummins, W.A. (eds) 1988. *Stone Axe Studies 2*. London: CBA Research Report 67

Coles, B. 1998. Doggerland: a speculative survey. *Proceedings of the Prehistoric Society* 64, 45–81

Collens, J. 1994. Recent discoveries from the air in Cheshire, in P. Carrington (ed.) 1994. Chester: Cheshire City Council Archaeological Service Occasional Paper No 2, 19–25

Collingwood, R.G. 1933. An Introduction to the Prehistory of Cumberland, Westmorland and Lancashire-North-of-the-Sands. *TCWAAS* 33, 163–200

Coltman, V. 2006. Representation, replication and collecting in Charles Townley's late eighteenth-century library. *Art History* 29.2, 304

Comaroff, J. and Comaroff, J. 1989. The colonization of consciousness in South Africa. *Economy and Society* 18(3), 267–95

Conkey, M.W. 1990. Experimenting with style in archaeology: some historical and theoretical issues, in M.W. Conkey and C. Hastorf (eds) *The Uses of Style in Archaeology*. Cambridge: Cambridge University Press, 5–17

Coombs, D.G. 1982. Excavations at the Hillfort at Castercliffe, Nelson, Lancs., *TLCAS* 1982, 81, 111–30

Coope, G.R., Robinson, D. and Roe, F. 1988. The Petrological Identification of Stone Implements from Lancashire and Cheshire, in T. Clough and W.A. Cummins (eds) *Stone Axe Studies* volume 2. London: CBA Research Report 67, 60–66

Coppock, J.T. 1976 (2nd ed.). *An Agricultural Atlas of England and Wales*. London

Courtney, T.W. 1978. *A Stone Age Site: Unstone, Derbyshire*. North Derbyshire Archaeological Committee

Cowell, R.W. 1991a. The prehistory of Merseyside. *Journal of the Merseyside Archaeological Society* 7, 21–60

Cowell, R.W. 1991b. Wetland survey in Merseyside: Winter 1990–91. *NW Wetlands Survey Annual Report 2*. English Heritage/Lancaster University, 13–20

Cowell, R.W. 1992. Wetland survey in Merseyside 1991/92: aspects of the Mesolithic and Neolithic settlement, *North West Wetlands Survey Annual Report 1992*, 29–36

Cowell, R.W. 1995. Some Neolithic and Bronze Age Finds from Merseyside and the North West. *Journal of the Merseyside Archaeological Society* 9, 25–44

Cowell, R.W. 1996. The Upper Palaeolithic and Mesolithic, in R. Newman (ed.) *The Archaeology of Lancashire: Present State and Future Priorities*. Lancaster: Lancaster University Archaeological Unit

Cowell, R.W. 2000a. Brook House Farm, Halewood, in R.W. Cowell and R.A. Philpott, *Prehistoric, Romano-British and Medieval Settlement in Lowland North West England: archaeological excavations along the A5300 road corridor in Merseyside*. Liverpool: National Museums and Galleries on Merseyside, 27–66

Cowell, R.W. 2000b. The late prehistoric period in the north west, in R.W. Cowell and R.A. Philpott *Prehistoric, Romano-British and Medieval Settlement in Lowland North West England: archaeological excavations along the A5300 road corridor in Merseyside*. Liverpool: National Museums and Galleries on Merseyside, 169–174

Cowell, R.W. 2002. *Romano-British and Late Prehistoric Excavations at Duttons Farm, Lathom, West Lancashire, Second interim report. 1999–2001*. National Museums Liverpool unpublished report

Cowell, R.W. 2003. *Prehistoric and Romano-British Excavations at Duttons Farm, Lathom, West Lancashire, Third interim report. 1999–2002*. National Museums Liverpool unpublished report

Cowell, R.W. and Adams, M. 2000. *Romano-British and Late Prehistoric Excavations at Duttons Farm, Lathom, West Lancashire*. Unpublished report, Liverpool Museum

Cowell, R.W. and Innes, J.B. 1994. *The Wetlands of Merseyside. NW Wetlands Survey 1*. Lancaster: Lancaster Imprints 2

Cowell, R.W., Milles, A. and Roberts, G. 1993. Prehistoric footprints on Formby Point beach, Merseyside, in R. Middleton (ed.) *NW Wetlands Survey Annual Report 1993*. Lancaster: Lancaster Imprints, 43–48

Cowell, R.W. and Philpott, R.A. 2000. *Prehistoric, Romano-British and Medieval Settlement in Lowland North West England: archaeological excavations along the A5300 road corridor in Merseyside*. Liverpool: National Museums and Galleries on Merseyside

Cowell, R.W. and Warhurst, M.H., 1984. *The Calderstones: a Prehistoric Tomb on Merseyside*. Liverpool: Merseyside Archaeological Society

Cowling, E.T. 1946. *Rombalds Way: a Prehistory of Mid-Wharfedale*. Otley

Craig, C.R., Knüsel, C.J. and Carr, G.C. 2005. Fragmentation, mutilation and dismemberment: an interpretation of human remains on Iron Age sites, in M. Parker-Pearson and N. Thorpe (eds) *Warfare, Violence and Slavery in Prehistory*. Oxford, BAR International Series 1374, 165–180

Cross, M. 1938. A prehistoric settlement on Walney, *TCWAAS* 38, 160

Cross, M. 1939. A prehistoric settlement on Walney Island, Part II, *TCWAAS* 39, 262–283

Cross, M. 1942. A prehistoric settlement on Walney Island, III, *TCWAAS* 42, 112–15

Cross, M. 1946. A prehistoric settlement on Walney Island, IV, *TCWAAS* 46, 67–76

Cross, M. 1949. A prehistoric settlement on Walney Island, VI, *TCWAAS* 49, 1–9

Cross, M. 1950. A prehistoric settlement on Walney Island, *TCWAAS* 50, 15–19

Cummins, W.A. 1980. Stone Axes as a Guide to Neolithic Communications and Boundaries in England and Wales. *Proceedings of the Prehistoric Society* 46, 45–60

Cundhill, P.R. 1981. The history of vegetation and land use of two peat mosses in south-west Lancashire. *The Manchester Geographer*, new series, 2(2), 35–44

Cunliffe, B. 1978. *Hengistbury Head*. London: Elek

Cunnington, M.E. 1923. *The Early Iron Age Inhabited Site at All Cannings Cross Farm, Wiltshire*. Devizes: Simpson and Co

Davey, P.J. 1976. The Distribution of Bronze Age Metalwork from Lancashire and Cheshire. *JCAS* 59, 1–13

Davey, P.J. and Forster, E. 1975. *Bronze Age Metalwork from Lancashire and Cheshire, Work Notes 1*. Liverpool: University of Liverpool Department of Prehistoric Archaeology

Davies, M. 1941–3. A preliminary survey of local upland peat deposits in relation to the Mesolithic occupation of the area around Rochdale. *Transactions of Rochdale Literary and Scientific Society* 21, 83–97

Dawes, N. 1851–2. British Burial Places near Bolton, County Lancaster. *Transactions of the Historical Society of Lancashire and Cheshire* 4, 130–2

Dawkins, W.B. 1875. On the Stone Mining Tools from Alderley Edge. *Proceedings of the Literary and Philosophical Society of Manchester* 14, 74–79

Dawkins, W.B. 1876. On the Stone Mining Tools from Alderley Edge, Cheshire. *Journal of the Anthropological Institute of Great Britain and Ireland*, vol. 5, 1876, 2–5

Dawkins, W.B. 1900. On the exploration of prehistoric sepulchral remains of the Bronze Age at Bleasdale by S. Jackson esq. *TLCAS* 18, 114–24

De Rance, C.E. 1877. *The Superficial Geology of the Country Adjoining the Coasts of South-West Lancashire*. London: Memoirs of the Geological Survey of England and Wales

Deans, T. 1933. Tardenoisian sites on Oxenhope Moor. *Naturalist*, 223–7

Dickens, C. 1995 [1854]. *Hard Times: for these times*. London: Penguin

Dickson, E. 1888. Geological notes on the Preston Docks Works and Ribble development scheme. *Proceedings of the Liverpool Geological Society* 5(4), 869–76

Dietler, M. and Herbich, I. 1998. Habitus, techniques, style: an integrated approach to the social understanding of material culture and boundaries, in M.T. Stark (ed.) *The Archaeology of Social Boundaries*. Washington: Smithsonian Books, 232–63

Dimbleby, G.W. 1975. Summary and general conclusions, in J.G. Evans, S. Limbrey and H. Cleere (eds) *The Effect of Man on the Landscape: the highland zone*. CBA Research Report No. 11

Douglas, M. 1966. *Purity and Danger. An analysis of concepts of pollution and taboo*. London: Routledge

Douglas, M. 1973. *Natural Symbols: explorations in cosmology*. Harmondsworth: Penguin

Drewett, P. 1980. Black patch and the later Bronze Age in Sussex, in J. Barrett and R. Bradley (eds) *Settlement and Society in the British Later Bronze Age*. Oxford: BAR 83, 377–96

Duckworth, W.H.L. and Shore, L.R. 1911. Report on human crania from peat deposits in England. *Man* 11, 134–40

Dungworth, D. 2000. A note on the analysis of crucibles and moulds. *Historical Metallurgy* 34, 83–86

Dumayne, L. 1995. Human impact on vegetation in northern Cumbria since the Bronze Age: relating palynological and archaeological evidence. Cumberland. *TCWAAS* 95, 23–33

Ecroyd Smith, H. 1868. An ancient British cemetery at Wavertree. *Lancashire and Cheshire Antiquarian Society*, 1868, 130–146

Edmonds, M. 1990. Description, understanding and the *Chaîne Opératoire*. *Archaeological Review from Cambridge* 9(1): 55–70

Edmonds, M., Evans, H., Lund, J., Maxwell, R. and Star, M. 2002. Evaluation of Landscape Features on Sizergh Fell. *Archaeology North* 20, 13–15

Edwards, B.J.N. 1969. Lancashire Archaeological Notes, Prehistoric and Roman. *Transactions of the Historical Society of Lancashire and Cheshire* 121, 99–108

Edwards, B.J.N. 1973. Quernmore. *Antiquity* 47, 298–301

Edwards, B.J.N. 1978a. Bronze Age Site, Pilling, the Finds 2: flint and pottery, further work. *Lancashire Archaeological Bulletin* 4.3, 16

Edwards, B.J.N. 1978b. Bronze Age Site at Pilling, the Finds 1: flint. *Lancashire Archaeological Bulletin* 4.4, 73

Edwards, B.J.N. 1979. A new Bronze Axe from Pilling. *Lancashire Archaeological Bulletin*, 4.3, 16

Edwards, B.J.N. 1992. Bond's Farm, Pilling, Lancashire. *North West Wetland Survey Annual Report 1992*. English Heritage/Lancaster University, 42–3

Edwards, B.J.N. 2007. A report on excavations at Bonds' Farm Pilling, in P.J. Cherry (ed.) Studies In Northern Prehistory: Essays In Memory Of Clare Fell, *TCWAAS*

Edwards, K.J. and Hirons, K.R. 1984. Cereal pollen grains in pre-elm decline deposits: implications for the earliest agriculture in Britain and Ireland. *Journal of Archaeological Science* 11, 71–80

Edwards, W. and Trotter, F.M. 1954. *The Pennines and Adjacent Areas. British Regional Geology.* London: HMSO

Ehrenberg, M. 1989. The interpretation of regional variability in British and Irish Bronze Age Metalwork, in H.A Nordstrom, and A. Knape (eds) *Bronze Age Studies.* Museum of National Antiquities Stockholm Studies 6, Stockholm, 77–88

Ehrenreich, B. 1997. *Blood Rites: origins and history of the passions for war.* London: Virago

Elgee, F. and Elgee, H.W. 1933. *The Archaeology of Yorkshire.* London

Ellis, H. 1943. *The Road to Hel. A Study of the Conception of the Dead in Old Norse Literature.* Cambridge: Cambridge University Press

Ellis, P. (ed.) 1993. *Beeston Castle, Cheshire: Excavations by Laurence Keen and Peter Hough 1968–85.* London: English Heritage

Engels, F. 1986 [1884]. *The origins of the family, private property and the state* (West, trans.). London: Penguin Books

English Heritage 1990. *Monuments Protection Programme.* http://www.eng-h.gov.uk/mpp/mcd/pic.htm

Eriksen, T.H. 1993. *Ethnicity and Nationalism: Anthropological Perspectives.* London: Pluto

Evans, H. 2004. Where is the Cumbrian Neolithic? in V. Cummings and C. Fowler (eds) *Neolithic Traditions of the Irish Sea.* Oxford: Oxbow

Evans, H. and Coward, D. 2004. A Prehistoric occupation site at Sandscale Haws, Barrow-in-Furness. *Archaeology North* 22, 16–18

Evans, H. and Edmonds, M. 2003. *Interim Report on archaeological fieldwork undertaken on Sizergh Fell, South Cumbria, July 2003.* Sheffield University unpublished report

Evans, J. 1881. *The Ancient Bronze Implements, Weapons and Ornaments of Great Britain and Ireland.* London: Longmans

Evans, J.G. 1975. *The Environment of Early Man in the British Isles.* London

Fairburn, N., Bonner, D., Carruthers, W.J., Gale, G.R., Matthews, K.J., Morris E. and Ward, M. 2003. Brook House Farm, Bruen Stapleford: excavation of a first millennium BC settlement. *JCAS* 77 (for 2002), 9–57

Feather, S.W. and Manby, T.G. 1970. Prehistoric Chambered Tombs of the Pennines. *Yorkshire Archaeological Journal* 42, 396–7

Feeley-Harnik, G. 1989. Cloth and the creation of ancestors in Madagascar, in J. Schneider and A.B. Weiner (eds) *Cloth and Human Experience.* Washington D.C.: Smithsonian Institution Press, 73–116

Fell, C.I. 1953. A Beaker burial on Sizergh Fell, near Kendal. *TCWAAS* 53, 1–5

Fielding, J.T. 1905. A record of rambles, historical facts, legends and nature notes. *The Rambler.* Darwen: Darwen Rambling Club vol 1

Fishwick, H.1889. *The History of the Parish of Rochdale.* Rochdale: privately published

Fitzpatrick, A. 1997. Everyday life in Iron Age Wessex, in A. Gwilt and C. Haselgrove (eds) *Reconstructing Iron Age societies: new approaches to the British Iron Age.* Oxford: Oxbow Monograph 71, 73–86

Fleming, A. 1971. Bronze Age Agriculture on the Marginal Lands of North-East Yorkshire. *Agricultural Historical Review* 19, 1–24

Fletcher, M. 1986. A fortified site at Castle Steads, Walmersley, Bury. *Greater Manchester Archaeological Journal* 2, 31–40

Fontijn, D.R. 2002. Sacrificial landscapes: cultural biographies of persons, objects and 'natural' places in the Bronze Age of the southern Netherlands *c*.2300–600 BC. *Analecta Praehistorica Leidensia* 33/34

Ford, T.D. and Rieuwerts, J.H. (eds) 1983. *Lead Mining in the Peak District.* Bakewell: Peak Park Joint Planning Board

Forde-Johnston, J.L. 1957. Megalithic art in the north-west of Britain: the Calderstones, Liverpool. *Proceedings of the Prehistoric Society* 2, 20–39

Forde-Johnston, J. 1962. The Iron Age Hillforts of Lancashire and Cheshire. *TLCAS* 72, 9–46

Fowler, C. and Cummings, V. 2003. Places of transformation: building monuments from water and stone in the Neolithic of the Irish Sea. *Journal of the Royal Anthropological Institute* 9, 1–20

Fox, C.F. 1932. *The Personality of Britain: its influence on inhabitant and invader in prehistoric and early historic times.* Cardiff: National Museum of Wales

Fraser, D. 1983. *Land and Society in Neolithic Orkney*. Oxford: BAR British Series 117

Freke, D.J. and Holgate, R. 1988. Excavation of two second millennium BC mounds. *JCAS* 70, 9–30

Freke, D.J. and Thacker, A.T. 1988. The inhumation cemetery at Southworth Hall Farm, Winwick. *JCAS* 70, 31–8

Frere, S.S. and Cotton, M.A. 1968. *Buckinghamshire Archaeological Society Records of Buckinghamshire: Journal of the Architectural and Archaeological Society for the County of Buckinghamshire* 18, 187–203

Gale, S. and Hunt, C. 1985. The stratigraphy of Kirkhead Cave an Upper Palaeolithic site in northern England. *Proceedings of the Prehistoric Society* 51, 283–304

Gale, S. and Hunt, C. 1990. The stratigraphy of Kirkhead Cave an Upper Palaeolithic site in northern England: a discussion. *Proceedings of the Prehistoric Society* 56, 51–6

Gardner, W. and Savory, H. N. 1964. *Dinorben: a hill-fort occupied in Early Iron Age and Roman times.* Cardiff

Garland, A.N. 1987. The skull on the moss. *Medioscope* 65, 32–3

Garner, A. 1994. The Alderley Edge Shovel: The Finders Story. *Current Archaeology* 137, 172–3

Garner, D. 2001. The Bronze Age of Manchester Airport: Runway 2, in J. Brück (ed.) *Bronze Age Landscapes.* Oxford: Oxbow

Garstang, J. 1906. Early Man, in W. Farrer and J. Brownbill. *Victoria History of the Counties of England. Lancashire* vol. 1. London: Boydell and Brewer, 211–56

Garwood, P. 1999. Grooved ware in Southern Britain: chronology and interpretation, in R. Cleal and A. MacSween (eds) *Grooved Ware in Britain and Ireland*. Oxford: Oxbow Books, 145–176

Gatty, Rev. R.A. 1912. Pigmy flint implements: their provenance and use. *TLCAS* 30, 14–23

Gaythorpe, H. 1899. *Transactions of the Cumberland and Westmorland Antiquarian and Archaeological Society. TCWAAS* xiii, 164–66

Gaythorpe, H. 1900. Prehistoric Implements in Furness. *TCWAAS* os xiv 23

Gaythorpe, H. 1903. Notes on the Bronze Celts from Urswick and Bronze Spearhead from Piel Castle. *TCWAAS* ns iii 410

Gaythorpe, H. 1906. Prehistoric Implements in Furness. *TCWAAS* ns vi art 4

Geary, P. 1994. *Living with the Dead in the Middle Ages.* London: Cornell University Press

Gell, A. 1992. *The Anthropology of Time: cultural constructions of temporal maps and images.* Oxford: Berg

Gent, H. 1983. Centralised storage in later prehistoric Britain. *Proceedings of the Prehistoric Society* 49, 243–268

Gerritsen, F.A. 2001. *Local Identities. Landscape and community in the late Prehistoric Meuse-Demer-Scheldt Region.* Amsterdam: Free University of Amsterdam

Gibson, A. and Kinnes, I. 1997. On the urns of a dilemma: radiocarbon and the Peterborough problem. *Oxford Journal of Archaeology* 16, 65–72

Godelier, M. 1999. *The Enigma of the Gift.* Cambridge: Polity Press

Godwin, H. and Switsur, V.R. 1966. Cambridge University natural radiocarbon measurements VIII. *Radiocarbon* 8, 390–400

Gonzalez, S. and Cowell, R.W. Forthcoming. *Neolithic Coastal Archaeology and Environment in NW England*

Gonzalez, S. and Huddart, D. 2002. Formby Point. *Quaternary of Northern England* 25, 569–582

Gonzalez, S., Huddart, D. and Roberts, G. 1997. Holocene development of the Sefton coast: a multidisciplinary approach to understanding the archaeology, in A. Sinclair, E. Slater and J. Gowlett (eds) *Archaeological Science 1995.* Oxford: Oxbow Books, 289–99

Gosden, C. and Marshall, Y. 1999. The cultural biography of objects. *World Archaeology* 31, 169–78

Green, H.S. 1980. *Arrowheads of the British Isles.* Oxford: BAR 75

Green, H.S. 1984. Flint arrowheads: typology and interpretation. *Lithics* 5, 19–39

Greene, J.P. and Hough, P.R. 1977. Excavation in the medieval village of Norton 1974–76. *JCAS* 60, 61–93

Grimes, W. 1931. The Early Bronze Age Flint Dagger in England and Wales. *Proceedings of the Prehistoric Society of East Anglia* VI, 340–355

Haddon, A.C. and Maudslay, A.P. 1928. *Man*, vol. 28, 169–171

Hains, B.A. and Horton, 1969. *Central England. British Regional Geology.* London: HMSO

Hall, D., Wells, C.E. and Huckerby, E. 1995. *The Wetlands of Greater Manchester: NW Wetlands Survey 2.* Lancaster: Lancaster Imprints

Hall, B.R. and Folland, C.J. 1967. *Soils of the South-West Lancashire Plain.* Harpenden: Memoirs of the Soil Survey of Great Britain, England and Wales

Hallam, A.M. 1990. *The Bronze Age Pottery of North-West England and its Social Context.* Unpublished MPhil dissertation, University of Liverpool

Hallam, J.S. 1960. *The Mesolithic of the Central Pennines.* MA thesis, University of Liverpool

Hallam, J.S. 1970. The Prehistory of Lancashire. *Archaeological Journal* 127, 232–7

Hallam, J.S. 1988. *The Surviving Past: Archaeological Finds and Excavations in Central Lancashire.* Chorley: Countryside Publications

Hallam, J.S. 1995. The Pendleton legend, Craggs Farm footprints and Apronful Hill. *TLCAS* 91, 127–43

Hallam, J.S., Edwards, B.J.N. and Stuart, A.J. 1973. A late glacial elk with associated barbed points from High Furlong, Lancashire. *Proceedings of the Prehistoric Society* 39, 100–128

Halstead, A. 1893. *Singleton Thorpe: A Buried Village on the Blackpool Coast.* Blackpool

Harding, J., Frodsham, P. and Durden, T. 1996. Towards an agenda for Neolithic Studies in Northern England, in P. Frodsham (ed.) *Neolithic Studies in No-Mans Land.* Newcastle: Northern Archaeology 13/14, 189–201

Härke, H. 1994. A context for the Saxon barrow [on Lowbury Hill]. *Archaeological Journal* 151, 158–211

Harker, J. 1865. British interments at Lancaster Moor. *Journal of British Archaeological Association* 21, 159–61

Harker, J. 1877. British interments at Lancaster. *Journal of British Archaeological Association* 33, 125–27

Harris, M. and Hughes, B. 2005 (2nd edition). *The Ancient History of the Wyre.* Fleetwood: Fylde Country Life Preservation Society

Harrison, S. 1995. Transformation of identity in Sepik warfare, in M. Strathern (ed.) *Shifting Contexts, Transformations in Anthropological Knowledge.* London, 81–97

Harrison, W. 1892. Archaeological finds in Lancashire. *TLCAS* X, 249–52

Harrison, W. 1910. Leland's itinerary. *TLCAS* 28, 40–57

Haselgrove, C. 1996. The Iron Age, in R. Newman (ed.) *The Archaeology of Lancashire: Present State and Future Priorities.* Lancaster: Lancaster University Archaeological Unit, 61–73

Hearne, T. (ed.) 1710. *The Itinerary of John Leland the Antiquary.* Oxford: Thomas Hearne

Helms, M.W. 1988. *Ulysses' Sail: An Ethnographic Odyssey of Power, Knowledge and Geographical Distance.* Princeton: Princeton University Press

Helms, M.W. 1993. *Craft and the Kingly Ideal: art, trade and power.* Austin: University of Texas Press

Hey, G., Bayliss, A. and Boyle, A. 1999. Iron Age inhumation burials at Yarnton. *Antiquity* 73, 551–62

Hibbert, F.A., Switsur, V.R. and West, R.G. 1971. Radiocarbon dating of Flandrian pollen zones at Red Moss, Lancashire. *Proceedings of the Royal Society of London B* 177, 161–76

Higham, N.J. 1983. A Romano-British Farm Site and Field System at Yanwath Wood, near Penrith. *TCWAAS* 83, 49–58

Higham, N.J. 1985. Tatton Park: Interim Report on the 7th Season of Excavation of the Deserted Village. *Cheshire Archaeological Bulletin* 10, 75–82

Higham, N.J. 1992. *Rome, Britain and the Anglo-Saxons.* London: Seaby

Higham, N.J. 1995. *An English empire: Bede and the early Anglo-Saxon kings.* Manchester: Manchester University Press

Higham, N.J. and Cane, T. 1999. The Tatton Project Part 1: prehistoric to sub-Roman settlement and land use. *Cheshire Archaeological Society* 74 (for 1996–7), 1–62

Hills, C. 1997. Beowulf and archaeology, in R.E. Bjork and R.E. Niles (eds) *A Beowulf Handbook.* Exeter: University of Exeter, 291–310

Hird, F. 1912. *Lancashire Stories: containing all that appeals to the heart and the imagination in the Lancashire of today and of many yesterdays.* 2 vols. London and Edinburgh: T.C. and E.C. Jack. Vol 1, 205–208

Hodgkinson, D., Huckerby, E., Middleton, R.H. and Wells, C.E. 2000. *The Lowland Wetlands of Cumbria.* North West Wetlands Survey, Lancaster Imprints 8. Lancaster: Lancaster University Archaeological Unit

Hodgson, J. and Brennand, M. 2006. The prehistoric period resource assessment, in M. Brennand (ed.) The Archaeology of North West England, an Archaeological Research Framework for North West England: vol 1 resource assessment. *Archaeology North West* 8, issue 18 for 2006

Holden, T.G. 1995. Pollen analysis of the Lindow III food residue, in R.C. Turner and R.G. Scaife (eds) *Bog Bodies: new discoveries and new perspectives*. London: British Museum Press, 76–82

Holtorf, C. 2002. Notes on the life history of a pot sherd. *Journal of Material Culture* 7, 49–71

Holtorf, C. 2005. *From Stonehenge to Las Vegas: Archaeology as Popular Culture*. Walnut Creek, CA: Altamira Press

Hope Taylor, B. 1977. *Yeavering: An Anglo-British Centre of Early Northumbria*. London: Department of the Environment

Howard-Davis, C.L.E. 1996. Seeing the sites: survey and excavation on the Anglezarke uplands, Lancashire. *Proceedings of the Prehistoric Society* 61, 133–66

Howard-Davis, C.L.E., Innes, J. and Stocks, C. 1988. *Peat and the Past*. Lancaster: Lancaster Imprints

Howard-Davis, C. and Williams, J.H. 2005. Excavations on a Bronze Age cairn at Hardendale Nab, Shap, Cumbria. *Archaeological Journal* 161, 11–53

Huddart, D., Gonzalez, S. and Roberts, G. 1999a. The archaeological record and mid-Holocene marginal coastal palaeoenvironments around Liverpool Bay, in Edwards and Sadler (eds) *Holocene Environments of Prehistoric Britain*. London: Quaternary Proceedings No. 7, Quaternary Research Association, 563–74

Huddart, D., Roberts, G. and Gonzalez, S. 1999b. Holocene human and animal footprints and their relationships with coastal environmental change, Formby Point, NW England. *England Quaternary International* 55, 29–41

Hume, A. 1863. *Ancient Meols*. London: J. Russell Smith

Innes, J.B. and Tooley, M. 1993. The Age and Vegetational History of the Sefton Coast Dunes, in D. Atkinson and J. Houston (eds) *The Sand dunes of the Sefton Coast*. National Museums and Galleries on Merseyside, 35–40

Isbell, W.H. 2000. What we should be studying: the 'imagined community' and the 'natural community', in M.A. Canuto and J. Yaeger, *The Archaeology of Communities, a New World Perspective*. London: Routledge, 243–66

Jackson, J.W. 1909. Preliminary report on the exploration of "Dog Holes" cave, Warton Crag, near Carnforth, Lancashire. *TLCAS*, 1–32

Jackson, J.W. 1910. Further report on the explorations at Dog Holes, Warton, Lancs, with remarks on the contents of two adjacent caves. *TLCAS* 28, 59–81

Jackson, J.W. 1912. Third report on the explorations at Dog Holes, Warton Crag, Lancs. *TLCAS*, 99–130

Jackson, J.W. 1929–31. On the Discovery of a Shale Armlet on Flint Hill, near Blackstone Edge. *Transactions of the Rochdale Literary and Scientific Society* 17, 71–3

Jackson, J.W. 1935. The prehistoric archaeology of Lancashire and Cheshire. *TLCAS*, 65–106

Jacobi, R.M. 1976. Britain inside and outside Mesolithic Europe. *Proceedings of the Prehistoric Society* 42, 67–84

Jacobi, R.M. 1978. Northern England in the eighth millennium bc: an essay, in P. Mellars (ed.) *The Early Postglacial Settlement of Northern Europe*. London, 295–332

Jacobi, R.M. 1980. The early Holocene settlement of Wales, in A. J. Taylor (ed.) *Culture and Environment in Prehistoric Wales*. Oxford: BAR 76, 131–206

Jacobi, R.M. 1987. Misanthropic miscellany: musings on British early Flandrian archaeology and other flights of fancy, in P. Rowley-Conwy, M. Zvelebil and H.P. Blankhorn, *Mesolithic Northwest Europe*. Sheffield 163–68

Jacobi, R.M., Tallis, J.H. and Mellars, P.A. 1976. The southern Pennine Mesolithic and the ecological record. *Journal of Archaeological Science* 3, 307–20

Jacobi, R.M., Gowlett, J.A., Hedges, R.E.M. and Gillespie, R. 1986. Accelerator mass spectrometry dating of the Upper Palaeolithic finds, with the Poulton elk as an example, in D.A. Roe (ed.) *Studies in the Upper Palaeolithic of Britain and Northwest Europe*. Oxford: BAR International Series 296, 121–8

Jacobsthal, P.F. 1944. *Early Celtic Art*. Oxford: Clarendon Press

James, R. 1636 [1845]. *Iter Lancastrense*. Manchester: Chetham Society

Jenkins, R. 1997. *Rethinking Ethnicity: Arguments and Explorations.* London: Sage

Jewitt, Ll. 1886. *Reliquary* 23, vol 6, 137–8

Jones, A. 2001. Enduring images? Image production and memory in Earlier Bronze Age Scotland, in J. Brück (ed.) 217–28

Jones, A. 2002. *Archaeological Theory and Scientific Practice.* Cambridge: Cambridge University Press

Jones, S. 1997. *The Archaeology of Ethnicity.* London: Routledge

Jopling, C.M. 1846. A Letter to George Godwin on the Subject of Remains Ascribed to the Era of the Druids in Furness, North of Lancashire, 1846. *Archaeologia* 31, 448–53, fig. 448

Kaul, F. 1997. Skibet og solhesten. Om nye fund af bronzealderens religiøse kunst. *Nationalmuseets Arbejdsmark,* 101–14

Kear, B.S. 1985. Soil developments and soil patterns in North-West England, in R.H. Johnson (ed.) *The Geomorphology of North-West England.* Manchester. Manchester University Press, 80–93

Kendall, H.P. and Roth, H.L. 1912. Local Prehistoric Implements. *Bankfield Museum Notes.* Halifax, 12

Kenna, R.J.B. 1978. Early Settlement on the North Wirral Coastal Area. *Journal of the Merseyside Archaeological Society* 2, 27–34

Kenna, R.J.B. 1986. The Flandrian Sequence of North Wirral (NW England). *Geological Journal* 21, 1–27

Kinnes, I. 1979. *Round Barrows and Ring-ditches in the British Neolithic.* London: British Museum Occasional Papers 7

Kinnes, I.A. and Longworth, I.H. 1985. *Catalogue of the Excavated Prehistoric and Romano-British Material in the Greenwell Collection.* London: British Museum

Knüsel, C.J. and Carr, G.C. 1995. On the significance of the crania from the River Thames and its tributaries. *Antiquity* 69, 162–169

Knüsel, C.J. and Carr, G.C. 1996. Comment. *Antiquity* 70, 190

Kopytoff, I. 1986. The cultural biography of things: commoditisation as process, in A. Appadurai (ed.) *The Social Life of Things.* Cambridge: Cambridge University Press, 64–91

Kristeva, J. 1982. *Powers of Horror: an essay on abjection.* New York: Columbia University Press

Kristiansen, K. (ed.) 1985. *Archaeological Formation Processes. The Representativity of Archaeological Remains from Danish Prehistory.* København: Nationalsmuseets Forlag

Küchler, S. 1987. Malangan: art and memory in a Melanesian society. *Man* ns 22, 238–55

Lamb, H.H. 1981. Climate from 1000 BC to 1000 AD, in M. Jones and G. Dimbleby (eds) *The Environment of Man: the Iron Age to the Anglo-Saxon Period.* Oxford: BAR British Series 87, 53–65

Langley Roberts, W. 1931. *Legends and Folklore of Lancashire.* London: Collins

Law, R. and Horsfall, J. 1882. Discovery of Flint Implements on the Hills between Todmorden and Marsden. *Proceedings of the Yorkshire Geological Society* 8, 1–15

Leach, E. 1976. *Culture and Communication: the logic by which symbols are connected.* Cambridge: Cambridge University Press

Leach, E. 1977. A view from the bridge, in M. Spriggs (ed.) *Archaeology and Anthropology: areas of mutual interest.* Oxford: BAR Supplementary Series 19, 161–76

Leach, G.B. 1951. Flint implements from the Worsthorne Moors, Lancashire. *Transactions of the Historic Society of Lancashire and Cheshire* 103, 1–22

Leah, M.D., Wells, C.E., Appleby, C. and Huckerby, E. 1997. *The Wetlands of Cheshire: NW Wetlands Survey 4.* Lancaster: Lancaster Imprints

Leigh, C. 1700. *The Natural History of Lancashire, Cheshire and the Peak in Derbyshire.* Oxford: Printed for the author

Lemonnier, P. 1993. Introduction, in P. Lemonnier (ed.) *Technological Choices: Transformation in Material Cultures since the Neolithic.* London: Routledge, 1–35

Lewis, G.D. 1970. *The Bronze Age in the Southern Pennines.* Unpublished M.A. Thesis, University of Liverpool

Longley, D.M.T. 1987. Prehistory, in B.E. Harris and A.T. Thacker (eds) *A History of the County of Chester vol 1. The Victoria County History of the Counties of England.* Oxford: Oxford University Press, 36–114

Longworth, I.H. 1961. The Origins and Development of the Primary Series in the Collared Urn Tradition in England and Wales. *Proceedings of the Prehistoric Society* 27, 263–306

Longworth, I.H. 1967. A Bronze Age hoard from Portfield Farm, Whalley, Lancashire. *Brit. Mus. Quart* 32, 1–2 and 8–14

Longworth, I.H. 1984. *Collared Urns of the Bronze Age in Great Britain and Ireland.* Cambridge: Cambridge University Press

Lort, Rev. 1779. Observations on Celts. *Archaeologia* 5, 106–18

Lowndes, R.A.C. 1964. Excavation of a Romano-British farmstead at Eller Beck. *TCWAAS* 64, 6–13

Lucy, S.J. 1992. The significance of mortuary ritual in the political manipulation of the landscape. *Archaeological Review from Cambridge* 11(1), 93–105

Lucy, S.J. 1994. Children in early medieval cemeteries. *Archaeological Review from Cambridge* 13, 21–34

Lucy, S.J. 1997. Housewives, warriors and slaves? Sex and gender in Anglo-Saxon burials, in J. Moore and E. Scott (eds) *Invisible People and Processes: writing gender and childhood into European archaeology.* Leicester: Leicester University Press, 150–68

Lynch, F. 1966. The Pikestones, Anglezarke, Lancashire. *Proceedings of the Prehistoric Society* 32, 347–8

Lynch, F. 1970. Prehistoric Anglesey, in H. Ramage (ed.) *Studies in Anglesey History* 3. Llangefni: Anglesey Antiquarian Society Field Club

Malinowski, 1922. *Argonauts of the Western Pacific.* London: Routledge

Manby, T.G. 1964. Early Bronze Age Axes from Yorkshire. *Yorkshire Archaeological Journal* 41, 344–55

Manby, T.G. 1967. *The Neolithic Cultures of the North of England.* Unpublished M.A. Thesis, University of Liverpool

Manby, T.G. 1968. *TLCAS* 75–6, 224–5 fig. 54

Manby, T.G. 1969. Bronze Age Pottery from Pule Hill, Marsden, W.R. Yorkshire and Foot Vessels of the Early Bronze Age from England. *Yorkshire Archaeological Journal* 62, 273–82

Manby, T.G. 1974. *Grooved Ware Sites in Yorkshire and the North of England.* Oxford: BAR British Series 9

Manby, T.G. and Turnbull, P. 1986. *The Bronze Age in Western Yorkshire.* Oxford: BAR British Series 158, 55–82

March 1903 Flint implements. *Transactions of the Lancashire and Cheshire Antiquarian Society,* 20, 228–9

March H.C. 1874. *The Flint Implements of the Pennines of East Lancashire*

March, H.C. 1886. A Cinerary Urn. *Rochdale Literary and Scientific Society Annual Report*

March, H.C. 1887. Types of sepulchral urns. *TLCAS* 5, 272–86

March, H.C. 1912. Pigmy flints: their provenance and use. *TLCAS* 30, 8–13

Marriott, A.D. 1991. *Settlement in the Lune Valley.* Unpublished BA dissertation, University of Durham

Matthews, K.J. 1996. Iron Age sea-borne trade in Liverpool Bay, in P. Carrington (ed.) *Where Deva Spreads her Wizard Stream: Trade and the Port of Chester.* Chester: Chester Archaeology Occasional Paper No 3, 12–23

Matthews, K.J. 1997. Immaterial culture: invisible peasants and consumer subcultures in north-west Britannia, in K. Meadows, C. Lemke and J. Heron, *TRAC 96. Proceedings of the Sixth Theoretical Roman Archaeology Conference.* Sheffield 1996. Oxford: Oxbow Books, 121–32

Matthews, K.J. 1994. Archaeology without artefacts: the Iron Age and Sub-Roman periods in Cheshire, in P. Carrington (ed.), 1994, 51–62

Matthews, K.J. 2002. The Iron Age of North-West England: A Socio-Economic Model. *JCAS* 76 (for 2000–1) 1–44

Matthews, K.J. 2001. The Iron Age of North-West England. *JCAS* 76, 1–51

Mauss, M. 1979 [1950]. Body techniques, in G. Gurwich (ed.) *Sociology and Anthropology.* London: Routledge, 97–123

Mauss, M. 1993 [1923/1924]. *The Gift. The form and reason for exchange in archaic societies.* London: Routledge

May, J. 1976. *Prehistoric Lincolnshire.* Lincoln

May, T. 1904. Notes on a Bronze Age Barrow. *TLCAS* 21 (for 1903), 120–126

McCafferty, P. 2007. Cult in cometary context, in D.A. Barrowclough and C.A.T. Malone, *Cult in Context: Reconsidering Ritual in Archaeology.* Oxford: Oxbow, 229–233

McKay, J. 1888. *Pendle Hill.* London

McMann, Jean. 1993. *Loughcrew: The Cairns: a guide to an ancient Irish landscape.* Oldcastle, Ireland: After Hours Books

McKenny-Hughes, T. 1904a. On another tumulus on Sizergh Fell. *TCWAAS* 4, 201–4

McKenny-Hughes, T. 1904b. Some notes on mound opening, with a description of one recently explored on Sizergh Fell, Westmorland. *TCWAAS* 4, 71–9

Meaney, A. 1964. *A Gazeteer of Early Anglo-Saxon Burial Sites.* London: Allen and Unwin

Meaney, A. 1981. *Anglo-Saxon Amulets and Curing Stones.* Oxford: BAR British Series 96

Mellars, P.A. 1973. The affinities of the Sandbeds Mesolithic site. *Yorkshire Archaeological Journal* 45, 13–18

Mellars, P.A. 1976a. Fire ecology, animal populations and man: a study of some ecological relationships in prehistory. *Proceedings of the Prehistoric Society* 42, 15–45

Mellars, P.A. 1976b. Settlement patterns and industrial variability in the British Mesolithic in G. Sieveking, I.H. Longworth and K.E. Wilson, *Problems in Economic and Social Archaeology.* London, 375–99

Middleton, J. (ed.) 1990. *NW Wetlands Annual Report* 1990. Lancaster

Middleton, R. 1993. Landscape archaeology in the North West and the definition of surface lithic scatter sites. *NW Wetlands Annual Report* 1993. Lancaster: Lancaster University Press, 1–8

Middleton, R. 1996. The Neolithic and Bronze Age, in R. Newman (ed.) *The Archaeology of Lancashire.* Lancaster: Lancaster University Press

Middleton, R. 1997. Hunter-gatherers and early farmers in the Lancashire wetlands. *ANW* 12, 140–145

Middleton, R., Wells, C.E. and Huckerby, E. 1995. *The Wetlands of North Lancashire, NW Wetlands Survey 3.* Lancaster: Lancaster Imprints

Middleton, R. and Tooley, M.J. in prep. *The Wetlands of West Lancashire, North West Wetland Survey.* Lancaster: Lancaster University Archaeological Unit

Morris, E. 1985. Prehistoric salt distributions: two case studies from western Britain. *Bulletin of the Board for Celtic Studies* 32, 336–79

Morris, E.L. 2005. *Lancashire Earlier Prehistoric Pottery: Assessment for detailed petrological analysis.* Southampton: Unpublished Report for the author, University of Southampton

Mortimer, J. 1905. *Forty Years' Researches in British and Saxon Burial Mounds of East Yorkshire.* London: Brown

Mulk, I.M. 1997. Sacrificial places and their meaning in Saami society, in D.L. Carmichael, J. Hubert, B. Reeves and A. Schanche (eds) *Sacred Sites, Sacred Places.* London: One World Archaeology 23, 121–31

Mullin, D. 2002. Early Neolithic Pottery from Cheshire. *JCAS* 77, 1–7

Mullin, D. 2003. *The Bronze Age Landscape of the Northern English Midlands.* Oxford: BAR (British Series) 351

Munn, N.D. 1986. *The Fame of Gawa: a symbolic study of value transformation in a Massim (Papua New Guinea) society.* Cambridge: Cambridge University Press

Musson, C.R. 1991. *The Breidden Hillfort: a later prehistoric settlement in the Welsh Marches.* London: CBA Research Report No 76

Needham, S. 1982. *The Ambleside Hoard: A discovery in the Royal Collections.* British Museum Occasional Paper 39

Needham, S. 1990. *The Petter's Late Bronze Age Metalwork: an Analytical Study of Thames Valley Metalworking in its Settlement Context.* British Museum Occasional Paper 70. London

Needham, S. 1993. The Beeston Castle Bronze Age metalwork and its significance, in P. Ellis, 41–50

Needham, S. 1996. Chronology and periodisation in the British Bronze Age. *Acta Archaeologica* 67, 121–40

Needham, S., Bronk Ramsay, C., Coombs, D., Cartwright, C. and Pettitt, P. 1997. An independent chronology for British Bronze Age metalwork: the results of the Oxford radiocarbon accelerator programme. *Archaeological Journal* 154, 55–107

Nevell, M. 1988a. Arthill Heath Farm, trial excavations on a prehistoric settlement site 1987–88. *Manchester Archaeological Bulletin* 3, 4–13

Nevell, M. 1988b. Early Settlement in Northern Cheshire. CBA Group 5 *Newsletter* 56, 10–12

Nevell, M. 1991. A Field Survey of High Legh Parish. Part One, Prehistoric and Roman Evidence. *ANW* 1, 16–19

Nevell, M. 1992a. *A History and Archaeology of Tameside Volume 1: Tameside before 1066.* Tameside Metropolitan Borough Council with the Greater Manchester Archaeological Unit

Nevell, M. 1992b. *Settlement and Society in the Mersey Basin c.2000 BC to c.AD 400. A Landscape Study.* Manchester: Unpublished PhD, Department of Archaeology, Manchester University

Nevell, M. 1994a. Late prehistoric pottery types from the Mersey Basin, in P. Carrington (ed) *From Flints to Flower Pots. Current Research in the Dee Mersey Region.* Chester: Cheshire City Council Archaeological Service Occasional Paper No 2, 33–41

Nevell, M. 1994b. Rainsough. A Romano-British Site in the Irwell Valley. *ANW* 2, 11–15

Nevell, M. 1997. *The Archaeology of Trafford. A Study of the origins of Community in North West England Before 1900.* Manchester: Greater Manchester Archaeological Unit, University of Manchester Archaeological Unit and Trafford Metropolitan Borough Council

Nevell, M. 1999a. Iron Age and Romano-British rural settlement in North West England: theory, marginality and settlement, in M. Nevell (ed.) *Living on the edge of empire: models, methodology and marginality. Late-prehistoric and Romano-British rural settlement in North-West England.* Manchester, CBA North West Volume 3, University of Manchester and Chester Archaeology, 14–26

Nevell, M. 1999b. Great Woolden Hall: A Model for the Material Culture of Iron Age and Romano-British Rural Settlement in North West England, in M. Nevell (ed.) *Living on the Edge of Empire. Models, Methodology and Marginality.* Manchester: CBA North West Volume 3, University of Manchester and Chester Archaeology, 48–64

Nevell, M. 2001. The Edge of Empire: Late Prehistoric and Romano-British Settlement in North West England. A Study in Marginality, in N.J. Higham (ed.) *Archaeology of the Roman Empire. A tribute to the life and works of Professor Barri Jones.* Oxford, BAR International Series 940, 9–74

Nevell, M. 2003a. Legh Oaks Farm, High Legh. The Value of Sample Excavation on Two Sites of the late Prehistoric and Roman Periods. *JCAS* 77, 115–30

Nevell, M. 2003b. The late prehistoric and Romano-British settlement of the Mersey Basin: a study in marginality. *JCAS* 78, 1–21

Nevell, M. 2004. The Late Prehistoric and Romano-British Settlement of the Mersey Basin. A Study in Marginality. *JCAS* 78, 1–22

Nowakowski, J. 1991. Trethellan Farm, Newquay: the excavation of a lowland Bronze Age settlement and Iron Age cemetery. *Cornish Archaeology* 30, 5–242

Oldfield, F. 1960. Studies in the post-glacial history of British vegetation: Lowland Lonsdale. *New Phytologist* 59, 192–217

Oldfield, F. 1963. Pollen analysis and man's role in the ecological history of the South East Lake District. *Geografisca Annaler* 54, 23–40

Oldfield, F. 1969. Pollen analysis and the history of landuse. *Advancement of Science* 25, 298–311

Oldfield, F., Dearing, J.A., Thompson, R., Garrett-Jones, S.E. 1978. Some magnetic properties of lake sediments and their possible links with erosion rates. *Polskie Archivum Hydrobiologii* 25, 321–34

Oldfield, F., Appleby, P.G., Cambray, R.S., Eakins, J.D., Barber, K.E., Baltarbee, R.W., Pearson, G.R. and Williams, J.M. 1979. ^{210}Pb, ^{137}Cs, ^{239}Pu profiles in ombrotrophic peat. *Oikos* 33, 40–45

Oldfield, F., Tolonen, K. and Thompson, R. 1981. History of particulate atmospheric pollution from magnetic measurements in dated Finnish peat profiles. *Ambio* 10 (4), 185–88

Oldfield, F., Higgit, S.R., Richardson, N. and Yates, G. 1986. Pollen, charcoal, rhizopod and radiometric analysis, in I.M. Stead (ed.) *Lindow Man, the body in the bog.* London: British Museum Publications, 82–5

Olivier, A.C.H. 1987. Excavation of a Bronze Age funerary cairn at Manor Farm, near Borwick, North Lancashire. *Proceedings of the Prehistoric Society* 53, 129–86

Oxford Archaeology North, 2002a, *Priory Farm, Priory Lane, Hornby: Evaluation report.* Lancaster: Oxford Archaeology North unpublished report

Oxford Archaeology North, 2002b, *Holbeck Park Avenue, Barrow-in-Furness: Evaluation report.* Lancaster: Oxford Archaeology North unpublished report

Pacitto, A.L. 1968. The Excavation of Two Bronze Age Burial Mounds at Ferry Fryston in the West Riding of Yorkshire. *Yorkshire Archaeological Journal* 42, 295–305

Parker-Pearson, M. 1996. Food, fertility and front doors in the first millennium BC, in T. Champion and J. Collis (eds) *The Iron Age in Britain and Ireland: recent trends.* Sheffield: J.R. Collis, 117–32

Parker-Pearson, M. 1999. *The Archaeology of Death and Burial.* Stroud: Sutton

Parsons, D.W. 2004. *7 Nelson Square, Levens: Excavation Assessment Report.* Unpublished report, Oxford Archaeology North

Penney, S.H. 1978. Gazetteer. *Contrebis* 6, 43

Petch, J.A. 1924. *Early Man in the District of Huddersfield*. Huddersfield

Phelps, J.J. 1915. A gold pendant of early Irish origin. *TLCAS* 33, 192–200

Philpott, R.A. 2000. Brunt Boggart, Tarbock, in R.W. Cowell and R.A. Philpott (eds) *Prehistoric, Roman and medieval excavations in the Lowlands of North West England Excavations along the Line of the A5300 in Tarbock and Halewood, Merseyside*. Liverpool: National Museums and Galleries on Merseyside, 117–64

Philpott, R.A. and Adams, M.H. 1999. Excavations at an Iron Age and Romano-British settlement at Irby, Wirral, 1987–96, in M. Nevell (ed.), 64–73

Philpott, R.A. and Cowell, R.W. 1992. *An Archaeological Assessment of Land East of Telegraph Road, Irby*. Unpublished report, Liverpool Museum

Philpott, R.A., Simmons, P. and Cowell, R.W. 1993. *An Archaeological Evaluation at Southworth Hall Farm, Croft, Cheshire, February 1993 (Site 32)*. Unpublished report, Liverpool Museum

Piggott S, 1954, *The Neolithic Cultures of the British Isles*. Cambridge: Cambridge University Press

Pigott, M.E. and Pigott, C.D. 1959. Stratigraphy and Pollen Analysis of Malham Tarn and Tarn Moss, *Field Studies* 1, 84–101

Platt, S.S. 1900. Stone Axe Hammer found at Low House Farm, near Milnrow. *Transactions of Rochdale Literary and Scientific Society* 7, 95–7

Poole, S. 1986. A Late Mesolithic and Early Bronze Age site at Piethorn Brook, Milnrow. *Greater Manchester Archaeological Journal* 2, 11–30

Porter, J. 1876. *History of the Fylde of Lancashire*. Fleetwood: W. Porter

Powell, T.G.E. 1963. Excavations at Skelmore Heads near Ulverston, 1957 and 1959. *TCWAAS* 63, 1–30

Powell, T.G.E. 1972. The Tumulus at Skelmore Heads near Ulverston. *TCWAAS* 72, 53–6

Powell, T., Corcoran, J., Lynch, F. and Scott, J. 1969. *Megalithic Enquiries in the West of Britain*. Liverpool: Liverpool University Press

Powell, T.G.E., Oldfield, F. and Corcoran, J.W.P. 1971. Excavations in zone VII peat at Storrs Moss, Lancashire, England. *Proceedings of the Prehistoric Society* 37, 112–137

Preston, F.L. 1954. The Hill-Forts of the Peak. *Derbyshire Archaeological Journal* 74, 1–31

Price, T.D. 1978. Mesolithic settlement systems in the Netherlands, in P. Mellars (ed.) *The Early Postglacial settlement of Northern Europe*. London 81–114

Pryor, F. 1980. *Excavation at Fengate, Peterborough, England*, 3rd report. Northamptonshire Archaeological Society Monograph 1, Archaeological Monograph ROM 6, Canada

Pryor, F. 1982. *Fengate*. Aylesbury: Shire Publications.

Pye, K. and Neal, A. 1994. Coastal dune erosion at Formby Point, north Merseyside, England: causes and mechanisms. *Marine Geology* 119 (1994) 39–56

Radley, J. 1966. A Bronze Age Ring-Work on Totley Moor and other Bronze Age Ring-Works in the Pennines. *Archaeological Journal* 123, 1–26

Radley, J. 1968. A Mesolithic structure at Sheddon, with a note on chert as a raw material on Mesolithic sites in the south Pennines. *Derbyshire Archaeological Journal* 88, 26–36

Radley, J. 1969. The Mesolithic period in north-east Yorkshire. *Yorkshire Archaeological Journal* 42, 314–327

Radley, J. 1974. The Prehistory of the Vale of York. *Yorkshire Archaeological Journal* 46, 10–22

Radley, J. and Marshall, G. 1963. Mesolithic sites in south west Yorkshire. *Yorkshire Archaeological Journal* 41, 81–97

Radley, J. and Mellars, P. 1964. A Mesolithic structure at Deepcar, Yorkshire, England and the affinities of its associated flint industries. *Proceedings of the Prehistoric Society* 30, 1–24

Raistrick, A. 1929. The Bronze Age in West Yorkshire. *Yorkshire Archaeological Journal* 29, 354–65

Raistrick, A. 1933. The Distribution of Mesolithic Sites in the North of England. *Yorkshire Archaeological Journal* 31, 141–56

Raftery, J. 1972. *Iron Age and Irish Sea: problems for research*. CBA Research Report 9

Ralph, S. 2007. Broken Pots and Severed Heads: Cult Activity in Iron Age Europe, in D.A. Barrowclough and C.A.T. Malone, *Cult in Context: Reconsidering Ritual in Archaeology*. Oxford: Oxbow, 305–312

Redhead, N. and Roberts, J. 2003. Mellor; a new Iron Age hillfort. *Current Archaeology* 189, 400–403

Rega, E. 1997. Age, gender and biological reality in the Early Bronze Age cemetery at Mokrin, in J. Moore and E. Scott (eds) *Invisible People and Processes: writing gender and childhood into European archaeology*. Leicester: Leicester University Press, 229–47

Renfrew, A.C. 1979. Discontinuities in the endogenous change of settlement pattern, in C. Renfrew and K.L. Cooke (eds) *Transformations, Mathematical Approaches to Culture*. London: Academic Press, 437–61

Reynolds, P.J. 1979. *Iron Age Farm: the Butser Experiment*. London: British Museum Publications

Richmond, I.A. 1926. Britons, Angles and Norse in the Roch Basin. *Transactions of the Rochdale Literary and Scientific Society* 1926, 23–30

Roberts, G. Forthcoming. Hominid ichnology and associated vertebrate footprints: ephemeral, subfossil mammalian and avian tracks within intertidal-zone, flandrian sediment exposures at Formby Point, Sefton coast, North West England. *Ichnos*, forthcoming

Roberts, G., Gonzalez, S. and Huddart, D. 1996. Intertidal, Holocene footprints and their archaeological significance. *Antiquity* 70, 647–51

Robbins, L.M. 1986. Estimating height and weight from size of footprints. *Journal of Forensic Sciences* 31(1), 143–52

Robbins, L.M. 1987. Hominid Footprints From Site G, in M.D. Leakey and J.M. Harris (eds) *Laetoli: A Pliocene Site in Northern Tanzania*. Oxford: Clarendon Press, 497–502

Robinson, M.E. and Shimwell, D.W. 1996. *Radiocarbon Dates from Ashton Moss. A Supplementary Report*. Palaeoecological Research Unit, University of Manchester

Roe, F.E.S. 1966. The battle-axe series in Britain. *Proceedings of the Prehistoric Society* 32, 199–245

Roe, F. 1979. Typology of stone implements with shaft-holes, in T.H. Mck. Clough and W.A. Cummins (eds) *Stone Axe Studies*. London: CBA, Research Report 23, 23–48

Roeder, C. 1889–90. A new archaeological discovery on the Ship Canal at Stickling Island. *Transactions Manchester Geological Society* 21, 204–11

Roeder, C. 1907. Kersal Moor. *TLCAS* 25, 82–85

Rohl, B. and Needham, S. 1998. *The Circulation of Metal in the British Bronze Age: the application of lead isotope analysis*. London: British Museum Occasional Paper 102

Ross, A. 1967. *Pagan Celtic Britain: Studies in Iconography and Tradition*. New York: Columbia University Press

Rosser, C.E.P. 1958. Notes on recent field-work in Lancashire and Cheshire, 1958. *TLCAS* 68, 139

Roth, H.L. 1906. *The Yorkshire Coiners 1767–1783 and Notes on Prehistoric Halifax*. Halifax

Rowlands, M.J. 1993. The role of memory in the transmission of culture. *World Archaeology* 25, 141–51

Rowley, G. 1975a. Excavation of a Circle at New Farm, Henbury, *TLCAS* 78, 78–80

Rowley, G. 1975b. Brickbank Farm, *Cheshire Archaeological Bulletin* 3, 43–5

Rowley, G. 1977. The Excavation of a Barrow at Woodhouse End, Gawsworth, Macclesfield. *JCAS* 60, 1–34

Roymans, N. 1996. The sword or the plough. Regional dynamics in the romanisation of Belgic Gaul and the Rhineland area, in N. Roymans (ed.) *From the Sword to the Plough. Three Studies on the Earliest Romanisation of Northern Gaul*. Amsterdam: Amsterdam Archaeological Studies 1, 9–126

Rupke, N. 1994. *Richard Owen, Victorian Naturalist*. New Haven, Connecticut: Yale University Press

Rüsen, J. 1994. Geschichtskultur als Forschungsproblem [1992]. *Historische Orientierung*. Köln: Böhlau

Salisbury, C. 1986. Comments on Kirkhead Cave an Upper Palaeolithic site in northern England. *Proceedings of the Prehistoric Society* 52, 321–3

Salisbury, C. 1988. Late Upper Palaeolithic artefacts from Lindale Low cave, Cumbria. *Antiquity* 62, 510–13

Salisbury, C.R. and Sheppard, D. 1994. The Mesolithic occupation of Heysham Head, Lancashire. *TLCAS*, 141–147

Sayce, R.U. 1956. The Celtic Iron Age. *TLCAS* 66, 1–21

Schneider, J. and Weiner, A. (eds) 1989. *Cloth and Human Experience*. Washington DC: Smithsonian Institution Press

Self Weeks, W. 1917. Some legendary stories and folklore of the Clitheroe District. *TLCAS* 34

Semple, S. 1998. A fear of the past: the place of the prehistoric burial mound in the ideology of middle and later Anglo-Saxon England, in R. Bradley and H. Williams, The Past in the Past: The Reuse of Ancient Monuments. *World Archaeology* 30: 1, 109–126

Shee Twohig, E. 1996. Context and Content of Irish passage tomb art. *Revue Archéologique Ouest*, Supplement 8: 67–80

Shennan, I. and Andrews, J. (eds) 2000. *Holocene Land-sea Interaction and Environmental Change Around the North Sea*. London: Geological Society

Sheridan, A. and Davis, M. 1998. The Welsh 'jet set' in prehistory: a case of keeping up with the Joneses? in A. Gibson and D. Simpson (eds) *Prehistoric Ritual and Religion: essays in honour of Aubrey Burl*. Stroud: Sutton, 148–62

Shotter, D.C.A. 2004. *Romans and Britons in North West England* (3rd ed). Lancaster: Centre for North West Regional Studies, Lancaster University

Simmons, I.G. and Innes, J.B. 1987. Mid Holocene adaptations and later Mesolithic forest disturbance in northern England. *Journal of Archaeological Science* 14, 385–403

Simpson, J. 1983. Beyond Etiology: Interpreting Local Legends. *Fabula* 24, Nos 3 and 4, 223–32

Smith 1926. *Stone Age Guide*. London: British Museum

Smith, I.F. 1974. The Neolithic, in Renfrew, C. (ed.) *British Prehistory: a New Outline*. London, 100–36

Smith, B. and George, T.N. 1961. *North Wales, British Regional Geology*. London: HMSO

Sobee, F.J. 1953. *A History of Pilling*. Exeter: F.J. Sobee

Sørensen, M.L.S. 1991. Gender construction through appearance, in D. Walde and N.D. Willows (eds) *The Archaeology of Gender: proceedings of the 22nd Annual Chacmool Conference*. Calgary: Archaeological Association of the University of Calgary, 121–9

Sørensen, M.L.S. 1992. Gender archaeology and Scandinavian Bronze Age studies. *Norwegian Archaeological Review* 25, 31–49

Sørensen, M.L.S. 1997. Reading dress: the construction of social categories and identities in Bronze Age Europe. *Journal of European Archaeology* 5 (*1*), 93–114

Sørensen, M.L.S. 1998. The Atlantic Bronze Age and the construction of meaning, in S. Oliveira Jorge (ed.) *Existe uma Idade do Bronze Atlântico?* Lisboa: Trabalhos de Arqueologia 10, 255–66

Spencer, A. 1950–1. Preliminary report on archaeological investigations near Radcliffe, Lancashire. *TLCAS* 62, 196–203

Spikins, P. 1995. *West Yorkshire Mesolithic Project Site Report 1995*. West Yorkshire Archaeological Service for English Heritage and the National Trust

Spikins, P. 1996. *West Yorkshire Mesolithic Project Site Report 1996*. West Yorkshire Archaeological Service for English Heritage and the National Trust

Spikins, P. 2002. *Prehistoric People of the Pennines: Reconstructing the lifestyles of Mesolithic hunter-gatherers on Marsden Moor*. Leeds: West Yorkshire Archaeological Service

Spratt, D.A., Goddard, R.E. and Brown, D.R. 1976. Mesolithic settlement sites at Upleatham, Cleveland. *Yorkshire Archaeological Journal* 48, 19–26

Stead, I.M. 1968. An Iron Age Hill-Fort at Grimthorpe, Yorkshire, England. *Proceedings of the Prehistoric Society* 34, 148–90

Stead, I.M., Bourke, J.B. 1986. *Lindow Man: The Body in the Bog*. London: British Museum Publications

Stewart-Brown, R.D. 1911. *A History of the Manor and Township of Allerton, in the County of Lancaster*. Liverpool: E. Howell, 106–40

Stone, J.F.S. and Thomas, L.C. 1956. Use and Distribution of Faience in Ancient East and Prehistoric Europe. *Proceedings of the Prehistoric Society* 22, 37–84

Stonehouse, W. P. B. 1972. Rocher Moss South: report on a recently excavated Mesolithic flint site in Saddleworth. *Saddleworth Historical Society Bulletin* 2, 36–40

Stonehouse, W.P.B. 1976. Red Ratcher: the excavation of a Mesolithic site in the Peak National Park. *Saddleworth Historical Society Bulletin* 6, 15–22

Stonehouse, W.P.B. 1986. Dean Clough 1: a Late Mesolithic site in the Central Pennines. *Greater Manchester Archaeological Journal* 2, 1–9

Stuiver, M., Reimer, P.J., Bard, E., Beck, J.W., Burr, G.S., Hughen, K.A., Kromer, B., McCormac, F.G., Plicht, J. v. d. and Spurk. M. 1998. INTCAL 98 Radiocarbon Age Calibration, 24,000–0 cal BP. *Radiocarbon* 40, 1041–83

Sturdy, D. 1976. A ring cairn in Levens Park. *Scottish Archaeological Forum* 4, 52–61

Switsur, V.R. and Jacobi, R.M. 1975. Radiocarbon dates for the Pennine Mesolithic. *Nature* 256, 482–4

Sutcliffe, W.H. 1896–7. A Neolithic trader's store of graphite. *Transactions of the Rochdale Literary and Scientific Society* 5, 63–4

Sutcliffe, W.H. 1899. Urns found in East Lancs. and the implements associated with the men who made them. *Transactions of the Burnley Literary and Scientific Club* 17, 171–7

Sutcliffe, W.H. 1905. Flint implements. *TLCAS* 21, 111–119

Sutcliffe, W.H. and Parker, W.A. 1912. Pigmy flint implements: their provenance and use. *TLCAS* 30, 1–8

Tallis, J.H. 1975. Tree remains in southern Pennine peals. *Nature* 256, 482–484

Tallis, J.H. and McGuire, J. 1972. Central Rossendale: the evolution of an upland vegetation 1: the clearance of woodland. *Journal of Ecology* 60, 721–37

Tallis, J.H. and Switsur, V.R. 1973. Studies on Southern Pennine Peats, VI: A Radiocarbon Dated Pollen Diagram from Featherbed Moss, Derbyshire. *Journal of Ecology* 61, 743–51

Taylor, A. 2001. *Burial Practice in Early England*. Stroud

Taylor, M.W. 1881. On the discovery of prehistoric remains at Clifton, Westmorland. *TCWAAS* 5, 79–97

Taylor, J.J., Innes, J.B. and Jones, M.D.H. 1994. Locating prehistoric wetland sites by an integrated palaeoenvironmental/geophysical survey strategy at Little Hawes Water, Lancashire, in R. Luff and P. Rowley-Conwy (eds) *Whither Environmental Archaeology*. Oxford: Oxbow Monograph 38, 18–23

Thomas, J. 1996. *Time, Culture and Identity: an interpretive archaeology*. London: Routledge

Thompson, F.H. 1967. The Roman Fort at Castleshaw, Yorkshire (W.R.): Excavations 1957–64. *TLCAS* 77

Thompson, A. 1998. To here from eternity: Manchester airport second runway. *Rescue News* 75, 1–2

Thompson, A. 1999. *The archaeology of Manchester airport's second runway*. CBA North West 14

Thompson, F.H. 1974. The Roman fort at Castleshaw, Yorkshire (West Riding). Excavations 1957–64 *TLCAS*, 77, 1–13

Thornber, W. 1837. *An Historical and Descriptive Account of Blackpool and its Neighbourhood*. Poulton: privately printed

Thornber, W. 1851. An Account of the Roman and British remains found north and east of the River Wyre. *Transactions of the Historic Society of Lancashire and Cheshire* 3, 116–26

Tierney, J.J. 1960. The Celtic ethnography of Poseidonius. *Proceedings of the Royal Irish Academy* 60, 189–275

Tilley, C. 1996. The powers of rocks: topography and monuments construction on Bodmin Moor. *World Archaeology* 28, 161–76

Tindall, A. and Faulkner, P. 1989. Fairy Brow. An Early Bronze Age Cremation Burial at Little Bollington, Cheshire, in P. Faulkner (ed.) 1989. *South Trafford Archaeology Group 1979–89*. South Trafford Archaeology Group, 88–102

Tooley, M.J. 1970. The peat beds of the south west Lancashire coast. *Nature in Lancashire* 1, 19–21

Tooley, M.J. 1971. The evolution of the Fylde coast, in A.R. Wilson (ed.) *Aspects of Fylde Geography*. Blackpool, 1–7

Tooley, M.J. 1974. Sea-Level Changes during the last 9000 years in North-West England. *Geographical Journal* 140, 18–42

Tooley, M.J. 1978. *Sea-level changes. North-West England during the Flandrian*. Oxford: Oxford University Press

Tooley, M.J. 1985. Climate, sea-level and coastal changes, in M.J. Tooley and G.M. Sheail (eds) *The Climatic Scene*. London 206–30

Treherne, P. 1995. The warrior's beauty: the masculine body and self-identity in Bronze Age Europe. *Journal of European Archaeology* 3 (1), 105–44

Topping, P. 1997. (ed.) *Neolithic Landscapes: Neolithic Studies Group Seminar Papers 2*. Oxford: Oxbow Monograph 86

Turnbull, P. and Walsh, D. 1996. A Beaker burial in Levens park. *TCWAAS* 96, 13–26

Turnbull, P. and Walsh, D. 1997. A Prehistoric Ritual Sequence at Oddendale, Near Shap. *TCWAAS* 97, 11–44

Turner, R.C. 1986. Discovery and excavation of the Lindow bodies, in I.M. Stead, J.B. Bourke and D. Brothwell, *Lindow Man: the Body in the Bog*. London: British Museum Publications, 10–13

Turner, R.C. 1995. Recent research into British bog bodies, in R.C. Turner and R.G. Scaife (eds) *Bog Bodies: new discoveries and new perspectives*. London: British Museum Press, 108–122

Turner, R. 1989. Another Cumbrian bog body, found in Seascale Moss in 1834. *TCWAAS* 88, 1–7

Tyson, N. 1962. Irwell 814. *Bury Archaeological Group Bulletin* 4, February 1962

Tyson, N. 1980. Excavation of a Cairn at Wind Hill, Heywood, Lancashire. *Greater Manchester Archaeological Journal Publication* 1

Tyson, N. and Bu'Lock, J.D. 1957. The Iron Age Fortifications at Planes Wood, Whalley. *TLCAS* 67, 115–17

Uchibori, M. 1978. *The Leaving of this Transient World: a study of Iban eschatology and mortuary practices.* Canberra: Australian National University

Ucko, P.J. 1969. Ethnography and the archaeological interpretation of funerary remains. *World Archaeology* 1, 262–90

Vandkilde, H. 1996. *From Stone to Bronze, the Metalwork of the Late Neolithic and Earliest Bronze Age in Denmark.* Aarhus: Jutland Archaeological Society Publications XXXII

Varley, W.J. 1932. Early Man in the Cheshire Plain. *Journal of the Chester and North Wales Archaeological Society* 29, 50–65

Varley, W.J. 1938. The Bleasedale Circle. *Antiquaries Journal* 18, 154–71

Varley, W.J. 1964. *Cheshire Before the Romans.* Chester

Varley, W.J. 1976. A Summary of the Excavations at Castle Hill, Almondbury 1939–1972, in D.W. Harding (ed.) *Hillforts: Later Prehistoric Earthworks in Britain and Ireland.* London, 119–31

Wainwright, G.J. 1960. Three microlithic industries from south-west England and their affinities. *Proceedings of the Prehistoric Society* 26, 193–201

Wait, G.A. 1985. *Rituals and Religion in Iron Age Britain.* Oxford: BAR British Series 149

Waldron, T. 1989. The effects of urbanisation on human health: the evidence from skeleton remains, in D. Sarjeantson and T. Waldron (eds) *Diets and Crafts in Towns.* Oxford: BAR British Series 63

Warmenbol, E. 1996. L'or, la mort et les Hyperboréens. La bouche des Enfers ou le Trou de Han à Han-sur-Lesse, in *Archäologische Forschungen zum Kultgeschehen in der jüngeren Bronzezeit und frühen Eisenzeit Alteuropas. Ergebnisse eines Kolloquiums in Regensburg 4. 7 Oktober 1993,* 203–235

Watkin, W.T. 1883. *Roman Lancashire: or, a description of Roman remains in the county palatine of Lancaster.* Liverpool: Printed for the author

Watson, A. 2001. Composing Avebury. *World Archaeology* 33, 296–314

Watson, G.G. 1952. *Early Man in Halifax District.* Halifax

Wegner, G. 1976. *Die vorgeschichtlichen Flußfunde aus dem Main und aus den Rhein bei Mainz.* Kallmünz

Weiner, A.B. 1992. *Inalienable possessions: the paradox of keeping-while-giving.* Oxford : University of California Press

Welfare, A.T. 1985. The Milling Stones, in P.T. Bidwell (ed.) *The Roman Fort at Vindolanda.* London: HMSO

Wells, C.E. and Hodgkinson, D. 2001. A Late Bronze Age human skull and associated worked wood from a Lancashire wetland. *Proceedings of the Prehistoric Society,* 163–174

Wacher, J.S. 1964. Excavations at Breedon-on-the Hill, Leicestershire 1957. *Archaeological Journal* 44, 122–142

Wheeler, R.E.M. 1953. An Early Iron Age beach-head at Lulworth, Dorset *Archaeological Journal* 33 (1–2) 1–13

Wheeler, R.E.M. 1954. *The Stanwick Fortifications.* Oxford: Society of Antiquaries Research Report 11

Whimster, R. 1981. *Burial Practices in Iron Age Britain: discussion and gazetteer of the evidence, c. 700 BC-AD 43.* Oxford: BAR British Series 90

Whitaker, Rev. J. 1771. *The History of Manchester: in four books.* London: printed for Joseph Johnson and J. Murray

Whitaker, T.D. 1876 (4th ed.). *An History of the Original Parish of Whalley and Honor of Clitheroe.* London

White, A.J. 1974. Excavations in the vicus, Lancaster, 1973-74. *Contrebis* 2(2), 13-20

White, A.J. 2002. *Sir Richard Owen, The Dinosaur Man.* Lancaster: Lancaster City Museums

White, R. 1990. Scrap or substitute? Roman material in Anglo-Saxon graves, in E. Southworth (ed.) *Early Anglo-Saxon Cemeteries: A Reappraisal.* Stroud: Alan Sutton, 124–52

Whittle, A.W.R. 1980. Two Neolithics? *Current Archaeology* 70 and 71, 329–34, 371–3

Whittle, A. 1997. Moving on and moving around: Neolithic settlement mobility, in P. Topping (ed.) *Neolithic Landscapes.* Neolithic Studies Group Seminar papers 2. Oxford: Oxbow Monograph 86, 15–22

Wigley, A. 2001. Searching for the Cornovii in the Iron Age: a critical consideration of the evidence. *West Midlands Archaeology* 44, 6–9

Wild, C. 2003. A Bronze Age cremation cemetery at Allithwaite, Cumbria. *TCWAAS* 3, 23–50

Wilkinson, T. 1911. Interesting discovery near Burnley. *Lancashire Naturalist* 4, 223

Williams, H. 1998. Monuments and the past in early Anglo-Saxon England, in R. Bradley and H. Williams, The Past in the Past: The Reuse of Ancient Monuments. *World Archaeology* 30: 1, 90–108

Wilson, D. 1992. *Anglo-Saxon Paganism.* London: Routledge

Wimble, G., Wells, C.E. and Hodgkinson, D. 2000. Human impact on mid–late Holocene vegetation in south Cumbria, UK. *Vegetation History and Archaeobotany* 9(1), 17–30

Wolfram, H. 1994. Origo et religio. Ethnic traditions and literature in early medieval texts. *Early Medieval Europe, 3(1),* 19–38

Worsley, P. 1985. Pleistocene history of the Cheshire-Shropshire plain, in R.H. Johnson (ed.) *The Geomorphology of North-West England.* Manchester: Manchester University Press, 201–21

Wrigley, A. 1911. *Saddleworth: its prehistoric remains.* Oldham

Yeager, J. and Canuto, M.A. 2000. Introducing an archaeology of communities, in M.A. Canuto and J. Yaeger, *The Archaeology of Communities, a New World Perspective.* London: Routledge, 1–15

Young, R. 2002. The Palaeolithic and Mesolithic periods in Northern England: an overview in C. Brooks, R. Daniels and A. Harding (eds) *Past, Present and Future: the archaeology of Northern England.* Durham: Architectural and Archaeological Society of Durham and Northumberland Research Report 5, 19–36

Zvelebil, M. 1994. Plant use in the Mesolithic and its role in the transition to farming. *Proceedings of the Prehistoric Society* 60, 35-74

INDEX